To Dolly,

Thank you for sharing
in Heidi's story.

Catherine Adamsen

Heidi Dawn Klompas:

Missed Opportunities

By

Catherine S. Adamson

Catherine S. Adamson

Heidi Dawn Klompas: Missed Opportunities

ISBN 978-0-9737970-1-5

Catadam Publishing
4460 West 11ᵗʰ Avenue
Vancouver, BC
V6R 2M3

In loving memory of
Heidi Dawn Klompas

Contents

PART THREE:
Royal Columbian Hospital

PART FOUR:
The Aftermath

Forward

by Christopher R. Scott

This is a remarkable and heart rending story about an event few of us will ever be forced to experience, much less have the courage to share. This is not for the faint of heart and I believe many of you will cry along with me as you follow the many avenues of psychological, physical and mental anguish experienced by all of the participants. The horrific incident at Stokes Pit on the 13th of September, 1997, has left its cruel, indelible angst, sorrow and continuing pain among the many victims, witnesses and family members of those involved. After reading this book, you may agree that it could have also accurately been named, "Stolen Opportunities." The author, Ms. Adamson, reveals discrepancies, facts and procedures, and offers insights into the very complicated and ambivalent world of the College of Physicians and Surgeons of B.C. Many of these have only recently come to light in regards to the medical treatment of Heidi. You will, as well, be asked to form your own opinions on the very real possibility of malfeasance. You will share in the frustrations experienced with the Young Offenders Act, and get an insight not only into the Coroner's Investigation that determines the cause of Heidi's death, but also the Children's Commission's Investigation into her demise. The book also looks at the many facets of the organ donor transplant societies, as well as it gives us an introduction into the mandate and activities of MADD.

Ms. Adamson tells Heidi's story as an emotional tribute to her daughter, and also in a factual, circumspect manner as few others would have the nerve to do. You will also be invited to share in getting to know exactly who Heidi Dawn Klompas was and experience the very real sense of loss we all share in her death. You will rejoice in the story of young Vicram Ralh. As you learn about Heidi, you will come to realise and appreciate the joy she would have taken in knowing that in death, she has given life.

Having worked as a street cop in law enforcement for 28 years, mainly in accident and criminal code investigations, I believe this book should be mandatory reading and form a part of every high school curriculum. Each and every youngster in those tempestuous years should read this book and through it have a thorough understanding of the consequences of drinking and driving. Lives will be saved, I will assure you. Thank you, Ms. Adamson, for not only sharing your pain in Heidi's death, but for also sharing your joy in her life.

C.R. Scott LSM
R.C.M.P. (Ret)

Acknowledgments

This book could not have been completed without the help of several wonderful people. I would like to thank the following:

Ms. Kathleen Stephany, Investigator for the B.C. Coroner's Service, for investigating Heidi's unusual death and reporting the truth. I thank you for being so open and honest with me throughout the extent of your investigation and for not holding back information. I know this particular investigation was a difficult one for you and I thank you so very much for seeing it through to the end.

Mr. John Greschner, Deputy Commissioner and Chief Investigator for the B.C. Childrens's Commission, for investigating Heidi's death and the surrounding circumstances that led up to it. I thank you for your attention to detail and I want you to know that I appreciate the extensive time and effort you put into your report.

Dr. Marco Terwiel, for agreeing to give my book a "medical edit," so that I did not inadvertently misrepresent a condition, procedure, test, or a drug. Thank you, Dr. Terwiel for your exploratory examination of my book, and your kind suggestions for revisions. I am ever so grateful.

Constable Christopher Scott, Chilliwack RCMP, for volunteering to edit my book with a policeman's eye. I thank you for your candid critique as it has been very helpful. I also thank you for your generous Forward to my book. Your opinion matters.

My sister, Dawn Adamson, for always supporting my dreams. I thank you for contributing to the editing; your suggestions have been invaluable because they've allowed me to see these pages from a different perspective. Thank you, I love you.

Bill and Laura Klompas, Heidi's brother and sister, for your emotional support during these difficult past seven years. You held me up when I should have been the one supporting you. We have all come out of this tragedy as stronger people who now realise that life is too short to not be doing what we love and what brings us happiness. I love you both so much. I am very proud to be your mother. Thank you.

Kathryn Elden, or "Auntie Kathy," who supported our family, emotionally and nutritionally, during the three and a half weeks in Royal Columbian. I also thank you for helping me understand the medical jargon and attending meetings with the Coroner's investigator and my lawyer. Your love and support are most appreciated.

Les and Daunn Davis, of *Up and Running Computer Systems & Consulting* in Langley, for helping me format my manuscript and teaching me how to upload photographs, then edit and insert them into my pages. Your help has been invaluable and I appreciate you both coming to the rescue at a crucial time. I thank you both.

Dr. Surender Ralh, his wife Rajinder, and their children Manish and Neeharika for welcoming us into their family, through Vicram. I want to especially thank Dr. Ralh for taking the time to answer my many questions about Vicram's life. Your help and support were encouraging and I hope I have duly honoured your beloved son, Vicram.

My parents, Dorothy and Albert Adamson, of Langley, who

always provide a soft place to land when I am falling. Our combined tears over Heidi's loss could fill a lake. I love you both and thank the heavens for their gift of you as parents.

Last but not least, I wish to thank Heidi's friends for working past their discomfort and contributing to this book. I know it was difficult to go back in time to that most painful place, but I want you all to know how much I appreciate your thoughts, your memories and your written words. Heidi always treasured her friends above all else, after family, and she would be very happy to know that you have participated in her book. I thank Courtney, Jamie, Chrissie, Ryan, Victor, Tiffany and Leigh from my heart. I also thank the people I spoke with that were either at Stokes Pit that night, or who are the parents of the teens who were there. I appreciate all your thoughts and comments on this tragedy and I sincerely thank you all.

With love,
Catherine Adamson

Introduction

How do I tell you this story? How do I begin? I feel this story needs to be told for many reasons. Hopefully, people in positions of power will recognize themselves and stop missing so many opportunities to save lives. Adults who bootleg liquor for teenagers might consider the end results of their actions and think twice before buying for minors again. Parents will discover there are choices they can make while overseeing the emergency care of their injured children. Nurses and doctors might better understand why they must pay closer attention to the concerns of the parents of their patients. Our law makers, our politicians, must explore more diverse opportunities to improve our justice system. The RCMP might see opportunities to better serve and protect. And the College of Physicians and Surgeons of B.C. might readdress their mandate to protect the public. British Columbians, indeed, Canadians, might see themselves in the ordinary lives of the people in this story and realise this too could happen to their families.

I will begin at the beginning of the end for Heidi. I will also show you some wonderful snapshots of her life as you labour through the days leading up to her death. I thank you for taking this difficult journey with me.

This book represents *my opportunity* to speak the whole truth. Based on over 800 pages of hospital records and research papers, and, of course, my memories, this is what happened.

Catherine S. Adamson

PART ONE:

Stokes Pit

1.1   Man with a gun.

In the rural town of Langley, British Columbia, temperatures adjusting to the cooler fall season cause great banks of mist to lie
heavily over fields of tall grasses that cover the rolling meadows
found throughout this small township. Late at night and early in
the morning, these low clouds blanket our pastures and fields,
creating beautiful, surreal landscapes. It was on such a night
as this, in October of 1996, that Courtney and her cousin Judd
set out with their friend to explore the tall grasses in a farmer's
field. The two girls made Judd pull his car over to the side of
the road and the three of them jumped out, hopped over the
ditch, and climbed the fence to play in the thick fog. They were
running in the dark, hiding on each other, jumping up and over
the mist and popping in and out of sight. They were whoop-
ing with laughter as they frolicked like delirious six-year-olds.
Eventually they made their way across the field to the fence
on the far side. Walking alongside the fence, they didn't notice
the man approaching them until he ordered them to stop. Surprised, they listened attentively to what he was hollering about
but were taken aback over his accusations that they had been
damaging his fence-posts by knocking them over and removing them. While this irate farmer was accusing them of vandal-
izing his new posts, he lifted his gun and pointed it at them.
Courtney and Judd immediately backed away from this furious
man with a gun. Frightened, they ran back to the car, desperate
to get away from him; and Judd called out to their friend, "Come
on, let's go! Hurry up, he's got a gun!" Their friend ignored their
pleas to retreat and instead she bravely charged right up to the
armed man; and with her hands firmly planted on her hips she
shouted, "Shame on you!" "We are not thieves and you have no
right to point your gun at us. Besides, it's only a little pellet gun,
you creep. You don't scare me at all." The surprised man quickly

lowered his gun and hung his head; he silently turned away and started walking back to his house. With that done, the fearless girl turned around and marched back to her friends who were anxiously awaiting her back at the car.

This plucky sixteen year old girl had had the courage and the fortitude to confront and scold a total stranger, an angry and armed older man in a dark and misty meadow late at night. And she came out of this night with her head held high knowing she had defended her friends against a potential assailant.

Meet Heidi Dawn Klompas, my daughter.

1.2   Friday, September 12th, 1997

Friday afternoon, September 12th, 1997, Heidi and her friends are discussing getting together later in the evening with some friends from the other high schools. Rumours of a house party on 208th Street near 28th Avenue in south Langley are going around and the girls decide to check it out. There are several carloads of friends going to the party and this night Heidi decides to ride along with Kendra, who promises to do her duty as designated driver. The girls meet with a crowd in the parking lot of their high school, Langley Secondary School (LSS), after supper at around 8:00 o'clock. Some of the teens are having fun fooling around and pretending they are in a rock band. Heidi, Courtney and Jared are playing air-guitars and belting out their favourite songs. They are in party mode and some of the teens have started drinking their prized, contraband alcohol. Heidi is drinking "Stingers," a vodka lemonade drink that comes in four-packs. She proceeds to get tipsy this evening, but never becomes falling-down drunk. This is the beginning of their grade twelve year and they are celebrating their final year in school. They talk about all the great gags they will play on the rival high schools, the grade twelve pyjama party and sleep-over planned for the front lawn of the school, the graffiti, the parties, and the dances. It is going to be a great year at LSS. Heidi is on the yearbook committee and she's already starting to take pictures of the grads, which she'll develop later during her photography class. This is her fifth year at LSS, and the school is like a second home to her. She has close relationships with some of her teachers, especially Lynn Tansey, who encouraged Heidi to tutor math students last year. Heidi's brother, Bill, graduated in 1996. Heidi will be graduating in 1998 and her younger sister Laura will graduate in 1999. I also attended LSS in my grade eleven year when it was still just a senior secondary. My family moved the summer after grade eleven, and even though I had to attend a different high school for grade twelve, LSS would always be considered "my" high school. I am so glad my three children can attend the same school uninterrupted from grades eight through twelve. Things are going well for us. Until this one night in September.

The boy made infamous by the events of this evening cannot be named publicly because of the Canadian Young Offenders Act. So for the purposes of this book we'll call him "John," as in John Doe.

John and a male friend, both students at LSS, hear about the party on 208th and make plans to attend. John has just purchased his first car the day before: a full-sized burgundy, 1980 Cadillac Eldorado. He pays for the insurance, attaches the new license plates, gases up and is ready to have some fun with his newfound freedom machine. John and his friend pool their resources and find they have just enough money to buy a six-pack of oversized cans of beer. John drives them to the Langley Hotel on Fraser Highway and waits in the car while his friend stands outside the cold beer store next to the pub. The friend approaches a man as he exits the store and asks him if he will buy him the six-pack. The man does not hesitate; he takes the boy's money and re-enters the store. Minutes later he emerges with the beer in hand and turns it over to the seventeen-year-old who's now sporting a huge grin. The boys are off to a good start and the evening looks promising.

John and his friend make their way over to the boisterous

parking lot crowd of LSS students, and they have fun mixing with the others, making plans for the evening and showing off John's new car. Around 9:00 pm the students start drifting towards south Langley and the party on 208th Street. By 10:00 pm the party is in full swing with at least forty cars parked in the driveway and on the back lawn. The music is loud and the teens are even louder as they sing along, shout out greetings and generally try to outdo each other. A couple of fights break out, but it's nothing serious. Yet.

A neighbour calls the police at 10:28 pm to report the fighting and the noise. When police arrive, they discover that the party of forty teens has expanded to almost 200 people, and in one corner the fighting is now out of hand. People are getting hurt and windows are being smashed. Twenty-five police officers eventually arrive at the scene and three people are arrested. The others are all ordered off the property. The police do not check the drivers for alcohol consumption and although a couple of the boys question the officers about checking the drivers for sobriety, they are simply told, "That's their problem." John knows he has had too much to drink but he feels compelled to get into his car and drive away. He was not planning on driving while he was drinking; rather, he thought he would stay at the party until it was safe to leave. The presence of the Langley RCMP changes his plans for him even though John and his friends are not the ones fighting or causing trouble. He just wants to hang out and have some fun this night. So off he and his friend go, riding through the night in his Eldorado.

Many of the ousted partiers make their way to the gravel pit near the corner of 206th Street and 36th Avenue. John is there, as are Heidi and her friends. The homeowners across the street waste no time before calling the Langley RCMP to report this unwanted crowd of teens, and soon the prompt and efficient police officers arrive to disperse the crowd. This is called "fire-bombing:" when the police arrive and immediately defuse and scatter a crowd onto the streets. So they fire-bombed the crowd. Once again, this opportunity to check for inebriated drivers slips by the police as they usher everyone into their cars and off the property. Not once is a driver checked for alcohol consumption.

The crowd of teenagers next makes its way onto the stretch of road along Stokes Pit on 28th Avenue, between 192nd and 194th Streets. There are no homes along this stretch of pavement alongside the park, and no street lights, so the area is dark and quiet at night. There is lots of parking available for the men, boys, and families that enjoy fishing in the lake every day. The teens park their cars on the roadside and get out to socialize in peace. Heidi sees lots of her girlfriends from all the high schools that night. These are the girls Heidi knows from elementary school, softball, Girl Guides, soccer and church. Heidi apparently knows students from every high school in Langley.

John is also at Stokes Pit and he is now very drunk from drinking four of the six large cans of beer; he is also under the influence of some marijuana he smoked earlier with another person. When he decides to leave for home his friends try to stop him because they now realize he's very intoxicated. One of his friends takes his keys away from him and keeps them for awhile. John is feeling sick to his stomach and, according to one of his friends, he feels embarrassed when he throws up in front of the others. Now he really wants to go home. He grabs his keys back, his friends shout at him not to drive, and a struggle ensues. John is now in a bad humour and vigorously fights them off. Angrily, he takes off with a friend still sitting on his trunk. The friend rolls safely off the car and watches as

John heads east on 28th Avenue, going towards 200th Street and home.

The groups of teenagers party on until midnight, then some start going home. It is around midnight when Heidi first says she wants to go home with Kendra. Her friends beg her to stay a little longer. Vanessa offers to drive her home so Heidi decides to stay a few more minutes. Around 12:20 am, Heidi again starts to get into someone's car to be driven home but is persuaded to stay longer. She agrees and this ultimately proves to be the biggest mistake of her life.

1.3 Car rules for Heidi and her friends.

Heidi and her large group of buddies liked to party and drink on occasion. This may sound like irresponsible teens who were out of control, but they were just the opposite. Heidi and her closest friends were adamant about having a trustworthy designated driver. When Heidi borrowed my car for an evening with her girlfriends, I knew she would not be drinking. The girls have discussed this with me and I am confident they never compromised their rule of having a driver who abstains from drinking alcohol for the entire evening. This way, they all took turns driving, and they all took turns drinking in safety, knowing they would get securely home. The evening of September 12th, 1997, Heidi said she was going out with her friends and that they were picking her up. I knew she might be drinking that night, but I also knew she was with reliable friends who would ensure her safety. I was more worried about her newly extended curfew: from midnight to one o'clock. Her father and I disagreed on that one, and against my wishes he gave her permission to stay out until 1:00 am. Heidi and her friends always took precautions to keep themselves safe from harm but they couldn't have anticipated the events of that night in September.

What a difference an hour makes.

1.4 Accident scene

12:30 am, September 13th, 1997.

Many of the teens at Stokes Pit are on the road gathered in groups, socializing. Many others are on the sides of the road preparing to get into their cars to leave. Vanessa is getting ready to leave with Courtney and Heidi, and they are saying their goodbyes to their friend Jamie, who is about to leave with her boyfriend. Heidi is chatting with Courtney, Jamie, Jason and Vanessa. They are making plans for going home and talking about what they will be doing this weekend. Jamie says her goodbyes and walks across the road to her boyfriend, Ryan, who is motioning for her to join him. Jamie speaks with Ryan for only a few seconds before the accident happens.

John returns to Stokes Pit by travelling west along 28th Avenue from 200th Street. His friends are surprised to see him come back and they watch as his car heads towards the crowds. As the Cadillac goes past, several of John's friends see his head drop forward to rest on the steering wheel. John appears to be passing in and out of consciousness, although his car is still moving forward. The Cadillac veers off towards the side of the road where the largest crowds stand in tight groups. There is no moon out tonight and it is very dark as the Eldorado ploughs through the crowd just behind Jamie. As the big car smashes its way down the road, Jamie spins around and sees that her friends are gone. With one twist of her body she is transported out of a scene of happy farewells and into a scene of complete and incomprehensible mayhem. Bodies are flying.

John's car surges through the crowds of people, smashing and knocking them into the air. Then he crashes into another car that is preparing to leave. This is Camy's car, and she is about to take her three friends home when John rear-ends her Honda, forcing it into the group of friends she has just been speaking with. Her car hits two or three people and they flip up and smash her windshield with their bodies. John stops. He backs up his car and side-swipes the Honda as he attempts to move forward again. People are banging on his windows for him to stop and get out. Angry young men are threatening him; he is frightened now and starts to panic. He hits the gas. John's car takes off again through a hail of beer bottles thrown by those left standing. Drunk and dazed in his battered Cadillac, John heads for home.

Most of the teens become instantly airborne when the car's low bumper strikes their unprotected legs. In all, sixteen people are directly struck by the car and injured or killed. Many more are struck and injured by the flying bodies. Heidi's shins make contact with the bumper; she flips up, hits the windshield, rolls over the roof, and flies off the car. Heidi falls from the sky and lands hard on the road, skidding on her buttocks. Courtney lands by Heidi's feet and Vanessa thumps down a few feet away and then is pounded again by a body landing on her neck. Ashley Reber, 17, a student from Brookswood Secondary, is killed instantly when she lands on the road next to Heidi. Many of the teens land in the weed-filled ditches that line the road, or in the bushes further back; consequently, some of them are not immediately located.

Chaos takes over. The crowds are frantic as they scurry in the dark to locate friends and family members on this pitch-black stretch of road. Ashley's friends come to her aid and a boy and a girl alternately perform CPR (Cardio Pulmonary Resuscitation) on her broken body until the paramedics arrive. But she is gone. Jamie rushes to her friends' sides and tries to comfort them. Heidi is lying on her back and says her legs hurt. Jamie can see they look oddly crooked. She watches in astonishment as Courtney drags herself along the gravel and pavement, screaming in pain as she pulls herself up alongside Heidi's body. Courtney passes out several times while she tries to reach Heidi's head. With no small effort, Courtney curls herself into a fetal position around Heidi's head before losing consciousness again. Eventually, Courtney realizes something is terribly wrong with her leg when she sees that her foot is touching her knee. Her leg is bent in half between the knee and ankle and something sharp and white is protruding from her jeans. She is bleeding. It is a horrific sight and when she absorbs what she is looking at she faints again. Vanessa is calling out for help and Jamie rushes to her side. Vanessa screams that she can't feel anything and asks Jamie to lift her right arm. Jamie gently grabs her arm and upon instruction lets it drop to the ground; Vanessa starts screaming that she can't feel anything in her arms or her legs. She has no sensations in her hands or her feet. She is paralysed from the neck down and is becoming very, very frightened. Bodies are lying all over the road, each surrounded by large groups of frightened, hysterical friends.

Fortunately, many of the teens have cell-phones and police reports show that seventeen "911" calls are made before 1:00 am on the morning of September 13th. Eight more calls are made directly to the police stations, and emergency vehicles are soon on their way. The Langley RCMP are the first to arrive and they quickly assess the enormity of the situation. They call for as many ambulances as possible and for more police. The firemen are the next to arrive, then the ambulances. The paramedics take over the CPR for Ashley's friends but they soon realize she is beyond saving. The coroner is called. Vanessa and Courtney's injuries are assessed as the most serious, so the two seventeen-year-old girls are transported to Royal Columbian Hospital in New Westminster. Heidi and four others are taken to Peace

Arch District Hospital in White Rock. Several friends argue over who is going with Heidi to the hospital, however, the paramedics have their hands full with the injured and decide to not allow any friends to accompany those needing medical attention. Jamie sees each of her friends off and is left wondering what to do and where to go; she doesn't know which hospitals the girls are being taken to. Another five of the injured are taken to Langley Memorial Hospital and an additional four are taken to Surrey Memorial Hospital. Many more injured are not hurt seriously enough for the hospital, so their friends assist them home. Ryan and Jamie are first driven to Ryan's home, then later over to Jamie's. Ashley's mother is notified and a friend of the Reber family comes to identify Ashley's body, still laying on the roadside at Stokes Pit.

John somehow finds his way home. He arrives in a panic and decides to call the police and report that his car has been stolen. When the police arrive at his home they discover the car in his driveway; it is battered and smashed and has someone's purse hanging off the right side-mirror. John is arrested and taken into custody.

1.5   Heidi's Music

I believe in miracles
Where you from
You sexy thing
I believe in miracles
Since you came along
You sexy thing

By Hot Chocolate

Heidi loved this song so much it would pop into her head at any given time, especially when she was particularly happy about something. I can still hear Heidi, Courtney and Jamie singing this song together, giddy and laughing in the warmth of their love for each other. I can picture these three beautiful teenagers singing this trippy little love song as they drive to the 7-Eleven for candy and cigarettes on a Friday after school.

Heidi often sang in the car with her brother and sister when enroute to their games, schools, or friends' homes. We had an old Rolling Stones cassette in the car that the children loved and because we played it so often, Heidi knew the words to most of the songs. She liked "Under My Thumb," "You Can't Always Get What You Want," "Get Off Of My Cloud," "Ruby Tuesday;" and we had lots of fun with "The Spider And The Fly."

The girls liked Bob Seger's "Old Time Rock N Roll." Heidi liked the Matthew Good Band's "Symbolistic White Walls," which the girls referred to as the "overpriced bubblegum song." The opening lines are: "I'm tired of blood and overpriced bubblegum, mom." Heidi enjoyed Alternative music, which was just about anything her friends didn't like. She loved Pearl Jam, the Tragically Hip, and to her friend's horror, Paul Simon's "Graceland" album. Both Courtney and Heidi's mothers played Paul Simon at home a lot, therefore, both girls could sing along with most of his songs; "Diamonds on the Soles of Her Shoes" was a favourite. Heidi could also shock and amuse her friends with her rendition of Johnny Cash's "Ring of Fire," which was on a cassette in her father's car: a big lumbering white station wagon the girls took to the old Hillcrest Drive-In Theatre on many occasions. It became known as the party wagon. Heidi listened and sang to music wherever she was. Our family members are not Country & Western music fans, but Jamie's family is, so Heidi was forced to listen to lots of country twang when at the Hyde's. Whenever I took my children on long car trips, to the Okanagan or Quesnel to see their Uncle Bill, we made a habit of buying a new cassette at the gas station each time we filled up the tank. Some places only sell cowboy music, so we were forced to acquire some country.

Heidi was singing almost as soon as she was talking. She loved the way music made her feel and she would dance and sing on a whim, not noticing who was listening or watching, drifting away in her own world wherever the music took her. Our family also listened to some classical music, symphonies and operas. Heidi took ballet lessons when she was little and she danced like a ballerina to the Nutcracker Suite, especially after seeing a professional performance in Toronto when she was three. Heidi appreciated all kinds of music, from Beethoven to OutKast, and from The Rolling Stones to Shania Twain. There was nothing she wouldn't sing along to.

1.6   My arrival at Stokes Pit

It is getting close to 1:00 am and Heidi has not returned home yet; I am starting to worry. Laura and Bill are in bed and I am in my pyjamas, just finishing my reading and preparing to go to sleep. The children's father is away on a flight. The phone rings, startling us all out of our beds; it is 1:00 am and the caller is a boy named Kevin Dornan, a former boyfriend of Heidi's. He is upset and anxious as he tells me that Heidi has been hit by a car and that she has two broken legs. I ask where she is and he says Stokes Pit on 28th Avenue. I tell him I will be right there and look up to see Bill and Laura already in my bedroom listening to the end of the call. I tell them what has happened and we all jump into action. Our house, on 32nd Avenue, is just a three to five minute drive from Stokes Pit. Bill drives us west on 32nd, then south on 194th Street and makes a right hand turn onto 28th where we come to an abrupt stop. The scene is incomprehensible: completely surreal. There are fire trucks, police cars and ambulances lining both sides of the road. Crowds of teenagers are huddled together on the south side of the road while the emergency personnel do their work on the opposite side. As we get out of the car and walk towards the scene, the flashing red, white and blue lights from the emergency vehicles light up the road and spotlight the eeriest sight I have ever seen: a road covered with dozens and dozens of shoes and purses. They are everywhere. Some of the shoes are standing upright and next to each other in pairs, as if the occupants had just stepped out of them. Later, I realize the occupants of those neatly arranged pairs of shoes were knocked right out of them, leaving the shoes intact on the road where the people once stood. It is an eerie image that I cannot get out of my head; it just seems all wrong. My brain cannot comprehend what it is that I am seeing.

Kevin runs up to us and says that Heidi is already in an ambulance and that her legs look really bad. He doesn't know which hospital she is being taken to. I notice that some of the ambulances are starting to leave so I run up alongside of them, one after another, frantically jumping up to the windows to try and see if Heidi is inside. I bang on the sides of them, trying to make them stop long enough to find Heidi, but they don't stop. The ambulances leave one after the other and I ask some people if they know which hospital she is going to. No one knows. Walking up to two policemen standing off to the side of the road, I ask them if they know which hospital Heidi is going to. They say they don't know, however, they do tell me the teens are going to four different hospitals: Langley, Surrey, Peace Arch and Royal Columbian. Then I look down. Lying at their feet is a yellow tarp with two little white feet poking out from under its edge. It is Ashley. These two policemen are standing guard awaiting the arrival of Ashley's mother and the Coroner's Service. This is the moment when I realize how deadly this accident has been. The large train of ambulances is another clue. Now I am in an even greater panic to find my daughter. Bill and Laura support me as I stagger back to our car.

Bill, Laura and I decide to drive to Langley Memorial Hospital because it is the closest. As Bill drives, I call directory assistance on my cell phone to get the hospital's number so I can ask if Heidi has arrived. The hospital receptionist says she doesn't know yet, however, ambulances are starting to arrive so perhaps I should call back in an hour after they get the patients registered. I try calling my parents, but there is no answer. I call their home several times that night and become more and more frustrated because there is no answer. I am in crisis and I need my Mom and Dad. Next, I call Courtney's home and her mother says they too, are desperately trying to find Courtney. We both agree to call the other hospitals until we find our girls, and she suggests I come over to their house until we locate them. Bill calls his friend, Chris Sturgeon, and we pick him up at his home on the way to the Wilson's. We drive to Courtney's and by the time we arrive her mother has located Heidi at Peace Arch, but they are still searching for Courtney. I thank her and Bill drives Laura, Chris and I to Peace Arch District Hospital in White Rock.

1.7 Lost on the Skytrain.

Heidi was always getting lost on family outings. When she was five or six, she often wandered off when we went grocery shopping at Save On Foods in Langley. On one such trip, she got lost three times. That's right, three times during one grocery shop I heard over the intercom: "Attention shoppers, we have a lost girl in the store, and her name is Heidi. Would her mother please come get her at the service counter?" The third time she got lost we were at the checkout counter and I was unloading groceries from the cart onto the conveyor belt. Heidi was looking at magazines in the racks at the end of the counter, and without noticing what she was doing, she travelled around the curve, following the headlines until she was in the next checkout lane. She looked up, and not seeing her mother, she started crying again. When I heard the announcement broadcasting that Heidi was lost again, I looked around the magazine racks, and grabbing her hand, I brought her back around to once again stand with her family. She always had a fear of getting lost, but then she was the one of my three who was most adept at it.

A couple of years later when the children were aged 8, 9, and 10, they went with their Gramma K to Vancouver. Gramma decided to drive to the first (or last) Skytrain station, which at that time was the only Surrey station, located near the Pattulo Bridge that spans the Fraser River. On the platform, Gramma told the three children to wait for her before getting on the train. They agreed. So when the train pulled up Gramma held back but Heidi jumped on board; the doors closed and off she went across the Fraser River to New Westminster all by herself. According to the reports from Bill and Laura, Heidi had her face pressed against the window and screamed as the train whisked her away from her Gramma and her brother and sister. Luckily, many people on the train saw what had happened, and saw the screaming, jumping, and waving Gramma panicking on the platform. They helped Heidi off the train at the first New Westminster station and a kind woman waited with Heidi until her Gramma and siblings caught up to her on the next train. It all ended well, except for Gramma K's nerves.

And yet again, the next year when Gramma took them on a bus trip Heidi accidentally climbed aboard the wrong bus. But that time she got off before the bus closed its doors. Whew!

How many times did we lose Heidi? Too many to count.

PART TWO:

Peace Arch District Hospital

2.1   Arrival at Peace Arch District Hospital

Heidi arrives at Peace Arch Hospital in White Rock at 1:29 am, which is twenty-three minutes after leaving the accident scene at 1:06 am. Heidi must have been in one of the departing ambulances I was trying to inspect when I first arrived at Stokes Pit. It seems that I just missed her. She is examined and given her first morphine shot at 1:45 am. Dr. L admits her officially at 1:54 am. Upon arrival, her vitals signs are all within the normal range, except her legs, which are described by Dr. L in her records as "bilateral lower limb deformities!!" Heidi is on a clamshell: the flat board she was placed on at the accident site. Her legs are splinted and she is wearing a hard neck collar. Her temperature is 36.2 degrees Celsius and her oxygen saturation is 97%. She has a small swollen bump on her left forehead, a laceration on her right temporal area (temple), and an abrasion on her right cheekbone. She is fully conscious and aware of where she is.

Bill, Laura and I arrive at Peace Arch Hospital just after 2:00 am. The front admissions nurse directs us to the emergency room and we find Heidi in a bed, just back from having the first x-rays taken of her legs. She is very glad to see her family and the nurse tells me she has been asking for her Mom. She is alert and very much aware of what has happened to her. She says her legs really hurt, but when I look I can only see her feet sticking out from under her blanket. Heidi apologizes to Laura for ruining her new sweater that she had borrowed. Apparently the paramedics cut her sweater down the middle to get it off her. They do the same to her shoes, which also turn out to belong to Laura. The girls just recently bought their new back-to-school clothes and are used to swapping with each other. Heidi's blue-jeans are tucked under her hospital bed and it isn't until much later that I look at them closely and discover what they implicate.

Dr. L pulls back the sheet to let me see Heidi's legs. They are horribly misshapened, have turned purple and red and are swollen to more than twice their normal size. They are very painful to the touch and Heidi is given morphine through an intravenous (IV) drip they have already set up. Dr. L informs me that Heidi has sustained injuries only to her legs and that having looked at my daughter's head and spine; Dr. L is satisfied there are no further injuries. Heidi has a bloody scrape on her right cheek and a small bump on her left forehead, but they don't look serious. I ask about head injuries and Dr. L assures me that Heidi's head is okay. Heidi can move all extremities, wiggle her toes and turn her head from side to side. She is bright, alert and talkative. I am so relieved. I am so thankful my baby has come away from this horrific accident with only two broken shinbones. Thinking of what Ashley's mother must be going through at this time, I can't imagine her pain. But my Heidi is going to be okay. She is safe now.

The bed next to Heidi's contains JR, another victim from Stokes Pit. He and Heidi have been talking while waiting for their parents. He has one badly broken leg, similar to Heidi's. His mother and father are now with him. Around 3:00 am the x-rays arrive and the doctor takes all three parents to the lightboard to view them. When they put up JR's x-ray we can see that the fractures look bad but everything else appears normal. Then they put up Heidi's x-rays and suddenly JR's father needs to sit down. JR's mom and I stand amazed before Heidi's x-rays; the breaks are what the doctors are calling comminuted fractures: The bones of her tibias and fibulas, her shin bones, are jaggedly broken, twisted, and overlapping.

The following photographs of Heidi's x-rays are two separate films overlapped to give you the best impression I can of what her injuries looked like:

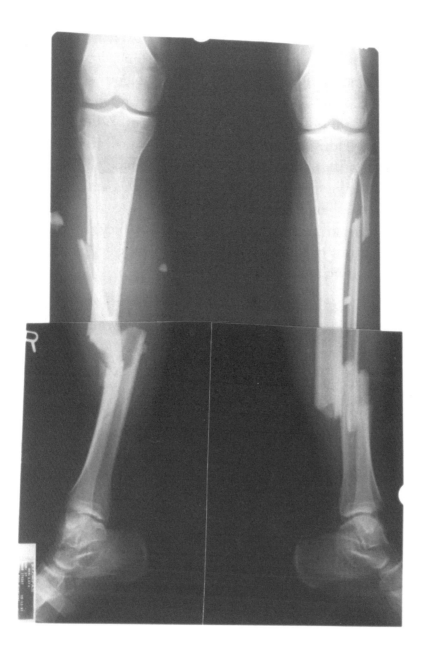

The clinical terms for Heidi's broken legs are described in Dr.
R's (Medical Imaging Consultant) report as follows (the italic
print is mine):

> Right side—There is a mildly comminuted *fracture*
> of the right tibia just distal to the mid-point. Distal
> main fragment shows 2.5cm medial and posterior
> displacement along with slight anterior and lateral
> angulation. In addition, there is evidence of 90 degree
> rotation of the fracture fragment.
>
> There is also a comminuted *fracture* of the mid-shaft of
> the fibula at this level, distal main fragment showing
> anterior and lateral angulation.
>
> Also noted is an oblique *fracture* of the proximal shaft
> of the right fibula at the junction of proximal one-third
> with the middle one third. Distal fragment shows
> approximately 1cm lateral displacement and moderate
> medial angulation.
>
> Left side—There is an irregular transverse *fracture* of
> the distal shaft of the tibia at the junction of the distal
> one third with the middle one third. There is marked
> anterior and lateral displacement of the distal fragment
> by complete width of the shaft as well as 90-degree
> rotation. There is also overriding of the fragments by
> about 4cm. Also there is a transverse *fracture* of the
> distal shaft of the fibula at the same level with complete
> anterior and lateral displacement of the distal fragment
> by width of the shaft and 90-degree rotation.
>
> Also noted is the presence of an oblique *fracture* of the
> proximal shaft of the fibula at the junction of proximal
> one fourth with the distal three fourths. Distal

fragment shows medial displacement by complete
width of the shaft and there is approximately 2.5cm
overriding of the fragments. (PADH, 13)

These are really nasty breaks that obviously require immediate
attention. I ask the doctor if Heidi can have her legs corrected
immediately and she tells me she has already called the
orthopaedic surgeon who is on call that night, a Dr. H. I enquire
as to when she called him and she says about a half hour ago, at
2:30 am, and she tells me he promises to be right in. We wait
for his imminent arrival, but it doesn't come. About two hours
later, at 4:45 am, I ask the doctor to call him again and I watch
as she goes over to the phone and makes the call. She reports
back to me that he'll be right in. Again we wait. I am getting
insistent because Heidi is in a lot of pain, so Dr. L calls Dr. H
again around 5:00 am and he says he'll be in soon. But he doesn't
come in. The nurses are upset with Dr. H's no-show and the
emergency room doctor is clearly upset. Before going off shift at
7:00 am, Dr. L calls Dr. H one last time and then she tells me he
assures her he will be in by 9:00 am. At this point I ask one of
the nurses if Heidi can be transferred to another hospital where
she can have her surgery done immediately, but the nurse says
no because Dr. H will be in by 9:00 am to do Heidi's surgery,
and she wouldn't get operated on any earlier at another hospital.
This makes sense to me so I stop asking. My big mistake.

Heidi is in a lot of pain. She is given 2.5mg (milligrams) of
Morphine intravenously (IV) at 1:45 am, plus 25mg of Gravol
(antinauseant). She tells the doctor her pain is unbearable
ten minutes later, and at 1:55 she is given another 2.5mg of
Morphine. At 2:05 and 2:10 she is given additional Morphine
at 2.5mg each, because the pain in her legs refuses to relent. At
2:35 am her neck collar and sand bags are removed when she
returns back from radiology, and she is given another 2.5mg of

Morphine for her pain. She receives 2mg of Ancef (antibiotic) and another 2.5mg of Morphine at 2:55 am. At 3:20 Heidi receives 2.5mg of Morphine as well as another 10mg Gravol. At 3:35 am her legs are put on back slabs and her ankles are wrapped in tensor bandages. Her pain remains unbearable. At 4:40 am she is given 2.5mg of Morphine and again 2.5mg of Morphine at 6:10 am. In total, she receives a whopping 22.5mg (9 x 2.5) of Morphine within four and a half hours: from 1:45 am to 6:10 am. Heidi is groggy and starting to get confused. No wonder. But she is still experiencing a lot of pain in her legs. She can't stand for them to be touched; even a slight breeze over her legs causes her pain. It hurts when someone breathes on them; the skin is so taut that the leg hairs are standing straight up and just the tiniest breeze from my breath when I'm looking at them moves the hairs, and even this causes her excruciating pain. This extreme pain is an indication that her leg muscles are developing something called **Compartment Syndrome.**

Here is an explanation from MEDLINEplus Medical Encyclopedia: Compartment Syndrome: (italic type is mine for emphasis)

> Definition: Compartment Syndrome involves the compression of nerves and blood vessels within an enclosed space, leading to impaired blood flow and nerve damage.

> Causes, incidence, and risk factors: Thick layers of tissue called fascia separate groups of muscles in the arms and legs from each other. Inside each layer of fascia is a confined space, called a compartment, that includes the muscle tissue, nerves, and blood vessels. (They are surrounded by the fascia much like wires surrounded by insulation).

Unlike a balloon, fascia do not expand, so any swelling in a compartment will lead to increasing pressure in that compartment, which will compress the muscles, blood vessels, and nerves. If this pressure is high enough, blood flow to the compartment will be blocked, which can lead to permanent injury to the muscle and nerves. If the pressure lasts long enough, *the limb may die and need to be amputated.*

Swelling leading to compartment syndrome is associated with high-energy trauma, such as from a *car accident* or crush injury, or surgery. Compartment syndrome may also occur due to *tight bandages* or casts.

Compartment syndrome is most common in the *lower leg* and forearm, although it can also occur in the hand, foot, thigh and upper arm.

Symptoms: The *hallmark symptom* of compartment syndrome is *severe pain that does not respond to elevation or pain medication.* In more advanced cases, there may be decreased sensation, weakness, and paleness of the skin.

Signs and tests: Typically, severe pain will occur when a muscle running through a compartment is passively moved. For example, when the doctor *moves the toes* up and down, a patient with compartment syndrome in the foot or lower leg will experience *severe pain.* The skin overlying the compartment will be *tensely swollen and shiny.* There will also be pain when the compartment is squeezed.

The test that will absolutely diagnose this condition

involves directly measuring the pressure in the compartment by inserting a needle attached to a pressure meter into the compartment. When the compartment pressure is greater than 45mmHg or when the pressure is within 30mmHg of the diastolic blood pressure (the lower number of the blood pressure), the diagnosis is then made. When chronic compartment syndrome is suspected, this test must be performed immediately after the activity that causes pain.

Treatment: *Treatment* for both acute and chronic compartment syndrome *is usually surgery.* Long incisions are made in the fascia to release the pressure building inside. The wounds are generally left open (covered with a sterile dressing) *[fasciotomy]* and closed during a second surgery, usually 48-72 hours later.

Expectations (prognosis): If the diagnosis of compartment syndrome is made promptly and surgical release performed, the outlook is excellent for recovery of the muscles and nerves inside the compartment. However, the overall prognosis will be determined by the injury leading to the syndrome.

If there is a delay in diagnosis, there can be permanent nerve injury and loss of muscle function. This is more common when an injured person is unconscious or *heavily sedated* and incapable of complaining. *Permanent nerve injury can occur after 12-24 hours of compression.*

Complications: Complications include permanent injury to nerves and muscles that can dramatically impair function.

In more severe cases, limbs may need to be amputated because all the muscles in the compartment have died from lack of oxygen.

Prevention: While there is probably no way to prevent compartment syndrome, being very aware of this condition and *early diagnosis and treatment* will help to prevent many of the complications.

Therefore, *early diagnosis and treatment are the best ways to prevent,* or at least reduce, the injuries sustained to the muscles.

While I am urging Dr. L to keep trying to get Dr. H to come into the hospital, Laura calls my sister Sandy at 6:00 am. Sandy picks up our sister Margie and the two arrive at the hospital around 6:30 am. They help me comfort Heidi, and upon instructions from the doctor, they use nail polish remover to clear Heidi's nails. Sandy takes the polish off Heidi's fingernails, while Margie removes the multiple layers of toenail polish. Heidi expresses extreme pain when her toes are touched, and her Aunty tries ever so carefully not to move her toes while removing the polish. We remove her rings and wristwatch and I tuck them away for safekeeping. We call Heidi's Gramma K and Bill leaves to bring her to the hospital. Sandy and Margie say hello to Gramma K when she arrives and then they leave just after 9:00 am.

Five teens are brought to Peace Arch Hospital that morning. Only Heidi and JR have broken bones. The other three are badly bruised up and I see one of the girls go by in a wheelchair as she pauses to speak with Heidi and JR. She is lucky—she is going home.

During the early morning hours, Heidi speaks with me about the accident and tells me that she thinks a girl died. I tell her it is a girl named Ashley, but neither of us knows her. She also discusses what she has learned about the driver of the car and accurately names John. Prior to my arrival, Heidi had been speaking with the other four injured teens brought in from Stokes Pit. She explains that she knows John, that he is in one of her classes at school, and that he's a really nice guy who wouldn't deliberately hurt her or the others. She says it must have been a horrible mistake, or maybe something was wrong with his car in order for such a disaster like that to happen. She clearly states that she is not mad at him because she knows he would never hurt others on purpose. She asks that I not be angry with him. I am so proud of her in that moment.

Heidi asks repeatedly about her friends, Courtney Wilson and Vanessa Glasser, and wants to know how they are doing and where they are. Around 9:00 am, I call Courtney's house again and this time get her older sister on the phone who informs me that Courtney and Vanessa were taken to Royal Columbian Hospital in New Westminster. Courtney's parents are there with her now, and they had called the sister earlier to report that Courtney, so far, has a broken pelvis in two places, one broken leg, at least two broken ribs and a broken shoulder. She is in surgery now. They are taking good care of Courtney at Royal Columbian. Vanessa appears to be paralyzed from the neck down and has been transferred to the Spinal Unit at Vancouver General Hospital. Heidi is relieved to find out her friends are alive but is very concerned about their injuries.

Heidi repeats that she doesn't want me to be mad at John for causing the accident. She mentions this several times as the news comes in about the others that are hurt. She realizes the enormity of this tragedy and expresses her sadness that a girl died this night. She doesn't know Ashley because they never played sports together and they were attending different schools. Heidi tells me that she was lying beside, or near, the dead girl. This affects her profoundly, to have been that close to death.

2.2 Sidewalk Snack

We lived in Ontario for the first four years of our marriage, moving there when Billy was six weeks old. Both girls were born there. We made frequent trips to B.C. to visit with our families and on one of these visits to B.C. we were staying with my in-laws: Gramma and Grampa K. The neighbours were over having a visit and we all watched adoringly as little Billy and baby Heidi played in the sunny backyard (Laura was yet to be). Heidi was wearing a cute little blue dress, pink tights, and sporting a straw hat on her head. She was just over one; thirteen months old and as cute as a button. Mr. O'Grady from across the street was admiring our beautiful children when he noticed Heidi bending over to pick something up from the sidewalk. She quickly popped it into her mouth and he shouted for us to take it out. But Heidi was too fast; she chomped on her crispy treat and swallowed. Then she looked down and walked a few steps before finding another tasty morsel. We watched in horror as she picked up a stiff, sun-dried worm off the sidewalk, placed it between her lips and snapped it in half, relishing the salty (I assume) flavour. I managed to grab the other half out of her hand before she devoured it. Mr. O'Grady was shouting that we'd better make her spit it out, but, of course, she had chewed and swallowed before we could intercept. We adults discussed whether or not we thought the worms were harmful and decided they were not; she seems to have enjoyed them immensely. It had rained the previous night and we discovered many more worms had suffered the same fate on the sidewalk on this hot June afternoon. I found a broom and swept the rest of them into the grass where they would be harder to find. We later teased Heidi about her taste for worms when she was old enough to laugh at her antics as a baby.

2.3   Fluids

The nurses at Peace Arch Hospital tell Heidi she needs to have a catheter installed because she will not be able to get up and go to the washroom. She protests loudly, saying she does not want anyone touching her down there. JR, in the next bed over, was going through the same ordeal but he already submitted to the procedure and was over the embarrassment. Upon hearing that JR was okay with it, Heidi finally relents and allows the nurses to insert a Foley catheter into her urethra. But she is not happy about it and says so. She soon calms down. Heidi's urine is clear and yellow and the tests show no infections. (It isn't until years later while reading the hospital reports that I discover she was also tested for pregnancy. The urine tests show that Heidi is not pregnant).

The nurses earlier installed an IV drip to hydrate Heidi and to aid in the quick administration of drugs. The IV is infusing Normal Saline (N/S) into Heidi's body and it is measured for volume intake, while the catheter allows for urine to flow out, which is measured as volume output. Heidi receives a large volume of fluid, but the nurses and doctors fail to notice the lack of output. She is approaching fluid overload and no one is noticing. Normally the intake and the output are close to the same in measured volume, but Heidi's fluid measurements are irregular. She receives 4500cc (4 ½ litres) of fluids while at Peace Arch, but her urine output is only 500cc (½ litre) The difference of four litres is huge: think of a gallon of milk. Still, no one seems to notice this.

Heidi's care at Peace Arch Hospital is interrupted by the antics of a man brought into Emergency for a drug overdose. He is put in a bed two down from Heidi's and needs the supervision of two attendants. When he is left alone for a moment, he jumps out of his bed and runs wildly throughout the emergency department, naked and with a parade of medical personnel chasing after him. He is shouting and flailing his arms as he runs about the other patients' beds and deftly dodges the staff. It is quite a scene for a few minutes; in the end they tackle him, sedate him and put him back in bed, this time with restraints. He causes quite an uproar before he succumbs to the new drugs and falls back asleep. I find this event a little unnerving.

2.4   Dr. H's Arrival

While taking a break from Heidi's bedside, I decide we need to find Heidi's father and let him know what is happening. At 5:00 am I call the home of our friends, John and Kathy Elden, and ask John how to get in touch with Air Canada. John, also a pilot with Air Canada, says he'll call Crew Scheduling and relay the instructions for Heidi's father to come directly to Peace Arch Hospital when he lands at Vancouver airport later this morning. The Air Canada dispatcher decides to wait until his plane lands before giving him this upsetting news. They hold onto this message, and as it turns out, he never receives it.

Bill and Gramma K are with me at Heidi's bedside when Dr. H finally shows up at 9:15 am. He uncovers her legs, pokes and prods them to Heidi's great discomfort, then orders lateral x-rays. Her legs are now swollen like bent, overstuffed sausages. They are very purple and extremely painful to the touch. Heidi is in a lot of pain and I want the operation done NOW. But Dr. H calmly explains to us that he wants to do a hip operation in Langley first and then he'll come back to Peace Arch and start on Heidi's legs sometime between 2:00 pm and 4:00 pm, depending on whether or not he can reschedule a knee operation here. He explains that he doesn't use rods, but will correct Heidi's fractures with metal plates and screws. He is concerned about compartment syndrome and tells the nurse to watch for Heidi's foot responses (pedal pulses). At this point Heidi has diminishing sensations in her feet but they are still reacting somewhat to stimulus. Dr. H says he'll look at the new x-rays when he gets back from Langley, but in the meantime Heidi should be given more morphine for the pain. He does not seem concerned about the extra five to seven hours Heidi will have to wait for her surgery. He leaves and we never see him again. We assume he is on his way to Langley but it turns out this is not the case.

Heidi is very, very uncomfortable. She squirms and says her back hurts and she wants to rest on her side, but of course she can't because her legs are not splinted for safe movement. She is still lying on the flat board from the ambulance. I ask the nurses and doctor several times if Heidi should have ice-packs on her legs to reduce the swelling, so to placate me a nurse brings in a small plastic sandwich bag filled with ice-water and plops it on a small section of one leg. It does not have any affect whatsoever on these legs that look ready to burst.

Bill and Laura take Gramma K home after the conversation with Dr. H, knowing they should return before Heidi's operation at 2:00 pm: Dr. H's earliest estimation. Heidi is taken into the x-ray department and I accompany her into the room. This new jostling causes her legs more pain, but she only whispers to me, "Mom, it really hurts." I tell her to be strong, to just endure the pain for a little while longer until her operation; then she'll be healing and the pain will diminish. She promises to be brave for me and tries not to cry. When she says, "I love you, Mom," it sends a shiver up my spine and I realize I don't want to hear those words. They sound too much like a farewell. I can only think of the next phase of getting my daughter back to her normal, feisty, teenaged self. (I cannot remember if I said it back. I hope I did, but I'm not sure). They are signalling me to leave the x-ray room now and I tell Heidi I'll be waiting just outside the doorway. I tell her to be brave and it'll all be over soon. She says "Okay, Mom, I'll try to be brave now." and those are the last words I will ever hear from my Heidi. I kiss her goodbye, stroke her forehead one last time and I leave the room as instructed.

2.5   Zippity Do-dah.

My father-in-law died suddenly in February of 1983. He was play-ing with Heidi and her brother Billy at the time, and his heart attack came as quite a shock to us all. Heidi's father was in the midst of a transfer from Toronto to Vancouver and I brought the children out to Vancouver for their grandparents to look after when I returned to Ontario to help with the move. When Gram-pa K died, Heidi's father and I decided it might be best to move in with Gramma K for awhile until we found a house of our own. We had to wait a few months, which turned into a year, for our house in Milton, Ontario to sell first. This was the big real estate mar-ket slump of 1983 when mortgage rates went up over 18% and house sales dropped. We settled into his old home for fourteen months before we were able to afford our own home again. Dur-ing this time, Billy started Kindergarten at the neighbourhood school and Heidi was enrolled in a dance class for pre-schoolers. She was just three years old in the fall of 1983, and so very sweet. She loved her dance classes and would proudly practice for us: putting on costumes, singing, and going through the various and elaborate hand motions for certain songs. She performed the Hawaiian Christmas Song, "Mele Kalikimaka" complete with hula dancing, at age three.

One of her all-time favourite songs was "Zippity do-dah" (…zip-pity-ay, my oh my what a wonderful day, plenty of sunshine coming my way, zippity do-dah, zippity-ay …Mr. Bluebird on my shoulder…). Readers my age and older will surely recognise this delightful old song. Heidi would get us all singing this song whenever we went for car rides, especially on outings on sunny days. Never failing to cheer us up, it was our favourite song to sing when we went boating and camping over the years. My parents and I still think of Heidi when we hear this song, and we picture her with her round chubby cheeks, wild curly hair, great big blue eyes, and that famous gap-toothed grin. She was such a little treasure at that age and so full of joy. She had the deepest, heartiest laugh ever heard coming from a little girl.

I can hear it still, when I am very quiet inside.

2.6   Seizure

I am told to wait outside the x-ray room while they shoot the x-rays, so I walk down the hall towards the payphone. The Radiology Technician, a Ms. T, is puzzling over why Heidi's legs are not splinted separate from her body. She makes the assessment that Heidi's legs are not properly supported with the correct splints, and because of this, she is afraid the bones might burst through the taut skin if her legs are moved. She decides not to attempt the lateral x-rays that Dr. H has ordered. Nurse S brings Heidi into the x-ray room and notices soon after that Heidi's eyes are rolling back. Realizing that something is terribly wrong, she leaves Heidi unattended for the few seconds it takes to run through the x-ray doors and call for help. At 9:40 am, according to Ms. T, she is alerted by Nurse S and agrees to call ER—STAT. A technician sees Heidi vomit up a large amount of brown fluid and start to seizure. Nurse S returns to Heidi and, together with Nurse K, they turn Heidi's upper torso onto her right side. The nurses are later confused as to whether or not she vomited. An x-ray technician is the only person who claims to have seen this happen.

I see medical personnel rushing into the x-ray room. I try to follow, but am pushed back and told to stay out. Dr. C finds me in the hall about a half hour later and explains there is nothing to worry about. Heidi has had a seizure, but it's a common occurrence when someone is in extreme pain. He says it's just her brain reacting to the pain in her legs and that she'll be okay. He leaves to go back and I see them wheel her into a side room in emergency. They won't let me see her. There are still a lot of people moving in and out of the room and I don't know what's going on in there.

Heidi is met by Dr. P as she is returned to the emergency room during her seizure, with her limbs rigid and her jaw clamped tight. Nurse S claims there was no vomiting in the radiology department, but then Ms. T says there was no vomiting in the emergency room. Nevertheless, Heidi has certainly aspirated (vomited and inhaled) and her lungs are now in trouble. Dr. P discusses her condition with Dr. D and they re-apply a neck collar and sedate her with 5mg of Valium (muscle relaxant/ sedative). Dr. P struggles to insert an oral airway, mainly because Heidi keeps clenching her jaw down on it. Her blood oxygen levels are starting to drop and the doctors are getting alarmed at her negligible neurological responses. She makes no verbal responses and will not open her eyes to her name being called. At 10:10 am her blood oxygen saturation is 97%; at 10:10 am her oxygen saturation is 96%; at 10:20 am her oxygen saturation is 93%; and by 10:30 her blood oxygen saturation levels drop to 92% in spite of the 100% oxygen being given orally. Her lungs are not functioning properly. At no time are her lungs suctioned for vomit.

At 10:00 am, Dr. P calls Royal Columbian and speaks with a neurosurgeon, Dr. M. He continues to monitor her condition, but she is still unresponsive. At 10:10 am Heidi starts to open her eyes when her name is called, and she is now responding to pain by withdrawing all four limbs when stimulated. Her only verbal response is a loud groaning to the pain. Her hands remain clenched. At 10:10 am I am allowed in to see Heidi briefly, but long enough to witness the nurse cutting her hands on the broken glass and sharp gravel imbedded in Heidi's back. Portable chest x-rays are ordered, and as the nurse slips the x-ray plate under Heidi's torso she jerks her arms back at the sudden pain. We both look at her bleeding hands and realize that Heidi has been lying on gravel and broken glass since the time of the accident at 12:30 am. No wonder she was squirming and complaining her back hurt. But there would be no more complaining from Heidi. At 10:30 Dr. P makes a STAT call to Royal Columbian's Dr. M, neurosurgeon, then arranges with their ER receiving physician to have Heidi transferred immediately. An ambulance is called. It is decided that she will need assistance with breathing throughout the trip to New Westminster; therefore, Dr. C will accompany her.

At 10:50 am Dr. P arranges for Dr. G (Anaesthetist) to intubate Heidi (insert an airtube deep into her trachea). At 11:05 am, Dr. G sedates Heidi with 200mg of Fentanyl (narcotic analgesic), 100mg of Lidocaine (antiarrhythmic), and 120mg of Succinylcholine (neuromuscular blocking agent). Then, at 11:10 am, he gives her 5mg of Diazepam (muscle relaxant/sedative), and 8mg of Pavulon (neuromuscular blocking agent). She is now in a drug-induced coma. Next, Dr. G intubates her with a # 7.5 endotracheal tube (ETT), and she is thereby manually hyperventilated with 100% oxygen until she arrives at Royal Columbian.

After another half hour or so, Dr. C comes to speak with me. He says Heidi is in a coma and they are transferring her to Royal Columbian Hospital in New Westminster (RCH). I don't understand. He says they are worried about her brain and have arranged for a neurosurgeon to see her when she arrives at RCH. He says she will be transferred shortly by ambulance and that I should arrange to go there soon. He is going in the ambulance with Heidi to ventilate her, and he will ensure she arrives safely at Royal Columbian. He allows me a brief visit with my now comatose daughter. I am so scared I feel sick. I don't stay very long at her bedside.

After taking Gramma K home, Bill and Laura go back to our house to pick up some clothes for me, as I am still bra-less and in a crumpled sweatshirt. They decide to rest awhile at home because they know Heidi won't be operated on until the afternoon. They notice the flashing red light on the answering machine indicating there are messages, so they press "play." What they hear will continue to haunt them for many years to come. They listen to Heidi's voice calling from the hospital, crying and pleading for someone to pick up the phone. She is crying for Mom and trying to tell us what has happened to her. She says there was an accident and that her legs are broken. She keeps calling out for Mom, louder and louder, hoping to wake us up. Then Laura and Bill listen as a nurse in the background tells Heidi to hang up, that no one is home, but Heidi insists there must be someone home and refuses to hang up. Then the connection is cut off. A second call from Heidi repeats the same desperate plea for her mother, but this call is louder and she is sobbing on the phone, trying to find her family. She is screaming, "Mom, Mom, Mom, where are you? Wake up, somebody please come to the phone! Mom, Mom, Mom, Mom! I'm hurt, Mom, where are you? Mom, Mom, Mom...." Laura and Bill are very shocked and upset. They have never heard their sister sound so frightened and desperately in need of her family before. Her two messages profoundly affect them. Shaken, they decide it would be best to erase the messages before I can hear them: a good call. They try to rest, but cannot. About an hour later they get the call from me to return to the hospital as soon as possible. Just as they hang up from my call, the phone rings again and this time it's Bill's friend, Caleb Weitzel. Bill explains what is going on and they agree with Caleb's offer to drive them back to Peace Arch. While they are waiting for Caleb to arrive they receive two more calls from me begging them to come quickly. Bill and Laura are nervous wrecks by the time they rejoin me at Peace Arch. I am surprised to see Caleb but understand that they are equally as upset as I am and they felt it was best to leave my car at home and let Caleb drive.

While we wait for them to prepare Heidi for the trip to New Westminster, Bill calls Air Canada and tells them that Heidi is being transferred to Royal Columbian Hospital in New Westminster. Unfortunately, this new dispatcher does not know about the first message that is waiting for Heidi's father and he forwards the message straight into the cockpit via the fax machine. The children's father is the First Officer on the 767 and he is descending as he prepares to land at Vancouver Airport when the fax machine spits out this message: "Heidi has been transferred to Royal Columbian." That's all the information he receives. He takes his hands off the controls and turns the landing over to the captain. It is common knowledge in the lower mainland that Royal Columbian is the trauma hospital that all the worst accident victims get taken to. Heidi's father knows this is going to be bad. He calls Dispatch and tries to get more information, but the new dispatcher on duty doesn't know anything about the first message and can tell him nothing. He is frantic. The plane lands safely and he runs out of the airport, gets into his car and drives as fast as possible to New Westminster.

At 11:30 am, Caleb drives us to RCH and about half way there the ambulance carrying Heidi passes us. We try to stay close behind it all the way into New Westminster. The trip takes us about twenty-five minutes whereas it would normally take about forty. We screech into a parking stall in the emergency area and run into the hospital. We arrive just before noon.

Nurse K accompanies Dr. C with Heidi in the ambulance to Royal Columbian and continues to make notes on her chart. At 11:20 she writes that Heidi's "total fluids in since admission [is] 4500cc NS—output 500cc." She underlines the numbers for emphasis. 11:30 am is the time noted for leaving Peace Arch District Hospital and arrival is noted at 11:55 am. Heidi's airway is continuously manually bagged (ventilated) by Dr. C during the ride and two IV lines continue to run Normal Saline into her system. Heidi arrives at Royal Columbian in what Nurse K describes as "stable condition" (PADH, 29).

2.7   Stitches

Our family lived in the City of Mississauga and then in the town of Milton, both in the province of Ontario, from 1979 to 1983. Heidi and her sister Laura were born in Mississauga General Hospital, whereas their older brother Billy was born in British Columbia just before our move east, at Abbotsford's MSA Hospital. A year before our return to B.C., we bought our first house in the small town of Milton, located just outside Mississauga in the Toronto area (close to the airport). One evening shortly after our move to Milton we were entertaining our friends, John and Kathy Elden, and their daughter Kristy. Heidi and Kristy were born two months apart and Kathy and I had enjoyed going through our pregnancies together. Laura was still tiny, about six months old, and partially mobile in her walker. The two two-year-old girls were playing with Billy and running around the house when Heidi tripped while rounding a corner of the coffee table. She fell face-first on its sharp edge and received a slash just above her left eye. It bled profusely with the increased blood pressure from all the screaming, and we decided she might need stitches. We thought it best if her father took her to the hospital while I stayed home with the baby and Billy. I couldn't handle the thought of watching while they stitched up my little girl. Heidi's father later described the experience as harrowing, and he was absolutely exhausted when he arrived home. The doctors made him hold down a sobbing Heidi on the table while they put just one staple under her eyebrow. She was quiet when she returned home; and her eyelid and brow turned many different colours over the next week. It looked awful on her pretty little face. We thought that was a really bad day for our young family. We had no idea.

PART THREE:

Royal Columbian Hospital

3.1   Arrival at Royal Columbian Hospital

We enter the RCH emergency room at about 11:55 am, just behind Heidi and a group of medical personnel. We slip into the curtained cubicle to see Heidi, but it is so crowded with doctors and nurses that Bill and Laura decide to wait in the family room, just offside the general emergency waiting room. Standing next to Heidi, I watch as the assisting orthopaedic surgeon, Dr. W, removes the blanket to expose Heidi's legs. He shouts, "Oh my God, look what they've done to her legs!" Alarmed, I ask him what he means. He points to the tensor bandages that are tightly wound around each ankle, and as he quickly tries to remove them he tells me they are cutting off her circulation and nerves; she could lose the use of both of her feet. I am taken aback. I do not fully absorb this information until Dr. O, the attending orthopaedic surgeon, agrees and speaks angrily about the Peace Arch doctors who did this. Again, I have no medical background, no schooling, and no experience with these kinds of injuries. I am becoming increasingly frightened. These doctors at RCH appear alarmed. I am feeling really scared right now. Heidi is still in a coma and her brain is not responding well. Her blood oxygen levels are continuing to drop because her lungs will not function properly. Suddenly, her legs are the least of her worries.

Heidi's father, wearing his full pilot's uniform, rushes into the emergency cubicle just as they mount the x-rays on the lightboard. I have already seen the films, but he hasn't, and his reaction is similar to that of JR's father at Peace Arch. He needs to sit for a few minutes and a nurse gives him a paper bag to breathe into because he starts to hyperventilate. He retreats to the family room to join Bill and Laura, taking his paper bag with him.

Bill and Laura are surprised to see two boys from school also waiting in the emergency room. The brothers, Francis and Sean McCann are there waiting for word on Courtney and Vanessa, and now Heidi. Francis and Heidi dated briefly the previous year. They are nice boys, and like the rest of the students from Langley's high schools, they are very concerned about the welfare of those injured in the previous night's horrible accident at Stokes Pit. Unbeknownst to us, and since the early morning hours, details about the accident are being continuously broadcast on all the local radio and television stations. It seems everyone knows that a drunk driver has hurt fifteen to twenty teenagers. Rumours start making their rounds, twisting and turning with each telling, such as: Heidi has had a heart attack, Courtney has had a leg amputated, Vanessa will be a quadriplegic for the rest of her life, etc. Of course none of these rumours are true. The community of Langley is in turmoil over this accident and an information meeting is scheduled for students, parents and police at H.D. Stafford Secondary School on Grade Crescent for the following day, Sunday, September 14th.

I question the doctors and they are very forthright with me about her multiple injuries. Dr. M, the emergency room doctor, Dr. M, the neurosurgeon, and two orthopaedic surgeons, Dr. O and Dr. W, are attending Heidi. Between 12:00 noon and 1:00 pm they perform a myriad of tests, take fluid samples and have her x-rayed. Heidi's chest films (x-rays) show congestion that indicates fluid overload; and the films show some patchy air space in her left and middle upper lung zones that are consistent with aspiration/pneumonitis. The doctors cannot figure out how her lungs were damaged and a consultant, Dr. Q, guesses that perhaps she had aspirated; but there is no indication of this on the paperwork that comes from Peace Arch. Her lungs are in serious trouble. Dr. M, the neurosurgeon, finds that he cannot perform a complete neurological examination because she has been given the drug, Pavulon. He orders a CT scan (cat-scan) of her head, which shows no abnormalities at this time. Dr. O determines that she, indeed, has compartment syndrome in her right leg and that he will probably perform four compartment fasciotomies in addition to the plates, screws and rods he will use to realign her tibias and fibulas. It is questionable at this time whether or not he will need to do a fasciotomy on her left leg. At 2:00 pm they make the plaster back slabs to splint both legs, which finally stabilizes them. She continues to receive small doses of morphine every hour or so for the pain.

The surgeons decide it would be best to operate on the legs as soon as possible as they will need to do a lot of work. They are concerned with her problematic brain activity but at this point she shows no signs of brain damage or skull fracture so they feel her legs can be attended to now. Heidi goes into the Operating Room at 3:55 pm. Dr. O performs a fasciotomy on Heidi's right leg to relieve the compartment syndrome, followed by the open surgical reduction of her bone fractures. A plate is bolted on the double break on her right tibia and a titanium rod is inserted into her left tibia. The right leg is left open (fasciotomy) to allow for the drainage of excess fluids from her muscles. The open flesh is covered with saline packs to keep the wounds fresh and to prevent infection. The left leg doesn't seem as bad, so he closes it up. The smaller bones, the fibulas, are found to be shattered and Dr. O decides to leave some of the fragments misaligned, concentrating instead on the larger tibias. The diagnoses from all doctors are right compartment syndrome with bilateral tibia/fibula fractures. This has now been corrected with the surgery. Dr. O asks that Heidi's left leg be closely monitored during the night for signs of compartment syndrome. She is out of surgery around 8:30 pm and is taken to the Post Anaesthetic Care Unit (PACU) for monitoring. She is ventilated on a respirator. Her vital signs are stable and her urinary output is good, but her oxygenation status is still poor.

It is a long operation. We are waiting outside the Operating Room for her to emerge, but it seems to take forever. Finally, Dr. O finds us and says the operation went well and that her bones are strong and he expects a full recovery. He explains again what the fasciotomy is for and that he hopes to close up her leg in a day or two. We are so relieved. Heidi is still unconscious when we go in to see her, but we are assured everything will be okay. Bill and Laura decide to go back home with Caleb. It has been a long, exhausting day for them. Heidi's father and I spend the evening making many phone calls to family members and friends and updating everyone on what is happening to Heidi.

3.2   Starfish on Sucia

Heidi's father bought a boat when she was five years old. It was about 16 feet long and had an outboard motor. Once we started exploring Georgia Strait and the Gulf Islands, we planned every summer around our boating and camping trips. We traveled as far north as Hornby Island and the great beach at Tribune Bay; this exotic white beach with its clear turquoise waters is as close to a Hawaiian beach as B.C. gets. Then we explored south to the Juan de Fuca Strait, the area around Victoria, and across to the United States' San Juan Islands. One of these islands is known as Sucia—a little paradise accessible only by private boat. We enjoyed camping there a couple of times.

Our most memorable moment on Sucia, apart from discovering the fossils and petroglyphs, was the time Heidi and Laura were searching for starfish at low tide. The girls and I gingerly made our way across a rocky breakwater as we could see lots of purple starfish clinging to the rocks at the water line. I watched as Heidi bent over to pry a starfish off when a big wave rolled up and crashed into the rocks. This huge wave washed over Heidi and suddenly sucked her out to sea. Laura and I panicked. Heidi, who could swim, was afloat and screaming for Mom. I was frantically stretching my hand out to reach her, as far as I could without falling in. Another wave brought her closer in to the rocks and I almost touched her hand, but then she was washed out again. I was getting ready to jump in when the next wave threw her back onto the lower rocks and I was finally able to grasp her arm and haul her back to safety.

First we were screaming, then we were crying. And then we were all laughing at our near disaster. What a moment in a child's life, to be carried out to sea while watching your mother's hand stretching out for you, just out of reach. And for me to see my little girl sucked out to sea, barely beyond my grasp. Well, it was a horrifying experience. We gave up on catching a starfish that day and retreated to the calmer sandy beach. We almost lost her that day.

3.3   End of the first day.

After her leg operations, Heidi is kept in the recovery room in order to be closely monitored. We are waiting outside one of the family rooms near the Operating Rooms that line the corridor. This area is a very busy place for anyone to spend extended time in. We visit with our comatose daughter in the recovery room between making phone calls and receiving incoming visitors.

Courtney's parents, Dianne and Grant Wilson, find me near the family room while taking a walk from their daughter's wardroom in another section of the hospital. They say that Courtney's operations went well, but that she is in a lot of pain. Through her morphine haze she has been asking for Heidi, so her parents have promised to find some news to take back to her. They find me and I fill them in. Dianne reports that Courtney has a broken pelvis in two spots, front and back. Her right shoulder is broken, and two ribs on her left side are broken as well as one or two ribs on her right side. Dianne tells me Courtney's right tibia and fibula are broken, but that they were repaired that morning. Her leg break was a bad one; her fractured tibia was sticking out of her leg at the accident scene. She has a titanium rod inside her tibia to hold it together; and although there is a gap in the bone where she broke it, they are hopeful it will knit together over the next month or so. They tell me Vanessa has been transferred to Vancouver General Hospital's Spinal Unit. Vanessa cannot move anything from the neck down. She is alert and aware of what is going on and she is, understandably, very frightened and upset. Vanessa's prognosis is not good, but then again the doctors do not know the willpower of Vanessa Glasser. We are all very worried about our daughters but we joke nevertheless about Heidi and Courtney sharing a hospital room while they recover; and we imagine the antics they would likely be getting into: harassing nurses, wheelchair races, and in-room parties with their friends. At this point we feel secure that both our daughters will recover.

By 8:40 pm, the nurses notify Dr. O that they are unable to palpitate Heidi's left pedal pulses and that her left foot now appears mottled and discoloured. The compartment syndrome in her left leg is now making its presence known, so arrangements are made to perform a fasciotomy on her left leg. At 8:50 pm Heidi is trying to wake up and is showing some signs of consciousness. She is still ventilated and breathing spontaneously. The nurses note that thick yellow secretions are suctioned out of her lungs and that when she is suctioned her oxygen saturation drops to 86%. She is put back on 100% oxygen. Another portable chest x-ray is taken at 9:30 pm and it shows the type of congestion consistent with fluid overload. At 9:51 pm Heidi's lungs are suctioned again and at this time the nurses note that thick, chunky yellow sputum is coming up, accompanied by a cough. Could this be some of the vomit she inhaled at Peace Arch? Heidi gives the nurse a rough time when she tries to insert an oral tube for ventilation: Heidi keeps biting down on the tube and effectively closing off the oxygen they are trying to give her. My girl is fighting.

Heidi has not yet recovered from the effects of the anaesthesia and the doctors are concerned. Dr. O informs us that her left leg needs a fasciotomy, and just past midnight, she returns to the operating room for this procedure. The operation is a success and her circulation shows marked improvement almost immediately. She is moved back to the Post Anaesthetic Care Unit at 1:00 am and more portable chest x-rays are taken at 1:14 am and then again at 5:53 am. These films show that the mild congestion (fluid overload) is resolving itself but that the patchy air space in her mid upper lung zones (aspiration pneumonitis) is still present. Her Hemoglobin is low (84) in spite of the transfusions she receives during surgery.

We see Heidi for just a few minutes after her second fasciotomy, around 1:00 am. She appears to be sleeping restfully, so we decide to go home for a few hours to catch some sleep and change our clothes.

3.4 Ups and downs with Mom's car.

Heidi earned her driver's license when she was sixteen; she took some lessons and passed her driver's test on the first try. With her license came a newfound sense of freedom for both Heidi and her friends. I trusted her to drive safely and often let her borrow my car: a 1989 black Hyundai Sonata with a sunroof. She loved going for long drives. Once in a while I would notice some subtle changes in the way my car operated after a night with Heidi. The shocks would be a little rough, as would the brakes on occasion. I thought it was just my imagination and didn't think much of it. One day she came home from Courtney's in tears and called me out to the carport to see what had happened. The front left corner was smashed in. The headlight cavity was exposed and the turn signal light was torn off. Heidi explained, in tears, that she didn't see Courtney's sister's boyfriend's truck parked on the curb next to Courtney's driveway, and when she backed out and swung over onto the street she crashed into his truck. Apparently there was no damage to his much tougher truck. But Heidi was devastated by what she had done to my car, which I needed on a daily basis for my real estate job. I asked her if anyone was hurt and when she said "No" I was relieved and told her not to fret so much. It was only a car. I never stopped allowing her to borrow it because I trusted her to continue showing such honesty.

What I didn't know until years later was that Heidi loved to drive along 32nd Avenue, just west of the Pacific Highway (176 St.), and fly over the big wavy bumps in the road. If she went fast enough she could get some "air" and the car would come crashing down and bounce when it landed, to the great delight of Heidi and her passengers, who have all relayed this story to me. It was like riding a roller coaster, with all the ups and downs, the flying through the air and the bouncing on the ground. Sometimes they would see sparks when the car landed, which thrilled them even further. Heidi's sister Laura, and friends Courtney, Jamie, Tiffany and Leigh have all gone on these joyrides with Heidi in my car. They have assured me they always felt safe and that Heidi really wasn't going that fast; the road just had many humps close together in a row. That explains the worn out shock absorbers and the weary suspension system. But looking back, I'm so glad she was able to have that kind of fun, to take a calculated ride on the wild side and experience the kind of car rides she didn't get when her mother was driving. (For all the teenagers reading this I'm sorry to inform you the Highways Department has since corrected the waves along this stretch of 32nd Avenue).

Even though it was wrong, and possibly dangerous, I am delighted to see that Heidi was a normal, thrill-seeking teenager who grasped at the chance to have some clean fun. After all, it was only a car.

3.5   Sunday, September 14

Kathy Elden picks me up at 6:00 am this Sunday morning to drive me into New Westminster because I am too distraught to drive; I want to be back with Heidi as soon as possible. We stop for coffee at a Starbucks on King George Highway in Surrey on the way to the hospital, and we take this time to catch up on the events of the past thirty-six hours. This is the first chance I've had to speak at length with Kathy, and she is horrified to discover that Heidi had been at Peace Arch Hospital all that time yesterday. She tells me that their emergency room has a less than stellar reputation in the medical community and that had she known earlier she would have come down there and insisted Heidi be transferred immediately. I am surprised at her vehement statements, but later I will come to understand just how accurate her assessment of Peace Arch is. Up until noon yesterday, I felt the doctors and nurses were doing a good job, which only demonstrates my complete lack of medical knowledge at this time.

Heidi is installed in the Intensive Care Unit, ICU, at 7:30 am, Sunday, September 14th. She is still ventilated but is now experiencing troubles with her heart. She shows a tachycardia (abnormally fast heartbeat) of 100 to 140 beats per minute (normal heartbeat is 70 bpm). Her temperature is elevated at 38.3 degrees Celsius. She is given Morphine every hour or two for pain and to relax her body as it accepts the mechanical ventilation. The sputum is analyzed and found to contain +2 pus cells; Heidi has a lung infection. A doctor speculates that her lung problems stem from aspiration and perhaps fat emboli (congestion of the lungs that often follows long bone fractures). Her delayed recovery from anaesthesia is guessed at this point to be caused by fat emboli to the brain (fat embolism syndrome). Heidi is unresponsive to stimuli, with no sedation. She has an electrocardiogram (ECG) of her heart and it shows no irregularities, except a non-specific T-wave abnormality.

An ECG is a recording of the electrical changes that occur in the heart muscles (myocardium) during a cardiac cycle (heartbeat). When the SA node (the heart's pacemaker) signals (every 0.85 seconds), the atrial fibres produce an electrical change called the P wave. The P wave indicates that the atria are about to contract. Then the QRS complex signals that the ventricles are about to contract (the spike seen on ECG). The electrical changes that occur as the ventricular muscle fibres recover produce the T wave. (Mader 130-1). Heidi's T-waves are abnormal. Her heart is experiencing difficulties: it is beating too fast and it's not recovering properly.

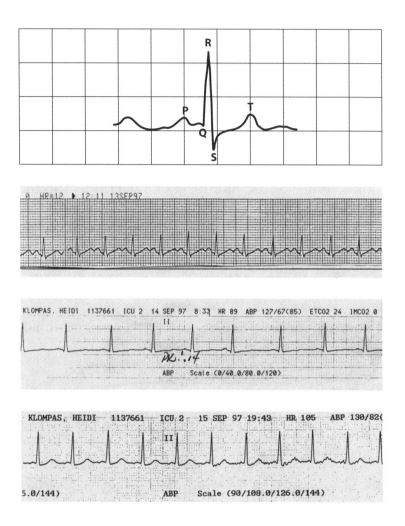

The above shows a normal heartbeat and the next three tapes show Heidi's heart activity on September 13th, 14th, and 15th. Note the change on September 14th.

I am anxiously waiting outside the Intensive Care Unit for the tests to be finished so that I can visit Heidi. They allow me in during a break between tests, and I am told I can only spend about five minutes with her. I whisper to her to hang in there, that she'll be okay soon. She doesn't respond at all to my voice; she appears to be in a deep sleep. I believe it is the drugs that are keeping her under, when in fact it is her brain that is not responding.

At 8:15 am, she is suctioned for a moderate amount of yellow, greenish sputum and again the culture is collected. At 9:05 Heidi is taken for a Catscan (CT scan) of her head, and it shows some brain swelling. It indicates multiple emboli and possibly fat embolism due to the multiple bone fractures. Specifically, the CT scan report reads:

> "Multifocal areas of low density are identified throughout the posterior fossa, and also scattered areas of both cerebral hemispheres. The largest area of low density is seen in the left inferior parietal region, and this may be associated with some minimal hemorrhage. Most of the low density changes are peripherally located near the grey/white matter junction. The appearances are in keeping with multiple emboli and the possibility of fat embolism is raised in this patient with a history of multiple orthopedic injuries" (RCH, 217).

Heidi is developing Fat Embolism Syndrome (FES). Here are some explanations of fat embolism syndrome from medical texts and articles. The italic type is mine, for emphasis.

> Fat embolism syndrome occurs when fat from the marrow of a broken bone enters the bloodstream and forms an embolus that lodges in the lungs. Classic signs and symptoms include confusion, decreased PaCO2, an unexplained *increase in temperature,* dyspnea [shortness of breath], and air hunger. The patient may also have *tachycardia* [rapid heartbeat], rales [rattling,

bubbling sounds with breaths], wheezing, and a cough. As the condition progresses, *petechiae* [red rash] in the chest and neck develop (RN, 85).

"Fever, tachycardia, tachypnea, altered mental status, and respiratory distress arise soon after..." (Ganong, 209).

Increased pressure in the marrow cavity resulting from trauma, *motion of bone fragments...* forces the marrow into venous sinusoids from which the fat travels to the lungs and occludes pulmonary capillaries; smaller fat droplets (7 to 10 um in diameter) may travel through the pulmonary capillaries into the systemic circulation and hence to the brain and other organs. Neurologic manifestations of fat embolism are diverse and nonspecific, ranging from irritability and confusion (common) to focal deficits, *seizures, and coma* (infrequent). A rare clinical scenario is *lack of recovery from general anesthesia.* Any change in CNS [Central Nervous System] status in a trauma patient should alert the physician to the possibility of fat embolism. Cerebral edema [brain swelling] caused by a combination of hypoxemia, embolic ischemia, and toxic free fatty acids-induced cerebrovascular [blood vessels in the brain] disruption contributes to the neurologic deterioration. T-wave changes [in the heart] have also been seen and are usually caused by hypoxia. [In the lungs], the most common finding is a diffuse, bilateral infiltrate, which can be interstitial or alveolar, sometimes referred as a snowstorm pattern. In trauma patients with FES rapid splinting and immobilization of the injured limbs can minimize complications. Another factor in the etiology of fat embolism is the time of operative fixation of the fracture. Several studies have observed a decrease incidence of FES in fracture patients treated with *early internal fixation* compared to a control group treated nonoperatively. This difference may have been due to reduction of local tissue pressure around the fracture brought about by opening and draining the fracture hematoma. In addition this approach prevents recurrent fat embolization produced by movement of fracture fragments during management with skeletal traction (Anon, 2-6).

The principal clinical features of fat embolism syndrome are: *Respiratory failure,* Cerebral dysfunction and Petechiae. The onset of FES is sudden, with restlessness and vague pain in the chest. *Fever* occurs, often in excess of 38.3 C [Celsius] (101 F), with a disproportionately [high] pulse rate. Otherwise unexplained dyspnea, tachypnea, arterial hypoxemia with cyanosis and diffuse alveolar infiltrates on chest x-ray. *Unexplained* signs of cerebral dysfunction, such as confusion, delirium or *coma.* Petechiae over the upper half of the body, conjunctive, oral mucosa and retinae. Management of fat embolism syndrome... consists primarily of ensuring good arterial oxygenation. *Supplemental oxygen* is given to maintain the arterial oxygen tension in the normal range. *Restriction of fluid intake* and the use of diuretics can be done to *minimize fluid accumulation in the lungs. Prompt surgical stabilization* of long bone fractures... reduce the risk of the syndrome. The mortality rate from fat embolism syndrome is 10 percent or less. (Prazeres, p.1-2).

Fat embolism and FES are also *more likely to occur after*

closed, rather than open, fractures. *Multiple fractures* release a greater amount of fat into the marrow vessels than do single fractures, increasing the likelihood of FES. Clinical fat embolism syndrome presents with *tachycardia,* tachypnea, *elevated temperature,* hypoxemia, hypocapnia, thrombocytopenia, and occasionally mild *neurological symptoms.* A petechial rash... is considered to be a pathognomonic sign of FES, however, it appears late and often disappears within hours. It results from occlusion of dermal capillaries by fat, and increased capillary fragility. CNS signs, including a change in level of consciousness, are not uncommon. They are usually nonspecific and have the features of diffuse encephalopathy: acute confusion, stupor, coma, rigidity, or convulsions. *Cerebral edema contributes to the neurologic deterioration.* Hypoxemia is present in nearly all patients with FES, often to a PaO2 of well below 60 mmHg. The chest x-ray may show evenly distributed, fleck-like pulmonary shadows (Snow Storm appearance), increased pulmonary markings and dilation of the right side of the heart. The most effective prophylactic measure is to *reduce long bone fractures as soon as possible* after the injury. Maintenance of intravascular volume is important because shock can exacerbate the lung injury caused by FES. Mechanical ventilation and PEEP may be required to maintain arterial oxygenation (Odegard, 1-3).

Unexplained hypoxia in the perioperative period where there is a long bone or pelvic fracture may be due to fat embolism associated with the release of intramedullary fat into the venous circulation from the fracture site. This can occur at any time following fracture, *but is more common if surgical fixation is delayed for longer than 8 hours* (Wilson, p.9).

Incidence of the fat embolism syndrome today is far lower than it was a few decades ago, early recognition of the symptoms is still of major importance in preventing morbidity and mortality in patients with single and multiple skeletal injuries. The clinical diagnosis of the syndrome, which means that two out of three main symptoms (pulmonary [lung] distress, cerebral confusion, petechial rash) must be clinically evident, has been reported in 0.5-3 per cent of the patients who sustained a single long-bone fracture. In *multiply* [sic] *injured patients, percentages of up to 30 per cent* have been reported. The incidence increases with the *number* of fractures. *Early open reduction*[s]... are believed to reduce the risk of developing major pathophysiological disturbances, such as the fat embolism syndrome [and] ARDS [adult respiratory distress syndrome]. Several so-called minor symptoms accompany the clinical picture fairly consistently. The most important ones are: *early fever* (over 38.5 degrees), sometimes already present at the first presentation of the patient in the emergency room, an unexpected *decrease in haematocrit* [proportion of red blood cells to a volume of blood] from day 1 onwards, retinal changes, jaundice, renal changes and *tachycardia* [rapid heart beat]. Whereas the main symptoms can be explained relatively easily by the embolization theory, the minor symptoms, such as *early fever and accelerated haemoglobin loss,* pose more of a problem. Nevertheless these minor signs may be of crucial importance in reflecting the onset of pathophysiological disturbances, because they often precede the pulmonary and neurological signs. Therefore the *early recognition* of symptoms that represent or accompany the fat embolism syndrome is of the utmost importance, because early supportive pulmonary therapy and other resuscitative measures may prevent deterioration of the pathophysiological process and so reduce morbidity and mortality (ten Duis, 77-85).

The Neurosurgeon, Dr. M, explains that fat from Heidi's bone marrow has entered her bloodstream and is making contact with her brain and causing a series of mini-strokes that result in the swelling of her brain tissue. Heidi is given Mannitol (diuretic) to reduce the fluids and relieve the pressure, Vitamin K to improve clotting, the steroid Decadron (glucocortcoid and anti-inflammatory) to reduce the brain tissue swelling, Lorazepam (mild sedative) to keep her still, and large amounts of Morphine for the pain. At 11:10 am a nurse notices the petechiae rash on Heidi's chest, just below her breasts. She now has all the major symptoms of FES that are mentioned above: rapid heart beat, T-wave abnormalities, petechiae rash, low hemoglobin, low blood-oxygen, and swelling of the brain. Our Heidi is in big, big trouble and her condition continues to deteriorate throughout the day.

We visit Heidi at 9:00 am, then again at noon. Her neurological signs are diminishing. At 1:00 pm Dr. M speaks with us about FES and the possibility of putting in a brain shunt. The shunt will perform two functions: it will allow the doctors and nurses to monitor and record Heidi's inter-cranial pressure, or ICP; and it will allow for the drainage of excess cerebrospinal fluid, or CSF, when the swelling expands her brain. This will relieve the pressure and give her brain some room to swell into without causing too much damage. He wants to drill a hole into Heidi's head. We agree, knowing the risks of infection and further complications, but something must be done soon or we will lose Heidi altogether. I think about how mad she'll be when she wakes up to discover a big bald patch in the long curly hair that she loves so much. Small sacrifices.

A nurse makes arrangements for our family to have the 24 hour use of a private "Family Room," complete with a coded lock on the door. It has long cushioned benches inside, long enough to lie down on.

Heidi is closely monitored during the remainder of the afternoon. Her temperature is higher than normal, her heart keeps racing, she still has a cough reflex, and the nurses continue to suction up yellow secretions from her lungs. By 5:00 pm, her pupils are becoming sluggish and have an irregular, elliptical shape; her cough is weaker, and her reflexes are slower; her temperature is high: 38.3 degrees Celsius. At 7:45 pm, her lungs are suctioned for more yellowish-brown secretions. Her hemoglobin is still low, so she is given one unit of packed red blood cells (PRBC). At 8:40 pm, her heart rate increases to 140 bpm and her blood pressure soars to 160 over 100 (160/100). Her pupils are fixed and dilated to 5mm (on a scale of 1 to 8). The resident intern manually bags her with 100% oxygen and she is sedated for flexing and coughing. By 8:45 pm, five minutes later, her pupils have gone down to 3mm and are reactive. The sedation is repeated at 8:45 pm. Ten minutes later, at 8:55 pm, her heart rate and blood pressure go back up and sedation is repeated. She is again bagged by the resident, given Tylenol, and has cool cloths applied to her body to bring her temperature down. The intern pages the neurosurgeon, Dr. M, at 9:00 pm. Two minutes later Dr. M calls in to speak with the intern and they discuss what has happened. By five past 9:00 pm, Heidi's pupils are down to 3mm again, but irregular; she exhibits a slight gag reflex; she shows slight flexing of her arms, but has no cough. Her heart rate is down to 125 bpm and her blood pressure is down to 150/90. Seven minutes later, at 9:13 pm, Heidi's heart rate soars to 160 bpm and her blood pressure is up to a dangerously high 175/125. Dr. M tells the intern to send Heidi in for a CT scan of her head—STAT—and says that he is on his way into the hospital. At this time, Heidi has no cough or gag reflexes nor any limb flexing or corneal reflexes.

During this day, many friends and relatives have come and gone. I am exhausted. My parents come in to see us late in the day, having just driven for ten hours from Prince George through to Langley only to discover a note left on their door telling them that their granddaughter Heidi is hurt and at Royal Columbian. They drop off their bags and drive another hour into New Westminster to be with us. They arrive amid this crisis.

Later, I discover that my brother Darren, who is up in Fort Nelson hunting with our older brother Bill, has found out about the accident by looking over the shoulder of the man standing in front of him in a line-up at a McDonald's restaurant. The man is reading the headline story on the front page of the Sunday Province newspaper. Darren gets an uneasy feeling and decides to call his wife, Karen, in Aldergrove, and is told the bad news. Darren and Bill drive as quickly as they can the long distance from Fort Nelson to Quesnel, where Bill is dropped off at his home. Then Darren carries on south to Aldergrove where he picks up Karen and heads into New Westminster. By Sunday night, most of our family is united in the family room at Royal Columbian. This is the first serious accident in our family's history. Collectively, we've not had more than a few bone breaks, a couple of concussions, and a few fender benders with no major injuries. Our immediate family has never experienced cancer or any other dangerous disease. We are a healthy lot, therefore, the seriousness of Heidi's injuries catches us unawares and ill-equipped to handle these feelings of anger, helplessness, and extreme fear. We are quiet in our panic, but I can smell the sweaty stench of fear in the room.

By 9:18 p.m., Heidi's heart rate goes up to a dangerously high 170 bpm and her blood pressure is 180/120. The intern comes to tell us that they are having problems keeping Heidi's heart rate and blood pressure down. Heidi's father insists on seeing her and the intern assists him into the Intensive Care Unit to see her. Her father is very upset and needs help sitting down. After only a minute or two he is unable to handle the situation and tries to leave but finds he needs a nurse's assistance in getting back to the family room. He is a wreck, and we all register his anguish when we see him helped into the room. I run to the washroom. It seems each time the news gets worse I break into a sweat, my bowels loosen and liquefy, which causes me to race to the toilet, often just making it in time. I am so scared. Finally, our well-meaning crowds of loved-ones leave for their homes, allowing us some quiet time. I try to get some rest, unsuccessfully.

At 9:25 pm, Heidi's heart rate is up to 195 bpm, her pupils are blown to 5mm and are fixed, and her blood pressure is up to 190/120. The intern orders Mannitol. Twenty minutes later, at 9:45 pm, she is given the Mannitol and some more sedation. She is prepared to be taken for her CT scan, and leaves the Intensive Care Unit at 9:55 pm. An intern continuously bags her with 100% oxygen along the way. Fifteen minutes later, at 10:10 pm, Heidi returns from the CT scan with her pupil dilation down to 3mm, her corneals are present, she has a cough reflex, but no motor responses. Dr. M arrives at 10:20 to assess Heidi and decides to insert the Inter Cranial Pressure catheter, or shunt.

He speaks with Heidi's father and gets the consent signed. The Operating Room (OR) won't be ready until 11:00 pm. The drugs kick in and her heart rate goes down to 130 bpm and her blood pressure drops to 105/60. She is more stable.

At 10:45 p.m., Heidi is given 1000mg of Dilantin, an anti-convulsant, to prepare her for surgery. At 11:00 p.m. she is taken into the Operating Room to have a ventricular drain and an intracranial pressure (ICP) monitor inserted by Dr. M, assisted by Dr. Q. The shunt is positioned on the front right side of her skull, just down from the top. About a four inch diameter area of hair is shaved off, and a hole is drilled through her skull to access the area between her brain and her skull to drain cerebral fluid. It will also allow the ICP monitor to slip in between the folds of her brain and record the pressure inside. The operation is completed at 12:30 am (now Sept.15th), and Heidi is returned to the Intensive Care Unit at 12:45 am, still being continuously bagged with 100% oxygen by the resident intern. They set up the monitors and start to see what is happening with her brain.

Her intracranial pressure first registers at a high 19-20 mmHg, and at 1:15 am, Dr. M opens the ventricular drain (EVD) to release some cerebral fluid and ease the pressure. It works: Heidi's ICP drops to 9 with the release of some sero-sanguineous (blood-tinged fluid) drainage. The EVD is reclamped. She is given another unit of red blood cells. At 1:30 a.m., the clamp is reopened to relieve the pressure, then reclamped. At 1:45 a.m. Heidi's ICP rises to 21 and the clamp is reopened, allowing the ICP to drop to 8; the nurse decides to leave the EVD unclamped. Heidi's blood pressure is down to 110/60.

By 2:15 am, Heidi seems to be more stable. She flexes her arms to pain, she has a weak cough, her corneals are present, and her pupils are 3mm. The nurse changes the dressings on her brain shunt site, and on both her legs. She notes a large amount of sero-sanguineous fluid has been draining from her legs. This is good because it indicates the compartment syndrome in her calf muscles is being resolved. Her legs are on the mend and that's one less thing to worry about. Funny thing is, for the last ten hours I haven't given her legs a moment's notice.

At 4:00 am, Heidi's temperature is still high at 38.8 degrees Celsius, so she is given Tylenol. Her heart rate is down to 120 bpm, which is still high, however, this is considered an improvement. Her blood pressure is back down to a relatively normal 120/70. She is given another unit of packed red blood cells (PRBC) to help bring up her hemoglobin count. Heidi's face and arms are beginning to show a slight edema, or swelling. Her lungs sounds are coarse and she is suctioned for thick creamy secretions. By 6:15 am, her temperature is down to 37.9 C, her vital signs are stable, and she shows some response to pain (nailbed pressure). By 6:50 am, her hemoglobin is up to 96; my Heidi Dawn seems to be stabilizing.

And "Dawn with her rose-red fingers shone again" (Homer, 271). A new day has begun.

3.6 May Queen

Our town, Langley, originated on the site of the old fort at Fort Langley. Fort Langley was originally one of the many fur trading posts established by the Hudson's Bay Company in Canada during the 18th and 19th centuries. The Fort was built in 1827 on the south banks of the Fraser River near the Salmon River, and it contained several buildings enclosed within a formidable fortress of tall, upright, sharpened tree trunks. It was named after Thomas Langley, a director for the Hudson's Bay Company. This location on the river allowed the Company to trade with First Nations' people for salmon and beaver pelts; and the Fort was very prosperous for many years. The Fort Langley area expanded into Langley Prairie where settlers could farm crops and raise livestock to supply food for the growing community year-round. Fort Langley was designated as the first Capital of the newly established British territory until Victoria, on Vancouver Island, was later named the Capital city. The Fort was declared a national historic site in the 1950's, and it has been renovated and restored many times since the mid-1900's. The Fort at Fort Langley remains a major tourist attraction in the Langley area.

The town of Fort Langley celebrates its history each year in May by hosting the May Day Parade and Celebrations. The parade boasts many multicultural groups, dancers and musicians, and celebrates the farmers and pioneers who founded Fort Langley. After the parade ends everyone converges onto the fairgrounds for a country-style fair with amusement park rides, competitions, May-Pole dancing, music, antique car displays and lots of home-made pies and preserves. Each May the elementary schools put forward one grade seven girl to compete for May Queen: an honour and a privilege held in the highest regard. I remember the excitement over Langley's May

Queen contests when I was in grade school. This was always a big event for the girls in the community.

Heidi's school sent notices home to all the parents, which requested signed permission for their daughters to try out for the school's May Queen. Heidi wanted to put her name in the draw, so I agreed to allow this, thinking that she only had a one in fifteen chance at winning. Well, she won. Heidi's name was drawn out of the hat and she would represent Langley Central Fundamental School in the parade. This also meant that she would go to the Fort and compete for the big title of Langley's May Queen. She was so excited!

Heidi would need a new dress for the parade, a wide-brimmed hat and a pair of white gloves. We went shopping and found the hat and the gloves. Not satisfied with the dresses she tried on in the stores, Heidi decided she wanted me to sew a special dress. We spent an entire afternoon at Fanny's Fabrics, first selecting the perfect pattern, then choosing a pretty fabric and matching thread. Heidi chose a simple summer frock in crisp cotton with a small floral pattern. She helped me cut out the fabric and I guided her in sewing some of the seams. We tried it on several times throughout the process and ended up with a good, but loose, fit on her tomboy-ish figure. She was so happy with her good fortune.

We met the other girls at the Fort a few days before the parade and we were hosted by a group of women who descended from the first pioneers; I think they are called the Pioneer Daughters of Fort Langley. These wonderful older women taught this group of gangly twelve and thirteen year-olds, most of whom had mouths full of metal braces, some basic etiquette. They prepared the girls for their ride on the float (keep your legs closed when wearing dresses!), and for their attendance up front during the many speeches by visiting dignitaries (no talking or chewing gum!). Then they drew the names. Heidi was not chosen as Langley's May Queen, but she and all the others were happy to remain as May Day Princesses. There were no hard feelings because the Queen was chosen by draw, not by votes.

Heidi rode in the parade on the May Queen Float amongst the girls in pretty dresses, and flowers and ribbons. And she had a great time doing the "Queen's wave," just like Queen Elizabeth: a gloved hand that slowly passes back and forth in front of her face. She and the princesses had a ball. They were treated like royalty: they were fussed over, photographed for the local newspapers, and served cake and tea. The day was a complete success and we (the moms) were all so proud of our princesses.

The kids back at school honoured Heidi as their very own May Queen. She did the school proud. This all added up to an exceptionally joyful end to her grade seven year and elementary school life. In the fall she would enter high school on the heels of having been a princess for a day.

3.7   Monday, September 15

Early Monday morning, at 7:15 am, Heidi's intracranial pressure, her ICP, goes up when they close the clamp on the EVD to collect the drain-off of cerebrospinal fluid. It settles down again when they reopen the clamp. At 7:20 am, the orthopaedic intern, Dr. W, comes in the see Heidi and decides to hold off on closing her fasciotomies until the next day. He notes that she is not yet neurologically stable enough to withstand the leg surgeries. The leg wounds appear fresh and clean so there is no hurry to close them.

In Intensive Care, the usual practice is to assign one nurse to each patient; and she must sit at the end of the bed and continuously monitor the patient's vital signs, reflexes, respiration and ventilation. The nurses take extensive notes and confer with the various doctors who specialize in different parts of the body: respiratory, cardiac, orthopaedic, neurology, etc. The nursing shift-changes occur between 7:00 and 8:00 am each morning, then again in the evenings from 7:00 to 8:00 pm. The nurses coming on duty must go over the previous twelve hours of notes with the retiring nurses, and as I am told this is not the best time for me to be visiting Heidi, I try to come in either before 7:00 o'clock or after 8:00 o'clock, morning and night. The nurses rotate their patients every day, therefore, I have a new person to direct my questions to every twelve hours. I find this somewhat annoying, but when I ask one of the nurses why they don't stick to the same patient each day she says they don't like to get too attached to ICU patients. I understand now.

At 8:00 o'clock this Monday morning, Heidi's vitals are taken and she appears stable as long as her EVD clamp is kept open. When clamped, her ICP spikes up to 21. Closed, her ICP stays between 4 and 12, which is closer to our normal brain pressure.

Her pupils are still sluggish and slow to react to light; she has a weak cough and flexes her limbs to pain. The nurse has trouble checking for a gag reflex because Heidi keeps biting down on the tube. She has a generalized edema to her extremities (she is puffy), her chest still crackles, and her lungs are suctioned for white secretions. She is seen by Dr. DC at 8:10 am, then by the neurosurgeon at 8:35 am. Dr. M notes that her ICP goes up to 22 with clamping. At this time her pupils are 2mm, and she is withdrawing her limbs to pain. He orders another CT scan for this afternoon. At 8:50 am, a physiotherapist works on Heidi's chest to loosen the congestion; she also checks on her legs.

Heidi's father comes in with Kathy Elden to visit with Heidi for awhile this morning. Kathy has been at the hospital off and on since Saturday, and she has been most helpful with interpreting the medical jargon for us; years ago, she used to work as a lab technician here at Royal Columbian. Only family members are allowed into the Intensive Care Unit, so we tell the nurses that Kathy is Heidi's aunt. This works well for us.

Later this morning, a portable echocardiogram (similar to ultra-sounds used for pregnancies) is utilized to see into Heidi's heart. Dr. McC, an Internist and Head doctor of the ICU, sees her at 10:45 am, along with some other doctors. The echocardiogram reveals no evidence of a patent foramen ovale (a hole in the heart from birth), as was suspected. It does reveal a marked biventricular dysfunction in the moderate range and a mild mitral regurgitation. A doctor explains to us that they were looking for a small hole in her heart; and if there was one, she would have been born with it anyways, so it wouldn't necessarily present as a life-threatening problem at this time. Apparently, it is a fairly common anomaly and we are told to not worry about it. After examining her, this doctor concludes that Heidi has aspiration pneumonia and orders the antibiotic, Flagyl, 500mg IV, to be added to her already extensive medications.

Heidi's calcium and phosphorous levels have been persistently low since her arrival at Royal Columbian and the doctors decide to resolve this through a dietary intervention that is supplemented with potassium phosphate. At 11:30 am they insert a feeding tube, the NG (nasogastric) tube, up through her left nostril, leading it down through her oesophagus to her stomach and position it in her duodenum (where the stomach ends and the small intestine begins). Heidi resists this procedure and quite purposefully moves both hands up to her face. She clearly demonstrates that she doesn't like having a tube shoved up her nose. The person from Nutritional Services believes that early supplemental feeding will circumvent any catabolic response to her injuries. Starting today, tube feedings of Traumacal (thick white liquid that is dyed a blue-green) is started and measured at 70cc per hour. Depending on lab results, this rate is adjusted over the next few days.

Dr. O sees Heidi at noon and decides she is still not neurologically stable enough to have her fasciotomies closed today. He will keep checking on her progress and operate when he feels she can handle it. At 2:00 pm, Heidi is taken for another CT scan. Dr. M comes in at 2:45 to check on her and discuss the CT scan with the nurses, doctors, and our family. He notes that her ICP keeps going up into the 20's when clamped, which is not good. He writes orders for the EVD to be left open to allow continuous drainage of cerebrospinal fluids. The CT scan shows some scattered haemorrhages deep in the right cerebral hemisphere as well as, possibly, a small amount of subarachnoid (arachnoid: middle of three membranes that cover the brain) blood. She is kept on regular doses of Morphine, Versed, Mannitol, Decadron, Flagyl, Ancef, and Dilatin.

The rest of the afternoon is uneventful and her leg dressings are changed just before the shift change. The nurse notes her wounds are clean and still draining moderate amounts of fluids. Heidi is turning her head to sounds. Another x-ray makes sure the NG feeding tube is in the correct position. In the early evening her heart rate is 105 bpm and her blood pressure is 130/82. She remains fairly stable. At 8:20 pm, the new nurse notes that Heidi's ICP goes up as high as 32 when the EVD is clamped. She leaves it open and the pressure goes down. Heidi is unresponsive to pain, withdraws her legs only slightly, and has no gag or cough reflexes. Her skin is pale but her face is flushed. Her left hand is now very puffy. Her lungs are still making coarse sounds. Once the x-rays of her stomach are confirmed by a clinical associate, the feeding commences. I come in to see Heidi at 10:30 pm, just before going to sleep, and the nurse explains her status to me, and the reasons for the feeding tube.

The blue feeding tube travels from a suspended sack in through Heidi's nose and down into her stomach via her oesophagus. She has another larger tube, the endotracheal tube (ETT), which enters her mouth and goes into her trachea to assist her breathing. This oral tube is tied with straps around her head to keep it in place, and I see the straps cutting into the corners of her lips, making them bleed. Another tube, the EVD, drains fluids from her brain. Yet another tube, the Foley catheter, drains urine from her urethra. She has two IV needles inserted into her right wrist area, and another into her left wrist. Both lower legs are still open, like filleted fish, to drain the excess fluids from her soft tissues. Heidi's poor little body has been completely invaded and this is getting very hard for me to bear. The nurse is going to give her a bath this evening and I inform her I have just recently looked at the blue-jeans Heidi was wearing on the night of the accident; the fabric from both buttocks is torn and worn right through. It looks as though she was dragged by the car or else she slid on the pavement for enough of a distance to wear through the denim. I am concerned that the flesh on Heidi's buttocks might be injured. The nurse then gently lifts Heidi's left side posterior and we are both shocked at the devastation. Her buttocks are absolutely raw and bloody. They had not been attended to at Peace Arch or at Royal Columbian, and I suppose this was because of her other, more serious, injuries. But still! The nurse promises me she'll clean and dress Heidi's backside this evening. This is just one more insult to add to my damaged daughter's list of injuries.

Heidi's father goes home for the night and I try to get some rest in the family room. At 1:00 am, I am sleeping soundly when a loud alarm goes off and a voice on the intercom repeatedly shouts, "Code Blue." I leap out of the family room door and into the main corridor to see doctors and nurses running down the hall towards the Intensive Care Unit. Panicked, I run after them down the hall and around the corner and watch as they run past the ICU doors and enter the Cardiac Unit. Oh, thank God, it's not Heidi. I am so relieved I cry. I walk unsteadily back to my room and try to still my hammering heart enough to lie back down and try to sleep. Around 5:00 am, another alarm goes off but this time I see the people running *away* from the ICU and towards another part of the hospital. I notice the woman staying in the family room beside mine is doing the same thing. We glance at each other's heads poking out of our doors, and with just enough time to register the naked fear, we quickly retreat back inside and slam shut our doors. I didn't like the look on her face and I'm sure she didn't like the look on mine. I try but I can't get back to sleep.

Heidi is given a thorough bed bath and linen change around 11:00 pm. Somewhere in Heidi's unconsciousness she must be enjoying this new cleanliness and comfort for her body. At midnight the nurse removes the IV from her left wrist, as it has no blood returns anymore. She inserts a new line into the right wrist. Heidi's brain continues to drain clear fluid and her lungs seem clear except for the scattered coarse sounds heard. At 3:55 am, she spontaneously coughs up some greyish mucous. At 5:00 am, the nurse notices some thick, blood-streaked oral secretions. Other than that, Heidi is in fairly stable condition with no traumas to report for this evening. I am back in before 7:00 am to see how she faired during the night. A new day begins.

3.8   Tuesday, September 16

Tuesday, September 16th, begins uneventfully. After visiting with Heidi for a little while, I leave the Intensive Care Unit because the nurses need to change shifts and go over Heidi's records. I find my way down to the coffee shop in the lobby and buy myself a muffin and a large café latte. I pick up a newspaper and try to relax in the relatively quiet atmosphere of the café.

This day is quiet so far. Heidi is being continuously assessed and she seems stable. The nurse is still having trouble assessing a gag reflex because Heidi persists in biting down hard when her mouth is probed. Her pupils react briskly and are dilated to 3mm. After the 8:00 am examination by the incoming nurse, Heidi is deemed to be in stable condition. Her lungs are suctioned for a moderate amount of greyish-white secretions. I am wondering about these grey-coloured secretions from her lungs and am thinking back to when I quit smoking at age twenty-one. I had only been smoking for three years when I quit and I never was a heavy smoker; nonetheless my lungs coughed up good amounts of grey and brown gunk over the two weeks following my last cigarette. Heidi is a part-time smoker; although she rarely smokes at home, she smokes when she is with her friends. And now she is going into her fourth day cigarette-free and is coughing up great amounts of grey-brown mucous from her lungs. I think the fact that she smokes doesn't help her lung problems at all, and I'm wondering now if the doctors took this into consideration. I do not, however, recall discussing this with anyone.

Dr. McC sees Heidi on his rounds at 10:30 am. He notes the improvement to her lungs and finds the infiltrate in her lungs has cleared. He assesses her as neurologically stable while the clamp is open, but finds she still is spiking to 20mmHg when the EVD is clamped shut. He decides she should still wait another day or two before having her fasciotomies closed by the orthopedic surgeons. Her pneumonia is clearing up and her fever is down. He orders medication for her hiccoughs.

Heidi's father and I take turns visiting her around 11:00 am. We spend time speaking with family and friends on the phone, giving updates on Heidi's condition. Heidi's father makes arrangements with Air Canada to miss work until she is better. I talk to Cos Van Wermeskerken, Chairman of the Langley School Board, about missing the next few School Board and committee meetings. (I am a School Board Trustee). The Board has a policy that stipulates Trustees can only miss three public School Board meetings in a row before something must be done, such as: stepping down and leaving the seat vacant, or electing someone new to serve the rest of the term (3 year terms). I promise not to miss more than three consecutive meetings. I also speak with my partner in Real Estate, Bent Hanson, who also covers work for me. Bent and his wife, Bev, visit us at the hospital many times during this ordeal. I appreciate the support.

Bill and Laura are unable to concentrate at school. They prefer to be either at home close to the phone so they can speak with us, or be here at the hospital; and both options are stressful for them. We are visited by our friend, John Scholtens, Mayor of the Township of Langley, and his advisor and friend, Gregory Thomas. Councillors May Barnard and Karen Kersey also come in to see how we are holding up. Everyone is being so supportive, yet I hardly notice who is here because I'm constantly watching to see if Dr. McC, Dr. O, or Dr. M are coming back to speak with us.

It is on day four that I realize I stink. I have been wearing and sleeping in the same clothes and underwear for three stressful days and nights and it's time to change. My hair hasn't been washed since last Saturday and is full-on greasy. I go home for a few hours to scrub down; and once I am refreshed I return to the hospital, bringing along a fresh change of clothing. I also bring along my yellow roses stitchery project to keep my hands busy during the long waits between visits with Heidi. The family has given me a gorgeous bouquet of my favourite flowers, yellow roses, and I find these in the family room in a big glass vase, awaiting my return. These are Heidi's birth flowers, her yellow roses, and I am delighted to have them in the room with me. Somehow, they give me comfort: a constant connection with Heidi.

On my way back to the hospital I buy a bottle of my favourite perfume, L'Air du Temps; and I spray myself before visiting with Heidi. For over twenty years this has been my one perfume, my smell. Later, when I lean in to kiss Heidi's forehead, her nostrils flare out and I know she recognizes the smell. Her bottom lip pushes out and a single tear rolls down her cheek. She knows I am here. She knows and I am comforted.

Heidi's blood pressure starts to drop around 4:00 pm, and Dr. McC is made aware of this by the nurse. At 103/63, it is still in the acceptable range. Her heart rate is good at 86 bpm. She still doesn't respond to verbal commands, but does flex to nailbed pressure. Her ICP bolt continues to drain clear cerebrospinal fluid. She has a generalized edema and her left elbow is quite swollen and looks bruised today. Heidi's chest sounds are still coarse and at 8:15 pm her lungs are once again suctioned for large amounts of greyish yellow secretions. Her mouth is producing lots of thick blood-streaked secretions. A bite-block is inserted in her mouth to keep her from biting down on her airway tubing.

I visit Heidi again at 9:00 pm and try to touch her skin, but it is hard to find a spot that doesn't have needles or tubes protruding from it. Finally I decide to rub her tummy just like I did when she was little, although this time it's through a hospital gown. It probably gives me more comfort to touch her than it does Heidi. I want to hold her so badly I ache for it. There are so many machines and IV stands in the way that it's hard getting close enough to smell her, let alone touch her. I just want my baby to wake up; I am so unhappy.

The leg dressings are changed at 10:30 pm, and her bedding is changed afterwards, along with a washdown. Heidi is now menstruating. I worry about how mortified she will be when she finds out other people have been changing her sanitary napkins. What next? She is not tolerating any EVD clamping and her brain pressure is now rising dangerously to close to 40mmHg when it's clamped. It quickly goes back down to a stable 7 or 8 when opened, so they decide to keep it open. Heidi's blood pressure starts to rise around midnight and her heart-rate reaches 100 bpm by 2:00 am. An intern is called and Heidi is given chlorpromazine to relieve the hiccoughs, and more Mannitol to keep the brain pressure down. The rise in blood pressure does not seem to alarm anyone at this hour. Our Heidi has a fairly restful evening.

3.9   Tea Parties

Heidi and her cousin Jana spent many happy hours playing under the cedars and firs in the front yard of our home on 196B Street in Langley. Our first home we owned in Langley was on a beautiful half acre with lots of trees in the front and back yards. The home was on a quiet cul-de-sac street and this proved to be a safe haven for our three children to grow up in, with plenty of room to practice riding their first bicycles. The area was filled with young families like ours with lots of small children running around the neighbourhood during the daytime; it was nice and quiet at night. The front yard had a stand of mature trees along with large rhododendrons, tropical plants and ferns. When the girls were small, between the ages of six and twelve, they would enjoy many private tea parties inside the circle of trees on a tiny patch of lawn that caught the afternoon sun. This small sunny enclosure would glow within the dark trees and it became the secret garden for the two little cousins. Heidi and her sister Laura made good use of the miniature ceramic tea set that their Gramma K gave them, and this is what Heidi would set up for her special parties with Jana. I would provide them with lukewarm tea for the teapot, and let them fill the sugar pot and the creamer to take outside. They usually convinced me to let them have a plate of cookies to nibble on: something we kept secret from the other siblings and cousins in the backyard. These two darling cousins would play with their Barbie dolls and spend hours and hours talking and playing with each other as they basked in the solitude and the peace of this front yard oasis. These were special, private moments for Heidi and Jana that were not shared with the other children, and they are dearly treasured.

Heidi and Jana had a close bond that lasted well into their teen years. Jana was born four months after Heidi (to my sister, Dawn), so they were the same ages and were in the same grades at school. On the night of September 12th, 1997, both girls were out with their friends: Heidi in Langley and Jana in Yarrow (near Chilliwack). At half past midnight the next morning, September 13th, both girls were involved in motor vehicle accidents. We already know what happened to Heidi. Jana was sitting on her friend's lap in the crowded cab of a pick-up truck while another friend drove. The driver was drunk. The truck crashed into a ditch at exactly 12:30 am., the same time as the drunk driver struck Heidi and sixteen other teens at Stokes Pit. Jana's head smashed through the windshield of the truck, and had her friend not grabbed her tightly around the waist, she would have flown through the windshield and very possibly have died. She received a slight head concussion and extensive bruising on her torso and needed a few days of bed-rest to recover. Luckily, she was not seriously or permanently injured. This accident has haunted Jana ever since: she was in a vehicle with a drunk driver and she lived; her beloved cousin was not as lucky. The coincidence of the dates, circumstances, and times of the crashes is eerie, to say the least. Jana did not tell her mother about this accident until almost two years later.

3.10   Wednesday, September 17

I begin this day by visiting Heidi at 6:30 am. She has had an uneventful night and looks peaceful this morning and this pleases me. I only stay fifteen minutes because someone comes in to take some blood for testing. I am not allowed in the Intensive Care Unit whenever they are doing something to Heidi, so I go off in search of my first cup of coffee of the day.

At the 8:00 am shift change, the nurse notes that Heidi is stable but showing little response to nailbed pressures. She is still experiencing occasional hiccoughs and now both arms appear swollen. Her right hand is very puffy. Her oxygen saturation is at 96%, but her lungs still have crackle sounds. Heidi's heart rate and blood pressure are normal this morning, as is her temperature. Her intracranial pressure, ICP, remains at a comfortable 9mmHg, although she is not yet responding to verbal commands.

I visit Heidi again at 9:00 am and I'm still worried that she isn't waking up. She seems to be stable, so I go for a walk inside the hospital to try and find Courtney's room. I wind my way through seemingly endless corridors, take an elevator up a couple of floors and find myself in a different tower. Courtney is in a lot of pain, but glad to see me. We talk about Heidi's problems, and she gives me an update on Vanessa over at Vancouver General (VGH). Vanessa's spinal injuries are serious and she is almost completely immobile from the neck down. But she is starting to move her toes on one side and this small accomplishment is giving Vanessa and her doctors some hope that she just may recover some movement in her limbs. Perhaps her spinal injuries are not permanent after all. Vanessa has broken three vertebrae in her neck and the initial prognosis is not good. We wish her well. I discuss going over to VGH to see her, but I really don't want to leave this hospital and be that far away from Heidi. Visiting Courtney is as far as I want to venture at this time.

Courtney says she will come to see Heidi as soon as they let her leave her room. Courtney's broken leg was fitted with a titanium rod, just like Heidi's, and by the same orthopaedic surgeon, Dr. O. She is taking lots of morphine for the pain as her cracked pelvis, ribs, shoulder, and the badly broken tibia and fibula start to heal. She worries about the schoolwork they are missing and tells me that many of their friends have been visiting her, so I assume there are lots of LSS students missing school this week. Some of those same friends have been coming to the ICU area but so far have not been allowed in to see Heidi. After about twenty minutes I'm itching to get back to Heidi, so I say goodbye and leave Courtney to her pain and her healing.

Dr. McC makes his rounds at 11:30 am and notes that Heidi's ICP still goes up sharply when clamped, so the EVD is left open. Her hemoglobin is still low and more PRBCs (packed red blood cells) are ordered. He checks her slightly extended abdomen, makes queries about her blood loss, and notes there is no obvious source for this; so he orders an abdominal Ultra-Sound for this afternoon. He has Heidi's badly swollen left elbow x-rayed to check for fractures, and they find none. He checks her echocardiogram and orders a Cardiology Consult to help resolve Heidi's heart problems. By noon her ICP is ranging from 9 to 12 without stimulation. It goes up when she is suctioned, or when her responses to pain are tested, such as nailbed pressures to see if she withdraws to the pain. Her limbs are withdrawing slightly to stimulation, but this infliction of pain also makes her blood pressure go up, which is dangerous for her brain.

The afternoon begins with a 12-lead ECG attached to Heidi's

chest and back to monitor her heart. Her EVD is clamped for the procedure and she doesn't tolerate this very well. Next, she is give the first unit of blood that was ordered earlier; then at 4:10 pm Dr. McC supervises while a portable Ultra-Sound is administered over Heidi's abdomen. When he sees the results he notifies Dr. N to come quickly to give his opinion. Dr. N examines her belly and agrees that it appears she may have a splenic hemorrhage; Heidi's spleen seems to be leaking blood. The doctors opine that she may have suffered a laceration (a tear or rip) in her spleen during the accident. It is explained to me that the spleen tends to bleed easily and it is almost always the first organ to act up when the body has been traumatized in an accident. They will watch her spleen over the next few days, but they expect it to eventually stop bleeding on its own without surgery. Dr. N decides to continue with the feeds infusion. So now Heidi has another problem for us to worry about. Her legs, her lungs, her brain, her heart, and now her spleen is in trouble. Suddenly it dawns on me: I have been rubbing her tummy each time I visit her, trying to comfort her. This can't have helped her injured spleen! I wonder if my actions have inadvertently contributed to the bleeding. Oh my God, I didn't know. I am feeling weaker by the minute in this never-ending house of horrors. Now I can't touch her anywhere.

This is day five of our ordeal and Heidi is showing no signs of coming out of her coma. I have been living in this hospital day and night, washing myself in the basin in the women's washroom, changing my clothes in there, praying in there, and sleeping on the hard benches in the family room. During the day I sit on the benches in the corridor outside the family room furiously stitching while vigilantly watching for one of Heidi's doctors to come by and tell me she's improving. I buy my morning coffee at the little shop in the main foyer of the hospital on the ground floor, and my food at the cafeteria in the hospital's basement. I am an emotional wreck by this time and my tolerance level for jerks has dropped to zero.

Enter ICBC (Insurance Corporation of British Columbia) claims adjuster, Mr. John C. On this day he somehow gets the phone number for the family room and rings me up. He tells me he is downstairs in the hospital's main lobby and that he wants me to come down and meet him there. I ask him what this is about. He says he has the papers ready and if I'll just come down and sign them, "We can settle this today, right now." At first I believe he means to settle the claim. I cannot believe this man's gall. Heidi is still in a coma! What is he thinking? That I am so stupid or emotionally distraught that I will sign ICBC papers without council? This makes me very angry and I tell him he has no right interfering with me when my daughter's life is in the balance. How dare he do this to me; I am very upset with him and tell him to call Garry MacDonald, my lawyer in White Rock; then I hang up on him. Later, I realise he probably wants my signature to *initiate* the claim only, not to "settle" it. I was, however, in no condition to read or sign any legal papers at this time and he should have known better. I have since heard many stories about aggressive ICBC lawyers and adjusters and none of these stories have been complimentary. Not even close.

Meanwhile, back in the Intensive Care Unit, Heidi's dressings are changed at 6:20 pm and the nurse notes a large amount of very yellow serous and sanguineous drainage from her legs. This is healthy. The petechiae rash is still present on her chest. Later, the nurse notes that Heidi turns her head away when stimulated, and this is good. Her heart rate is 86 bpm and her blood pressure is up to 144/89. Her ICP is 15mmHg and the EVD is now draining blood-tinged cerebral fluid. Her lungs are suctioned for small amounts of white secretions. And she continues her menstruation cycle.

Dr. B, a Cardiologist (heart specialist), sees Heidi at 9:00 pm and checks the ECG done earlier in the day. As she assesses the T-wave abnormality, the evidence of moderately decreased systolic function, and the mitral regurgitation, Dr. B concludes that Heidi is suffering from a myocardial contusion (bruised heart). It does not, however, require any treatment. She recommends a transesophageal echocardiography once Heidi is neurologically stable, but states that it is not urgently needed. Dr. G, also a Cardiologist, sees Heidi at 9:30 pm and agrees with Dr. B's assessment that although Heidi's heart is bruised, no immediate medical intervention is necessary. The bruising is expected to resolve itself over time. My baby's heart is bruised. So is mine.

Later this evening, the intern suggests to me that Heidi may have suffered a blunt chest trauma that affected her heart and caused the laceration to her spleen. This is probably an accurate assessment considering most of the people struck by the car became airborne and hit the pavement, gravel, or ditches hard. Heidi landed on the north edge of the road where the pavement blends into the packed gravel shoulder. She would have landed hard, although I still wonder about her being dragged for some distance after hitting the road. I guess we'll never really know exactly what happened to her body after being struck by the car, but the suggestion that her chest suffered a blunt trauma sounds plausible.

Dr. McC discusses Heidi's condition with us and is cautious with her prognosis. They are still monitoring her closely and trying to keep her brain pressure out of the danger zone by bagging her when needed. He tells us about her bleeding spleen and suggests this is the reason her hemoglobin keeps dropping. Another abdominal Ultra-Sound is scheduled for tomorrow. She is given two more units of red blood cells to help increase the hemoglobin count, as well as three units of Pentaspan (synthetic blood volume expander). Her hemoglobin count rises to 75 after the transfusions. He explains, again, that Heidi's heart is bruised but he feels it is nothing to worry about at this time. We are reassured that Heidi is receiving the best possible care and our hopes are restored for our daughter's full recovery.

I have been communicating with family members over the phone throughout the day. They are suffering just as we are. They have come to dread the phone calls because they seem to be bringing worse news each time. First I call about the struggles with her brain pressure, next I call to say her spleen is bleeding into her abdominal cavity, and then later this night I call them to say Heidi's heart is bruised. This is hard on everyone, and our phones are kept active all day long within our large family network.

Heidi remains hypotensive (low blood pressure). She is bathed and has her dressings changed as per the usual nursing routine. At 4:30 am her ICP goes up to 20 and she is given an IV analgesic to eliminate any pain signals reaching her brain. She bites down on the airway when stimulated and responds to nailbed pressure. Her ICP persists at 20 and the nurse notices that Heidi has slipped down the bed a little. Once that is resolved and her EVD is releveled, her ICP goes down (with more analgesic at 5:00 am) to 12-16. At 6:10 am her ICP is back up and she is bagged, which quickly brings the pressure back down to 12. At 6:20 her ICP is up again and the nurse bags her to bring it back down; but once the bagging stops, the ICP races back up again. She is given Mannitol at 6:45 am and this doesn't seem to make any changes to her brain pressure. Dr. G is made aware of the high ICP at 7:00 am and he orders another CT scan. The EVD tube is draining some blood and tissue from her brain now. The EVD is drained and cleared. At 7:15 a.m., Heidi's legs dressings are changed again and some blood work is taken for the new day. This day is not beginning too well for our Heidi.

3.11 Thursday, September 18

Heidi has had a rough night with her ICP (brain pressure) persisting in the high ranges; consequently, she requires frequent bagging by the nurses to bring it down to a safe level. She is getting another CT scan this morning and leaves the ICU at 7:40 am, accompanied by the ICU resident and two registered nurses who keep assessing her on the portable monitor, and who keep bagging her to keep the ICP down. Dr. G is present for the CT scan and is fully aware of her delicate neurological condition. The CT scan report reads:

"Multiple low density lesions are noted in the subcortical and periventricular white matter of both cerebral hemispheres. Low density change is also noted in the cerebellar hemispheric white matter. This has increased since the previous study of September 14, 1997" (RCH, 220).

This shows an increase in fat embolism damage from the last CT scan. Her brain is not doing so well: the swelling has increased. Heidi returns to the ICU at 8:25 am.

During the morning nursing shift-change it is noted that Heidi no longer responds to painful nailbed pressures. There is no longer any limb movement and her corneals are weak. The ICP bolt is checked and the EVD is drained for sero-sanguineous fluids, with a slight clot near the bolt. Petechiae is noted on both breasts, and some bruising is noted around the peripheral IV in her right hand, which is still puffy. Her left elbow also remains puffy, and her face is flushed. Coarse crackles are heard in her lungs but no suctioning is done because of the high ICP, which is aggravated by any procedures being performed on her. Her abdomen is distended, but still soft.

Dr. M comes in to see Heidi at 9:15 am, and he notes that her

ICP rises to a dangerously high 42mmHg when the EVD is clamped. She flexes slightly to pain, her corneals are present, and her pupils are 2mm. He orders a regimen of Mannitol and Decadron to maintain a lower brain pressure. We come in to see Heidi and speak briefly with Dr. M about her condition. He is cautiously optimistic due to her brain's response to the drugs, so he will keep her on them as long as she needs them.

At 9:45 am, Heidi's pupils increase in size and become fixed and unequal: a sign of brain trauma. Her blood pressure, heart rate and ICP all climb upwards. Her heart rate soars to 180 bpm, her blood pressure goes up to 230/153, and her ICP is spiking at 42. She is bagged by the resident and given more Mannitol. Ten minutes later her ICP drops to 18, and her heart rate and her blood pressure follow. Dr. M is called.

Dr. M soon arrives back at Heidi's bedside and adjusts the EVD level down to 12mmHg. Her ICP stabilizes but her heart rate and blood pressure are still higher than normal. He calls for a consult with Pharmacy regarding barbituate coma information. R. S. from Pharmacy responds and writes his assessments and suggestions down for the doctors to consider. The plan is that if Heidi's ICP doesn't settle down, she may be put into a drug-induced coma to keep all sensory information from affecting her brain. The drug is called Patobarbital, and this will keep the brain in a deep sleep-like state, giving it the time needed to recover from the damage caused by the fat embolism. Dr. M explains to us how serious Heidi's condition is, but I really don't fathom this information nor do I absorb what it could mean.

Between 10:20 and 10:30, Heidi's IV line is taken out of her swollen right hand and replaced by a new line in her upper right arm. At 11:00 am, her pupils dilate again; she is bagged and given Mannitol. Her heart rate and blood pressure go up again and the resident helps to bring her ICP back down. Dr. McC sees Heidi at 11:30 am during his rounds, and he notes that her CT scan from this morning shows increased cranial edema (brain swelling), along with the fluctuating ICP that keeps spiking. He notes she responds to the increase in Mannitol and Decadron and adds that the nurse can increase the Mannitol further if needed. He says she is not fit for an abdominal CT or for TEE (RCH, 66).

I come in at noon to see Heidi lying so still in her hospital bed. She is very unstable and I cannot stay for very long. The nurse explains that she isn't doing well, that she is a very, very sick girl. I don't allow myself to consider what she is trying to tell me at this point. Soon after I leave, at 12:30 pm, the nurse notes that Heidi's pupils are unequal and that her limbs show no movement at all to stimulus. Dr. H, the ICU intern, sees Heidi at 1:45 pm and assesses her condition. He notes that Heidi's condition deteriorated overnight and that her cerebral edema is progressing. From a neurological point of view, she is worsening. At around 2:00 pm, her temperature is elevated at 38.2 degrees Celsius, her heart rate is 102 bpm, her blood pressure is 140/90, and her unclamped ICP is 20. Her pupils are unequal: right pupil is dilated to 5mm, and left pupil is 4mm. Both are slow to react. She has no cough or gag reflexes and remains unresponsive to pain stimuli. The intern agrees with Dr. M's instructions for increased Mannitol, and notes that she may require barbituate coma and decompression. The abdominal bleed can be handled with transfusions when her hemoglobin gets low, but if the bleeding becomes severe she will need general surgery. Her heart situation is best handled in consultation with Dr. B, the Cardiologist. I am having difficulty in handling this new information. I just want Heidi to wake up.

When I arrive back at the family room after lunch, I discover that both my perfume and my beautiful yellow roses, complete with glass vase, are gone. Someone has taken them while I was out of the room. My aching heart receives this new blow as I realize that some thief is pillaging the family rooms while we visit our sick loved ones in the ICU. What next?

At 2:40 pm, Heidi's pupils blow again and she is bagged and given more Mannitol. It is becoming increasingly hard for the nurses to bring down her brain pressure with each recurrence. Dr. McC calls Dr. M on the phone and discusses Heidi's condition with him. At 3:45 her dilated pupils remain unequal, she has some corneal reflexes but no response to nailbed pressure. By 4:10 pm, her ICP is trending upwards and she is quite unstable. Her pupils are blowing frequently, she has no gag or cough reflex, no limb movement to pain, her temperature is up again to 38.2, and her face is quite flushed. She is suctioned for a small amount of white secretions from her lungs, and suctioned for yellowish sanguineous secretions from her oral airway. Dr. H is made aware of her status. Dr. N, from surgery, sees her at 5:00 pm. Dr. H speaks with Dr. M in the Operating Room about Heidi's condition. Everyone is quite concerned about her worsening condition.

Around 4:00 pm, a nurse comes out to the hallway to speak with our family. Heidi's father, brother and sister are there with me as she warns us not to expect Heidi to survive the night. She explains how badly Heidi's brain is swelling and that it is becoming increasing difficult for them to keep the pressure down. The blown pupils are an indication that her brain stem is being squeezed by the pressure inside her skull. The brain stem is the centre for life-giving impulses: her breathing and her heart beats. She is now in great danger, and according to this nurse, there seems to be no hope for recovery.

This is the first time anyone has said that Heidi might die. This is the first time I allow this information into my conscious state. My brain reels with this new information. I do not take it well. I argue with this nurse and tell her that Heidi *cannot* die, that she only had two broken shin bones and that it is impossible for her to die. She assures me that Heidi only has a few hours left and that she is certain she will not make it through the night. After she leaves us, I try to walk down the corridor but find I have to hold onto the walls for support. My legs aren't working properly. My knees are literally wobbling in and out like they were made out of soft rubber. I stagger down the hall to the family room, lie down on the bench, curl up into a fetal position and cover my ears with my arms wrapped tightly about my head. It is decided the children and I will go home this night.

I need an Oprah hug: an all-encompassing Mother-earth, Goddess-like hug that will assure me everything will turn out okay. This nurse has stolen my Hope, and I need someone larger-than-life, someone like Oprah Winfrey who understands such a pain as this, to reach into the depths of the universe to find and restore my Hope. I am collapsing without it. Hope is my life-force. How could this nurse steal this mother's life-force? I need to find my Hope because I know, I know, I know Heidi will die without it. And, already, I feel *myself* dying in its absence.

The 8:00 pm nursing shift change is uneventful, with the new nurse doing her series of checks, vitals signs, dressing changes, and general assessment of the patient. She notes that Heidi is only moving her left arm slightly to deep nailbed pressure and that none of her other limbs are responding. She makes a note that no suctioning is to be done unless necessary. Heidi's chest is still making coarse sounds.

Dr. M comes in to see Heidi at 8:10 pm and then speaks with us in the family room about her condition. He is cautiously optimistic that they can keep her ICP down long enough for this to pass. He tells us that fat embolism usually abates within seven to ten days. This is day six. It still might get worse before it gets better. She is in a very delicate state and no one can know what the outcome will be. He asks us to consider, if absolutely necessary, allowing him to perform a lobectomy: the removal of a portion of one or two lobes in Heidi's brain. I am now thoroughly and completely horrified. He calmly explains how this procedure would give her brain additional room to swell into without damaging the brain stem. Reluctantly, we agree to this emergency-only plan. Dr. M and his drastic, terrifying plan somehow restore in me a glimmer of the Hope I thought was lost. I can breathe again, although it's mostly in ragged gasps and sighs.

My friends, Bent and Bev Hanson come in to see us and arrive just as Dr. M is leaving. We tell them the bad news and the nurse's prognosis of impending doom. Kathy Elden also arrives to hear the frightening news; it is decided that she will stay overnight with Heidi's father to keep checking on Heidi throughout the night. Meanwhile, the Hansons will take the children and I home. I insist on staying a little while longer, to make sure Heidi is going to be okay. Unbeknownst to me, Heidi's father signs the consent forms for both a lobectomy and organ donation at 9:00 pm. The children and I stay until just after 10:00 pm.

At 10:00 pm, Heidi's heart rate goes up to 130 bpm, her pupils are dilated at 5mm and fixed, and the nurse calls Dr. McK. She is given more Mannitol, her EVD is drained, and this brings the ICP back down to a manageable 13 -14. Dr. M speaks to me on the phone in the family room and explains what has just happened. They will keep Heidi on Mannitol and bag her each time she spikes, and hopefully, this will be enough to keep her brain safe while the fat embolism works its way out. He assures me again that he will only consider a lobectomy if her life is in immediate danger.

I am absolutely drained and it is finally time for me to go home. I need help manoeuvring through long corridors of the hospital and across the acres of parking lot to Bent's car. Bent and his wife sit in front and we three sit in the back. My head drops back onto the headrest and I take slow, deep breaths as I try to stay calm. I am not functioning well at this point; my mind is reeling.

Before going to bed at home this night I do something that I am later ashamed of. Late in the night, I telephone John Scholtens (Langley's Mayor) and scream at him to pray for my Heidi. John and his family are devout Christians and I tell him, I order him, to pray to his God to save my Heidi. I am sobbing on the phone and John tries to calm me down with his words of comfort, but by this time I am absolutely inconsolable. Poor John. This is such an unfair thing for me to do to him and his family and I sincerely apologise now for my hysterical behaviour this night. But John does as I ask and he has his entire family kneel and pray and plead for Heidi's life long into this scary, dark night. At home, I just howled at my God all night long, making demands, offering promises, anything, if He'd just keep my baby safe for one more night. "Oh God, give Heidi one more day, oh please, please, please. Keep her safe. Don't let her die. I'll kill you if you let her die! Oh, God, I'm sorry, I didn't mean that. I'll do anything you ask of me but please just save my baby this night!" I am out of my mind with fear. I don't remember sleeping but I must have passed out eventually.

Back at RCH, it is midnight and Heidi's pupils are back down to 3mm, with sluggish responses, and her corneals are present. She is withdrawing both hands to nailbed pressure now. Her EVD is still draining sero-sanguineous fluids. She continues to need hyperventilation. Some blood work is taken at ten past midnight, and then no notes are made in the records until 4:00 am. Heidi appears to be stabilizing. At this time she is given a sponge bath and seems to tolerate it well. Heidi's arms are now showing a weak withdrawal to nailbed pressure and her pupils are at 3mm with sluggish to brisk responses. She is still menstruating, so at least one of her systems is functioning normally.

At 5:00 am, Heidi's right arm moves spontaneously up towards her face. She coughs and her lungs are suctioned for a moderate amount of thick light brownish, yellowish secretions. At 7:00 am, more blood is taken for testing. She has had a more stable night than was expected. She surprises everyone by surviving. That's my girl! Thank you, God. Thank you, John. Is it possible our prayers worked?

3.12 Friday, September 19

This is the first day I cannot face going into the hospital. I spent most of the previous night praying or phoning the family room at Royal Columbian and speaking with either Kathy or Heidi's father. I manage to sleep for a few hours in the early morning. It feels good to be home, good to shower and change, good to do a load of laundry, good to spend some time with Bill and Laura, and good to go for a walk in the park nearby. I am amazed at the huge number of flower bouquets that have filled up the kitchen, dining and living rooms. I spend some time reading the accompanying cards and I savour the heartfelt love that is being sent our way. It seems the whole community of Langley is concerned for Heidi's health. Adding to this florist's shop that was once my home are the numerous newspaper articles about the accident and the progress made by Heidi, Courtney and Vanessa. Most of the other teens that had their legs broken have already gone home. Ashley Reber's funeral was last Wednesday and close to a thousand people turned out to say goodbye to her. I was unaware of her funeral while inside Royal Columbian, otherwise I would have gone to pay my respects as well. Bill and Laura have been making several attempts to go back to school: Laura in grade eleven at LSS, and Bill in first year aviation at UCFV (University College of the Fraser Valley in Abbotsford). Neither of them has been successful; the stress on our family is too great. They cannot concentrate.

The one thing our family has not been without is food. A bounty of food keeps arriving at the door. Wonderful dishes of lasagne, casseroles, salads, and lots and lots of desserts. The children decide that Sheryl Strongitharm, Rich Coleman's assistant, is by far the best meat dish maker (beef stroganoff); and Shirley Van Meer, my fellow SBRA member (South Brookswood Ratepayers Association), is voted the best cake maker (lemon chiffon).

Thank you, ladies; your love-filled dishes nourish our hearts. The goodies keep arriving in such abundance we end up storing lots of the food in our freezer. This has been such a blessing as I had completely forgotten about providing nourishment for my other two children at home this past week. They ask me if they can skip school and I say yes. We'll work on catch-up after Heidi comes home. This provides them with some much-needed relief and now they will not have to stress over exams or assignments for the next week or two.

My heart is lifted by the news that Heidi has survived this awful night. The nurse was wrong. Actually, I think the nurse was wrong on many levels. She had no right to tell me when or if my daughter will die. The doctor who is primarily looking after Heidi's neurological care is Dr. M, and he has yet to give up hope. He has always tried to stay optimistic even under the worst conditions and I really appreciate this aspect of Dr. M. He renews my hope when others try to dash it. Hope is all I am hanging onto these days. Hope that the fat embolism is through with Heidi and ready to leave her alone. I see this fat embolism as some hideous monster that keeps attacking my child: this invisible beast who is trying to steal her away. Right now, for me, Dr. M is the proverbial knight in shining armour, or white coat, armed with the skills and knowledge to slay this beast and save my princess. This is the stuff that nightmares are made of; and just like nightmares, this experience is surreal, frightening, and seemingly never-ending.

This ordeal keeps me in a state of sweaty tremors, with legs that don't function, and a heart that hammers relentlessly in my ears. This fear is physical. It manifests itself in everything I do: I startle easily; I'll scream out loud with the slightest surprise; I have a dry mouth that no amount of coffee, juice or water can hydrate.; my bowels are becoming violent in their discharge;

my head aches and my armpits are pouring sweat that smells odd; I brush my teeth often but I always have a foul taste in my mouth; I hyperventilate; and I hold my breath for long periods without noticing, until I gasp out loud. This is killing me. I just want my Heidi back. Then I'll be okay again.

Back at Royal Columbian Hospital, Heidi's father and her "Aunt" Kathy are recovering from a relatively sleepless night. The 8:00 am nurse runs through her routine and notes that Heidi still does not respond to any verbal commands, her legs do not respond to pain, but she notices her arms *do* withdraw slightly to nailbed pressure pain. She has a weak cough but no gag reflex. At 7:30 am, Heidi's heart rate fluctuates between 96 and 118 bpm. Her blood pressure is 142/90. She is receiving lots of Ativan for her heart. Her face is still flushed and her arms still show some swelling (edema). She still has congestion in her lower lung fields and is suctioned for clear to slightly brown coloured secretions from both her lungs and her mouth. She is not taking any spontaneous breaths yet: the ventilator is doing all her breathing for her.

At 8:10 am, the orthopaedic surgeon, Dr. O, visits Heidi and decides that if she requires any other surgery he will authorize the closure of the fasciotomies in the Operating Room at the same time. He instructs the nurse to inform the resident orthopaedic surgeon if this occurs. Otherwise, her legs can wait until she is neurologically stable. The saline packs are keeping the wounds fresh and although this is an unusually long time to prolong the closures of the fasciotomies, the first priority is her brain activity; therefore, her legs will have to wait.

Dr. McC does his rounds and visits Heidi at 10:10 am. He instructs the nurse to continue with the prescribed plan of: hyperventilation, increase her tube feeds, monitor her hemoglobin, and use PEEP due to the atelectasis that showed up on her morning chest x-ray. The left lower lobe of her lung is collapsing (LLL atelectasis).

Heidi is taken for another CT scan and remains stable during the transport. At 12:10 pm her EVD is clamped for the CT scan, so she is manually bagged by the resident to keep her ICP down. It remains down between 19 and 25, but fluctuates occasionally to the high 20's. She is sedated for the CT scan and is still receiving Ativan. The CT scan reveals:

"The ventricles may have very marginally increased in size. Multiple low density changes are noted involving the cerebral and cerebellar hemispheres, predominantly in the white matter, and affecting also the thalami. This is in keeping with the clinical diagnosis of fat embolism. There is no evidence of new lesions" (RCH, 222).

Heidi returns to the Intensive Care Unit at 12:25 pm. At 12:35 pm the nurse assesses her and she seems stable although her blood pressure and her ICP are slightly elevated. She remains fairly stable over the next few hours. Her dressings are changed and her legs continue to drain serous fluid. The legs are looking good and appear healthy at this time.

At 4:20 pm, Heidi's ICP suddenly spikes up to 30 and 34 despite having no agitation. She is given Mannitol and sedation but three minutes later there still is no change in her ICP, so the resident manually bags her. Her ICP then drops to 17. At 5:10 pm, her ICP spikes again to 23, so she is bagged again, has the EVD drained, and her position changed. Ten minutes later her ICP is still high and more Mannitol is given. By 6:10 pm her ICP stays up; she is given sedation, her EVD drain is open, and her body position is corrected. Fifteen minutes later, at 6:25 pm, her ICP remains high and they give her more sedation plus manually bag her again. Five minutes later she shows no signs of lowering her ICP. She is given yet more sedation and Mannitol. Finally, at 6:40 pm, her ICP begins to drop to 18 while she is being bagged; but it goes back up again when the bagging is stopped. At 6:50 pm she is put back on the ventilator and her ICP fluctuates between 11 and 17mmHg.

The neurosurgeon, Dr. M, arrives at 7:00 pm to see Heidi. He tells the team to keep up the regimen of Mannitol, sedation and bagging, and to continue monitoring her very, very closely. Dr. M sees Heidi's father in the hallway and they discuss her status. Heidi's father calls me at home to let me know how she is coping today. I plan to go in and see her in the morning, while her father plans to come home tonight as he needs to get some real rest.

Shortly after Dr. M leaves Heidi's bedside, her ICP spikes again and she is given more sedation medication. Her ICP remains between 19 and 25, and even more sedation is given. At 7:15 pm, the ICU resident, Dr. H, arrives at her bedside to check on her and he is made aware of her fluctuations in the ICP over the last few hours. He pages Dr. M five minutes later, at 7:20 pm. By 7:30 pm, Heidi's ICP rises up to 27 and stays there, so she is given Mannitol then manually bagged until it drops again. She is proving to be a lot of work for the nurses and doctors and I'm sure they must all be thoroughly exhausted by the end of their 12-hour shifts.

The new nurse for the 8:00 pm shift change gets acquainted with Heidi's progress throughout this day and runs the series of routine checks on her. Heidi's heart rate at 9:00 pm is 95 bpm, her blood pressure is 137/74, and her ICP is 20. She notes that Heidi is still on a 30 degree incline on her bed and that the safety rails are up, as is usual. Heidi has a strong cough, but no gag reflex. She flexes her arms to nailbed pressure, her toes are pointed downward and some muscle movement is noted in her thighs with pressure to her toes. Heidi has a continuous Ativan infusion. Her EVD is draining a clear fluid with some bloody streaks in it. She seems manageably stable.

Kathy Elden is proving most helpful in interpreting some of the medical jargon for us. She knows what all the drugs are for, and what the tests are for that are done on the blood, sputum, urine, and other bodily fluids. She visits Heidi at 9:10 pm, just before leaving for the night. She calls me on her cellular phone on her way home to give me a progress report. I am so grateful for Kathy. Heidi's father leaves the hospital for home at about the same time.

Our Dr. M is taking the weekend off work, so another neurosurgeon, Dr. C, sees Heidi at 9:30 pm to assess her condition. A half hour later, at 10:00 pm, Heidi's ICP goes up and she is given Mannitol. At 11:15 pm her ICP goes up over 30 and she is manually bagged, given sedation and Mannitol. By 11:30 pm her ICP drops below 20, giving the nurse and the ICU resident time to catch their breaths. Her leg dressings are changed. At 12:55 am her ICP spikes to 27 and Mannitol is started again in her IV. By 1:30 am the ICP is back down below 20, but fifteen minutes later it spikes again. The intern, Dr. H, is there at her side. He instructs the nurse to give Heidi Tylenol and to put a cooling blanket on her.

Just before 2:00 am Heidi's pupils enlarge and are elliptical in shape. She is non-reactive, has no cough, no response to pain. Her ICP is now dangerously spiking up between 35 and 40. Her heart rate is up to 135 bpm. At 2:20 am her blood pressure is labile (unstable, falling) with her systolic pressure dropping to 88. Systolic pressure is the highest arterial pressure reached during the ejection of blood from the heart. Diastolic pressure occurs while the heart ventricles are relaxing. Normal resting blood pressure for a young adult is said to be 120 mm mercury (Hg) over 80mm Hg, or simply 120/80 (Mader, 132). Heidi now has a dangerously low systolic pressure. A few minutes later her blood pressure drops to 80/50 and her heart rate is 115 bpm. Dr. H instructs the nurse to call Dr. C, the neurosurgeon. At 2:30 am a cooling blanket is put on Heidi and a new IV is started in her right forearm. Dr. C comes in to see Heidi at 2:45 am and assesses her.

In the early morning hours the phone rings on my bedside table at home. At 3:25 am this is the scariest sound in the world. Heidi's father leaps over me and snatches the phone receiver to speak with the hospital. It is Dr. C and he tells him that Heidi is crashing fast and that we should get to the hospital as soon as possible as it doesn't look good. I watch as this news registers on Heidi's father's face, then I curl up into a fetal position and rock back and forth, crying, "No, no, no, no, no!" He tries to tell me what the doctor is saying, but only blurts out a few key words: "crashing,.... not going to make it,.... going down fast." He listens as the doctor speaks with other medical personnel in the background and tries to give me the information as he receives it. We are told to come in quickly. My heart is pounding right out of my chest, forcing its way up into my throat; I can't breathe. My brain is blacking over. I can no longer hear properly, there is a loud rushing sound inside my head. Heidi's father is quiet for a few seconds as he presses the phone tightly against his ear and intently tries to listen to what is going on at Heidi's bedside. Suddenly, Dr. C says, "Wait, wait a minute, she's coming back,... yes, now the ICP is dropping again. Okay, I think we have her back... yes, you don't have to come in right now; maybe you should wait until the morning. It looks like she's going to be okay now." Then he says goodbye and hangs up. Heidi's father's hand is frozen to the telephone receiver. He is trying to catch his breath as he tells me they got her back and that she isn't going to die right this minute. We are both upright, kneeling on our bed, hyperventilating; both of us are absolutely white in the face and our hearts are hammering in our chests. This is the most frightening phone call of our lives. It takes us more than an hour to settle down enough to try and go back to sleep. But there will be no more sleep for us this night.

Back at the hospital, all efforts are made to save Heidi's life. Her system is shutting down, but they somehow circumvent death by bagging her, giving her drugs, and by just being completely on top of her at all times. I now recognize the heroic efforts made on my daughter's behalf and I want the medical personnel to know I deeply appreciate all they are doing for her. After the 3:25 am crisis, Heidi does it again at 5:05 am. She doesn't immediately respond to the bagging and sedation and by 5:15 am her ICP is up at 25, and her blood pressure is registering at 160/95. She is given more Mannitol. This brings the ICP down somewhat, but again at 6:15 am, her ICP spikes and more Mannitol is given. Fortunately, by 6:30 am her ICP finally drops in response to the increased Mannitol.

At home, I cannot sleep. I am worried about Heidi being alone in the hospital, which is ridiculous because I know she is surrounded by doctors and nurses who are watching her every breath. I guess what I mean is that there are no family members at her bedside and I fear that she might sense this. I decide to get an early start and leave for New Westminster before 6:00 am. I arrive at Heidi's bedside just before 6:30 am, and have a brief visit with her. I whisper in her ear, "Just breathe, Heidi; all you have to do is just keep breathing." She is not breathing spontaneously and still requires full ventilation with the help of the machine.

At 7:15 am, Heidi's ICP spikes again, going up to 27. She responds to the bagging only momentarily and Mannitol is started again in her IV. Fifteen minutes later, at 7:30 am, her ICP drops in response to the Mannitol. Somehow, Heidi survives another harrowing night. She is stable once again, but for how long?

3.13 Science World

In grade eleven Heidi participated in a work-practice program in which students are placed in a job for two weeks to learn how to interact on the job and to learn new skills. Heidi's first placement was at Science World in Vancouver. This complex was built for Vancouver's Expo '86 World Exhibition, and it remains as a permanent Vancouver landmark. The building is easily recognizable by its large geodesic dome structure, which houses the Imax Theatre. Science World hosts many learning programs for busloads of elementary students throughout the year and Heidi worked in this area in addition to hosting the shows in the big screen theatre. Part of her duties in the science area included assisting the person who was performing the demonstrations.

Heidi and Courtney had earlier paid to have long acrylic fingernails professionally applied to their nails. For a few months both girls had extremely long fingernails that they loved to experiment and play with. Heidi made this really irritating clicking noise with her nails when she wanted to bug me; and she would use them as daggers if anyone bothered her enough. I'm embarrassed to admit the girls talked me into getting these false nails also, but mine were shorter and only lasted a month until I was fed up with them and had them removed. The girls held out longer, and as it turned out, this was a good thing.

One day after she returned home from Science World I asked Heidi what she did that day. She answered: "I had to pick leeches off the newts!" I laughed and asked how she managed to get them off. She responded, "I used my fingernails to pick them off and I never once had to touch them with my fingertips. The newts didn't like being picked up by my nails, but too bad, I wasn't going to touch them with my hands!" So the long fake nails proved useful after all. It wasn't too long after her stint at

Science World that Heidi had her acrylic nails removed. They had served their purpose.

One of the things Heidi most enjoyed at Science World was standing before the audience in the Imax Theatre and speaking into a hand-held microphone to introduce the film they were about to see. She took to this task much easier than to the newts and leeches. The nice young man who was operating the Imax show invited her behind the big screen during the film and he took her to the staircase that goes all the way up to the top. She told me it was scary going up so high, but she was okay with it. Heidi described how she could see the people in the audience through the thousands of tiny holes in the big screen. She thought this was a fantastic experience. So, to the young man at the Imax, I send you my thanks for giving my daughter such a wonderful new look at the world from high up behind the big screen. She was truly thrilled when she came home that day. Thank you, thank you, and thank you again for putting a big smile on her face that lasted for days.

3.14   Saturday, September 20

I can't sleep after that horrifying phone call from Dr. C, so I get up for good at 5:00 am, shower, eat breakfast, read the newspapers, and leave in my car before 6:00. I see Heidi around 6:30 am in the Intensive Care Unit. She is not doing so well. My nerves are all over the place.

I give a photo of Heidi to the nurse and watch as she tapes it to the wall above her bed. I want those who are attending Heidi in the ICU to see what she *really* looks like: when her shining eyes reflect the smile on her beautiful face, framed by a long, thick cascade of shiny chestnut-coloured hair. Later on, an intern asks me who is in the photo and he's shocked to learn it's his patient in the bed below; the patient with a lump of orange bandaging on her partially shaved scalp where the two tubes emerge; the patient with the white, sweaty face with the blue tube up her nose and the ETT strapped to her mouth, and the face in which her blue eyes never open; the patient whose bruised arms have four or five IV lines puncturing the flesh at all times; the patient whose splinted legs continue to drain fluids from the open filleted muscles; and the patient whose Foley catheter drains urine into the sack hanging off the side of her bed. It's no wonder he doesn't recognise the fresh, beautiful face in the photograph.

Upon our return to Royal Columbian Hospital, we find we have been ousted from the convenient Family Room. Other families need it now, and besides, we've had almost a full week of free accommodations at Hotel Royal Columbian. We are guided into the other waiting room for ICU family members: an open room with telephones and enough benches for a large group. As I walk past this room on my way to see Heidi, I notice it is filled with a rough-looking crowd who are very upset and are being very noisy about it.

Heidi has a new roommate on her right: The Tattoo Man. He was brought in last night suffering from a heroin overdose. One of the doctors tells me it's his seventh or eighth overdose this year and this time his recovery is doubtful. This man, in his late twenties or early thirties, is covered in tattoos. They are brightly coloured and decorate his arms, legs and torso, front and back. He is decorated in fish, skulls, knives, women, smoke and marijuana leaves. It is an amazing sight. He smells really bad. His body is wracked with convulsions and it takes two doctors to hold him down while they administer medications. The doctor tells me that a lot of heroin addicts know that most emergency paramedics carry medicine to counteract drug overdoses, so they push their heroin dosages to the limit, confident they'll be saved if and when they overdose. This makes the doctors and paramedics angry. He tells me they are sick of these people who willingly harm themselves. This time the potency was too high and it looks like Tattoo Man has fried his brains for good.

Heidi lies in her hospital bed, sleeping, and is oblivious (hopefully) to what is occurring next to her. I don't stay very long amidst this commotion, and after my visit I go into the new waiting room to work on my stitchery while waiting for my next visit after morning rounds. The Tattoo Man's friends are in turmoil as they try to grasp what has happened to him. They are from Surrey. A very thin and bedraggled woman is on the phone and speaking loudly to whomever she is calling, and she is discussing the overdose. She says that she is sure the seeds were okay and that they've never had a problem with their mixture before. She can't understand what went wrong with the process because she thought the strength was just right. She says maybe they should be extra careful with the rest of the batch and use it in smaller doses. She tells the person on the other end of the phone that she doesn't think the heroin should be thrown out though. That would be a waste.

I cannot believe what I am hearing. This emaciated young woman looks years older than she should. Her voice is coarse, her long hair is matted and oily, and her clothes hang on her like rags. She is coughing, her nose is running and she appears to be shaking. She is a mess and appears to be in need of another fix, and soon. She is openly talking with her friends in the room about making their own drugs, and now she's upset because the drugs may have cost her friend his life. There are no concerns about who is listening to this conversation, or maybe they just don't notice I'm here in the room with them. After about a half an hour of listening to drug recipes and methods of production, I leave. The other family room, although plagued by thieves, was at least private. It also smelled better.

I travel between visits with Heidi to the cafeteria, over to see Courtney, or outside for brief walks. Heidi's father decides to stay home this morning, so I'm on my own until visitors come by. Bent and Bev Hanson come by every few days, as does Kathy Elden, who brings us dozens of her homemade buns to eat. This crisis creates a need to keep our hands busy; I concentrate on my stitchery while Kathy tries out every recipe she can find for her new bread-maker machine. She keeps us in baked goods for the duration of our stay at RCH. We have frequent visits from John Scholtens and Gregory Thomas, and it's good to catch up on the political news. Some of Heidi's friends come by too, and they are frustrated they cannot visit with her like they can Courtney and Vanessa.

After I leave Heidi in the ICU, the nurses do their shift change and the usual procedures follow. The new nurse is updated on Heidi's rough night and she notes the lack of response in her patient. Heidi is only weakly responding to deep nailbed pressures, and her corneal and gag reflexes are absent. Her lungs are suctioned for a moderate amount of greyish secretions, and are still making coarse sounds. Her LLL (left lower lobe) is not working properly. Her abdomen is no longer distended but is flat and soft, which is good.

I come in to see Heidi again at 8:45 am and speak with the nurse. I try to talk to Heidi, but her ICP goes up when I am there, so I don't stay long. At least she senses I am there, so I know she has some brain function. If only she would wake up. Dr. C is in to see Heidi right after I leave, and he comes out to the hall to speak with me. Contrary to what Dr. M has suggested Dr. C does not feel that a barbiturate coma is a good idea because he feels the doctors would thereby be unable to accurately assess the patient. Nor does he like the idea of a lobectomy because it "will not be effective in diffusing bilateral swelling"(RCH, 77). He tells me that the removal of a lobe will allow room for the brain to swell into, but that it causes movement of other parts of the brain, including the brain stem, and this presents the possibility of massive damage. He is the neurosurgeon on duty this weekend and he informs me he will not perform a lobectomy on Heidi no matter what happens. He lets me know in no uncertain terms that Heidi is gravely ill and that we cannot be too optimistic about her recovery. He discusses her management to date and believes it's the best course of action: Mannitol, sedation, and bagging. This has worked so far and saved her many times over the last few days, so they will continue with same.

Dr. G and the intern, Dr. C, make 10:00 am rounds this Saturday. They are made aware of the events of the night and agree to continue with the status quo in treatment. The intern notes that upon viewing the previous day's CT scan, he assesses the increase in ICP as secondary to fat embolism, but perhaps also to a shear injury. He agrees the scattered swellings in her brain are consistent with fat embolism syndrome, and notes there is a small port hemorrhage. Heidi's brain has suffered some damage, but it is still too early to know if this damage will be permanent or not. There *is* hope.

Heidi remains unstable throughout the morning and at 11:00 am the nurse notes her ICP fluctuates dramatically between 11 and 27, sometimes within seconds and with no provocation. At 12:15 pm her temperature is starting to rise, and her chest sounds remain coarse throughout. At 1:55 pm she is given a complete bed bath and linen change. She continues to menstruate. The nurse notes erosion of skin in the creases of her groin, and when she is turned, it is discovered that Heidi's entire buttock area is reddened and excoriated (skin falling off). A large amount of skin is sloughing off and the nurse calls the intern to see her. Some creams are put on her buttocks and fresh dressings applied. She tolerates this well. She remains stable throughout the afternoon and into the early evening up to the end of this shift.

This evening the new nurse assesses her condition as mainly unchanged: weak or no responses to pain, no gag reflex, edema to hands, forearms, ankles and feet, and coarse breath sounds. She notes a difficulty in threading the suction catheter into the OETT (main trachea tube). She is suctioned for a small amount of yellow-white secretions, after which her chest sounds are clearer. She notes a large area of bruising to Heidi's left upper thigh, hip and buttock. She sees yellowish bruising on her left foot as well. She applies Nyotatin cream to her red, raw buttocks area from her tailbone to her anus, and in her groin creases. White-yellow skin is sloughing from this region of her body. She is repositioned to help this situation.

Heidi's father comes in to see her at 8:50 pm and he is very upset when updated on her condition. He receives emotional support in the Intensive Care Unit. Dr. C, the ward doctor, is at Heidi's bedside and speaks with her father. She is hanging in there and the treatments seem to be keeping Heidi alive. Her temperature is 38 degrees Celsius, her heart rate 96 bpm, and her blood pressure 115/65. Dr. C orders more antibiotics to combat the fever and the infection found in the lab results from her aspirate. The results show: "endotracheal tube aspirate + 1 gram negative cocci, + 3 pus cells, Haemophilus influenzae + 2, and Candida species + 1" (RCH, 277). Her lungs and trachea are badly infected, but the doctors are aware of this and, I assume, treating the infections accordingly.

Heidi's evening is uneventful and she is given an analgesic and a sedative before the nursing care begins at 11:00 pm. Her dressings are changed on her legs and they are noted to be healing well. At 11:15 pm her ICP goes up and the intern is immediately at her bedside; but her ICP drops before any treatment is needed. This is a good sign. Around 11:50 pm she is given a complete wash and the nurse notices there are open areas of sloughed skin on her left buttock, with clusters of pinpoint blisters on her left hip, some of them open. She applies a soothing paste to her buttocks, hips and groin area.

Just past midnight, Heidi's ICP spikes, so she has her head realigned. She is given Mannitol and her ICP drops and stabilizes. She still has some petechiae on her right breast region. Her ICP fluctuates throughout the early morning hours and sometimes it spikes spontaneously. Sedation helps. Her lungs are suctioned for a small amount of sputum and she tolerates this well, neurologically. More antiseptic paste is applied to her buttocks, and blood work is taken at 7:20 am. She has had a much more stable night than the previous one.

3.15   Sunday, September 21

This Sunday dawns with a renewed light for us. Heidi has had a relatively uneventful night and has survived to see a new day. Now that we are no longer allowed to stay in the family room overnight, I begin a new routine. I leave home around 5:30 am and drive to Koko's Cappuccino Shop in Langley; I get a large café latte for the drive into New Westminster and a container of fresh-squeezed fruit juice for Courtney. Courtney's sister is dating the son of the owner of Koko's, and he is happy to see me early each morning to get an update on our girls. I'm sure he puts an extra dollop of love into Courtney's juice. I am in the hospital before 7:00 am most mornings, and stay until around 7:00 pm most nights. It is good to sleep in my own bed at night, and it is better for me to have some breaks from the suffocating atmosphere of the hospital. When I'm in the hospital, I see Heidi every three or four hours, albeit briefly. When I'm at home I call the ICU nurse once before going to bed, then once in the night if I wake up, usually around 2:00 am; and I call again as soon as I'm awake in the morning, around 5:00 am. This is less stressful on me than staying inside the hospital twenty-four hours a day. I enjoy visiting Courtney in the mornings after my first check-in with Heidi and her nurses.

The shift change is uneventful and at 7:45 am the new nurse is doing her routine with Heidi. She notes that Heidi's ICP responds quickly to sedation, so she is now in a more manageable state. Neurologically, she is not yet responding to pain, but her pupils are mid-sized and reactive. She still shows no spontaneous respiration effort and remains on full ventilation. Her chest sounds are coarse and she is suctioned for a moderate amount of thick yellow-green secretions. Her urine output is good and her legs are healthy.

At 9:30 am Heidi's heart rate is at a reasonable 94 bpm, her blood pressure is a healthy 120/68, but her temperature remains elevated at 38.1 degrees Celsius. At 10:00 am, the new ICU doctor works his rounds and is updated on her condition, which is stable at this time. Her ICP goes up when she is turned and she receives Mannitol and sedation; within five minutes her ICP returns to normal. At noon her temperature has dropped and she is receiving a Morphine infusion along with her regular Ativan infusion. Her chest sounds seem less coarse to her left base, although she still needs the ventilator to help her breathe. At 1:30 pm the nurse notes that Heidi's perineum is very red and excoriated. She applies more Ihles paste to soothe the reddened areas and she changes her dressings.

It is very hard for the nurse to insert the suction catheter into the OETT tube, and she makes a note of this at 3:55 pm. Heidi has no cough reflex. The good news is that her neurological status has been stable all day. Samples of the cerebrospinal fluid (CSF) are sent to the lab and she tolerates the brief clamping of the EVD. At 4:40 pm Heidi's ICP goes up and she is given extra sedation and a dose of Mannitol. The resident is there by 5:00 and is aware of what is going on. The EVD is flushed out because some brain tissue has been noted in the tubing. By 5:20 pm her ICP is improving. Again, at 5:40 her ICP increases and a call is put in for the neurosurgeon, Dr. C. He calls in at 6:10 pm and is made aware of the tissue in the EVD tubing but he does not want the catheter flushed at this time. Her ICP is fluctuating between 15 and 40 mmHg. An hour later, at 7:10 pm, the ICP stabilizes. The nursing shift-change begins.

Today's chest x-ray report reads: "This patient demonstrates persisting minimal subsegmental atelectasis in the base of the left lower lobe with a small pneumomediastinum" (RCH, 243). Heidi's white blood cell count is elevated at 18.1 (RCH

262); the normal range is 3.9 to 10.2. Dr. MC, the ICU doctor, orders the anitbiotic, Cefuroxime, to be given in place of the Ancef every eight hours for her pulmonary infection.

The new nurse takes over the note-making at 7:55 pm, and begins her long, detailed write-up on Heidi's various conditions. Heidi shows very weak withdrawal of her right hand to nailbed pressure, she has no cough or gag reflexes, and has weak corneal reflexes. Her EVD is draining a clear to slightly pink-tinged fluid, with sediment and tissue seen in the tubing. Both pupils are at 4mm and brisk. Her temperature is 37.2 degrees Celsius. Her breath sounds are coarse and her left lower lobe is still not functioning correctly. The nurse has difficulty advancing the in-line suction tube, so the resident uses a single-line catheter, which proves effective for bringing up a small amount of white sputum. She notes the bruised skin on Heidi's thigh and hip, and notes that the alternating foot splints, which pulsate to aid circulation, are now working on her patient.

I leave shortly after seeing her at 7:00 pm, and Heidi's father comes in to see her at 8:35 pm. Again, he needs emotional support from the nurse; and she writes this in her notes. He leaves for home soon after.

At 9:12 pm, Heidi's heart rate is 87 bpm, her blood pressure is 111/60, and her ICP is 18. She is stable. At 9:35 pm her ICP fluctuates upwards so she has her head realigned on the bed and is given sedation. Her ICP slowly creeps up to 25, but soon stabilizes. At 11:00 pm her fasciotomy dressings are changed and then she is given a full wash and linen change. Her skin is washed with mineral oil to remove the old Ihles paste and then is rinsed before the nurse reapplies more salve to the damaged skin on her buttocks, perineum, and groin areas. Two areas have opened up on Heidi's skin: a 1x2 inch spot on her left buttock and a 1/2 inch gash on her coccyx (tailbone). Her EVD is flushed out to clear the brain tissue debris. Her heart rate at midnight is 91 bpm, and blood pressure is 141/75. I find this encouraging.

At 1:00 am the nurse notes that Heidi's oxygen saturation level has dropped to 91%. Her chest sounds are coarse and she is suctioned for scant white secretions. She is given 100% oxygen and her saturation levels improve. Again, at 1:30 am her oxygen saturation is down to 91% and her chest sounds remain coarse. The nurse tries to suction and gets nothing. She has trouble advancing the suction catheter, so she calls the resident for help. By 2:00 am, the resident is successfully suctioning her lungs. They note that her left lung expansion is less than her right lung. The nurse sends blood samples to the lab to see where Heidi's blood gas levels are. Oxygen saturation is up to 95% by 2:20 am. At 4:00 am Heidi's oxygen saturation is markedly improved at 97 to 99 %. It is noted at this time that Heidi has a pink rash on her left breast and her right thigh. Her fasciotomy dressings are changed again at 6:30 am, and more blood work is taken at 6:55. Morning has arrived and Heidi has made it through another night without any serious trauma.

3.16 Florida

Our family went on a trip to Florida in February of 1989. We needed some sunshine after a long and wet B.C. winter, and we also wanted to catch up with our old friends from Langley: the Gillrie family. Heidi was best friends with Anne, while our Laura was buddies with Laura Gillrie, and Bill was friends with their older brother, Adam. The Gillries had five children with the sixth on the way, and their eldest children were the same ages as my three. Their mother, Jan, and I became close friends for the short time they lived in Langley and our children attended the same elementary school. Mr. Gillrie was transferred to the Tampa Bay area in Florida, and the children soon missed their good friends after they moved away. So we were especially excited to be seeing them after a year's absence. While in Florida, we packed in as many tourists' sights and activities as we could in just seven days. We enjoyed: two days on the beach with the Gillries; an exciting day at the GatorLand Jumperoo Show; a day at the Epcot Centre; a trip to the Kennedy Space Center at Cape Canaveral where we saw the Space Shuttle, Discovery, standing tall on the launch pad (we missed takeoff by three weeks!); a memorable dinner at the Medieval Times where Heidi caught the winning knight's flower (big thrill!); and, of course, Disney World.

We brought along a travel diary and Heidi added her perspective to our trip by filling in a few pages. Each of us contributed to the journal and it is now something I dearly treasure. Some excerpts from an almost nine-year-old Heidi:

"Now we are on the airplane; there have been some bumps but now they are over. We have just flown over Lake Ontario into the U.S. It will take us 3 hours to get to Florida. We are staying in the Sea Spire [motel] and we got to go in the ocean. Then we went for dinner and we walked to the restaurant. There are lots of lizards here and lots of different kinds of palm trees. It is warm out…The Gillries came and we had a lot of fun. The Gillries and us went swimming in the pool at the hotel. It was Valentine's Day. Laura said Happy Valentine's Day. Laura [Gillrie] said Merry Christmas. Billy saw a lizard on a branch and he caught it; the lizard turned out to be a male gecko that Billy had read about, so he let him go."

These are some of the highlights of our Florida trip from a child's perspective. The Medieval Times was also a lot of fun for Heidi and her siblings. We sat in the green section and cheered for the Green Knight and we all wore green crowns and ate with our fingers (no cutlery here) and drank soda pop from heavy goblets. The horse tournaments were excellent and throughout the evening each colour-coded Knight won at least one game. He then rode over to his cheering section and threw a red carnation to the fairest maiden in the crowd. Our Green Knight threw his carnation to Heidi and she caught it easily, with a loud whoop and a squeal over her good fortune. She talked about this for months afterwards. For this brief moment she became the princess of fairytale legends.

St. Petersburg Beach was another thrilling find for our family. The massive white sand beach stretches for miles and miles and the water is warm enough to swim in, even in February. As much as we love our beaches and coastline here in British Columbia, nothing compares to the glorious beaches in Florida. And the heat: oh my, did we love the heat! B.C. is not weather-friendly in February and this was a heavenly escape from the damp and the cold. I am so thankful we took this opportunity; we took our children out of school and slipped into another world for one glorious week. I am grateful we were able to do this for our children (and Gramma K who accompanied us). These little moments now seem colossal in retrospect. This was seven days of intense joy for our young family.

3.17 Monday, September 22

Heidi comes out of a quiet night and I am so relieved that she is stabilizing. This is day ten and surely to God this fat embolism Beast will soon relinquish its hold on my daughter's brain. I am more hopeful today than I have been for the past week. Heidi hasn't crashed for two days now and I'm thinking that the worst is over, that now we will start to see our daughter emerge from this black pit she was thrown into ten days ago.

At 8:00 am Heidi's temperature is slightly raised but overall she is stable. The morning routine reveals no change in her neurological responses. Her ICP still occasionally spikes up to as high as 29 from a steady 14, with no stimulation, but they get it back down soon enough. The new nurse notes a small amount of brain tissue in Heidi's EVD line. Heidi's legs muscles are now twitching to pain, but even better, her arms are showing a slight movement to stimulus. Her cheeks are flushed this morning and her buttocks are still red and excoriated. Her breath sounds are still coarse and she remains on full ventilation. She is suctioned for a small amount of white secretions from her lungs. Her belly is rounded and moderately firm today.

Heidi's neurosurgeon, Dr. M, comes in to see her at 10:00 a.m., and he orders another CT scan for today after reviewing the events of the weekend. I am at her bedside speaking with Dr. M when I notice his bandaged left thumb. I ask what happened and he explains that while building a tree-fort for his children over the weekend he bashed his thumb with a hammer. I tell him I think neurosurgeons have no business wielding hammers, given the delicate work their hands and fingers do in surgery. He laughs and agrees it was a dumb move, but what could he do? His children wanted a tree-fort. It is nice to have a normal conversation with this doctor, about family life and the usual misadventures that happen to us all. He seems like a good father, a nice man.

Dr. McC and his team do their rounds at 10:30 am and they note that Heidi is deeply comatose and remains unresponsive. During their examination, Heidi's heart rate is 89 bpm, blood pressure is 119/64, and ICP is 21. Her ICP always goes up when she is having things done to her. They note her abdomen has a mild distension, but is soft. Her ICP drops down to 13 during their visit and continues to fluctuate up and down. She is to continue with her course of drugs to stabilize her ICP, and the nurse is asked to closely monitor her hemoglobin, which is at 111 today. Once again, they speculate that she has "a splenic contusion or small vessel injury" (RCH, 83). Her orthopaedic surgeries will have to wait another day at least, unless she goes into the Operating Room for another procedure.

Heidi remains stable and I visit her around 2:00 pm. As I whisper to my daughter I can't help overhearing a conversation between the two nurses about the dashingly handsome Dr. M, the neurosurgeon. They are giggling and gushing over him like two schoolgirls. The pretty blonde with long lacquered nails that are "newt-worthy," as Heidi would say, tells me they are very happy Dr. M is Heidi's neurosurgeon because now they get to spend lots of time near him. I find I am irritated by this conversation and I think it's because I don't want Heidi's nurses to be distracted while they care for her. I apologise if I sound unkind, but it doesn't take much to irritate me these days and I have no patience for workplace flirtations (In Dr. M's defence, the flirtations are one-sided: he's oblivious to them). I am probably being unreasonable to expect the nurses to focus 100% on my daughter for their entire 12-hour shifts.

Heidi is readied for her trip to the CT scan. Her ICP is still erratic but she tolerates the trip well and returns to the ICU at 4:15 pm. Dr. M comes in to see her again at 6:15 pm and discusses today's CT scan. The CT scan is summarized:

"The periventricular white matter hypodense changes are more extensive[ly] consistent with fat embolism, but the hypodense changes within the cerebellar hemisphere, although still present, are not as prominent today. There is also evidence of increased intracranial pressure" (RCH, 223).

Heidi's brain is struggling with the fat embolism, but seems to be improving. Hooray!

A chest x-ray is taken and it shows "worsening of atelectasis in the basal segment of the left lower lobe" (RCH, 244). Heidi's lower left lung is collapsing. This is not good.

The 8:00 pm nurse notes that Heidi is now slightly diaphoretic (sweating) and warm. Her temperature is 37.9 degrees Celsius, heart rate is 87 bpm, and blood pressure is 125/65. Her belly is distended, and she continues with her entube feedings. Her T-waves have dampened, as seen on her heart monitor. She is still unresponsive. Her left ankle is badly bruised, and she has scattered bruising on her arms and legs; I have no explanations for these bruises. The skin on her thighs remains red and excoriated. The nurse doesn't check her buttocks nor her back at this time. At 8:35 pm she is suctioned for scant amounts of clear secretions, with no cough. She is deeply comatose. Her leg dressings are changed, and they are still draining small amounts of fluid. She is repositioned to relieve pressure on her buttocks, one side at a time.

At 11:45 pm Heidi receives a full bed bath and linen change. After her wash, more Ihles paste is applied to her buttocks and perineum. It is noted for the first time that her axilla (armpits) are excoriated as well. Her ICP levels go up during her bath time. By 12:15 am her ICP settles with more sedation and Mannitol. She is still not taking any spontaneous breaths and remains unresponsive. Her abdomen is now quite distended.

Around 4:00 am Heidi's ICP goes up and then resolves spontaneously. The nurse notes that her ICP is not correcting with the IV sedation and Mannitol. She still has no cough or gag reflexes. Her fever is still present and her skin feels hot and dry now. By 4:40 am the nurse repositions Heidi onto her back from her right side because her ICP keeps going up. She is now laying on her back on a 30 degree incline, as before. She stabilizes for the remainder of the early morning. More blood samples are taken to the lab at 6:45 am. A portable chest x-ray is taken at 7:10 and her leg dressings are changed again at 7:20 am. A rather uneventful evening is behind us and a new day begins with a glimmer of hope that the worst is truly over.

3.18 Skiing in Winter

Heidi's family took great advantage of seasonal sports. We boated and water-skied in the summer, and in the winter we downhill skied. Our home in Langley is just an hour or two from several wonderful mountains that offer a variety of ski slopes for different level skiers. We often made day-trips to Cypress, Seymour, Grouse, Baker (in the U.S.), and occasionally Hemlock and Whistler, which are longer drives. Heidi and her siblings always joined the ski trips their elementary and high schools organized. The school groups usually went to Whistler/Blackcomb, north of Squamish. Because of our proximity to these mountains, the children had lots of snow time each winter, starting at about age six.

We went on a couple of Christmas-break trips in which we rented a hotel or condominium for a week of non-stop skiing. One year we stayed at the Big White resort, just east of Kelowna; and a couple of years later we stayed at Silverstar Mountain, near Vernon in the Okanagan. Heidi, Bill and Laura were inexhaustible on these trips. They would gulp down breakfast then race out the door to start skiing first thing. Later, they would meet up with us for a quick lunch, and then up they went again on the chair-lift. We would rarely see them until it was starting to get dark, around 3:30 to 4:00 pm. These were wonderful, wonderful holidays and we are left with some exquisite winter memories that we'll always treasure. Heidi was particularly fond of the resort at Big White because our hotel had an indoor pool. Our children loved the water and as soon as the sub-zero slopes closed outside they changed into bathing suits and spent the rest of the evening playing in the hotel's steamy hot pool. I would bring a book down to the pool area and read while watching over the children; we were all so deliriously happy then. When I finally put them to bed each night, they would pass out as soon as their heads hit the pillows. For our little family, these times were as close to pure bliss as it got. Well, except for the summers.

3.19   Tuesday, September 23

This Tuesday morning begins with my usual 7:00 am visit with Heidi in the Intensive Care Unit. She has had a restful night and the new day looks promising for her tired, battered body. The new nurse notes she is showing slight movement in her left hand in response to pain but otherwise there is no movement in her limbs. Her corneal responses are very weak, and she still has no cough or gag reflexes. She turns her head to the right when the nurse cleans her mouth, or changes the ties that hold the air tube (OETT) in place. A small amount of tissue is seen in the EVD tube from her brain. Her ICP varies spontaneously, going up to 25 then down to 11 within 30 seconds. She is not assisting the ventilator yet. Her skin is warm, pink, and dry. Heidi's buttocks are still reddened but are improving from the previous day. Her lungs are making coarse breath sounds and are suctioned for a small amount of white secretions. Her belly is rounded and distended. Heidi continues to receive liquid food from the entube feedings, but has not had a bowel movement since entering the hospital. In other words, she has not had a bowel movement since September 12th: eleven days! This can't be good for her. I am worried about the distended abdomen, as it cannot possibly be beneficial to her overall health.

Dr. N, general surgeon, is filling in for Dr. B in the ICU. He notes that she is stable. Dr. M comes in next and assesses her, neurologically. He notes she is more stable today and therefore gives permission for an abdominal Ultra-Sound and an Echocardiography for later in the day, or tomorrow. He schedules another CT scan for tomorrow, Wednesday. He considers allowing the closure of her fasciotomies soon, and if her ICP is stable, perhaps he will disconnect her EVD. He speaks with me and tells me she is definitely improving. This is good news. My daughter is coming back to me. I knew it!

Dr. McC does his rounds at 10:30 am and notes that she will have an abdominal Ultra-Sound soon, and perhaps the Echocardiogram to check her heart. He questions whether or not her heart size seemed smaller in the last chest x-ray. He wants a Doppler done on her legs.

Heidi's father and I take turns visiting her around 11:30 am. She is showing very little improvement and the nurse tells me they will give her an enema today to help move her bowels. We hope she can tolerate the procedure neurologically. At noon she is given a sodium phosphate enema but there are no immediate results. She has a quiet day, and at 2:00 pm, her leg dressings are changed and it's noted that they are still draining small amounts of serous fluids. At 4:15 pm Heidi's temperature is 38.5 degrees Celsius and she is given a cool bath. There is some mucous drainage coming from her rectum, but no stools yet. Her skin is very warm to the touch. A small amount of clear secretions are suctioned from her lungs. The lab results show that the endotracheal tube aspirate contains " +4 pus cells" and "Candida albican +1" (RCH, 277). On this day her white blood cell count is 18.9. I come in at 6:30 pm to see her before I go home for the day. Her ICP still goes upwards when I'm next to her; and as scary as it is to be causing a small spike in her brain pressure, it reassures me to know that *she* knows her mother is at her side. Heidi knows she is not alone as she struggles to emerge from this murky darkness. I only hope it is soon.

Jamie and some of Heidi's friends come into the hospital today to see if they can visit with Heidi. I ask the nurse in the Intensive Care Unit and she says no, strictly family members only are allowed into the ICU. So Jamie, Ryan, and the gang are disappointed because they brought in a framed collage of photographs of Heidi's friends for her to enjoy. They want to place the picture next to her bed so she'll see it when she wakes up. The picture is amazing and it makes my eyes misty again. All her friends are in it. Many of them are posing for Ryan or Jamie's cameras, blowing kisses and waving hello. Lots of friends are gathered together in group photos for Heidi.

Within this collage I see two photos of Heidi. The main one is the swimming pool scene taken last August when the girls were in Osoyoos. Their skin is glowing in the golden rays of the setting sun. From left to right, they are: Heidi, Jamie, and Courtney. They are wearing bikini tops with their shorts and are dangling their legs in the pool at Jamie's aunt's home in Osoyoos. The girls are laughing. This is how I most remember my daughter, laughing with her best friends. The other little shot of Heidi is curious: she is in a white t-shirt and has her back to the camera and her right arm holds her long hair out of the way as she kisses the boy in the baseball cap (Kevin D.). I never did get to see her kiss a boy and I'm grateful for this evidence that she did indeed enjoy a little smooching in her teens. I'm sure this photo is included as a teaser just to bug Heidi when she sees it. This is a wonderful compilation of Heidi's closest friends and she will love it when she sees it. I am so grateful to Jamie and Ryan for putting this collage together, both for Heidi's sake and mine. Heidi is loved by so many who can't wait for her to be well again.

The Cardiologist, Dr. B, comes to see Heidi at 6:45 pm and is satisfied enough with Heidi's heart function that she cancels the Echocardiogram. Great! Heidi's bruised heart is improving.

The 8:00 pm shift change reveals no new developments. Heidi is still comatose. Her skin is hot and dry. Her heart rate, blood pressure, and ICP are stable and at reasonable levels. She still has some swelling on her arms and hands, and her belly remains distended. There remains a large bruise on her left ankle and scattered bruising on her arms and legs. Heidi's inner upper thighs are excoriated, although less so than last night. The resident doctor suctions her lungs and brings up moderate amounts of thick, yellow secretions. She has no cough reflex, which would usually occur with the suctioning.

Heidi's bowels finally loosen after 8:30 pm. She starts to leak brown liquid, is cleaned up and her buttocks, groin and perineum areas are redressed with a soothing cream and fresh compresses. At 10:35 pm Heidi's face is diaphoretic (sweating) at times, so she is given Tylenol to bring down the fever. Her leg dressings are changed for serous drainage and she is resettled. At 11:40 pm she releases a large amount of stool and they decide to insert a Bardex rectal tube into her rectum to facilitate the removal of her bowel contents. She drains liquid stool for a quite awhile. Then she is given a complete bed bath and linen change. By midnight Heidi is clean, and her ICP is brought back down within five minutes with the infusion of Mannitol to her IV.

Early into the next day, Heidi's ICP is stable, her blood pressure is normal, and she is suctioned for more yellow secretions. Her skin is still hot and she is sweaty. Her abdomen remains distended. The Bardex continues to drain liquid stool. At 2:00 am her feeding tube is flushed and clamped; the feeds are off until after she has her Ultra-Sound in the morning. One of the IVs in her right arm is not functioning properly, and a technician is called in at 3:30 am to restart a new IV line in her hand. She tolerates this well and the procedure is effective. By 5:25 Heidi's ICP remains stable; however, she seems determined to hang onto this high fever of hers. Her belly is still distended, but less so than earlier. The Bardex is still draining small amounts of liquid stool. Blood work is taken and the leg dressings are changed at 6:55 am. Our Heidi survives another night in the Intensive Care Unit.

3.20 Wednesday, September 24

Wednesday morning begins as they all do these days. Heidi is stable after an uneventful evening. I am glad she is finally moving her bowels and I see that her tummy is less distended this morning. At 7:47 am her heart rate is a nice 80 bpm, her blood pressure is 120/64, and her temperature is still slightly elevated at 37.9 degrees Celsius. She is suctioned for a small amount of white secretions, with no cough or gag reflexes. Her head turns to the right when the nurse performs mouth care, and her ICP seems less erratic today. Heidi's abdomen remains somewhat distended and the Bardex tube continues to drain liquid diarrhea.

When I touch the side of her face, Heidi jerks her head the other way. She is reacting to touch on some level. I wonder if she can hear me; does she know I am here?

Dr. O, the orthopaedic surgeon, comes in to see Heidi at 10:00 am, and he is willing to wait a little longer to close her fasciotomies. Her legs are draining only small amounts of fluid now and the wounds are still fresh and clean with no infections so far. This has been an extraordinarily long time to maintain open fasciotomies when the normal practice is to keep them open for only 48 to 72 hours. This is day twelve for Heidi.

Dr. McC and his team do their rounds at 11:00 am and they are satisfied Heidi is stable. Her ICP is staying down on its own most of the time now and her heart seems to have settled down to a more normal rhythm. Her temperature is still elevated, so she is kept on antibiotics.

The abdominal Ultra-Sound is done on Heidi at 1:45 pm, and she tolerates the procedure well. Her tube feeds are restarted after she returns. The Ultra-Sound reveals marked improvement since the last test and Dr. N notes the following: "Only a small sliver of free fluid now visible medial to the spleen which itself appears normal. No other free fluid visible anywhere in the abdomen and pelvis. [It] is greatly improved since the previous exam. Liver, pancreas, CIB & CHD, kidneys all appear normal" (RCH, 88). A satisfyingly positive report.

The day is fairly routine with dressing changes and another chest x-ray. Today's x-ray is similar to the previous day's in that it reveals persistent atelectasis in Heidi's left lung's lower lobe. A physiotherapist works on Heidi's lungs later in the day, around 4:30 pm, to loosen the congestion in her chest. Heidi's IV lines are changed again as they seem to keep plugging up. She also had an IV line changed the night before.

I come in to visit Heidi at 6:45 pm, and spend some time with her before going home for the night. I try to touch her but I am afraid to after the spleen incident. So I slip my hand alongside her inner right forearm, being careful not to jostle the two or three IVs in her arm and hand on that side. Then, miraculously, I feel Heidi's arm pressing my hand against her body. She is definitely responding to my touch; she knows I am here with her. I speak softly to her and watch amazed as tears start rolling down her cheeks. I know she is aware; she wants so badly to wake up but her brain is not yet ready to release her. This is how I feel, intuitively, as a mother. The nurses tell me she has no responses, but I know better. My baby is coming back to me. This little pressure from her arm and her tears renew my hope that the brain damage is only temporary and that she'll soon make a full recovery. The waiting is killing me. I don't want to leave her side, but the nurses are starting their shift change and have lots of busy-work to do, so once again I say my goodbyes for the night. Before prying myself away from her bedside, I promise I will see her first thing in the morning.

At 7:55 pm Heidi is stable and her temperature has gone down to 37.2 degrees Celsius. Her lungs are suctioned for a small amount of yellowish-green secretions; perhaps the physiotherapy loosened some infected mucous from her lungs. She continues making coarse wheezing sounds from her lungs. Her dressings are changed and the large bruising is noted on her left ankle. The edema is still present on both hands. Once again Heidi turns her head while receiving oral care. Heidi gets a full bed bath just before midnight and the nurse notices a large area of sloughed skin on her buttocks and coccyx area. She is still having her menses.

At 1:00 am Heidi is suctioned for a small amount of whitish secretions. Her chest sounds remain the same. At 6:20 am she is coming out of a stable night and has her leg dressings changed. Her breath sounds are still coarse, especially in the left base. Blood work is taken at 6:45, and a portable chest x-ray is done at 6:55. The tapes on the OETT are changed just after 7:00 am, after I had raised my concerns about the ties cutting into the sides of Heidi's mouth. I bring in a toothbrush and toothpaste for the nurses to use on Heidi's teeth and the nurse promises to use them.

3.21 Daisy's Puppies

Our Golden Retriever, Daisy, gave birth to eleven puppies in June of 1990, when Heidi was ten years old. The children were thrilled to watch the birthing process that lasted well into the night. Our veterinarian thought she might have six puppies, so when Daisy kept pushing after the sixth, seventh and eighth puppies, the whole family was suspended in this state of wonderment we had never experienced before. The children refused to go to bed until we were sure Daisy was finished. We couldn't believe it when the eleventh pup came out. She was a good mother, tending to each pup, tearing open the sac and licking her new baby until it was breathing on its own. She chewed through the umbilical cords and cleaned the mess by lapping it up with her tongue. (Ugh!) Poor Daisy was exhausted after the last one came, and she collapsed on an old sleeping bag we'd placed on the floor of the mud room for her in the basement. I gave her lots of water and tried to interest her in food, but she didn't want any just yet. The children came down to see the spectacle and to count the puppies one last time before going to bed. They couldn't wait until morning and had trouble sleeping through the night.

One of the puppies was born deformed with an almost backward-facing leg. The next morning I called our vet and he said to bring the lame puppy in along with two of the healthy ones so he could do an assessment. He didn't think the lame pup would survive so he took it into the back and promised he'd put it gently to sleep. The rest of the puppies were examined and found to be normal and healthy. Dogs have ten teats, so this reduced number now meant that each pup got equal time with their mom's milk supply. When they were all lined up suckling, they looked like little loaves of bread. Daisy's puppies were absolutely adorable. Once word got out, our house had a constant stream of neighbourhood children, often with their parents, who wanted to see the ten puppies. Everyone loved these puppies. Once they were up and running about, we built a make-shift enclosure out of chicken wire out on the lawn in the backyard where they could play during the day; we always brought them in at night.

Once the pups were in the backyard, the neighbours' children would ask to go into the enclosure to play with the puppies. These lucky little pups had children to play with them every single day until they were adopted out to new families at six and seven weeks. The children were always gentle with the pups and we had no accidents, mostly because of the strong mutual love between the dogs and the children. My three children loved this special time with the puppies, and benefited from this experience by caring for, feeding, cleaning up after, and grooming these tawny bundles of joy.

Heidi was no exception. She was downstairs in the mudroom first thing in the morning and out in the yard in the afternoon after school, cuddling her puppies. She liked to lie on the grass and have the puppies crawl all over her, nuzzling her face, chewing her hair, and pulling at her clothes. By four weeks we let the puppies explore the larger backyard and go into the bush. They would all respond when we called out, "Puppies," by turning around and running towards us in unison. It was a glorious sight. We kept a close eye on our puppies and they grew into healthy little dogs, fully weaned at six weeks. It was a sad few days when the new owners started taking them away. We had names for all of them and the children talked about their puppies for months afterwards. Daisy's puppies provided us with some of the best learning opportunities for our children. If love were tangible it would be soft and warm, fuzzy and chubby, snuffle and lick your ears.

3.22 Thursday, September 25

Thursday begins with more hope than I've had for a long time. Heidi is responding to me and I know her brain is recovering. The morning run-up reveals a fairly stable Heidi with a lowered temperature. Her corneals are brisk, and she moves her head to the right when touched. The EVD is draining clear fluids now, an improvement over the sanguineous (bloody) fluids draining from her brain the previous week. She is showing a generalized edema, especially in her hands. She looks somewhat puffy everywhere, in my opinion. Her breath sounds are bronchial with persistent crackles. The lungs are suctioned for a small amount of white secretions. Her abdomen is rounded and slightly firm. Heidi's buttocks are still reddened and continue to slough skin.

I come back in to see Heidi after the new nurse is finished with her tests and procedures. Today I bring in my camera so that after her recovery I can show Heidi what she looked like when she was in the Intensive Care Unit. I have every confidence she will make a full recovery and I think these photos will be important to her, especially after losing a couple of weeks in a coma. I ask permission and have to wait until someone signs a consent form allowing me to take photographs in the ICU. Obviously, I cannot take photos of the other patients. So, I proceed to take five or six shots of Heidi from different angles. I try to include the vast array of medical equipment at her bedside, from the ventilator machine, the heart and ICP monitors, the IV sacs of fluids connected to at least three sites in her arms and hands (today she has an IV line in her right thumb!). I get a close-up of the massive orange bandaging covering the EVD and ICP bolts in her head. I get shots of her legs in the splints, but not uncovered. I want to document every little detail I can, for Heidi's personal history. A few years

earlier I took photographs of Bill's friend Ben, when he was
in Royal Columbian with serious head injuries. He had bright
orange tape around the EVD bolt near the top of his head, just
as Heidi does now. Ben survived the multiple fractures to his
skull, and the photos are a reminder of the day he recklessly went
cliff-jumping with his friends (and my son) at Alouette Lake in
Golden Ears Park. The photographs of him in the hospital are
important to his history, and to ours. But as it turns out, these
photographs of Heidi never get developed.

A physiotherapist works on Heidi's chest at 10:45 am. She is
concentrating on the left lateral chest area and Heidi seems to
tolerate this well with no increase in her ICP. Rounds at 11:00
am are conducted by Dr. McC and he writes new orders for the
day. The morning's chest x-ray shows persistent atelectasis of
the lower left lobe. Heidi's WBC, or, white blood cell count,
is rising and it is now at 25.7. This is an indication that her
body is fighting an infection. She is put on the antibiotic,
Ampicillan. Her oxygen saturation is under 95% and although
she no longer has a fever, her lungs are still struggling. He
notes that her diarrhea has stopped and that there is no need
for further abdominal investigation. He questions whether to
start weaning her off the ICP treatment. He seems satisfied
with her progress and orders a Doppler test on her legs when
she can tolerate it.

The ward doctor sees Heidi and notes the higher white blood
cell count of 25.7. He writes: "Must consider other courses
of fever, if it persists: specifically DVT/PE as patient is on no
prophylaxes" (RCH, 90). Heidi's rising white blood cell count
is starting to concern the doctors.

Heidi's father and I are in and out throughout the day, and
between visiting her we go for long walks outside to get some

fresh air. The air inside the hospital is stifling; there is a smell of sickness and fear in here that makes me nervous. Although it feels good to leave the hospital, I worry about Heidi the whole time I'm away from her. I like to be nearby so the doctors can find me each time there is an update; when I visit with Heidi, the nurses are more cautious with what they tell me than the doctors are. So I regret missing a doctor's visit and often have to wait until the next day to speak with them.

The Purple Buddha arrived today; he is an extremely overweight man who is having some kind of heart or circulatory problems. It looks serious, and he is kept bare-chested, sitting upright in his bed directly across from Heidi. His skin is a vivid purple colour. Sitting up cross-legged like that, he looks like the familiar statue of a rotund, seated Buddha. Hence the nickname. I don't mean to sound unkind and I sincerely hope this man survives his stay in the ICU. But still, he becomes my "Purple Buddha" distraction for a few days. He is as hard not to notice as the Tattoo Man, both with their colourful skin tones. Very sick men surround Heidi in her quad unit, and she is like this sleeping beauty amongst the men. If she opens her eyes today she will not like this view: Purple Buddha sitting up across from her, huffing and sweating and staring straight at her. Tattoo Man lies in the bed beside Heidi, quivering and shaking with tremors as his brain struggles with his home-made chemical overload. Yikes! I find myself trying not to look at these men but I'm drawn by the same twisted fascination that makes me slow down and look at traffic accidents. I cannot help but notice the other people healing in Heidi's quad unit. Again, I hope they both recover.

At noon Heidi's breath sounds are still bronchial and louder on the left side. She is suctioned and only brings up instillate (tiny amounts). Her fasciotomy dressings are changed and her

clean wounds are draining mostly serous (clear) fluids. She is
given a bed bath at 2:30 pm and more Ihles paste is applied to
her buttocks. She still has some menstral flow showing. The
resident doctor applies new ETT tapes as the corners of her
mouth have cuts in them from the previous ties. Her morphine
infusion is decreased. She is suctioned for small amounts of
yellow secretions and now has a definite cough reflex when
being suctioned, and this is good.

Dr. M comes in to see Heidi at 6:30 pm and notes that her
ICP is steady between 8 and 12, and he demonstrates there
is now little change when the EVD is clamped. He clamps
her for three minutes and her ICP only goes up to 13, then
quickly, and spontaneously, recovers when unclamped. This is
very good. He orders another CT scan for tomorrow, and if it
shows improvement, he will consider removing the EVD over
the weekend. If she goes into the Operating Room to have this
done then she can have her fasciotomies closed at the same time.
She is improving, she is improving, she is improving! He finds
me working on my stitchery in the hall and tells me the good
news. My heart is lifting, I can breathe again this is such good
news. I visit her again after Dr. M leaves, at around 7:00 pm.
Heidi moves her head when I stroke her cheek. We connect. I
know she knows I am here with her, loving her and stroking
her face. I speak to her as if she is fully conscious, not knowing
what, if anything, she hears or understands at this time. But I
tell her to hang in there, it's almost over, she'll be awake soon,
her friends are waiting to see her; and Courtney wants to visit
with her before she is released from the hospital. I really, really
need her to wake up. For me. And soon.

The rest of her evening is uneventful, with a little sweating
noticed by the nurse. Her corneal reflexes are brisk, and she
is clamping down on the swab when the nurse is trying to

do some mouthcare. She turns her head, but still shows little response to nailbed pressures. Her temperature creeps back up to 37.4 degrees Celsius and by 8:05 pm her face is quite flushed. The new nurse suctions Heidi for a small amount of whitish secretions, and her chest continues making coarse sounds. The evening nurse changes the dressing on her left arterial line (IV), which is oozing sanguineous fluids. This has been a problem before and seems to be getting worse. It is cleaned and redressed. Her leg dressings are changed at 10:30 pm and are draining sero-sanguineous secretions in moderate amounts. The leg wounds remain clean and fresh looking. At 10:50 pm Heidi gives a weak cough during the suctioning. The nurse makes a note that she is again having difficulty passing the suctioning catheter down the OETT. By midnight Heidi is weakly flexing her right arm to nailbed pressure.

Early into the next morning Heidi remains stable. At 6:30 am her fasciotomy dressings are changed. At 6:50 am the OETT tapes are changed because they keep slipping off. Blood work is drawn. Heidi is given a partial bath. And this is when I come in unannounced, just before 7:00 am. I round the corner of her quad unit to see a large male nurse washing my daughter's fully exposed torso. The regular nurse at the end of her bed is not there. I am shocked at this unexpected sight. I am so upset I leave without announcing my presence. I don't know if I'm shaken by the surprise of seeing someone washing my daughter's naked body or by the fact it was being done by a large, muscular young man. This troubles me deeply. Why am I so upset? Maybe it is just the extremely masculine presentation of a large man hovering over her helpless body, touching her in a most intimate way. This is a picture, a snapshot I just cannot get out of my head. Why does it bother me so? It just seems wrong. I don't know why. Heidi has been seen by many different male doctors so why am I so disturbed by the sight of a male nurse bathing her? Where is this unease coming from? I just wasn't expecting to see a man touching my comatose daughter's naked body. Her body was also fully exposed to the three bedridden men around her and I know this would really bother Heidi if she knew. I hope she doesn't know this.

After her wash the nurse notes some small sanguineous fluid oozing from Heidi's anal area, as well as some bruising. I wonder about this. What is causing the bleeding and bruising? Could it be from the Bardex tube inserted into her rectum? I guess I will never know, but still, it bothers me. The nurse applies the Ihles paste to the large area of sloughed and reddened skin on her buttocks and coccyx. Heidi is making wheezing sounds, especially in the left base of her lungs. Her ICP goes up to 28 when she is clamped and the head of the bed is lowered for the linen change. It goes back down quickly when she's unclamped and when the head of the bed is back up to a 30 degree incline, which is where it has stayed for the past two weeks. This has been another relatively good night for Heidi.

3.23 Friday, September 26

Friday, September 26th ends up being a very busy day for us. It is my parents' 44th wedding anniversary and I call them from the hospital this morning to congratulate them. They and the family have hardly noticed what day it is. My brothers, sisters and parents have been riding this roller coaster with me the whole time, and they are heartened by the progress Heidi is now making. We are all nervous about Heidi waking up. We don't know what we will have at that point. There might be horrible changes to her personality, temperament, cognitive abilities and motor skills; or she might just be the same Heidi she was before the crash. We won't know for sure until months after she wakes up because an injured brain needs considerable time to heal itself. Right now we just want her to wake up.

Heidi's body is given the usual routine run of tests and checks this morning. Her heart rate, blood pressure and ICP are stable and at satisfactory levels. Her temperature is 37 degrees Celsius. She gives a weak cough when they suction her for a small amount of thick white secretions. No gag reflex yet. During her check, the nurse notes a dried laceration on Heidi's left hand, although no explanation is given. Her abdomen is rounded and firm.

I come in to see Heidi again at 9:15 am and I'm satisfied she is improving. At 9:30 the physiotherapist comes into work on Heidi's chest, so I have to leave. She uses mechanical vibrations to loosen the congestion in her chest. Dr. McC does his rounds at 11:30 am and gives orders for the Ampicillan to continue for a total of fourteen days. Heidi's white blood cell count is now extremely elevated at 24. He wants a Doppler test done on her thighs. Another doctor queries the existence of a pulmonary embolism. He notes she has "not been anticoagulated prophyactically" (RCH, 91), due to her brain injury. He agrees she needs a Doppler and a V/Q scan. By noon she is readied for her transport to the CT scan room, but this becomes delayed for reasons unknown to us.

Courtney is going home today. She is wheeled over to the ICU area by her mother on their way out of the hospital. Courtney, still in pain and sitting uncomfortably in her wheelchair, visits with me in the hallway and discusses whether or not she'll go in to see Heidi before she leaves. She starts to wheel herself towards the ICU doors, but then stops. She wrestles with herself and then turns around and comes back to us. Courtney tells me she'll wait to see Heidi until after she wakes up. They stay with me for over a half hour, during which time Courtney changes her mind several times. In the end she decides she doesn't want to see Heidi if she's still in a coma. She gazes longingly towards the ICU and finds it very difficult to leave the hospital without Heidi. I promise her I'll tell Heidi she was there and wanting to see her, but couldn't. Heidi will understand. Courtney is in great pain and great conflict. She's happy to be going home after fourteen days in the hospital, but she's very sad to be leaving Heidi behind. She's clearly suffering, both physically and emotionally. I am happy to see Courtney well enough to go home and I can see the weary relief on her mother's face. But we're all still pretty frightened about Heidi's condition.

The CT scan reveals: "There is persistence of periventricular white matter low density change, and this includes the posterior limb of the internal capsules bilaterally" (RCH, 224). Her brain is stable, and no additional damage is seen. The fat embolism has run its course and now the brain should start recovering. Dr. M explains the plans for the next day: Heidi will go into surgery and have a tracheostomy to aid in her recovery and to save her vocal cords from damage as she slowly recovers consciousness. The OETT tubing has been in her trachea for two weeks now, which is a long time. It passes through her vocal cords and when she wakes up she will try to make sounds, and this can cause permanent damage to the cords, hence the need for the tracheostomy. Dr. M informs me that he will perform the tracheostomy himself, instead of the usual team of specialists who do this, because he wants to position the hole lower down on her neck to reduce the visibility of what will surely be an unsightly scar. He tells me he prefers to do most of the tracheostomies on his own patients. I trust in his judgment as he has saved Heidi's brain, and her life, so far. He and this wonderful team of doctors and nurses have wrestled the seemingly relentless fat embolism beast to the ground and we are getting close to a victory. I agree to the procedure. In addition to the tracheostomy, Heidi will have her ICP and EVD bolts removed. At the same time, the orthopaedic surgeons will close her fasciotomy sites on both legs.

Oh my God, I can't believe this wonderful news! Heidi is definitely improving and the doctors are more optimistic now for a full recovery than they ever were before. I am so happy today I can't stop smiling. Tomorrow holds great promise for my girl.

Today, Heidi receives a new roommate; he's in the bed next to Purple Buddha and across from Tattoo Man. I call him "Traction Man." This unfortunate man, fifty-something in years, I'm guessing, has been in a horrible accident and has arrived with lots and lots of broken bones. His head and neck are in a brace; all four arms and legs are encased in plaster casts and hang suspended above the bed by a series of wires, cables and pulleys. He has extensive bandaging over his entire head and I can see that the tiny bits of face peeking through the gauze are horribly discoloured. Traction Man is very quiet, save when they move his limbs; then he groans softly. One eye is tightly swollen shut, the other is puffy with a small slit to see from. He is in a great deal of discomfort and I feel badly for him. His chest is wrapped in bandages, so I'm assuming he has broken a few ribs as well. Poor fellow. Traction Man's arrival now completes Heidi's quad unit in the ICU. She is indeed the sleeping beauty amongst these three battered and broken men. Heidi's injuries are much more subtle than the men's injuries. You cannot tell by looking at her that her brain is swollen, her heart is bruised, her lungs are infected, and her tibias have rods and plates holding them together. The men's injuries are much more overt: the tremors, the discoloration and the casts and cables. For someone with a non-medical background, this place takes on a surreal atmosphere for me and each additional guest here in the ICU quad unit fills me with wonder and curiosity. I pray they all recover.

At 3:20 pm the nurse tries to suction Heidi's lungs, but she can't advance the catheter far enough, so she tries deflating and re-inflating the cuff in case it is herniated. This seems to work and the lungs are then suctioned for creamy thick white secretions. A weak cough is present during the suctioning. But Heidi's oxygen saturation levels suddenly drop to 88-87%; she is put on 100% oxygen until her saturation levels reach 97%. At 3:30 pm she is again suctioned for a moderate amount of yellow secretions. Dr. McC is made aware of the drop in oxygen saturation. A portable chest x-ray is taken of Heidi's chest at 3:40 pm, and Dr. McC reads the x-ray report at 4:10 pm and notes an increase in the collapse of her lower left lobe. He orders the PEEP to be increased, more physiotherapy on Heidi's chest, a Doppler and a V/Q lung scan.

Again, at 4:30 pm, Heidi's nurse is having trouble with the suction catheter, so she uses a smaller one and manages to bring up a small amount of white secretions. Her breath sounds are coarse, especially in her left lower lobe. Her oxygen saturation is now at 95%; blood samples are sent to the lab. Heidi's dressings are changed at 5:00 pm, and more Ihles paste is applied to her damaged buttocks.

Heidi's father and I come in to say good-bye earlier than usual today because we are going out to a dinner party with our political friends. I see her at 5:30 pm and discuss the plans for tomorrow with the nurse, who then has me sign consent forms for tomorrow's operations. Once they operate, they will start weaning her off the sedation drugs, and hopefully, she will emerge from this dark fog she is in. I am so excited I can barely contain myself. I am nothing but hopeful and optimistic. I do not consider any negative thoughts and cannot even imagine anything else going wrong. We are so close now. So very close.

The nurse calls Dr. M at 7:00 pm and tells him the consent forms are all signed, and the plan remains that the operations will take place Saturday morning.

The 8:00 pm shift change is normal, and the new nurse notes that Heidi is showing some slight withdrawal to pain with all four extremities. She is moving her head a little, her corneals are present, and her ICP is fluctuating between 5 and 15. At 7:40 pm her temperature is down to 36.8 degrees Celsius, but at 8:20 pm the nurse notes her oral temperature has risen to 38.3. Heidi is wheezing so she is suctioned for a small amount of thick white secretions; and she coughs. She is given a Tylenol elixir to help ease her fever. She has a bed bath at 11:00 pm and her skin is still in rough shape. The reddened skin is still sloughing off of her buttocks, coccyx, and anal areas. Now there are open patches of raw skin, and the nurse applies more Ihles paste and wraps them in fresh dressings. The fasciotomy sites are changed and the nurse notes the wounds are pink and red in places.

In Langley we shower, change, and make the short drive to the Domaine de Chaberton Winery on 216th Street, near 8th Avenue in South Langley. The mayor has arranged a dinner for his political team: the Langley Leadership Team (LLT). Everyone from our team is there from the Langley Township Council and the Langley School Board, along with their spouses; and they all stand and applaud us when we arrive late. After all the hugs, kisses and pats on the back, we thank them for the love and support they have shown us during this excruciating time at Royal Columbian. We are served many, many courses throughout the evening, each with its own accompanying wine. This is the first time I have ever tasted Coq 'au Vin (wine-marinated rooster), and it is truly a taste sensation. It is also the first time I taste Domaine de Chaberton's Ice Wine and I am amazed at its wonderful, silky flavour. The conversation is mostly about Heidi's progress, and I don't really remember any political issues being discussed, however, knowing this crowd I am sure plans for Langley's future were discussed. We spend a few hours basking in the warmth of our good friends, then leave for home.

It is midnight at RCH and Heidi's temperature is lower: 37.2 degrees Celsius. Heidi continues to cough each time she is suctioned, which is a good sign, neurologically. She has a very quiet evening, and again at 4:00 am the nurse notes she is coughing. Now her temperature has dropped to 36.9 degrees Celsius. Her IV sites are working well and her ICP is steady and low, although her tummy is once again distended and firm. At 7:00 am blood work is sent, dressings and ETT ties are changed. Heidi is doing well this morning.

3.24 Brownie Camp

Girls join Brownies at age six or seven. Heidi wanted to join when she was six and a half and I happily signed her up. A few weeks later I received a call from the Fir District Commissioner telling me the Pack's leader, the Brown Owl, had quit and if they didn't find a new leader the Brownie Pack would close down. We had already purchased Heidi's new uniform and she was excited about joining because she saw how much fun her brother was having in Cub Scouts. So, I reluctantly agreed to take on the roll of Brown Owl on the provision that Girl Guides of Canada provide me with some training. And that they did.

Girl Guides of Canada is a wonderful, empowering organization for young girls, young women, and the mothers who volunteer to lead. I worked with many fine women—mothers all—who assisted our girls with their weekly tasks, songs, games and crafts. Some of Heidi's friends from school joined her pack; and every Wednesday after school, dressed in their brown dresses and orange maple-leaf ties, the girls gathered in the gym at Bradshaw Elementary School for fun and fellowship. Laura joined the next year and she brought along some of her school friends as well. We had five or six constant mothers who pitched in with their various skills.

The big event of each Brownie year was the camping weekend away from home. Girl Guides of Canada owns many camps throughout the Lower Mainland, and our favourite site was Camp Tsoona, near Chilliwack in the Fraser Valley. This is where I camped when I was a Brownie myself, and I have many fond memories of this magical place. Camp Tsoona is a log building with a Long House: a large meeting room complete with a fireplace where the girls meet to eat their meals and participate in indoor activities. Camp Tsoona sits on the side of a mountain surrounded by wilderness. There are many outbuildings, hiking trails through the old-growth forests, obstacle courses, and outdoor campsites.

Heidi loved Camp Tsoona. We camped there twice when she was a Brownie and once when she was a Girl Guide, and this place always provided a good time for all. The bunk rooms sported four beds each: two sets of stacked bunk beds. The girls supplied their own sleeping bags and pillows and kept their belongings in their knapsacks. The washrooms had rows of toilets (flushing!), and sinks for washing up. The large kitchen was well-equipped with a fridge large enough for a weekend's worth of food for thirty people. The stove had a huge griddle-top: room for dozens of pancakes.

Heidi and her friends spent some of their down-time in the bunkrooms, telling stories, singing songs and playing tricks on each other. One of the funniest tricks played on Heidi was when Marin Reith squeezed her whole tube of toothpaste through an open knot-hole in the pine-log wall between bunkrooms; and it plopped down on Heidi as she was sitting on a bunk in the next room. Thinking it was something horrible like fresh bird poop, Heidi screamed at the sight of this white stuff gobbed on her shoulder and arm. When the peppermint smell made its way into her brain she realized what it was and had a good laugh. The other girls in the room thought this was hilarious, and I didn't find out about the subsequent toothpaste war until many years later. Apparently, Heidi retaliated the next night while Marin was sleeping. The girls laughed about this well into their teens.

Heidi and the pack loved putting on skits and this became a big part of their entertainment in the evenings. Sometimes other Brownie Packs or Girl Guides were camping in the neighbouring buildings and we would invite them over to the Long House for an evening of fun and revelry. Usually this entailed tricking their leaders into participating in one of our skits that involved splashing, splattering, or smearing something objectionable all over them. These surprise attacks always brought on the biggest uproars of laughter from the girls, especially when they saw their leaders covered in gooey jelly, sticky chocolate syrup, blobs of whipping cream, or gobs of garish makeup. The messier the more shocking and fun it was.

Heidi made friends with many of the girls she met during her years as a Brownie and a Girl Guide. These friendships, rooted in camaraderie, were especially solid because of the tight bonds made at these camps.

3.25 Saturday, September 27

Saturday morning dawns more brightly than I can ever remember. Last night I told my friends that it feels like opening a Christmas present: you're excited with anticipation even though you don't know what you are going to get. Heidi is going to be weaned off her drugs and we will soon find out what her neurological status is. I can't wait to get to the hospital this morning.

At 8:00 am Heidi is stable and getting ready to go into the Operating Room. Her vitals signs are good, although she still needs the head of her bed kept raised at a 30 degree incline to maintain a low ICP. Heidi is transferred to the Operating Room at 10:00 am in the company of a nurse, a resident doctor and an OR porter.

Dr. M, Heidi's neurosurgeon, performs the tracheostomy operation and describes it through his dictation (dictated November 11th) as follows:

> Skin incision made with the #20 blade and skin edge hemostasis [surgical stoppage of bleeding] achieved with bipolar cautery. Platysma was divided and strap muscles identified. The thyroid was mobilized superiorly the second and third tracheal rings identified. A Bjork flap was placed in the trachea and stay sutures were placed with 2-0 Prolene. A #8 Portex was then used to cannulate [insertion of tube] the trachea. Endotracheal tube was withdrawn as the tracheostomy introduced. Hemostasis was insured and skin closed with 3-0 Prolene. Standard dressing was applied. (RCH, 174).

The tracheostomy is a success, but Heidi's ICP goes up during surgery so Dr. M decides to leave her EVD and ICP bolts in place for the time being. Dr. P performs the fasciotomies on her legs and they are closed up without any complications. The leg wounds look healthy and are expected to heal nicely.

Dr. M and the anesthetist accompany Heidi back to the Intensive Care Unit at 11:15 am. Dr. M tests her EVD by clamping it and keeping her bed at a lower elevation of 10 degrees. She seems to tolerate this well, so he asks that it is kept at 10 degrees and that the EVD remain clamped throughout the day as long as her ICP remains below 6. She is being weaned off the Mannitol and the Decadron. At 11:40 am, Heidi is still sedated from the surgery but she's moving her head now. Her oxygen saturations are satisfactory, and she is suctioned for whitish, yellow creamy secretions. And she coughs, although weakly. Her eyelids are flickering. She is trying to open her eyes! Heidi is coming back to us!

Heidi is given a bath in the afternoon and while this is being done the nurse notices that her blood pressure is going up. Her systolic (highest) pressure is over 180, then her ICP goes up over 20 so the nurse gives her more sedation, which soon brings the two pressures down. A small amount of sanguineous fluid is coming out of the tracheostomy site. Heidi is now coughing intermittently, and she is bringing up sputum. The nurse cannot test for a gag reflex because Heidi is now clamping down her teeth and not allowing anyone to prod her mouth to see if she gags. The nurse notes that her labia is swollen. Again, there is no explanation for this swelling, and this troubles me. Her buttocks continue to shed skin, however, the new skin appears healthier and less reddened. This problem is starting to improve for Heidi. Some Ihles cream is applied and the nurse notes there is some bleeding from a small hemorrhoid now.

A sequential splint is attached to each of Heidi's lower legs. These devices apply and release pulsating pressures to the muscles on her legs, stimulating blood flow and muscle movement to prevent atrophy. She seems to tolerate this new activity with no increase to her ICP.

Heidi is taken to have the Doppler ultra-sound done on her legs to test for DVT, or, Deep Vein Thrombosis. The test reveals no problems; her legs are going to be okay. She comes back to the ICU at 4:15 pm with her EVD clamped. She doesn't tolerate this very well and her ICP quickly goes back up to 24. Her bed is raised to 30 degrees again and this seems to settle her intracranial pressure.

Heidi's white blood cell count is still at a high 19 today. She is taken off the Ampicillin and put on the antibiotic, Ancef. The tracheostomy tube aspirate is sent for a gram stain and shows: " + 1 gram positive cocci and +4 pus cells" and it later grew "mixed coliforms +1, respiratory flora +1 and a few colonies of aspergillis species" (RCH, 277-8). This is not good.

The 8:00 pm shift change is the usual run-up of tests and checks. Her corneals are weak but present and she is showing a weak withdrawal of all four extremities to pain. Her temperature is high, up at 39.2 degrees Celsius, and she is given Tylenol to bring it down. The sequential compression stockings applied to her lower legs are set on 'cool.' Cold cloths are placed on Heidi's forehead. The bruising is still present on her ankles and heels, and her hands are still edemic. Her chest sounds coarse and she is suctioned for a small amount of thin secretions. Her tracheostomy site is draining a small amount of old sanguineous fluids. At 10:00 pm an IV site on her right hand is noted as reddened and swollen, so an IV therapist is paged. The IV nurse starts a new IV line and this resolves the problems with the previous IV site.

Dressings are changed around 11:30 pm and more Ihles paste is applied to Heidi's perineum and buttocks. At midnight Heidi's temperature is up at 38.9 degrees Celsius and more Tylenol is given, plus ice packs are placed in her axillae (armpits). At ten past midnight, Heidi's blood pressure is elevated and her ICP goes up to 25. They open her EVD and all pressures are resolved within a few minutes. Her temperature goes down to 37.9 degrees. Heidi spontaneously coughs at 5:00 am and her lungs are suctioned. At this time her temperature is back up to 39.5 degrees but her other vitals are normal. More Tylenol is infused into her IV and ice packs are reapplied to her armpits. Cool cloths are placed on Heidi's forehead.

When the 6:00 am tracheostomy care is done the nurse notices a large amount of purulent, foul-smelling draining coming from the site. She sends swabs of the drainage to the lab. At 7:00 am blood work is obtained and sent to the lab, as well as some cerebral fluid from the EVD collection. And so begins a new day.

3.26 Hydrangea

A big, beautiful, blue-flowered Hydrangea bush grew between the driveway and the sidewalk leading to the front door of our home on 196B Street in Langley. This was a lovely home on a half acre that the children and I cherished. Their father parked his boat in the carport and often worked on it there. This one day in the summer, between boat trips, Heidi's father decided to name the boat the "Miss Piggy," due to its voracious appetite for marine gas and its rough exterior. This boat was a patchwork of fix-up jobs that adhered to the program of trial and error. There were Fibreglass patches here, epoxy plugs there, wood supports for downriggers here, and aluminium braces for rod-holders there. Although sea-worthy, it was a mess of a boat and we all felt "Miss Piggy" was an appropriate name for it. I agreed to paint the Sesame Street character on each side of the bow, dressed as a mermaid perched on a rock in the ocean, with her name printed beside her.

At this time I was still using my oil paints to paint the occasional picture, usually landscapes, and the children were always warned not to go near them as they were toxic and dangerous. Also, oil paints are expensive and I used them sparingly, trying to make them last a long time. My brushes were old but good sable ones that I had had for years and always took great care of by cleaning them properly. This day of painting the namesake on the boat was a typically busy day in the life of a family of five, with many of the children's friends coming in and out of the yard all day. I had almost finished the logos on the boat when it was time to go in and make supper for the family. I carefully placed my palette on the sidewalk next to the tubes of paint and wrapped my brushes in oiled rags so they'd still be soft after supper, when I planned to continue. In I went. This was in the front of the house and because the children were all playing in the backyard I didn't worry about my paints.

During dinner we noticed the crows were back again, raiding the robins' nests and killing the baby birds. This was a recurring event, which greatly upset the children and myself: the crows would snatch a baby robin, place it on the back lawn in full view of our kitchen table, and proceed to peck it to death. Then it would leave the dead baby and go fetch another to do the same with. The crows never ate the baby birds, they just killed them. Heidi's father had a pellet gun he used to shoot at them with, so he said he and Billy would try to shoot a crow after supper, which made us all feel better about the carnage on the back lawn. After supper the children went outside to play, I assumed, while I cleaned the dishes.

When I went out later to resume my painting I discovered that my palette was all used up, the paints were mixed together, and my good brushes were caked with thick globs of paint. Then I saw the Hydrangea bush. Its leaves were painted all the colours of the rainbow. Some little pixies had carefully painted each individual leaf, this one blue, this one red, this one yellow, pink, purple, brown, orange, white and black. It was an amazing sight. But I was angry over the waste of my good paints and the damage done to my brushes. I returned inside and went downstairs to the basement where I could hear the girls in the washroom. As I burst into the room the startled girls began crying and saying that they were so sorry. In my washroom stood Heidi, Laura and a neighbour girl. They were frantically trying to wash the oil paints off their hands, arms and faces with wash cloths and water. Horrified, they discovered the oil paint had not washed off as they expected, instead it simply smeared further and further over their skin. The paint was everywhere. They had rubbed their eyes, touched their hair, and wiped hands on their clothing and their legs, not to mention my sink and towels. What a gigantic mess this was! They begged me not to get mad and said they were sorry over and over. I told them there was going to be some kind of punishment, but I didn't know what it was going to be yet. At this moment, when I said there was certainly going to be a punishment, Heidi's father and brother came to stand in the open doorway. They saw Heidi's father clutching his pellet gun and they started screaming, crying, and begging their father not to shoot them. I started laughing, as did their father and brother because we knew how ridiculous this was; of course their father wouldn't shoot them! But they were so upset with what they'd done they believed he just might. I feel bad now that they actually thought for a second their father would shoot them with a pellet gun, but at the time this preposterous idea just tore the lid off my anger and I laughed until I cried.

The girls and I spent the next hour trying to clean off the oil paints with turpentine, soap and water. I worried about the turpentine burning their skin and was especially careful to keep it away from their eyes. I sent the neighbour girl home over an hour later and was surprised I didn't hear from her mother; I guess she didn't tell. Eventually, I finished the Miss Piggy mermaids that long summer evening but that was the last time in many, many years I used my oil paints. The next week I went out and purchased a set of acrylic paints that were non-toxic, water soluble and easy to clean up. I also treated myself to some new brushes. I continued to paint in acrylics for the next fifteen years and have only recently returned to oils.

The Hydrangea's painted leaves drew many admiring and amused comments from our neighbours and visitors for the rest of the summer. The paint didn't wash off in the rain and only killed a few of the leaves before autumn took care of the rest. Heidi, the instigator, was justifiably proud of her painting project and showed it off to her friends and cousins all summer long. Oh, Heidi. My only regret is that I didn't take any photographs of her painted hydrangea.

3.27   Sunday, September 28

This Sunday begins much the same as the previous day. Yesterday was my sister Sandy's birthday and I forgot all about it. Sorry, Sandy. Heidi has had a very good night and is demonstrating increased responses. Her limbs withdraw weakly to pain stimulus, her corneal reflexes are present, and she moves her head when her face is touched. Her ICP still goes up when the EVD is clamped, thus, it remains open. Her heart rate is 108 beats per minute, and her blood pressure is low at 115/56. Her lungs are still making troublesome sounds when she breathes. Heidi's tracheostomy site is suctioned for small amounts of white secretions and a small amount of dark sanguineous ooze is noted on the tracheostomy dressings.

At 10:30am Heidi's temperature spikes up to 40 degrees Celsius. Her ICP goes up so the Mannitol is restarted. The ICU doctors plan to install a central IV line in her neck later in the day as the other IV lines in her swollen hands and arms keep clogging. Dr. McC comes by on his rounds at about 11:00 am and awaits the results of the cultures. Her white blood cell count is elevated at 20.2. At noon Heidi is running a temperature, is febrile, and ice packs are again applied to her armpits. Her tracheostomy dressing is changed for a "large amount of very, very foul smelling drainage, greyish brown in colour" (RCH 563).

Dr. McC is back at 3:00 pm and helps insert the new central IV line into Heidi's jugular vein in her neck. The usual routine for visiting the Intensive Care Unit is for visitors to ring the intercom outside the door and await instructions. I say who I am and whom I wish to visit. The nurse at the main desk then confers with the nurse attending the patient, and if she gives her the okay, the visitor is granted permission to enter. On this day,

I unthinkingly enter the ICU without permission and walk in on the above procedure. In shock, I stand and watch silently. Blood is everywhere as they hover over Heidi and struggle with the long needle, trying to position it just right. When the doctor and nurse finally notice me rooted to the floor next to Tattoo Man's bed, they shout at me to leave immediately. My mistake. It was a gruesome sight and I now understand why I have had to wait outside the doors so often, sometimes for very long periods, while the nurses and doctors complete their tests and procedures and scurry to make Heidi presentable again. It was upsetting for me to witness them trying to insert this long, scary IV needle into her neck. I understand that the IVs in her hands and arms have not been functioning properly lately and this is why the jugular IV needed to be installed. It was a shocking sight. I go out and sit back down in the hallway and begin stitching and waiting, stitching and waiting, stitching and stitching and stitching.

More chest x-rays are ordered to confirm the placement of the tracheostomy tube and cuff. They show the tracheostomy tube is in a satisfactory position but also that there is extensive opacification (clouding) of the left lower lobe, consistent with atelectasis and/or consolidation. The rest of her lungs are clear. At 3:00 pm the tracheostomy site is cleaned again because it continues to "ooze foul smelling greyish brown drainage" (RCH 563). The nurses note that Dr. McC has been made aware of this discharge coming from her tracheostomy site. At 4:30 pm Heidi is seen by a physician who confirms the placement of the tracheostomy apparatus. Heidi's bowels are reluctant to move in spite of the glycine suppository and this continues to be a problem for her. The new jugular IV seems to be working well at this time.

In the early evening, Heidi's oxygen saturation levels drop to

89%. Her lung sounds are coarse and she is suctioned for a small amount of creamy secretions. A creamy coloured secretion is still coming out from around the tracheostomy site. At 7:00 pm Dr. P sees Heidi about the purulent spot on her left knee, although it is not a big concern at this time. Some creamy foul drainage is suctioned from the back of her mouth. A gram stain of the swab taken from the stoma of the tracheostomy tube reveals "+3 gram positive cocci, +4 gram negative bacilli, and +2 pus cells. Cultures later reveal haemophilus influenzae +3, and mixed enteric[intestinal] organisms +2" (RCH, 279). Heidi's high fevers are currently consistent with this high bacterial count, as is her elevated white blood cell count. These infections are getting nasty.

The 8:00 pm shift-change tests show that Heidi still has a weak cough, and that she withdraws her limbs to nailbed pressure, albeit very slightly. Her lungs continue to make very coarse crackle sounds. She is trying to assist the ventilator with breathing, but she is not strong enough to make her own breaths yet. Her temperature is up again to 39 degrees Celsius, heart rate is 127 bpm, and her blood pressure is 132/54. Her tracheostomy site is dry, but there is some yellowish drainage still coming from the site. Her belly is distended and her ankles are bruised and swollen. She is considered to be in good condition. When I visit her I ask the nurse about the yellow ooze coming out from around the tracheostomy site, and the nurse tells me this is normal and not to worry. But I do worry. I gently lift a corner of the gauze covering the site and see lots of creamy yellow discharge; I question the nurse again because I find it hard to believe this is "normal."

At 8:20 pm Heidi is given a fleet enema to help her move her bowels again. It doesn't immediately work. Her ICP goes up to 17 when her head is lowered and her EVD is clamped. Also, her blood pressure and heart rate go up when work is being done on her but they go back down when she is left alone. She is given a bed bath at 11:00 pm, and receives care to her buttocks area with the application of some soothing Baja cream. She is left on her side for a while to give her buttocks some air. When the nurse cleans her tracheostomy site she notices a foul-smelling yellow drainage coming from the opening. The physiotherapist works on her chest again, with vibrations.

Heidi gives a strong cough at 11:20 pm, and fair amounts of thick, purulent looking yellow secretions are suctioned out. At midnight she is tested for reflexes and gives a weak response to deep nailbed pressure with all four limbs. She remains tachycardia (has a rapid heart beat) and feverish and is given more Tylenol. Her chest remains coarse sounding in spite of the large amount of infected discharge that has been suctioned out. At 12:40 am she is turned onto her back again because her blood pressure is going up; and the turn seems to resolve the problem. The chest physiotherapy resumes at 3:30 am, and now Heidi is giving a much stronger cough. She is suctioned for a large amount of purulent looking yellow secretions. Afterwards, her chest sounds clearer, except for the left base. She is sweaty but no longer feverish.

At 6:45 am another portable chest x-ray is taken. Heidi's trachea site is now oozing copious amounts of foul-smelling, purulent-looking drainage. Her cough is stronger and productive, bringing up a good amount of thick yellow secretions. Another tenuous day begins for Heidi in the Intensive Care Unit.

3.28 Monday, September 29

Heidi fights a high fever all day. The 8:00 am nursing assessment reveals that she is diaphoretic off and on throughout the morning. Her chest sounds are quite coarse and she is suctioned for a small amount of creamy white/yellow secretions. Her abdomen is again distended this morning, and she has not had another bowel movement in spite of the fleet given last night. Heidi moves her limbs slightly to pain, but otherwise her muscles remain fairly flaccid. Her corneals are weak and slow to react. Her jugular triple lumen central line IV is intact. Her ICP, unclamped at 7:45 am, is recorded at a low 3, which is excellent. Heidi's heart rate is 111 bpm, and her blood pressure is 120/67. She is doing very well.

Dr. B, respiratory specialist, does his rounds at 10:30 am, and tries clamping the EVD at 10:40 am. She tolerates this with no sharp increase in ICP. Heidi is given another glycerine suppository to help with bowel movements.

I come in to see her at ten minutes before 11:00 am and spend some time speaking with the nurse, then speaking to Heidi. Heidi turns her head towards me when I speak to her; she realizes I am there! My heart skips a beat as I absorb this wonderful new development in her neurological status. This one small thing has the power to make me so happy. I whisper to her, "Keep trying to wake up, honey, try and open your eyes for me." It doesn't happen yet. I leave when the nurse tells me she needs to do her work.

I am becoming increasingly aware that my visits disrupt the routine of the nurses assigned to Heidi and that they are getting weary of my constant questioning. I find I need to be told things more than once because the terminology is new to me and because my exhausted emotional state interferes with my absorption of this new information. We are into week three and I am a wreck. I leave my house at 5:30 each morning and don't return home until after 8:00 pm. I have one, sometimes two meals in the hospital cafeteria each day, then some leftovers when I get home. I'm in bed by eleven. This is gruelling.

At noon Heidi's EVD is unclamped again because her ICP keeps creeping back up over 20 mmHg. When unclamped, her EVD drains clear fluids briskly and then her ICP drops to a safer level. Her temperature has gone down slightly, but she is still diaphoretic. Her lungs are checked again and found to be still coarse throughout. She has a very weak cough and is suctioned for a minimal amount of secretions. Her tracheostomy site is oozing purulent drainage again and her dressings are changed.

I come in again at 12:50 pm and spend more time with Heidi. Sometimes when I visit, her blood pressure and ICP go up, so I have to leave right away. Today it is better and I stay with her for longer periods.

At 2:40 pm some diarrhea is noted when the nurse is cleaning Heidi. At 4:00 pm the nurse notes that her EVD is draining a large amount of CSF (cerebrospinal fluid). She has very weak withdrawals to nailbed pressure. She coughs when suctioned for scant secretions. Her tracheostomy site continues to drain a large amount of purulent secretions.

Dr. M comes to see Heidi at 5:40 pm. He clamps her EVD and instructs the nurse to continue trying to clamp it during the evening. He gives me an update on my daughter and I am happy that he is so optimistic about Heidi's chances for a full recovery. Her white blood cell count is down to 14.7 and her hemoglobin is up to 99; these numbers indicate improvements in infection and blood-oxygen levels. He tells me he might remove the brain shunt on Wednesday or Thursday if she keeps improving. Good, good, good. I'm afraid to let myself get too excited and I try to quell my enthusiasm before going to see her again at 6:20 pm.

Heidi's bowels finally discharge some loose stool at 6:40 pm, and her body is turned on its side so that the nurse can attend to her bottom. Heidi's eyes open when she is turned! Her pupils are large, but are now very reactive. I come in again at 6:50 pm and am thrilled when I see she is opening her eyes for me! Oh my God, I can't even begin to describe how this feels. I am ecstatic. But her ICP soars upwards when she sees me, prompting the nurse to open her EVD again. Thankfully, her ICP goes back down. My daughter is clearly reacting to my presence, but this is causing her blood and brain pressure to go up. I am told I will have to stay away for a while. I would love to stay at her bedside overnight just in case her eyes open again, but not if it causes further trauma to her brain. Frustrated, I go for a long walk. I am just not ready to leave for home yet; I am too excited about her opening her eyes. My nerves are jumping all over the place.

The 8:00 pm shift-change reveals the usual assessments but the new nurse notes that Heidi's eyelids flicker when stimulated, although they remain closed at this time. Her teeth clench down when the nurse tries to gage a gag reflex, her knees flex to painful stimulation, and both these reactions indicate increased brain function. Her heart rate is a little elevated (tachycardia) at 101 bpm, and her temperature has gone up again to 38.2 degrees Celsius. Her blood pressure is normal. She remains diaphoretic. Her jugular triple lumen distal port IV site is now oozing a purulent looking drainage. Heidi's oxygen saturation is under 97% and her lungs are suctioned for small amounts of thick yellow secretions. Her abdomen remains distended. At this time her EVD is clamped and her ICP stays down at a comfortable level between 4 and 6. Heidi's brain is showing concrete signs of improvement, but the infection in her lungs remains troublesome.

At 9:00 pm I come back in to see Heidi. She is very stable and I stay for over an hour this time. This is one of the longest visits I have been able to have in the Intensive Care Unit. Her ICP is staying down with the clamping and I enjoy just being next to her for this extended time. I can smell her, stroke her arms and speak to her even if she doesn't know I am here. But I think she does. I want my baby back so badly my chest aches with the longing. We are getting so close now. I reluctantly leave at 10:15 pm when the nurse says it's time to bathe her. I call home to relay the good news while I'm driving through the dark towards the house of pins and needles, suffocating floral arrangements, and warmed-up casseroles.

Heidi's bed bath at 10:15 pm reveals more thick purulent yellow discharge coming from the tracheostomy site. It is cleaned and new dressings are applied. Heidi's leg dressings (remember her legs?) are changed and they are still draining scant amounts of sanguineous fluids, but otherwise the skin closures look very healthy. Another glycerine suppository is given at this time. Her ICP goes up during this routine, sometimes as high as 20, but only for 5 seconds or less and then it goes back down.

At midnight the EVD is clamped again and she tolerates it. Her temperature is 37.4, still high. Her lungs sound coarse and are suctioned for thick yellow secretions; she coughs when suctioned. At 1:15 am vibrations are applied to her right side and she is suctioned for more thick yellow secretions. At 2:00 am her jugular IV site is cleaned for a small amount of sero-sanguineous drainage. She is very diaphoretic although her temperature has dropped to 36.8 degrees. Her EVD has remained clamped since midnight with no ill effects. At 4:00 am she is tested for pain withdrawal and all four limbs react.

At 5:00 am Heidi's tracheostomy dressings are changed for a moderate amount of thick yellow drainage. By 5:20 am she is moving her head from side to side and coughing spontaneously. Her blood pressure goes up to 170/100 and the nurse gives her sedation, which settles her down a bit. Ten minutes later, at 5:30 am, she is very restless and triggers the ventilator. She moves her head from side to side and flexes her arms. Her pupils are large: 6 and brisk. Morphine is given at 5:45 am for the restlessness and her pupils are uneven at 6 and 7mm, but both react briskly. She is coughing and is suctioned for thick yellow secretions. She continues to move her head from side to side. Within ten minutes, at 5:55 am, Heidi's pupils are smaller, at 5mm each, and brisk. She receives a mini wash and complete linen change at 6:00 am.

I am there at 6:30 am to see my restless daughter. This is the most active she has been since the accident and I think to myself what a shame it is that she has to be sedated again, just when she's coming around. But her movements are potentially harmful, so she must be slowed down for her own good. The intern comes in and I'm asked to leave the Intensive Care Unit for awhile as the shift change is to follow.

Once I'm out of the room, at 6:45 am, blood work is taken as per usual and sent to the lab. Chest x-rays are done at 7:00 am. What will this new day bring?

3.29 Grad Dates

In June of 1997, Heidi and Courtney were finishing their Grade Eleven while Jamie, a year younger, was finishing her Grade Ten year. These three friends were very popular and good looking girls in the high school: something the boys certainly noticed. Three Grade Twelve boys who were graduating in June asked the girls to be their dates for the graduation dinner and party. This was the big formal affair in which the girls wear glamorous evening dresses, the boys wear tuxedoes and new suits, and everyone arrives at the Hotel Vancouver in limousines. The girls were thrilled to be invited by these senior boys. Heidi's date was her good friend Jung-Mo Kang; Courtney was escorted by Matt Bell; and Jamie was escorted by her friend Dan Edge, from Poppy High (also in Langley).

Heidi asked me if she could attend and after some hesitation I said yes. The hesitation? The cost of a new dress, a hair stylist, a boutonnière for her date, having her make-up professionally done (at Heidi's insistence and in Vancouver no less!) and new shoes. The cost was going to be high and I wondered about having to do it over again the next year when she actually graduated. But I knew these boys were respectable and because Heidi, Courtney and Jamie were so excited about being dates for the senior's grad, I finally capitulated. Thank God I did.

So off the girls went on a shopping spree to buy fancy new dresses. Courtney wore a gorgeous light green full-length silky dress and looked like a movie star. Jamie wore a full-length body-hugging black dress with short sleeves and a scooped neckline and she looked absolutely fabulous. Heidi wore a short black silky cocktail dress with a black wrap and looked very sophisticated and much older than her seventeen years, which of course made her very happy. Heidi and Courtney made arrangements to go into Vancouver during the day to have their makeup done and their hair styled. Courtney had her straight hair curled and Heidi, to be contrary, had her long curly hair straightened, with the top half put into an updo. They looked like they belonged in Hollywood. While Heidi was in Vancouver, Jamie came over to our house and Laura and I helped her with her hair and makeup and soon had her looking glamorous. Jamie didn't have a boutonnière for her date, so I quickly clipped a red rose from the garden, added some greenery, wrapped the stems in florists' green tape, found a long pin and, voila, we had a boutonnière. Jamie was pleased but pointed out that Heidi and Courtney's boutonnières came in boxed clear plastic containers from the florists. Therefore, when the boys showed up in the limo we waited for Heidi to give Jung-Mo his boutonnière first; then, telling him she'd get rid of the box for him, she brought it into the house. We put Jamie's boutonnière inside, taped it up, and Jamie delivered it to her date with no one the wiser. Excellent. The boys were happy to have three of the most popular girls in high school as their dates. For the girls, it was another fun adventure for the three of them.

Nine people shared the limo, so the costs were minimal. The driver took them into the city of Vancouver to the Hotel Vancouver. I had attended the dinner portion of Bill's grad the year before and found that the hotel's big ballrooms really make nice settings for the final send off from high school for our teenagers. There were the usual speeches, group and single photo shoots, the formal sit-down dinner served by people in uniforms, and the dance afterwards. Around midnight the students started leaving the hotel and found their limos for the ride back to Langley and the big house party that one of the parents agreed to host. A battalion of parents had volunteered to supervise this "Safe Grad:" alcohol would be allowed, but absolutely no one would be driving out of there except parents and taxi drivers. The party went well except for the rain, which had an amusing affect on the girls' hair: Courtney and Jamie's curls were straightened and Heidi's straight hair kinked back up into its usual ringlets and curls. So much for the expensive hairdos!

The girls had a marvellous time, the boys were well mannered, and they all arrived safely home the next morning. It was a blast and the girls were so glad they were allowed to participate. They had lots of gossip and funny stories to tell us. One of these stories involved a group of students who returned to their limo expecting their ride back to Langley only to discover that their limo driver was stinking drunk. Someone called the police to deal with the driver and then the parents were called into Vancouver to fetch their children. The parents were not amused, but the young people sure were.

I am so grateful to Jung-Mo for inviting Heidi to his graduation as his date. This meant that Heidi did not miss out on a right of passage that most teenagers expect to enjoy at the end of their Grade Twelve year. She was thrilled to attend and was always comfortable in his company; and the evening was a complete success. Thank you, Jung-Mo Kang, for your generosity, your kindness, and your love for my Heidi.

3.30 Tuesday, September 30

This morning I try not to intrude too much. Heidi is now opening her eyes when she is turned and she is giving a weak cough and withdraws her arms and legs to pain. Her jugular IV central line is in better shape this morning, but she is still diaphoretic. The nurse tries weaning her off the ventilator and finds Heidi is now assisting in her own breathing. She is receiving frequent physiotherapy on her chest to help clear her lungs of congestion and infection: they still crackle. Only a scant amount of secretions are brought up with the morning's suctioning of her lungs. At 8:30 am her oxygen saturation is down, so she is suctioned after the physiotherapy and finally they bring up moderate amounts of yellow secretions from her lungs. Heidi's oxygen saturation improves markedly after suctioning.

I anxiously try to bide my time while the nurses change shifts and perform their morning routines. I am not allowed back into the Intensive Care Unit until 8:55 am. I bend to speak softly to my sleeping beauty and immediately her ICP goes up. I am forced to leave. Damn it! The nurse opens the EVD and her ICP quickly drops down again. She leaves it unclamped for an hour and then re-clamps it without incidence. At 11:00 am Heidi gets a fleet enema via the rectal tube. This causes her ICP to go up again and the EVD is reopened. Even though she is improving neurologically, her brain is still very sensitive to outside stimuli.

More assessments are made at noon, and Heidi's blood pressure responds to the activities on and around her body. As a result, she is sedated again. Her face is flushed and diaphoretic and she develops a low grade temperature. Her lung sounds are still very coarse and she is suctioned for clear secretions. At noon her bowels have not yet responded to the enema and suppositories, thus, her belly remains distended.

Dr. M comes in at 1:00 pm to assess Heidi and he re-clamps the EVD. He speaks to me about her condition and I am again encouraged and hopeful. Today's chest x-ray shows a partial clearing of the left lower lobe atelectasis, so he leaves instructions to start weaning Heidi off the ventilator. This is promising news. Heidi is starting to breathe on her own; she is getting stronger by the hour. I am increasingly thrilled with each tiny improvement Heidi makes.

Finally, at 1:30 pm, her bowels start to move and she is then washed and turned. During this cleanup the nurse notes the reddened perineum and applies more Ihles paste to the area. The physiotherapist works on Heidi at 2:00 pm, trying to loosen her chest and resolve the crackles. At 2:30 pm Heidi has a large, messy bowel movement of liquid diarrhea. The nurse reinserts the Bardex tube, but this time Heidi is actively pushing it out. Again, she is washed and turned.

Some days I seem to spend endless hours watching the comings and goings of the maternity ward while I sit on the hallway benches. The other day I saw a young couple gingerly leave the elevator and shuffle towards the maternity ward. The enormously pregnant woman was concentrating on her breathing while her white-faced husband held her arm, trying to be strong. Two days later I see this same couple coming towards me down the hall; he is pushing a wheelchair as the new mother sits serenely in her wheeled throne and gazes adoringly into the face of her newborn infant. Each time I see this scene played over and over again I am reminded of the many old world paintings of the Madonna, the Virgin Mary, dressed in blue and gazing down on her newborn son. These new mothers appear to glow within this immense, spiritual love; and the damp-eyed new fathers grin and strut with pride over this, their greatest accomplishment.

I find these moments a wonderful reprieve from the Intensive Care Unit. This constant flow of new life keeps me sane and often puts a smile on my face. One day a very, very large woman was wheeled into the maternity ward with an anxious husband at her side. A week later I see this couple walking the baby-pageant route with not one, but two babies cradled in her arms. The father's grin is so wide I think it must be hurting his ears. I see two little bundles of joy wrapped up in pink blankets and snuggled against their mother's bosom. What a wonderful sight this is. Sometimes I walk down to the maternity ward and gaze through the window at the new babies. But this usually makes me cry, so eventually I stop doing this. Still, the parade of babies going home makes me so happy for such brief moments. They bring me a jolt of joy which manages to pierce through some of my darkest days on this floor. I am so thankful for these small miracles.

At 4:15 pm, Heidi's lungs are making coarse sounds so she is suctioned again for moderate amounts of sticky yellow secretions. She tolerates this and no changes are noted with her ICP. At 4:30 pm she expels more liquid stool, and is washed and turned. Her ICP goes up when she is laying flat, but promptly goes down when her head is elevated. She is not out of the woods yet.

I visit one last time today, at 6:30 pm, and I am feeling satisfied with Heidi's progress. Dr. M joins us at her bedside ten minutes later, and he is very pleased with her neurological progress. He will decide tomorrow if the shunt can come out. I am reassured and I am happy, for now.

At 7:05 pm the tracheostomy site is cleaned for lots of purulent drainage. Her jugular central line IV dressing is changed and the nurse sees that the area on her neck is slightly red. Heidi's blood pressure goes up with this stimulation and she is given more sedation medication.

The new nurse receives Heidi into her care at 7:45 pm. She notes that Heidi's eyes flicker to voice stimulation, but do not open at this time. Her chest sounds are good except for the fine crackles heard in the lower left quadrant. Her abdomen remains rounded and soft. The red rash is noted on her buttocks and perineum, and the skin continues to peel off her buttocks. Her vital signs are stable.

At 8:50 pm, a physician is unable to insert an arterial line IV into Heidi's right arm. He attempts it again at 10:30 pm but is unsuccessful. The blood vessels in Heidi's arms and hands seem to be worn out and are no longer capable of supporting IV needles. At 11:00 pm, the tracheostomy site is cleaned for moderate amounts of yellow secretions, and the nurse notes the skin around the tracheostomy opening appears to be reddened. Vibration physiotherapy is performed on Heidi's lungs this evening. Between 11:00 pm and midnight, I call the nurse from home to check on Heidi's temperature and she reassures me Heidi is doing well. I can go to sleep now.

Heidi receives a bed bath and linen change at 11:45 pm. Her various dressings are changed: legs, buttocks, neck, and head. The staples in her legs are intact and the wounds are clean and healing as well as could be expected, with a little fluid still seeping out. At half past midnight she is still restless and, depending on the amount of activity, her blood pressure fluctuates from 95/60 to 160/100. She is sweaty at this hour. More vibration therapy loosens her lungs and she is suctioned this time for a large amount of thick creamy yellow pus at the tracheostomy site. Her neurological status is checked at 4:00 am and she is found to be stable. The tracheostomy dressing is changed again at 5:25; the skin around this site still appears red and is noted so.

I call the Intensive Care Unit at 6:25 am to check on Heidi and the nurse tells me she is doing quite well. Blood work is drawn and sent to the lab and a chest x-ray is taken soon after. Heidi is sponged down at 7:00 am, due to her excessive sweating, and gets another linen change at this time. She has had a relatively stable night.

3.31 Wednesday, October 1

Today is my Mother's birthday but I don't remember it. (I'm sure she forgives me.) Today is also Vicram's birthday, but I'll tell you about him later. This morning Heidi's heart rate is elevated: 122 bpm at 7:55am; her blood pressure is also high at 160/100. The nurse notes that she cannot test for a gag reflex because Heidi will not open her mouth: she's clamped down. Whenever I'm told this I always give a little silent cheer for my daughter who appears to be exhibiting some protest over the invasive and painful prodding she receives each time the nurses conduct their assessments. Just because her muscles don't respond to the nailbed pressures doesn't necessarily mean she can't feel the pain on some level. You go, Heidi!

Heidi's tracheostomy opening is suctioned for a moderate amount of thick, light yellow, purulent secretions; and her trachea site continues to ooze more yellow secretions. By 8:30 am, Heidi is making spontaneous rigid movements with both arms, and because of this she is sedated. At 11:00 am, she is again sedated for more spontaneous extensions of her limbs. Her blood pressure goes down with the sedations. Dr. B, Respiratory Specialist, does his rounds at 11:00 am and her ICP stays under 20 throughout this morning's assessments. When I come in to see Heidi I discover that her hands have been tied down to the sides of her bed because of her erratic movements. Apparently, whenever the sedation starts to wear off she quickly brings her hands up to her throat and tries to grab at the trachea apparatus. I am shocked to see my daughter tied down on her bed. This doesn't seem right and I'm not very happy about it. I complain to the nurse but she says it's for her own good. I want them to stop sedating Heidi so that she can wake up, but each time she starts to wake up she becomes too active and must be sedated again. This has become a horrible Catch-22. When she starts to emerge from this murky blackness she signals her awareness by moving her limbs; but then she is pushed back down under with more sedation because she is moving her limbs! My head feels like it's going to explode any second now. Heidi wants to wake up but they won't let her.

This morning's chest x-ray demonstrates almost a complete resolution of the atelectasis in the left lower lung lobe. Her lungs appear to be almost completely healed, however, the purulent gunk oozing from her tracheostomy site continues all day. The lab results for this day show that the samples from the left radial (forearm) arterial catheter tests "positive for +1 staphyloccocus coag negative, > [over] 100 CFU" at the insertion site; and the catheter tip tests "+1 gram pos cocci, +2 gram pos bacilli, and +1 pus cells" (RCH, 280-1). This IV site is not being kept very sterile and this troubles me.

At noon Heidi remains diaphoretic. She is responding to nailbed pressures and her ICP remains stable with sustained EVD clamping. Heidi goes for another CT scan at 1:00 pm and tolerates lying flat with no increase in her intracranial pressure, (ICP).

Today's CT scan report on Heidi's brain reads:

> The lateral ventricles are slightly more dilated today than they were on the previous examination [Sept. 26], with the left more than the right. Third is becoming a little more prominent as well, and there is mild dilatation of the fourth more so than before. The periventricular hypodense changes are relatively unchanged, and a small hyperdense hematoma that was noted just posterior to the monitor within the right centrum ovale is now isodense. The hypodense changes within the thalami are less prominent today

than they were on the previous CT scan. No new focal abnormality is seen otherwise (RCH, 225).

Although Heidi's brain is showing signs of recovery, it is still presenting as slightly swollen. We still need to tiptoe around her and be careful to keep stimulation at a minimum.

Heidi gets a sponge bath and a linen change this afternoon. The skin is still peeling from her buttocks and armpits and the Ihles paste is reapplied to the damaged areas. Her eyelids flicker with the activity, but she doesn't open them. Her ICP goes up over 20 briefly, but soon goes down when she is left alone. Fewer secretions are brought up with this hour's suctioning of her lungs. At 7:00 pm she is quite sweaty and the nurse sponges her down. She becomes incontinent and discharges a moderate amount of thick dark green liquid stool. I have been in and out of the Intensive Care Unit all day and am anxiously looking for any signs of consciousness; I am becoming extremely frustrated with the increased sedation. The 8:00 pm shift-change is probably a big relief for the day nurse because I have been in her face all day asking about the oozing from the trachea site and questioning her about the lab results for bacterial infection. Heidi's white blood cell count is lower today, although still higher than normal at 14.6; and the anitbiotics have changed from Imipenum to Tazocin. Upon Dr. M's orders, the Decadron dosages are to be decreased over the next week so that Heidi's brain can be safely weaned from this powerful drug. I am assured that everything is okay and I should stop worrying so much. I leave for home just before Dr. M comes in, probably missing him by fifteen minutes.

The new nurse notes that at 8:45 pm Heidi jerks and moves to the slightest touch, so once again she sedates her. Heidi's eyes flicker to the sound of the nurse's voice, but her eyes don't open yet. She has a strong cough, and again, will not allow the nurse to prod inside her mouth. She is still diaphoretic and her skin is warm and pink. The jugular IV is functioning better and is noted to be in good condition at this hour. Heidi is suctioned for a moderate amount of thick creamy yellow secretions at the tracheostomy site. Fine crackles are still heard from her left lower lung. Heidi's abdomen is soft and slightly distended, and she is cleaned up after eliminating a large amount of brown stool. She is still suffering from a red rash on her bottom, although this nurse notes that it is improving. Her axilla (armpits) are red, and skin is sloughing from her buttocks, still.

At 10:45 pm I call the hospital from home to check on Heidi and the new nurse gives me an encouraging update. I can rest this night knowing Heidi is stable and resting peacefully.

Chest vibrations are continued at 11:00 pm; then a bed bath, linen change and teeth cleansing are done soon after. More paste is applied to Heidi's buttocks. All dressings are changed at this time. At midnight more thick yellow secretions are suctioned from the tracheostomy site. All is stable at the 3:00 am check, and at 6:00 a partial sponge bath is given for the diaphoretic sweating and the most recent bowel movement. Her tracheostomy site is cleaned up at 6:35 am and there is still a large amount of yellow secretions coming from the opening. The skin around it on her neck is red. It is noted at this time that the rash on her back is improving.

Blood work is drawn at 7:00 am and the nurse notes she had a stable night. All seems good. But at 7:15 am, Heidi's blood pressure starts to drop: systolic pressure falls to the 80's. A physician is quickly notified of this new development.

3.32 Modelling

The boys at Langley Secondary School referred to Heidi Klompas as "The Model." It was well-known she had been taking modelling lessons during her teens and that she had participated in a couple of fashion shows and location "shoots." Heidi really wanted modelling classes and she started when she was thirteen. Once a week, on Saturdays, I drove her into Richmond to a modelling school. She learned to walk "the walk" for runways, and to apply make-up and style her hair in various ways: updos, formal, casual, straight, curly, etc. I was never very comfortable with the idea of my daughter exploiting her good looks for a career in modelling, but I had an ulterior motive: her self-esteem. Heidi had experienced a couple of really rough classes at school with teachers who took out their frustrations on certain students. Heidi's self-image took a hit as her grades began to drop and one day she revealed to me that she believed she was "stupid." I met with some of her teachers and soon realised the problems were mostly coming from one incompetent math teacher. We tried to move her into another class, but the damage was done. She expressed her desire to try modelling; therefore, I signed her up and committed myself to a few years of driving the hour each way between Langley and Richmond. This turned out to be a good idea. Heidi's self-esteem shot up and she was soon walking tall with her head held high and her shoulders pulled back. She began to feel good about herself.

Heidi was invited to participate in a fashion show in Steveston in the spring of 1995 and she asked her good friend Melissa Barr to come along and model also. Melissa was a year older than Heidi: the two girls were sixteen and fifteen, respectively. The fashion show theme was "Fashion since the 1940's," and the girls modelled many different ensembles from the 1940's, 1950's, 1960's and 1970's. They had lots of fun and we took a whole roll of photographs. They had to first walk across a stage to show off the clothing and then stroll around the tables on the floor, letting the audience get a good, close-up view of the fashions. We had a great time and it was a wonderful experience for both girls. A year later Heidi modelled for an exclusive dress-shop and wore their high-end clothing at an outdoor photo-shoot. Several of her photographs were published in the Delta local newspaper, covering several pages. These were exciting times for Heidi; on a small scale she was famous! She was happy, she felt good about herself, and her grades improved to the extent that she became a math tutor in grade eleven. I am so glad I took the opportunity to help improve my daughter's self-esteem in a way that was special and unique to her personality and character. She absolutely blossomed in this arena.

3.33 Thursday, October 2

This day begins with a blood pressure drop that keeps fluctuating up and down all day. At 7:35 am, Heidi's heart rate is 106 bpm, her blood pressure is 87/41, and her temperature is 35.8 degrees Celsius. A red rash is scattered over her back and skin is still sloughing from her buttocks. Heidi's lungs make coarse sounds and she is suctioned for a copious amount of yellow secretions. She is coughing strongly with the suctioning. At 9:00 am, her blood pressure first goes up, with stimulation, then goes back down again. Her ICP goes up a little at this time, and again the nurse gives Heidi more sedation.

Dr. B, from Respiratory, does his rounds at noon and he notes some eye movement to the noxious stimulation. When the nurse tries to do the mouth care, Heidi moves her head vigorously from side to side. She raises her right arm to her face and is given yet more sedation. She has been diaphoretic with a flushed face since 10:00 am. Heidi is starting to cough spontaneously and is bringing up moderate amounts of yellow secretions on her own.

At 12:15 pm, Heidi's tracheostomy is fitted with a T-piece, to enable her to be weaned off the ventilator. She can now breathe directly from the open T-piece.

I have been in and out all day and I am happy with her progress so far, but I am becoming increasingly worried about the ooze coming from around the tracheostomy site. I call Kathy Elden to discuss this and she tells me to ask the nurses for the lab results on this discharge and also to ask what her white blood cell count is. I do as instructed, but the nurses don't seem to like this questioning. I think they can tell I don't really understand what it is I'm asking for. They tell me this ooze is normal. Something inside tells me this is *not* normal; however, I defer to the nurses' expert opinions and stop harping on it.

Today, Dr. M is supposed to come in to remove the EVD bolt from Heidi's head. I watch and wait for him but he doesn't come in all day.

A sponge bath is given at 2:30 pm and the nurse notes the rash on her back is improving. Heidi's lungs are suctioned for a small amount of yellow secretions at 3:15. At 4:00 pm, Heidi opens her eyes when she is suctioned, and blinks them repeatedly. She is becoming aware of the activity around her. She is becoming aware! But Heidi's blood pressure and heart rate seem to go up whenever she gets closer to consciousness, and the nurse sedates her again to bring these numbers down. Her heart rate climbs to 160 and 170 bpm, so I understand why the sedation is necessary; and it does prove effective.

The 8:00 pm shift-change routine reveals that Heidi is now opening her eyes to pain. She resists any mouth care and clenches her jaw. Her corneals are present, her limbs are now withdrawing to nailbed pressures (pain!), and she continues to move her head when touched. Her skin is moist and warm and her sheets are found to be damp from the excessive perspiration. The sequential compression stockings continue to massage her leg muscles; her legs appear to be healing very well with good pedal pulses, blood flow and muscle reflexes. Her lungs are suctioned for a small amount of yellow secretions. The abdomen is soft and flat. The rash on Heidi's back and buttocks is red and the nurse cleans the area and applies more Ihles paste. After the assessment, Heidi's blood pressure is up again and she is given sedation at 9:10 pm to bring it down.

I have been visiting Heidi as many times as the nurses allow me all day. I am tired now, and at midnight I tell the nurse I am going home. I say my good-byes to my daughter and make the long drive home. I am confident Heidi is safe so I do not call the hospital during the early morning hours, as usual, to check on her.

Heidi's ICP goes up to 20 around midnight, just after I say goodnight, then drops within five minutes. Did I cause this? I don't know but I wonder about it afterwards. Her heart rate and blood pressure also go up with stimulation, but quickly drop with sedation. She is given a complete bed bath and small amounts of yellow secretions are noted coming from her trachea. At 12:30 am the intern is made aware of Heidi's persistently high heart rate of 130 to 145 bpm. She is given additional drugs to calm her heart.

At 12:45 am Heidi blinks her eyes when the nurse speaks to her. The nurse asks her to squeeze her hand and Heidi makes an attempt to follow orders. The nurse notes that she feels a pressure coming from Heidi, although it is a weak response. She feels that Heidi is definitely trying to squeeze her hand. Again, at 4:00 am, Heidi tries to squeeze the nurse's hand when asked to and this time the nurse notes a definite pressure coming from Heidi's hand. Heidi is coming back to us. She understands instructions and she is trying so hard to comply. This is a huge breakthrough in Heidi's brain recovery.

Rounds of checks are done on Heidi at 4:00 am, and the nurse notes that she is still diaphoretic. She is suctioned for a moderate amount of thick yellow plugs from her lungs. The nurse cleans a huge amount of thick creamy drainage from her trachea. With all this activity, Heidi's blood pressure goes up again and the intern is made aware of it by 5:00 am. A portable chest x-ray is done at 7:00 am, and blood is taken to the lab. Heidi seems to have made good neurological progress this night and the new day looks brighter than ever.

3.34 The Last Summer

The summer of 1997 was a good one. My friends Bent and Bev Hanson offered me the use of their condo in Osoyoos for a few days and I took them up on it. It is within walking distance to Okanagan Lake and close to the stores and restaurants in town. At the same time as I was making these arrangements, the Penticton Peach Festival was approaching and Heidi wanted to go with her friends, Jamie and Courtney. I agreed to let her go, knowing I would be nearby in Osoyoos. The girls planned to stay at Jamie's aunt's home in Osoyoos, and to travel into Penticton for two or three days during the festival. Jamie and Courtney drove with Jamie's parents to Osoyoos the day before. Laura, Heidi and I drove to Osoyoos on the Friday and we met up with the girls at Jamie's aunt and uncle's place later that day. Heidi was excited to be with her friends, enjoying the hot sun with the bonus of a pool in Jamie's aunt's backyard. The three girls appeared to be well chaperoned and I felt confident Heidi was safe. Laura and I stayed at the Hanson's condo to enjoy a few days of sun and beach for ourselves.

Heidi, Courtney and Jamie, however, had other plans. Driving Jamie's mom's red car, they left Osoyoos early Saturday morning and made their way to Penticton and the Peach Festival. They met up with some male friends of Jamie's from Burnaby, by accident, and ended up camping with them on a reservation. They had a great time. The girls drank what the boys provided at night around the campfire, and they spent the evenings singing and dancing to their favourite tunes. They made their way to the Peach Fest and enjoyed the music and the crowds in Penticton. The three girls had a wonderful two days of freedom together.

Once the girls were back at the aunt's place on Sunday, Laura and I picked up Heidi and headed west towards Langley. All the way home Heidi relayed one story after another about what a great time she had. She enjoyed the freedom of camping out with her friends, instead of always camping with family. She spent her time flirting with lots of boys, singing and goofing off. The one thing that she spoke often of, that she enjoyed the most, was the opportunity to hop over a fence and pick as much fruit off the orchard trees as she could eat. She filled up on free (stolen) peaches for two whole days. Heidi has always loved the fresh Okanagan fruit we get here in B.C., and this must have been like a taste of heaven for her. The sun, the heat, the boys, the music, the beach, and all the free, fresh, juicy peaches she could eat. These were days of enchanted ecstasy.

One of my most treasured memories of Heidi is the vision of this tanned teenager stretched out in the front passenger seat of my car as I drove home from Osoyoos in the sweltering summer heat. The windows were all rolled down, the sunroof open, and Heidi's legs extended out the window so the wind could cool her toes. With her long curly hair blowing in the breeze, she enter-tained Laura and I with her rendition of Shania Twain's "Any Man of Mine" (...better be proud of me...). We had the tape playing at full blast and she sang the song at the top of her lungs, with a country twang, to our astonishment and our great amusement. What a heavenly creature she was. Heidi was brilliantly happy that August of 1997.

3.35 Friday, October 3

Today is my brother Darren's birthday and I don't remember if I called or not. He'll forgive me. Today is a big day for us here at Royal Columbian.

At 8:00 am the new nurse starts her routine with Heidi and notes that her heart rate is up at 143 bpm and her blood pressure is 147/82, although her temperature is down at 36.9 degrees Celsius. During this time Heidi starts coughing up large amounts of green-coloured sputum. She is suctioned and her lungs produce a scant amount of loose white sputum. Again, her lungs bring up minute amounts of white sputum, but she coughs up lots of thick green sputum. It is my opinion the green sputum is not coming from her lungs, but from her trachea. She opens her eyes to pain and flexes all four limbs to nailbed pressure. The nurse notes that she does not follow instructions and I am thinking "Good for Heidi!" Every time the nurse does her assessment it involves inflicting deep pain into the bases of Heidi's finger and toe nailbeds. I too, would resist the approach of a nurse after three weeks of this. Heidi's nails have been black and blue with bruising for several days now.

Dr. B does his Respiratory rounds at 10:30 am and he's satisfied with her condition. At 11:00 am, Dr. M is finally ready to remove the ICP shunt. I am told to leave the Intensive Care Unit while this is being done, so I am left to wait anxiously outside the door for Dr. M to come out. When he emerges from the Intensive Care Unit he tells me Heidi no longer needs the EVD drain and ICP monitor because she has been keeping her ICP levels down on her own for several days now, without needing any additional Mannitol. He is confident she'll recover from this fat embolism syndrome that has ruled over our lives for the past three weeks. He removes the shunt and closes the wound with blue-coloured sutures. I think to myself, "If he's happy then I'm happy." He tells me Heidi is breathing completely on her own now and that the ventilator has been disconnected. She'll breathe through the T-piece for now, then it'll be removed when she's ready: in a few days, hopefully. I thank him and go back into the Intensive Care Unit to see her for the first time in 2 ½ weeks without tubes coming out of her skull.

Heidi's physiotherapy commences at noon and I speak at length with the physiotherapist. She says Heidi is making good progress and she demonstrates that when she lifts her leg and bends the knee, Heidi pushes back upon instruction. She is obeying orders! She is responding to straightforward commands now and I am so very happy to see this: I am absolutely thrilled! After I leave, the physiotherapist resumes working on Heidi's chest to loosen it up and release the mucoid.

Later, I meet Dr. W, the intern, in the hallway and he informs me that Heidi is being transferred to the Maxi Ward today because they need her bed for a cardiac patient. Heidi is breathing on her own and it is thought that she is ready to move to the next level down in nursing care. The Maxi Ward has four patients to a room, but only one nurse to watch over them, unlike the four nurses assigned to each quad section in the Intensive Care Unit. I am a little concerned about this because she has just had her brain shunt removed and she is still very delicate. But when I speak with the ICU nurse she assures me Heidi is ready to be moved out of Intensive Care. I trust and pray she is right.

At 1:45 pm the nurse removes the arterial IV line in Heidi's right arm, and it bleeds enough to need pressure applied for five minutes. At 2:00 pm Heidi is bathed and made ready for transport to the 3 North Maxi Ward. I walk into the Intensive Care Unit just as the two nurses are disconnecting the various tubes and monitors. I bend down to speak near Heidi's face and this is the first time I get a full whiff of air from the T-piece in her now-open tracheotomy site. The smell is putrid, rotten, and horribly foul. It reminds me of the smell of decomposing flesh. (As a child I lived on a turkey farm and sometimes the dead carcasses collected from the barns each morning had to sit in a pile in the sun for a few days before they could be incinerated; the scent of putrefying flesh never leaves one's memory). I am alarmed and express my feelings to the two nurses. The extra nurse is there to help transport Heidi to the Maxi Ward, and the regular nurse sits in her usual spot at the end of Heidi's bed. The extra nurse tells me the smell is strong because Heidi has been running a fever for a few days. But this is not right; she has been bathed and has had her linens changed on a regular basis. I tell them something is not right here, and once again they both say it is perfectly normal. I ask if a doctor has looked at her tracheostomy site, meaning, has a doctor looked inside her trachea? The nurses exchange a look and then both of them burst out laughing. The ICU nurse tells me Heidi has been seen by many doctors, then to prove her point, she reads off a long list of doctors who have been looking after her over the past several days. I am embarrassed. I am confused. I feel shamed and diminished in their eyes and I leave the room until Heidi is ready to be moved out. (Years later, now, as I read the nurse's notes I see there is no indication this conversation ever took place, nor are there any notes alerting a doctor to check the trachea for this strong, foul odour). I have no medical education and I remind myself I must defer to the experts. I force myself to stop fussing, and instead, I try to focus on getting reacquainted with my Heidi. This is another opportunity I miss: this smell is alerting me to take action but I do nothing. I feel so helpless in this moment. My gut is telling me something is terribly wrong here but my head is telling me to listen to the nurses; surely they know better than I.

Heidi is transferred to 3 North Maxi at 3:20 pm. This ward is in another tower, closer to where Courtney was. I am at Heidi's bedside as they start to roll her bed out of the Intensive Care Unit. As we head towards the door, I see that we are passing by a quad unit with four empty beds. I ask the nurses why these beds are not being used and they tell me it's because of budget cuts. Heidi is being moved out of the Intensive Care Unit because someone else needs her bed, meanwhile four beds sit empty. This is a result of the Federal and Provincial Health Care budget cuts, thanks to Jean Chrétien and Glen Clark. We pass by Tattoo Man, Purple Buddha and Traction Man one last time and out we go. I accompany Heidi to her new residence and stay while she is settled in. Heidi's heart rate is still high and the nurse in Maxi informs Dr. B, the Cardiologist. Once settled, Heidi coughs up more sputum, and does it so vigorously that she does not require any suctioning. A cool cloth is applied to her forehead at 5:50 pm. The visiting rules are different in the Maxi ward. Family can only visit twice a day: from 11:00 am to 1:00 pm, then from 3:00 pm to 5:00 pm. I stay a little past 5:00 pm, then head home for the night. I tell Heidi we'll be in to see her in the morning. She moves her head towards my voice and opens her eyes, and my heart lifts. I am soaring and I can't wait until tomorrow.

At 8:20 pm, the nurse in the Maxi ward checks Heidi's vitals and notices her heart rate is high at 145 bpm. The sequential compression devices are put back on her legs and Heidi tolerates this well. At 9:30 pm Heidi has a large, soft green bowel movement and the nurse cleans her up, does some dressing changes and applies more paste to her backside. At 11:30 pm her chest sounds coarse so she is suctioned for moderate amounts of yellow tinged secretions. She has a good cough and that helps to loosen the mucoid. At 2:00 am she is checked and is found to be neurologically stable. Heidi spontaneously moves her left hand up and shows a little movement in her right hand. She is suctioned again. At 3:50 am the nurse notes she is diaphoretic with a flushed face. Her heart rate is up to 150 bpm now. Heidi's eyes open and her chest makes noisy crackles, so she is suctioned again. Ten minutes later, at 4:00 am, the nurse gives her Morphine to help settle her down. Ativan is added at 4:30 am, and her face becomes less flushed and her heart rate slows down. By 5:20 am she appears more relaxed and the heart rate is 140 bpm, lower than the previous hour, but still unusually high. At this time she is less diaphoretic and more restful. **Heidi has had a busy night in the Maxi ward, but is relatively stable and neurologically lighter. This new day holds so much promise.**

3.36 Painting with Mom

My conversion to acrylic paints meant that the children could now safely join me in painting on canvases. Of my three children, Heidi was the child who most enjoyed painting with me. I would take my paints with us whenever we went camping and boating, and always brought along a few smaller canvas boards for the children to paint on. We painted little landscapes and seascapes of Pirate's Cove, Cabbage Island, Sidney Spit, and other marine parks in the Gulf Islands. I would settle in and paint while watching the children play on the beach, and when they needed a break from their siblings they would join me. These were some of the most idyllic summer days of our past. We also went on day trips to Cultus Lake, White Rock and Crescent Beach where Heidi and I would paint or draw what we saw. She carried her artistic skills further by filling sketch books with drawings of her friends, family members and movie stars. She practised quite often, between school, sports and parties.

Heidi could see the beauty in everything and everyone. She delighted in flowers and loved to clip the roses and make beautiful arrangements for me. She loved the way the trees danced in the wind; she loved the sounds of the ocean; she loved the crunching underfoot as she walked on the crispy fallen skins of the red Arbutus trees on the islands. Heidi loved the smells of freshly baked bread, puppies, and oranges. She loved the tastes of mangoes, lemons, cinnamon and rhubarb. She loved the sounds of her friends' laughter and the warmth and smells of their closeness. She loved the outdoors, she loved the city, and she loved driving my car. I cherish the artwork Heidi left behind because it provides me with her vision of the world. She drew and painted what she loved, and in the last years she drew the beauty she loved the most: the beauty found in her friends' faces. Heidi loved beauty, and in loving it she personified it. She was beauty. Plato would have loved her.

3.37 Saturday, October 4

I am filled with renewed hope for my daughter. Heidi's family is happy and anticipating seeing her fully awake any time soon. After I arrived home the evening before, a reporter called from our local Langley Advance newspaper to ask how Heidi was doing. I told her that Heidi has been moved out of Intensive Care and that we are expecting a full recovery as she is breathing on her own and is starting to regain consciousness. The newspaper would run a nice article on Heidi's progress in their next edition.

As a family, we decide today that Heidi's father will visit with her in the morning and I will take Laura and Bill in with me for the afternoon visit. These new restrictions in visiting times will actually be easier on our family. I will be home more often and can resume making meals and tending to my other two children. Heidi's father leaves for New Westminster around 11:00 am, and around noon, Laura and I go the Save On Foods store in Langley to catch up on some much-needed grocery shopping. Bill stays at home to rest before going with us to Royal Columbian.

Heidi's morning involves the usual rounds of testing and cleaning. At 8:20 am her blood work reveals hemoglobin is in the normal range at 127; but her white blood cell count is back up to 14.8 (normal is 3.9-10.2), and her platelets are high at 469 (normal is 165-397) (RCH, 262). Her body is fighting an infection. An ECG (electrocardiogram) is done on her heart and shows no changes from the previous one done on October 2nd. Her right jugular IV line is removed due to the redness and swelling around it, and a swab from the tip is sent to the lab for culturing. A pressure dressing is applied to the sight. A new IV line is started in her right hand and the nurse notes that Heidi pulls back her right arm when the IV is being inserted. Dr. B is in to see Heidi at 11:00 am and he's satisfied all is well with her respiratory health. She is deemed stable this morning.

Heidi's father comes in at noon to visit and stays for an hour. Just before 1:00 pm he notices the T-piece in her neck is sitting askew, it's sitting quite crookedly in fact, and he points this out to the nurse. He watches in surprise as the nurse roughly jerks it back into position. This bothers him and he tells me about it later, when he realizes it might be relevant to what happens afterwards. Visiting hours are over at 1:00 pm and he kisses his daughter goodbye and tells her that Mom will be in to see her in two hours. He leaves for home.

After he leaves, the nurse does some work on Heidi. Her heart rate at 1:00 pm is recorded to be 119 bpm. Her lungs still make a coarse crackle so she suctions them for a moderate amount of yellow secretions. Heidi gives a healthy cough.

At 1:50 pm the nurse hears Heidi as she starts to cough again. The nurse looks over and sees that with each cough, bright red blood spurts out of Heidi's trachea. Within seconds the nurse recognises this is an emergency situation. She notes that fresh blood is filling Heidi's oxygen tubing and blocking her airway and she calls the Respiratory specialist, Dr. B, STAT, and any interns STAT. She then calls a Code Blue. Dr. H attends immediately. Within seconds, high pressure blood is pulsating out of the T-piece. Heidi is coughing, then choking, and soon she cannot breathe. She flails as she struggles for breath but the blood is filling her lungs at a rapid rate, and the nurses and doctors who arrive on the scene cannot immediately stop the flow of blood because they cannot locate the source of the bleeding. Heidi's pulse rate drops down to 50 bpm. Heidi's lungs expand with the influx of high pressure blood, as does her stomach. The rest of her blood keeps pulsating out of the trachea at a tremendous rate of pressure for about four minutes until finally her heart collapses. It is 1:54 pm and Heidi is now pulseless. There is no longer enough blood to sustain a heartbeat and she goes into full cardiac arrest. The medical team members perform CPR (Cardio Pulmonary Resuscitation) to keep her heart pumping, for over twenty minutes. Others are trying to insert IV needles into any accessible veins in her feet, hands, legs or arms; they desperately try to infuse liquids into her system to bring her volume up. They discover most of her veins have collapsed due to the lack of blood and they are having great difficulty in getting any fluids into her. She is pale and appears to be in shock. They cannot find the large needles, the #8 French central lines, so they opt to use the smaller #16 needles. Heidi's lungs are being suctioned for blood as well as being pumped with oxygen. She is not responding. Someone locates the source of the bleed and applies pressure. Now the fluids start staying in her blood vessels and, twenty eight excruciating minutes later, her heart begins to beat again. Her pulse comes and goes several times over the next few minutes. They locate the #8 French central line IVs in the tray and replace the #16s with the larger ones. Heidi's lungs require continuous suctioning for blood before they can begin to process oxygen again. Dr. S is notified to come to the scene, and once Heidi's pulse is back, this doctor goes to the Operating Room to arrange for surgery. Dr. Y says he'll arrange the Operating Room. Dr. B and Dr. Z are left in charge of Heidi while Dr. H leaves to consult with Doctors V and S about the impending surgery.

The room is in a terrifying state. Everyone and everything is covered in blood. The bed is drenched in a massive amount of darkening blood. The walls around the bed are splattered with great arcs of red blood. The floors are slippery with pools of blood. The equipment is coated in gore. The elderly woman in the bed across from, and facing, Heidi is being assisted for trauma after witnessing this horrific scene.

A massive amount of subcutaneous (beneath the skin) air is noted in Heidi's neck area; the air being forced into her trachea had to go somewhere else because her lungs were completely blocked with blood. The Resident eventually inserts a right femoral (large vein in groin) central line IV. They have trouble ventilating her manually. The tracheostomy tube is removed and replaced by a cuffed Shiley tube. During this extended resuscitation Heidi receives eight units of blood intravenously, in the form of packed red blood cells. A palpable pulse is not noted until 2:22 pm. Dopamine (vasopressor and inotropic agent) is started in an IV drip. After the resuscitation, Heidi's pupils are noted to be fixed and dilated. It is possible, and probable, that her brain has been deprived of oxygenated blood for as long as twenty eight minutes. Heidi's blood pressure is barely registering at 45/11. Everyone involved at the scene is traumatized by this unforeseen event.

Someone from Royal Columbian calls Heidi's father at home, and he and Bill leave immediately for the hospital. Laura and I are driving home from Save-On-Foods with a carload of groceries when I am paged to call the hospital. I call on my car's cell-phone and speak with someone in the Maxi Ward. This unknown person tells me that I should come in immediately as Heidi has suffered a bad bleed. I am told she is recovering, but her condition is very unstable. I tell him I will be there as soon as possible, and I drive as fast as I can along Fraser Highway to King George Highway in Surrey and across the Patullo Bridge into New Westminster. I remember driving so fast I am scaring myself. I honk other cars out of the way and weave in and out of traffic, getting to the hospital in under a half hour, which is twice as fast as usual. Poor Laura, she is so frightened, but she remains quiet during this erratic trip. We are scared out of our minds.

When Laura and I run into the Maxi Ward, Heidi's father and Bill are already there. I am met by a doctor in the hallway and he prevents me from entering Heidi's room, which has its doors closed. This doctor ushers me into a small office and as I am about to enter I am shocked when I see a nurse coming out of Heidi's room, assisted by a man. She is shaking and unsteady on her feet; she is covered in blood. Inside the office I see Heidi's father and brother and their faces are ashen. I know this is going to be bad. The doctor explains what has happened to Heidi, how an artery has burst open and caused this big bleed. He tells me her heart stopped for twenty minutes, and even though they tried to do CPR, he expects that her brain will be irretrievably damaged by this lack of oxygen for a sustained period. He tells me she most likely will be brain dead within a few days. He also tells me: "We don't keep vegetables alive in our hospital." He tells us we should be thinking of organ donation. They will, however, take her into surgery to fix the source of the bleed as soon as that can be arranged. At this point, he says he doesn't know exactly what happened, but surgery will give us more details.

There is this great howling noise inside my head as waves of black sounds rush through my brain. I don't know how to process this information. I am having trouble breathing and my heart is doing something weird with wild thumping and pain. He suggests we wait in the Intensive Care Unit's family room until Heidi comes out of surgery. I ask to see her and he refuses to let me into her room, saying I can see her later, after surgery. The door to her room is kept closed and with a guard outside. I see bloody footprints on the floor, leading away from my daughter's room. Oh my God. Oh my God.

As a group we stagger our way through the maze of corridors, towers and elevators back to that awful Family Room. I use the walls for support as I try to make my wobbling legs perform properly. The family room is unoccupied today, and we all lay down inside and rest for a few minutes before making the dreaded phone calls to family and friends.

It seems like an eternity waiting for Heidi to go into surgery. We catch the first glimpse of our devastated daughter at 3:30 pm when they wheel her past the family room and into the nearby Operating Room. They don't stop to let us see her but push past us in their hurry to operate. Heidi is covered with sheets and gauze and all I can see is one white hand poking out, punctured by several IV lines. My baby! What have they done to her?

We wait, pacing the halls for what seems like hours and hours. Heidi enters the OR at 4:05 pm. Inside the Operating Room the following occurs, as per hospital records:

> [Dr. V confers with Dr. S and they agree] the appropriate approach [is] a mediasternotomy with isolation of the innominate artery and ligature of the innominate artery and then repair of the tracheal fistula with a muscle flap of the anterior neck strap muscles and right stern mastoid muscle.

> [Dr. V scrubs] to assist Dr. S shortly after he control[s] the proximal innominate artery and the incision [is] then extended into the neck. The bifurcation of the innominate artery into the carotid and subclavian artery [is] mobilized and the innominate artery distally [is] closed just slightly proximal to the bifurcation in

order to maintain collateral blood flow from the right subclavian to the right carotid artery.

Dr. S then close[s] the proximal stump close to the aortic arch.

In the meantime the stern mastoid and the right neck strap muscles [are] mobilized. The tracheal opening [is] visualized, there [is] an opening post tracheostomy tube but there [is] also quite an extensive disintegration of the right anterolateral wall of the trachea at the place of the previous fistula.

The endotracheal tube, which was previously inserted by the attending anesthetist after the control of the innominate artery, was obtained; it [is] then advanced closer to the bifurcation in order to allow full vision of the trachea.

The anterior strap muscles and the right stern mastoid muscles [are] then used to repair the lateral wall of the trachea and we [the surgeons] then [use] adjustable flange, No. 9 tracheostomy tube which [is now], under direct vision, inserted through the previous tracheostomy opening into the trachea with the balloon position distal to the tracheal erosion and distal to the tracheostomy opening.

[Dr. V leaves] Dr. S prior to the closure of the thoracic cavity and the bronchoscopy will be performed through the tracheostomy to determine the location of the distal tip of the tracheostomy tube and then the x-ray will be ordered post operatively in order to position the adjustable flange to position the tracheostomy tube in exactly the right position (RCH, 38-9).

Heidi leaves the Operating Room at 8:30 pm.

At about 9:00 pm, Dr. S comes into the family room to speak with us. The operation was a long one, lasting over four hours, and we are anxious to hear if she survived. He tries to explain in layman's terms exactly what happened to her and what they did to correct it in surgery. He tells us that Heidi's trachea was extremely infected and this infection formed a fistula.

Fistula: "An abnormal passage from an abscess, cavity, or hollow organ to the skin or to another abscess, cavity, or organ" (Webster's Dictionary).

This fistula, or traveling infection, eroded a 3 cm diameter hole (the size of a Canadian two-dollar coin) through Heidi's trachea and then began working its way through the lining of her innominate artery. The innominate artery is a large blood vessel that branches directly off the aorta and serves as a link between the aorta and the carotid artery that serves her brain. When the erosion wore a hole through the wall of the innominate artery, which arcs in front of the lower trachea, the high-pressure blood quickly filled her lungs and stomach and then pulsated out of the trachea opening with each beat of her racing heart. That is why she exsanguinated (bled out) so fast, causing her heart to fail. This trauma happened very quickly and within four minutes of the first coughs her heart stopped beating. They called a Code Blue and all available doctors came to her aid. Dr. S assures us they did everything they could for her and he hopes the continuous CPR will have been enough to save her brain from damage. He tells us exactly what they did in surgery: how they opened up her chest by cutting through the sternum (mediasternotomy), how they looked at her heart and lungs directly to check for damage, and how they used her neck muscles to rebuild the huge hole in her trachea. The innominate artery had to be closed off and he hopes her brain will compensate with the blood delivered from her carotid artery on the left side of her neck. We will have to wait and see. When the brain has been deprived of oxygen for more than five or six minutes, such as in drowning accidents, is usually takes three to five days for the brain cells to shut down completely. Now we are left wondering if we are going to lose Heidi altogether, but we'll have to wait three to five days to find out. He gives us a very guarded prognosis.

The nurses looking after Heidi are monitoring her closely. She is not showing any neurological responses to pain. She has no cough reflex, no gag reflex. She has several IV lines inserted into various parts of her body. At 9:00 pm the nurse notes that she is very pale and cold and her temperature has dropped to 32 degrees Celsius. A warming blanket is placed over Heidi's body. At 9:30 pm a nasogastric tube is inserted via her nose into Heidi's distended stomach where it drains 150 cc of dark sanguineous fluid. It is attached to a low suction device and continuously drains the old blood from her stomach.

Finally, around 10:00 pm, we are allowed into the PACU (Post Anaesthetic Care Unit) to see Heidi. Her face is puffy and she has blood caked in her eyelids, her nostrils, her ears and in the folds of her neck. Blood has thoroughly saturated her hair. She looks brutalized. There are several nurses all around her, constantly moving up and down her bed, checking, prodding, making notes and adjusting monitors. Heidi looks awful. We are devastated. We are asked to sign a consent form permitting the hospital to test Heidi's blood for HIV; I am surprised they would be testing for this at such a late date but I guess it wasn't needed until the nurses and doctors were showered in it. The HIV test is for their protection; and not surprisingly, the results are negative.

Later that evening a nurse comes by to speak with me about the catastrophic events of the day. She tells me that Heidi's stomach filled with so much blood she looked nine months pregnant. It was a very traumatic event for the nursing staff and the doctors who answered the Code Blue. Everyone has been shaken up.

We decide we need to go home this evening, and we do so shortly after the nurse leaves. It is all I can do to keep breathing. I cannot think yet. I don't want to digest this new information. I cannot.

Chest x-rays reveal there is a small left pneumothorax with patchy densities noted in the left mid lung zone and left lung base. Pneumothorax: "The presence of air or gas in a pleural cavity, especially as a result of perforation or rupture of the lung tissue" (Webster's). Heidi's lungs are suctioned throughout the night and she is making a high-pitched wheezing sound on exhalation. Is it possible her lung has been punctured? I do not know the answer to this. Heidi's temperature is back up to 35.5 degrees Celsius by 1:00 am, and her skin is now pink and warm. The nurse questions the accuracy of the readings for Heidi's oxygen saturation levels because it shows a low 88% to 89%. Her lungs continue to make coarse sounds and she is suctioned often throughout the night for sanguineous sputum and clots. Her stomach is still distended and firm and the N/G tube keeps pumping out blood until the morning. The tracheostomy site is also draining sanguineous fluids. At 2:00 am, they try to bathe Heidi but her blood pressure and heart rate go too high for their comfort, so she is sedated and left to settle.

At 2:30 am Heidi starts to have small seizure-like activities on the right side of her face: her mouth and right eye are twitching. This twitching increases when the nurses or doctors approach her bed, so they try not to touch or move her too much. By 3:05 am she is moving her head from side to side, jerking it back and forth. She becomes incontinent and releases a large amount of green stool. By 3:20 am her right hand is twitching as well as her face. She is given Decadron 10mg IV, and Dilantin 500mg over a half hour. At 3:45 am they sedate Heidi before inserting a Bardex tube into her rectum. The Bardex immediately drains more liquid green stool. Her bedding is changed and they are extremely cautious when turning her. At 4:00 am the N/G tube stops draining, so it is irrigated and then begins draining dark sanguineous returns again. She continues to twitch. At 4:30 am Heidi is suctioned, which causes an increase in her respiratory rate, so she is sedated again. Blood work is taken and sent to the lab at 5:00 am; and at 5:30 am she is suctioned for a small amount of sanguineous sputum. Some sanguineous ooze is noted around the tracheostomy site.

Heidi remains stable when checked at 7:00 am, although her chest is still coarse sounding. Her lungs and stomach are suctioned and drained for more sanguineous fluids. The Bardex tube remains in place and continues to drain green liquids. Her face and hand are still twitching at 7:00 am.

Heidi at age fifteen

Girls in the kitchen: Courtney, Jamie, and Heidi

Heidi at one   Heidi at three

Heidi at four   Laura & Heidi with starfish on Sucia Island

Heidi the May Queen, 1993

Laura, Heidi and cousin Jana at Cultus Lake, 1988

Heidi's 17th Birthday

Collage of Heidi's friends made by Jamie Hyde and Ryan Kilby, 1997

Heidi with one of Daisy's puppies

Grad Dates '97: Courtney, Jamie, and Heidi

Whistler in summer: Bill, Heidi, and Laura, 1993

Heidi, Jamie, and Courtney in Osoyoos, August 1997

Cabbage Island Girls: Jana, Heidi, and Laura (with crab claw on nose)

Baby Heidi and her grandmother, Dorothy Adamson

Laura and Heidi in their driftwood fort on Sydney Island

Whale watching in the *Miss Piggy*

Beauford Harbour, South Pender Island:
Billy, Laura, and Heidi

First cross at Stokes Pit
Photograph by Rob Kruyt, Courtesy of the Vancouver Sun

Cross at Stokes Pit: Heidi's roadside
memorial, 2001

Heidi's gravestone at Victory Memorial Park

Vicram Ralh, age 20

Dr. Surender Ralh, Neeharika, Rajinder, Vicram, and Manish in back

Tiffany, Leigh, Vicram, and Jamie, 2002

Adamson and Ralh families, July 2002

3.38 Murder Mystery Party

Heidi's 13th birthday was near the end of her grade seven year at Langley Central Fundamental School. She wanted to do something different from the usual birthday parties she'd had in the past, so I suggested a theme party. She grasped onto this idea and after some considerable time spent ruminating over what could be the most fun, she decided to host one of those Murder Mystery evenings that was popular at the time. These games come in boxed sets for parties (usually adult oriented) and Heidi chose an airplane murder, thinking it would be especially fun for Marin and herself because they were both daughters of airline pilots. The game stipulated that all the guests receive instructions along with their invitations, and they had to arrive fully dressed and in character. This meant that half of the girls would have to come as men. These twelve and thirteen year old girls thought this was hilarious. No one knew which character was in each invitation, so we were all surprised when some of the girls showed up as a business men, a stewardess, a vamp, a pilot, a murderer and a victim. I can't remember all the roles they played but each character had a profession; they also each had a secret they didn't want the others to discover. What fun for a group of pre-teens. The game went well and everyone had a wonderful time. Only the murderer knew who she was, and only the victim knew who she was and how she gets killed. The girls had fun guessing from the clues, many of which were red herrings. After the game, which lasted for over two hours, we feasted on a quick dinner and lots of birthday cake and ice cream. Heidi's 13th birthday was a memorable blast.

This turned out to be a good idea for a party. Heidi's only regret was that the game was for eight people, so she had to limit her invitations to only seven girls. But what a way to celebrate the beginning of her teen years! Heidi and her friends knew how to have fun.

3.39   Sunday, October 5

I cannot bear to go in this morning. I call the hospital at 7:30 am and learn that Heidi has been fairly stable all night but she continues to twitch a little. Back at the hospital, her temperature is very high at 40.5 degrees Celsius, although her blood pressure is okay at 150/60. Her right femoral arterial line is oozing blood and this is being attended to again. Heidi's lungs are suctioned at 8:00 am for more bloody secretions and her N/G tube is still bringing up dark and bloody fluids from her stomach. The Bardex is still in place and draining large amounts of liquid stool. She is given a unit of platelets IV because of her low count (50). Hemoglobin is at 118.

Heidi is taken for a CT scan of her head at 9:00 am, and returns to the PACU by 9:35 am. Today's CT scan report reads:

> The right ventricular catheter has been removed and the ventricles appear very minimally enlarged in comparison with the study of September 26, 1997. However, sulci [shallow grooves separating the convolutions of the brain (Webster's)] are still visible.

> The other major change is that of a new infarct [an area of dying or dead tissue resulting from inadequate blood flow through blood vessels normally supplying the part (Webster's)] involving the left occipital and parietal lobe as well as the posterior temporal lobe. It is nonhemorrhagic. There is also a tiny infarct involving the right occipital lobe. Bilateral patchy low density changes are again noted in the sub cortical white matter. There is also some subtle low density in the region of the posterior limb of the internal capsule bilaterally.

Some faint hyperdensity is seen in the region of the
right caudate body in keeping with some minimal
hemorrhage. This is also a new finding. The small
amount of blood seen along the course of the
ventricular catheter on study of September 26 is no
longer visible.

Impression: New large nonhemorrhagic infarct
involving portions of left temporal, occipital and
parietal lobes and small focal right occipital infarct.
The ventricular size is increased slightly as well since
the study of September 26, 1997 (RCH, 227-8).

Dr. S comes to see Heidi at 10:00 am. Dr. V sees her at 11:30
am. Another neurosurgeon, a different Dr. S, is consulted and
he notes that:

Ms. Klompas has clearly sustained significant cerebral
hypoxia [damage from lack of oxygen] and associated
cerebral ischemia [damage from lack of blood]
subsequent to cardiac arrest and possibly the vascular
procedures required to stop the bleeding. This is on
the basis of premorbid cerebral edema subsequent to
fat embolism and I think one would have to say her
prognosis for making a functional recovery in terms of
her brain function is very guarded (RCH, 40).

The events from yesterday have definitely damaged her brain,
as evidenced by today's CT scan and consultant's report.

Heidi is transferred back into the Intensive Care Unit at noon.
Her heart rate is racing at a high 160 bpm, her blood pressure
is 104/54, and her feverish temperature persists at 40.5 degrees
Celsius. At this time her facial twitching has subsided. The
tracheostomy is suctioned for a scant amount of sanguineous

secretions. At 2:00 pm the bothersome right femoral IV line is removed by Dr. M, the ICU resident doctor, who then inserts a new IV line in Heidi's left radial artery. Dr. S, neurosurgeon, and Dr. B, respiratory specialist, come in to see her next.

I call the hospital and speak with Heidi's nurse around 2:00 pm and hear that her temperature is still a high 40 degrees Celsius. The nurse explains this might be a result of her body reacting to the trauma of the day before, it could be an infection, or it might be from a lack of oxygen to the brain. We'll have to wait and see. She is on a massive amount of antibiotics plus Tylenol to help with the fever.

Heidi's father calls the hospital at 3:30 pm and is told her temperature is still 40 degrees. At 4:00 pm her temperature drops ever so slightly, to 39.6. Heidi's blood pressure goes up with stimulation, and settles down with sedation. I call again at 6:30 pm and learn that her temperature is back up to 40.6 degrees. The nurse says she will be giving Heidi more Tylenol shortly.

The 8:00 pm shift-change brings us back to the usual routine in Intensive Care. Heidi's dressings are changed but now she has more incisions for the nurses to tend to. The massive wound from the incision down the middle of her chest seems to be clean and healing as expected. Heidi has two tubes draining fluids from her chest. The new wounds on the side of her neck were leaking fluids earlier but are now dry. The tracheostomy site is leaking air due to the low cuff pressure; however, she seems to be getting adequate ventilation so it's left alone. Her lungs are suctioned for some more sanguineous fluids. Her stomach is suctioned for a small amount of bloody secretions and is left on a low intermittent suction. Her bowels have finished draining, as per the Bardex tube. A cooling blanket is placed on her body to help reduce her temperature and this seems to work well. This evening another unit of platelets is administered IV, as well as two units of fresh frozen plasma.

At 10:00 pm I call again and the nurse tells me Heidi's temperature is down to 39 degrees. I tell the nurse I will be in to see Heidi in the morning.

By 11:00 pm Heidi's temperature drops enough for the nurse to remove the cooling blankets. Heidi is now opening her eyes occasionally and moving her head from side to side with 'noxious' stimulation. She is managing a good cough now. Again, her lungs are suctioned for more sanguineous secretions. Blood work is taken at 3:00 am. At 5:00 am the nurse notes her eyes are opening but not focusing. She moves her head with nursing care and extends her arms to nailbed pressure. She exhibits some sinus tachycardia (rapid heart beats).

Heidi's temperature is starting to increase again. She is trying to over-ride the ventilator with her own breaths despite the sedation medications. She is resistant to any mouth care and bites down, clenching her teeth down hard. More Tylenol is given for the creeping temperature. At 6:00 am, tracheostomy care is given and the nurse notes more bloody secretions from the site. Additional blood work is taken at 6:15 am. Chest x-rays are done at 7:00 am. This new day is filled with unknowns and uncertainties for Heidi.

3.40 Softball

Heidi and Laura played on many different softball teams over the years, starting when they were seven years old. I coached for four or five years, sometimes as assistant coach. I was successful in getting my Real Estate office to sponsor most of my teams for several years, which both supported the league and provided some free advertising for the company. Every second year Laura and Heidi played on the same team, due to their age categories.

We had many fantastically fun games over the years, few of which were stellar in performance, but we didn't mind. Our teams were the ones that had the most fun. We were playing junior ball, not Rep Ball, so there was no pressure to annihilate the opposing teams. We played for fun, camaraderie, and exercise; and we worked at improving ourselves and our skills, making sure every player got to try each position. Even the worst players (and there were many) had their time on the pitchers' mound and behind the batters as catchers. Our best players spent equal time in the outfields while the less talented honoured the coveted base positions. Our teams were for the children of parents with like attitudes; the competitive parents who couldn't tolerate seeing their children lose drifted off to the tighter-run, higher-scoring teams. I loved my days coaching girls' softball and Heidi loved playing it. She was a good pitcher but also played well on bases and outfield. Laura was the catcher in the family; squatting and jumping, whipping the ball to her team mates for a fast 'out.' If it was springtime, we were playing ball.

On one occasion during a regular season game we watched in horror as the other teams' catcher threw the ball to her third-baseman, whose head was turned. The ball smashed into her nose and snapped it sideways. We all heard the bone breaking.

Ugh! Big screams, blood gushing, everyone was running off the field and the game was stopped. Two of the parents rushed her to Emergency and she wasn't seen on the field for the rest of the season. Poor thing, that must have really hurt.

One year the thirteen year old brother of one of our girls took the umpire's course and worked as an umpire at league games. Once in a while he officiated at our games. He was a tall, gangly lad with a mop of red hair. He was very sweet and funny and all our girls liked him. He was a strict umpire, but fair. Being new, he stuck to the rules of the game and would not bend them for anyone, even his sister; he was tough. During one game when he was the umpire, the opposing coach (male) kept shouting at him and repeatedly tried to override his calls. One of the dads from that team was also heckling the umpire, calling him names and screaming at him each time he called a foul on one of their players. We noticed this harassment and were alarmed when it kept escalating. Finally, the young umpire had had enough and he threatened to expel the irate father from the game. Their coach started yelling at the boy, then shoved him and dared the umpire to hit him. This plucky kid told the coach he would end the game and award our team the winning credit if he didn't settle down. When they heard this, the father and the coach both pounced on our umpire and threw him to the ground. One of them straddled him and started punching him in the face. The other man was shouting and kicking the thirteen year-old as he lay pinned to the ground at home base. Well, by this time the nine and ten year old girls from both teams were screaming hysterically, leaving the field and running for their mothers. It took three or four dads to pull the coach and the father off of the umpire and drag them off the field. I had never seen anything like this at a junior level girls' softball game before. Everyone was upset. All the girls were crying. The umpire's mother was there (to watch her daughter) and she ran into the melee to see if her son was hurt; but she soon established he only had some scrapes and bruises. He wasn't hurt badly, but he certainly was shaken up. He called the game and even though our team was losing badly we were declared the winner. It took a long time to calm the girls down and Heidi, Laura and I stayed at the park for another hour while waiting for the rest of the parents to pick their daughters up at the regular time. The coach was later suspended and the father was banned from future games; soon all was back to normal. Heidi said maybe all dads should be banned from the games because they are the ones who interfere with the coaches and umpires. Sad, but true. Luckily, I never had to ask one of my parents to leave a game over all the years our girls played ball.

One of the odd things our team did consistently was to lose all season long then start winning games in the year-end tournaments. Maybe it was the lack of pressure, I don't know, but our girls laughed their way to 2nd and 3rd place in more than a few playoffs.

Heidi always had a nonchalant attitude at ball games and practices. I remember one game when it was her turn to give up pitching and serve time in leftfield. When we hit the field at the start of the inning she was swinging a head of long loose hair. When the inning ended, Heidi came off the field with her hair in an elaborate double French Braid. Once she had reached leftfield, she doffed her baseball cap and, assuming no one would hit the ball into the outfield, she proceeded to braid her hair. It was magnificent. Not a single hair was out of place. Heidi's Auntie Linda (Uncle Bill's first wife) had taught her how to French braid her hair the previous summer when we visited them in Quesnel. This girl was amazing. Her team mates were impressed. So was I.

Heidi often took the time to help new players learn the game and improve their catching, throwing and batting skills. She was always gentle with those less talented, especially the younger girls on the team. After playing softball in the spring, Heidi played soccer in the fall for a few seasons. But softball remained her favourite sport.

The playoffs meant the season-end party was approaching and we usually tried to have the party at the home of one of our girls who had a backyard pool. There were prizes and awards for each player and thank-you gifts for the coaches and parent helpers. Most of the prizes were for the goofiest of accomplishments, such as: loudest laugh, best sunburn for the season, worst throw that cost a game, best joke-teller, slowest base-runner, best song leader, most freckles, wackiest batter, best pre-game line-marker, most enthusiastic post-game cleanup crew, biggest bubblegum gob, best bubble blower, spitting the furthest sunflower seed and, of course, most injuries. These parties were a lot of fun and capped off the season with a splash and a bang. Heidi and her team mates made promises to try and get on the same team next year; sometimes they did and sometimes two years would go by before we saw one of our girls again. The girls came from all over Langley, so this was a nice way to make friends with girls from the other schools. By the time she was seventeen, Heidi had good friends in every high school in Langley. She loved this game.

3.41   Monday, October 6

I come into the hospital after not seeing Heidi for over 24 hours. I have missed her. When I find her in a new quad unit in the Intensive Care Unit, she is under a cool blanket to help bring her temperature down, and I watch as she is given more Tylenol. The nurses are very busy with her so I don't stay long for my first visit.

At 6:45 am it is noted that Heidi's hemoglobin is back down to 93, her platelets are 71, and the Albumin is 22. At 8:00 am, her heart rate is 137, blood pressure is 128/56, and her temperature is 38.9 degrees Celsius. Heidi's pupils are 5 and brisk and equally reactive. She gives a slight extension with her arms in response to pain. Her lungs are still coarse sounding and she is suctioned for a small amount of sanguineous liquid. Her two chest tubes are draining sanguineous fluids in moderate amounts.

Dr. M, Heidi's neurosurgeon, comes to see her at 9:30. He examines the CT scan results from Sunday and realizes the extent of the damage from Saturday's traumatic bleed. He finds me waiting in the hallway and we sit and discuss her condition for quite some time. He is visibly shaken by what has occurred, but remains hopeful that the CPR performed on Heidi will have been enough to supply a minimum amount of oxygen to save most of her brain. He tells me that the area showing the most damage is in the occipital lobe, the centre for eyesight, which is located in the lower back area of the brain. If she survives this catastrophe she might end up blind or at least have diminished eyesight. If blindness is the only damage from this event then we should feel lucky. He explains to me how the brain tissue reacts to a lack of oxygen: how the cells slowly die off over the course of a few days, usually in three to five days. We have to wait and see what happens over the next day or two. He tells me that miracles do happen sometimes, especially with children, so we should still hope for the best. He is cautiously optimistic and my hope is renewed that maybe we won't lose her after all. We can deal with her blindness if this is the case, but until then we will continue praying for her survival. I cannot even imagine our Heidi deprived of her eyesight. It's just too horrible to think about.

I go back in to see Heidi after speaking with Dr. M, and I'm thrilled to see she turns her face towards me when I speak. I place my hand on her cheek and she turns her head into my hand, pressing it against her pillow. She knows I am with her in what, to her, must now be a very dark house of horrors. On some level she is aware of my presence and I don't want to leave her side as she goes through this new and painful round of healing. I stay as long as the nurse allows, until she needs to do more work on her. I leave just past noon.

At 12:30 pm, the nurse notes Heidi's temperature has dropped to 38 degrees Celsius: a good sign. Dr. S, who performed the big operation to repair her trachea, comes in to see her at 3:00 pm. He is satisfied she is stable.

Kathy Elden comes in to see Heidi with me this afternoon. We both see good responses as Heidi opens her eyes to my voice and gives a slight pressure against my hand with her arm when I touch her. Kathy and I both agree Heidi is aware of us and that she is most definitely not anywhere close to being brain dead. We leave her room feeling confidant that Heidi is making a comeback.

I come back in at 4:00 pm, and the nurse decides to try and wash Heidi's hair. Another nurse helps as they place a basin under her head and pour water over her badly matted hair. It is caked with dried blood and is in terrible shape. They try to wash out most of the blood, the whole time watching to see if the activity affects her blood pressure, which it doesn't, and they rinse it as best they can. I help with the towels and with holding her head over the basin, as carefully as possible. Lots of blood is washed out, but the hair is horribly tangled with large matted areas. I try to comb out many of the knots, but without much success. I tell Heidi she might need a haircut and that I'm so sorry to do this to her wonderful long hair. I promise it will grow back eventually. The nurse gives me scissors and I clip out big clumps of hopelessly matted hairballs. I manage to leave most of her hair intact, so it isn't as bad as I thought it was going to be. I try to put her hair back into a braid, but it's a pretty fuzzy braid in the end. Well, we tried.

Heidi remains stable between 4:00 and 7:00 pm, and then I leave for the night as the nurses prepare for their shift change. The new nurse notes in her 8:00 pm routine that Heidi is extending both arms to nailbed pressure. Heidi's nailbeds are still badly bruised, black and blue, from almost three weeks of painful testing. She has good cough and gag reflexes, although they are weak. Her incisions are healing well, and no problems are noted at this time. Her lungs still make coarse sounds and she is suctioned again for a small amount of old blood. The chest drains are producing moderate amounts of sanguineous fluids. Her abdomen is rounded, but soft. She is stable.

At 11:10 pm Heidi is given a complete bed bath. Her dressings are changed: her legs, her groin for the femoral IV lines, her chest for the huge incision along her breastplate, her tracheostomy site for the ever-flowing ooze, her neck from where they took the muscles, and the numerous IV sites in her arms, legs and hands. Her blood pressure and heart rate go up with this activity and ventilation pressures are increased until they recede. After turning her, the nurse suctions Heidi's lungs for a large blood clot. Her pressures improve after the clot has been removed.

At 2:30 am Heidi's temperature starts to creep up. The nurse notes that the arterial line reading is inaccurate, so she uses the cuff and soon obtains a more satisfactory blood pressure reading. Her chest tube on the right side is suctioned for more sanguineous secretions. At 5:00 am Heidi's pressures go up again and she is suctioned with no improvements. The resident doctor tries to manually ventilate her, but has some difficulty. Eventually, she is successfully instilled and bagged and her pressures slowly go down. At 6:30 am tracheostomy care is done and the nurse notes that there is more sanguineous drainage from the site. More importantly, there is a large opening in her flesh just below the tracheostomy site. The nurse applies some gel and redresses the site.

Heidi has miraculously made it through another night at Royal Columbian.

3.42 Boating on the West Coast

The "Miss Piggy" was our ticket to paradise. The West Coast of British Columbia is littered with a flotilla of spectacular Gulf Islands: public and private, large and small, inhabited and deserted. There are many marine parks accessible only by private boat, and these islands became some of our favourite destinations during the long summers on the west coast.

One of these marine parks is called Cabbage Island; it's a short trip across Georgia Strait from Crescent Beach Marina in South Surrey. During extremely low tides this little island connects with the slightly larger Tumbo Island; and both these islands are located on the east side of the larger and inhabited, Saturna Island. Cabbage Island became our special day-trip destination due to its proximity to home. The island has a colony of seals at the north end, excellent salmon fishing just offshore in the Georgia Strait, and a protected sandy bay in which we'd anchor the boat and lay the crab net, on the west side. We would spend our days exploring the island and often allowed the children to circumnavigate the entire island on their own, which they did often enough to recognise all the landmarks along the way. We sat on the beach at dusk and watched huge bald eagles swoop down and pluck full-sized salmon from the bay. Heidi and her siblings would point out the Great Blue Heron nests in the trees lining the cliffs of Tumbo Island; and we'd delight in watching the otters frolicking as the sun went down in a blinding blaze of glory over the channel.

The waters of Georgia Strait are home to many pods of Killer Whales, or Orcas, and our family was privileged to see them many times. These magnificent beasts would swim up to, around, and underneath our boat. The big males would breach (leap out of the water), splashing water over us and making big enough wakes to rock the boat. We always turned off the engine when we spotted the whales so as not to injure them and, therefore, we became sitting ducks for whatever the whales chose to do. They are curious creatures who would come right up to the boat, yet we never felt threatened. Instead, we felt as if we were in the presence of some great, beautiful, divine beings who were honouring us with a visit. We felt blessed when we encountered our whales and the glow of wonderment would stay with us for days afterward. This was truly living.

Another favourite marine park Heidi and our family enjoyed was Pirate's Cove on DeCourcy Island, just off the northern tip of Valdes Island (near Naniamo). This marine park has camping sites, a fresh-water pump, and outdoor toilets. Now this was luxury! We'd tie up at the small dock while unloading our gear, then moor the boat in the opposite bay, closer to where we camped. We preferred our tents up on the cliffs for the spectacular view of the bay and the neighbouring islands. We camped under the trees and Daisy, our Golden Retriever, would have the job of keeping the raccoons out of our food at night. Often, we would awaken to the sounds of the Killer Whales swimming past the bay: "Spppooshhh, sppooshhh, sppooshh......" What a wonderful way to wake up! Heidi would jump out of the kid's tent and run excitedly down to the beach to get a better look. Soon all of us would be on the wet beach in our pyjamas, jumping up and down in our excitement over another whale sighting. We were on holidays and yet here we were, up at six in the morning, our adrenaline pumping and ready to start another great day on the island. When the tide went out the clam-digging started. The children took great pleasure in digging up lots of clams, which were kept fresh in buckets of sea water. Before cooking the clams I let them soak for a few hours in fresh water and this served two purposes: the live clams would filter out all the sand, salt and residue inside their shells and then, eventually, they would open up wide enough for us to access the meat for my famous clam chowder. Just clams, onions, and potatoes in water makes up the simplest and most delicious clam chowder when cooked slowly in a cast-iron pot over a driftwood campfire. This is what we ate when fresh salmon or crab were unavailable.

We enjoyed some extended (ten day) camps at Pirate's Cove, and the children were excited to learn the legends associated with this island. Early in the 20th century the island was inhabited by a man known as Brother XII, who ran a religious cult there. His "Aquarian Foundation" involved mysterious rituals and he, reportedly, lured many women over to join him. Legend has it that the island is littered with buried gold hidden by Brother XII before he was taken away by the authorities. Heidi and the gang spent many hours looking for this buried treasure but with no luck. The fun was in the looking. I made a few little paintings while on this island, and Heidi often joined me in the late afternoons while the others were taking naps or swimming. These were our special quiet times together, and we both savoured these stolen minutes. These moments alone with Heidi became the true treasures on this island; and I always found mine.

Heidi's father spent a good part of his days fishing off shore for salmon while the children and I explored the various islands we camped on. When he came back, it was time for some boating fun with water-skis, or the more popular Sea Biscuit: an inflated tube with an enclosed floor for sitting on. The boat would tow the tube and as the speed increased, so would the bouncing. Time and again the children achieved some good "air," and once in a while they would be thrown out of the tube altogether. This happened to Heidi in a place called Shark Bay when she was ten. We were coming back from South Pender's Bedwell Harbour and decided to let the children ride in the tube for most of the journey home. Laura was inside the tube and Heidi decided to join her. There really wasn't room for two and over Laura's protests Heidi climbed on top of her, and both girls struggled to hang onto the handles as the boat picked up speed. The tube was making small bounces when it suddenly hit a big wave and I watched as Heidi flew high into the air, somersaulting and screaming as she came down with a splash into the bay. She bobbed in the water (in her life jacket) and watched in horror as the boat sped away from her. We circled back immediately to pick her up, but she was so upset about being potential shark-bait that we decided to call it a day. We reeled in the tube, along with Laura, and headed for home. After her tears were dried, Heidi soon was laughing about it along with the rest of us.

Sidney Spit Marine Park is located on Sidney Island, just off the coast of Vancouver Island near the town of Sidney, which is just south of the Swartz Bay Ferry terminal. Sidney Spit offered us some great camping trips, although we had to dodge a few large ferry boats getting there: B.C. Ferries going to Tsawwassen, and the U.S. Ferries going to Anacortes. One day Heidi's father placed his expensive new shrimp-pot off the Spit and secured it well into Miners Channel. After anchoring Miss Piggy in Sidney Island's sheltered bay, he joined us on the beach to proudly point out the bright orange float that marked his new cage. We were all anticipating a tasty shrimp feast for dinner. As we watched the bobbing orange dot on the sea, the Anacortes ferry approached from the United States and ploughed right over the spot. After the ferry went by, the orange float was nowhere to be seen; we had lost our new shrimp-pot before even one shrimp was caught!

Sidney Island has a long thin spit that is sandy and offers good swimming. The beaches are littered with loads of driftwood and Heidi had fun making elaborate forts out of them with her sister and brother. They often built competing forts and decorated them with shells, pebbles and dried seaweed. Once in a while we discovered other forts built by unknown children, so Heidi, Billy and Laura would explore these foreign abodes and gather new ideas for better construction. Sidney Island also has extensive hiking trails that would lead us up-island into grassy meadows with wild deer running about, along rocky cliffs, into dense forests, and onto secluded sandy beaches. It is a wonderful small island with lots of camp sites for visitors. A pint-sized ferry boat brings foot-passengers over from Sidney on Vancouver Island, so day-trippers are there all the time. The children had no shortage of new friends to play with when we were at Sidney Spit.

The jewel in the Gulf Islands is Tribune Bay on Hornby Island. This bay is as close to a tropical beach as it gets on the coast of British Columbia. The large, crescent shaped bay is made of fine white sand and the waters are a crystal clear turquoise green, with no seaweed or kelp-beds to impede swimmers. The bay warms up in the summer, and floating on its salty waves is like being in heaven. We camped on this island only a couple of times during our boating years, mainly because it takes so long to get there. Hornby Island is located north of Naniamo and was too far to travel by sea, so we trailered the boat behind our station wagon. This entailed three ferry rides and lots of driving, so the trip was expensive, by our standards, and very time-consuming. But it was well worth it in the end. There are permanent homes on Hornby, and the residents are of the aging-hippie variety. Very sweet and gentle folks run the marina, gas station and grocery store. Hornby boasts a nudist beach at Whaling Station Bay, and it's considered no big deal within the atmosphere of this island. Many artists call Hornby home, and tourists have lots to choose from when purchasing mementoes and souvenirs: hand-woven tapestries and clothing, paintings, sculptures, carvings, hand-crafted musical instruments, hand-painted silks and linens, jewellery and many, many more items too numerous to list. Hornby is a state-of-mind that we all could use a dose of now and then. This paradise is almost too good to be true: everyone is smiling and courteous, the air is sweet and salty, the beaches are clean and hot and the waters are clear and warm. The government camp sites are well-equipped; therefore the tourists come in droves in July and August. No matter, they're good for the island economy and are mostly gone by Labour Day. Heidi and our family fell completely in love with Hornby.

We boated over to the San Juan Islands in the United States a few times and really enjoyed visiting the busier, tourist-minded Friday Harbour on San Juan Island. The shops are fun to look through as they are filled with lovely hand-crafted treasures. The food is good and the atmosphere was always in holiday-mode, so this was a fun way to fill a day while we camped on Sucia to the north. Island people are almost always friendly, no matter if the islands are on the Canadian side of the invisible aquatic border or on the U.S.A. side.

We also spent considerable time getting familiar with the Sunshine Coast: from Horseshoe Bay to Bowen Island, Gibson's Landing, and around to Sechelt. Our years of exploring the islands of B.C.'s Georgia Strait and the Strait of Juan De Fuca (off the coast of Washington State) gave us a lifetime of joyful memories we will cherish forever. These were the best times in Heidi's young life and she would often reminisce over the past summer's adventures while looking forward to the next season in the West Coast sun.

These are the opportunities we embraced to the fullest as our children were growing up. Heidi packed in more good living during her seventeen years than most people do in a lifetime. If our Heidi is now in heaven she's sailing in a boat, swimming with the Orcas, barking a chorus with the seals and sea lions, and soaring with the eagles as she oversees the salmon runs. She is swimming in turquoise waters and basking in the golden light of the setting sun, eternally. This is where I like to picture her now: in the happiest places of her childhood.

3.43 Tuesday, October 7

This Tuesday I am back at the hospital early in the morning. Heidi has had a stable night and I am increasingly hopeful she will miraculously arise out of this darkness. This becomes the last full day I will spend with Heidi. Early this morning she is still responding ever so slightly to my presence, although she seems weaker than yesterday.

The morning nurse notes that Heidi is opening her eyes, but that she is less reactive to painful stimuli. At 8:10 am her heart rate is 128 bpm, blood pressure is 162/88, and her temperature is still elevated at 38.5 degrees Celsius. Her lungs remain coarse sounding and she is making a wheezing noise when inhaling. Her lungs are suctioned for a trace of old sanguineous liquid. She has good cough and gag reflexes and her corneals are reactive. She remains on Decadron, Dilantin and Morphine. She is receiving feeds through the N/G tube again.

Dr. S sees Heidi at 8:45 am and finds her stable. The resident orthopaedic surgeon comes in to see Heidi at 10:30 am, and he gives orders for the nurse to remove the staples from her leg incisions. This is done promptly and the nurse notes her incisions are well-adhered, with only a scant amount of drainage from the staples. Heidi's legs look great, which is ironic considering that's what she originally came into the hospital for: to have her broken legs fixed. Rounds are done at 11:00 am and Heidi is maintained on a drug and fluid regimen to keep her stable.

I stay with Heidi all day between the rounds of doctors, technicians and nurses who must tend to her. Several days ago I gave the nurses some nice lotions for Heidi's skin and today the nurse lets me help massage the scented lotions into her arms and legs. The nurse keeps busy giving Heidi a manicure and then a pedicure. She files Heidi's nails and massages lotions into her feet and her hands. I think this is one of the nicest things I have seen a nurse do for Heidi so far. This nurse seems so caring and loving when touching my daughter and I want to thank her for this. I don't know her name, but she'll know who she is. Again, thank you for your kindness to Heidi on this most difficult day.

At 12:30 pm the assessment shows that Heidi's temperature is 37.9 degrees, and her lung fields remain coarse sounding. At 1:45 pm she is taken for another CT scan, and Heidi tolerates this well. At 2:30 pm I am back in with Heidi and spend my time speaking with her, telling her, "Just breathe, Heidi, just breathe." I repeat this over and over again. Nothing else is being asked of her on this day as her neurological signs slowly disappear with the hours. The nurse suctions out some foul-looking brownish drainage from the nares (nasal passages) at 2:30 pm.

A new nurse takes over at 3:30 pm and notes some short periods of spontaneous high respiration rates, but Heidi soon settles down again. Her lungs are still not functioning properly. By 6:00 pm she is giving only a weak cough. Her pupils are large but respond quickly to light.

There is this brief, soul-altering moment of absoluteness for me: as I am looking at Heidi she suddenly opens her eyes wide and stares straight at me and I feel this great rush of foreign energy pass through me like an invisible splash. It is hard to describe my feelings. I think to myself, "Oh God, no!" It's as if Heidi is telling me goodbye, that she is going now. I hold my breath and think, "This is it, I'm really losing her." I keep talking to her, but she's no longer responding. I tell myself I must have imagined it, but the memory and the feeling it invokes never ever leaves me, even to this day. I try to deny that my daughter is dying. I tell myself that I am tired, that my imagination is playing tricks on me. Of course my daughter is not dying. How could she be? This doesn't happen to our family, it happens to others, not to us. But I look at Heidi and is seems she is gone. I am having trouble breathing and my heart is pounding in my ears. Still, I deny.

I wait at the hospital all day hoping to see Dr. M and to hear the results of this morning's CT scan, but he doesn't show up. Exhausted, I leave for home around 7:00 pm. According to hospital records, Dr. M arrives at Heidi's bedside at 7:15 pm: I just missed him. A few minutes after I leave, Heidi's pupils become enlarged to 7mm and remain fixed. By 7:45 pm her pupils are fully blown: a sign her brain is shutting down. Her respiration rate drops and she is manually bagged. She is placed back on full ventilation as they watch her oxygen saturations go down to 90%. She is suctioned for small amounts of old bloody secretions, again from her lungs. She is no longer showing any neurological responses to pain. Her temperature is 38.6 degrees, and she is given Mannitol to bring down her cranial pressure. At this time, her heart is racing at 157 beats per minute and her blood pressure is 159/67.

Dr. M assesses Heidi and reads the results of today's CT scan. It is not good. The CT scan reads: "The main interval change is that of diffuse cerebral swelling with loss of gray-white matter differentiation, in keeping with global anoxic/ischemic injury" (RCH, 229-30). There is an increase in brain damage today, compared to two days ago. Dr. M phones our home and speaks with Heidi's father.

When I arrive home I am surprised to see my parent's truck in the driveway. I wonder what is going on. As I park my car, Heidi's father runs out the door to tell me the bad news. He says

Dr. M phoned earlier and told him Heidi is brain dead. She can no longer breathe on her own and her brain is quickly shutting down. I argue with him, insisting that Heidi was showing some responses in the morning and that she is just overly sedated. It must be the drugs, it couldn't be her brain. It just couldn't be. He takes me inside the house and I find my ashen-faced parents waiting for me, along with my two children. I look at them, turn, and pick up the phone. I call the hospital and demand to speak with Dr. M. He is right there in the ICU, and he repeats what he told Heidi's father earlier. It is after 8:00 pm and Heidi is not showing any signs of neurological activity. The CT scan today shows massive brain damage. She cannot breathe spontaneously and she has no response to pain. Her pupils are blown and unreactive. He tells me there is absolutely no hope for her survival at this point.

No hope. We have lost her.

He explains that tomorrow they will be conducting two series of tests to confirm brain death. He suggests we come in tonight to say goodbye to her but I am too exhausted to even consider this. I tell him we will be there in the morning. I hang up to the anguished faces of my parents, children and husband.

No hope left.

I am completely devastated. My mind is gone; I don't know anything anymore if I am not Heidi's mother. This is difficult for me to put into words. I know who I am: I am Catherine, the mother of Bill, Heidi and Laura; this is my place in my universe. Suddenly, I am no longer the mother of three children; I am only the mother of two. I feel that this must surely be happening to someone else. I no longer recognise myself because my soul has been altered. I am a stranger unto myself and I no longer recognise my world. Nothing makes any sense. This hole in my heart is bottomless, this pain eternal.

I look over at my camera sitting on the dining room table; I open the back and rip out the exposed film, ruining it in one quick motion. Those hospital photographs were meant for Heidi's eyes, Heidi's history, and Heidi's album; and now no one will ever see them. As a family we discuss what we are going to do, and my parents stay with us well into the night.

Back at the hospital, Heidi's brain is rapidly deteriorating. At 7:45 pm they notice she is having difficulty breathing and she is bagged on 100% oxygen. Her left pupil is 7mm and very slowly reacts to light; her right pupil is 8mm and does not react to light. The resident is called. She appears to be having tremors now. Dr. M is paged and he comes back in. She has no cough or gag reflexes. Her temperature is 38.4 degrees. The nurse notes she is hyperventilating herself, and her oxygen saturation drops to 88%. Her chest is coarse and she is wheezing and she is suctioned for old brownish blood from her tracheostomy site. They bring up copious amounts of brownish yellow frothy drainage from her nares. Her tube feeds are stopped. By 8:20 pm they manage to get her respiration rate back up to 20. At 8:23 pm her oxygen saturation level is 89%, which is dangerously low. At 9:40 pm she is given 100% oxygen and soon her saturation level climbs back up to 99%.

The nurse calls our home at 10:00 pm and I speak with her. She wants to know our feelings about organ donation and I tell her I want the heart recipient to be a young person, if possible. She says she will relay this information when necessary. She tells me Heidi is not showing any neurological responses at all and that she is gone.

The pain in my chest is making itself known and I need to lay myself down. I go to bed and Heidi's father insists I take one of the little white pills he got for me from our family doctor. It knocks me out and I don't see or hear anything until 6:00 am.

At 11:00 pm Heidi's temperature is up to 40 degrees Celsius. She is given a wash and has a cooling blanket applied to her body. Her blood pressure drops at around 11:30 pm and the resident gives her some medication. Her blood pressure is still low at midnight and it is noted she is not making any respiratory efforts any more. At 11:45 pm it is noted that she is no longer triggering ventilation. Her respiration rate drops to 16. Dopomine is started in her femoral IV line. Her blood pressure slowly falls.

A nurse calls the house at 12:30 am but does not receive an answer. She leaves a message with my pager service, but I do not hear my pager go off. They call my cell phone and do not get an answer (because my cell is installed in my car). At 1:15 am the nurse calls the home again and this time Heidi's father picks up. He is notified of Heidi's further deterioration, that her respiration rate has dropped and that they have to medicate her in order to keep her blood pressure up.

The nurses' notes read: "If an arrest situation develops, father does not want resuscitation. He would not remain on phone to allow resident to witness his wishes—but did repeat his wishes to a 2nd RN [ ] by telephone. Dr. M[ ] informed and agrees with no resuscitation" (RCH, 640). I am never, ever, told about this. I don't understand how they can issue a DNR (Do Not Resuscitate) order without the mother's knowledge or permission. A no resuscitation order is made in the notes and the witness to Heidi's father's order signs her signature to his statement: "I don't want Heidi resuscitated." (RCH, 640). I am completely unaware of this development and I do not discover this until three years later when I go through the RCH records.

The nurses and the doctors neglect to inform me of this Do Not Resuscitate order. Six years later it still appals me to think a nurse can issue a DNR without the mother's consent or knowledge. How is this possible? Why was this done?

At 1:20 am Albumin 5% is given for the low blood pressure. At 2:00 am Heidi's temperature drops and a warming blanket is applied. Both pupils are non-reactive. Her blood pressure is borderline and she remains on Dopomine. At 2:50 am a second unit of Albumin is started for the low blood pressure. At 3:00 am her pupils are fixed and dilated. At 4:00 am her blood pressure remains low and more fluids are given. At 5:00 am Heidi's urine is noted to be very diluted and the resident is called; her kidneys are not functioning properly. At 6:00 am they call our home again and speak with Heidi's father. He tells the nurse that our family will be in shortly. He wakes us up; we dress in silence and make our way to the car.

3.44 Heidi's birth

I realised I was in labour at 5:30 pm, May 5th, 1980. My husband took seventeen-month-old Billy over to Rosemary's, our next-door neighbour who had previously agreed to baby-sit him when I needed to go to the hospital. We left for Mississauga General Hospital (in Ontario) at 7:00 pm. The contractions were coming hard and fast and I knew this wasn't going to last long. We went into the labour room where I paced around for about an hour until the contractions were too difficult to handle on my feet. The doctor was not there yet because she thought it would be a few hours before the pushing started. But she was wrong. I was soon fully dilated and ready to push, but there were no doctors available to assist. We went into the delivery room with a battery of nurses and they prepared to assist the birth until the doctor arrived. Heidi's father, who had missed his son's birth by three hours, was panicking. He ran out into the hallway and grabbed the arm of the first man he saw wearing a white coat. He asked him if he was a doctor and the man said yes, so her father dragged this man into the labour room to help. The poor doctor was an anaesthetist, not a General Practitioner, Gynaecologist, nor an Obstetrician. He had no experience in birthing babies, so he slapped a blood-pressure cuff on my arm and started pumping away, inflating the cuff to get a reading. I paused in my pushing to look at him and he met my gaze with shock and apologized. He asked if I wanted any drugs. Not needing such a nuisance at this time, I ripped off the cuff and tossed it at him. He left the room in a hurry.

One of the nurses decided I should put my legs into the stirrups and when I refused she grabbed my right leg and tried to force it into the stirrup. I then placed my foot squarely on her chest and gave a great shove. She flew back, hit the wall and slid down; then she ran crying out of the room. But I didn't care, I had a baby to deliver. I asked the head nurse, who was between my legs, if I could have an episiotomy, as I felt myself tearing. She said she was not authorized to perform such a procedure and that I would have to wait for the doctor. I couldn't wait and on the next push there was this great ripping sound, like the tearing of a piece of fabric, as the baby's head emerged. At this point, Heidi's father's legs gave out and a nurse slipped a chair under him just as he was going down. I didn't notice this because the baby was emerging and I still had work to do. Just as Heidi's head came out, the doctor arrived. Dr. Margaret Adamson (yes, the same name as my youngest sister) took over and delivered the body and the placenta. She cut the cord and handed me my new daughter to hold while she stitched me up. My perfect baby girl was born at 8:26 pm, May 5th, 1980.

Prior to her birth, we had tossed around two possibilities for names: Heidi or Kirsten. But when I looked into her tiny, perfectly round pink face for the first time, I said, "This is a Heidi for sure." I chose "Dawn" as her middle name, to honour my older sister. Heidi Dawn was spectacular in her perfection.

The next day, over several hours, the head nurse brought three groups of student nurses by my room to meet me. Apparently I was known on the maternity ward as the woman who had given birth without any drugs: no spinal epidural, no painkillers, no sedation, and, oh yes, no stirrups. As a result my baby was alert, holding my gaze, and actively nursing at my breast within hours of her birth. I felt great, albeit a little sore, and couldn't wait to go home.

The next day Heidi's father brought me some flowers that caused quite a stir. The other women in the ward thought this was very funny; instead of a bouquet of roses, he brought a potted rose bush into the hospital, and in doing so, he left a long trail of dirt and grime from the garden shop on the hospital's floors. Even though the plant was too large and made a terrible mess I thought it was great. It was my favourite rose colour—yellow—and we planted it along the backyard fence of our Mississauga townhouse after I returned home. My stay in the hospital lasted exactly 36 hours, then I was out of there. Billy was thrilled with his new baby sister. The hearty yellow rose bush flourished over the next few years, giving us many vases full of deliciously scented blossoms from late spring through to early fall. This was Heidi's rose bush, and forever afterwards we associated yellow roses with our sweet Heidi.

3.45   Wednesday, October 8

Our family leaves the house at 7:00 am to drive through the early morning rush hour to our Heidi's deathbed. We arrive sometime between 8:00 and 8:30 am; I can't remember exactly. Heidi's father, sister and brother accompany me into her quad unit and the nurse draws the curtain around the bed for our privacy. We each take turns saying our goodbyes, whispering to her all those little endearments we never think to say otherwise. Heidi is warm and pink and looks like she is in a deep sleep. The respirator pumps a steady rhythm of forced air into her lungs. I watch as her chest rises and falls with each gust of false air from the machine. We are all crying. The children leave to wait in the hall. Heidi's father takes my hand and leads me towards the doors. I stop and run back to Heidi and sob uncontrollably as I stroke her face, over and over and over again. Finally, I have to leave. I say my last goodbye to my still-breathing, warm and pink-skinned daughter and make my way outside the double doors where her father waits for me. I collapse and he catches me before I hit the floor. My parents, my brother and my sisters witness this as they are seated on the hall benches, waiting for us to come out. I fall into my mother's arms and lay there stunned, unable to speak a word.

Dr. M comes to find us in the hallway, and he speaks with our family for a few minutes. He explains the procedures they are about to perform on Heidi: the Apnea tests that will be conducted by two separate physicians before they can legally declare her brain dead. He tells us how sorry he is for our loss, and expresses his regrets over Heidi's death. We thank him for the efforts he put forth to save Heidi's life. He is clearly suffering over this tragedy with Heidi.

One by one my family members go in to say goodbye to Heidi.

This is an unspeakably horrific day for our family. Never before have we experienced such pain and loss. Slowly, we make our way home. My heart is so heavy I can't understand how it continues to beat. My whole universe is collapsing in on me. I cannot imagine ever surmounting this kind of pain, or healing this soul-crushing rent in my heart.

In Royal Columbian Hospital, the doctors wait while the parade of family members makes their way to Heidi's bedside and slowly leave. At 10:05 am, Dr. S, neurosurgeon, under the supervision of Dr. M, is asked to do an assessment of Heidi's neurological status. He finds that both pupils are 8mm in size and are now non-reactive. No corneal reflexes are noted. No Doll's eye movements are noted with iced water stimulation. There is no limb response noted to painful stimuli. These examination results are in conjunction with the most recent CT scan results, and this leads Dr. S to conclude that the patient has sustained significant brain injury to be declared brain dead. Another neurological examination is performed on the heals of the first, by Dr. B, internist and respiratory specialist and these results are noted: pupils 8mm and non-reactive, no corneal reflex, no gag reflex, no cough reflex and no limb movement. An Apnea test is performed for ten minutes with no spontaneous respiratory effort. PCO2 goes from 37 to 81 during this period of apnea. Based on these findings and those of Dr. S, Heidi is declared brain dead at 11:20 am, October 8th, 1997 (RCH, 125-7, and Stephany, 13). This time is recorded as the official and legal time of her death.

Dr. M observes these tests and he agrees with the findings. Once she is declared, her body must be meticulously maintained for successful organ harvesting. Blood and tissue samples are taken throughout the day and sent to the lab as per instructions from PORT, the Provincial Organ Retrieval Team. Her temperature keeps going up, then down, and the nurses scramble first with cooling blankets, then with warming blankets. The Coroner's office is made aware of Heidi's death at 2:30 pm. She has another ECG and it shows her heart unchanged from the last ECG. Then an Echocardiogram is performed and it reveals:

1. Patient... is tachycardia with a heart rate of 122 per minute. Mildly decreased left ventricular systolic function with hypokinesis of the anteroseptal wall.

2. No significant valvular abnormality seen.

3. No atrioseptal defect seen.

4. Small posterior pericardial effusion.

5. Normal sized right ventricle (RCH, 215)

During the day Heidi receives three units of Albumin and two units of fresh frozen plasma. At 6:30 pm Heidi's blood pressure and heart rate go up and she is given more Dopomine. Her lungs continue to make coarse crackling sounds and it is noted at this time that she is "draining large amounts [of] purulent light brown drainage from both nares & around trach" (RCH, 644). A nasal dressing is applied. The tracheostomy culture from the lab shows, "gram neg [ative] bacilli +1; pus cells +4; and Enterobacter cloacae organism +3" (RCH, 278). Heidi's trachea is never cleared of infection.

Once we arrive back at home the day takes on a surreal quality with events and people coming in waves of activity. People arrive in droves. The press is calling. Our friend Gregory Thomas sets up his laptop computer in the kitchen and puts together an informative but eloquent press release for our family. He plugs into our phone line and sends the statements to the various media who are hounding us for information. While he is doing this, our friend Rich Coleman, MLA, is working to put together a scholarship fund in Heidi's name that people can donate to. We discuss this at length and decide the scholarships should go towards the continuing education of Early Childhood Education (ECE) students attending the Langley School District's own Langley College. My mother and two of my sisters (Dorothy, Dawn and Margaret Adamson) have participated in or have taught this program that certifies students for careers as daycare supervisors and pre-school teachers. The diploma program serves as a stepping stone towards the attainment of a degree in ECE. Rich makes arrangements with the Royal Bank of Canada, Brookswood Branch, and account number 100-202-1 trans 2900-003 is set up. By the end of the day we have a scholarship fund that the public can donate to at any Royal Bank in Canada. (The public can still donate to this fund). Once again, bouquets after bouquets of flowers start arriving at the house, and continue to arrive for the next week.

I make some important phone calls. First, I call the high school and let them know Heidi has died. Some of Bill's friends have arrived at the house, but Laura has no one yet, so I call a friend and ask if her daughter Katy would be willing to spend the day with Laura as I feel she needs someone to be with her. Laura and Katy have known each other since Kindergarten. My friend sends her husband to Langley Secondary School to fetch Katy. This mother couldn't handle seeing us at this time so she sent her poor husband who was speechless in his discomfort when seeing me. I thanked him and he said his wife was too distraught to come, but they both send their condolences. I understand completely. Next, I call Courtney's house and speak with her mother, Dianne. She tells me Courtney isn't home, but as we are talking Courtney arrives home with her sister. Dianne is crying and has to hang up to deal with a very frail Courtney who is about to get the worst news of her life. I call Judd, Courtney's cousin whom Heidi dated for a few months last year. I want Judd to hear this from me and not from the media. I tell him he always had a special place in Heidi's heart, and even though they broke up, a part of her would always love him. He is very distraught when I tell him she has died, and his mother ends up on the phone to get more details. My calls are leaving a swath of misery, but my thoughts are that certain people need to hear this from Heidi's family and not from the radio or this evening's television newscast.

At Langley Secondary School the staff has come around to the senior classes and announced Heidi's death. The whole school is in a turmoil. Many of Heidi's friends run screaming out of their classrooms and gather outside to hold onto each other while they cry. Some of the boys go to the wood-working classroom and together with their teacher they saw and carve out a large, heavy wooden cross with Heidi's name, birth and death dates etched and burned into it. When it is finished they transport it to Stokes Pit.

I call the mother of the boy who drove the car at Stokes Pit. John's mother is surprised to hear from me and she is sobbing on the phone as she tells me John has already heard about Heidi and he has curled himself into a fetal position in a corner of his room. He won't speak to her, won't say anything to anyone and she is very worried about him. I tell her the purpose of my call is to let him know I do not blame him for Heidi's death. Certainly he broke her legs, but Heidi never should have come even close to dying from her original injuries. I ask her to tell him I forgive him and again, to please tell him I don't hold him responsible for her death. She can't believe I am saying these words, she feels so guilty by association. This is the second girl to die from her son's drunk driving accident; and as his mother she is falling apart. She thanks me over and over again for forgiving her son. I wish them well and say goodbye.

I call VGH, Vancouver General Hospital, to speak with Vanessa. She doesn't handle the news too well. I have to repeat, loudly, that she must press the button to summon a nurse, and finally she manages it. When the nurse arrives at her bedside, I speak with her and inform her of what has happened and I stress that Vanessa needs a family member with her today. The nurse promises me she will call Vanessa's family immediately. I talk for some time with Vanessa, and she calms down enough to start telling me how her life has been since the accident. She is in a lot of pain and the emotional impact of Heidi's death doesn't do her body any good. She is wracked with sobbing and this causes her more pain. I wonder if I did the right thing in calling Vanessa, but I thought she would appreciate hearing the news calmly from Heidi's mother rather than from the television set in her hospital room. I don't hang up until she has calmed down and a nurse is in with her to stay until a family member arrives.

Our living room, dining room and kitchen are filled with wall-to-wall people. The flowers are suffocating and the never-ending dishes of donated food fill every available counter space. In a daze, I watch as my sister Sandra answers the phone and shouts at someone from the media to leave us alone. This makes me smile for a brief second. Various sisters, neighbours and friends are making and serving coffee and tea, washing dishes, making platters for serving lunch, snacks, dinner and late-night snacks. These wonderful women scrub out my bathroom and make sure throughout the day that there are fresh towels and replenished toilet paper rolls available at all times. We discuss, as a community, how and where we will have a funeral service for Heidi. We recognize that Heidi's father and I are not especially religious and that although I had attended Sharon United Church in Murrayville with our children several years ago, we had not been back for five or six years now. We don't know what to do so we decide to leave it for tomorrow after we've had some sleep. Our guests and family members slowly leave and go home for the night. I fall into bed exhausted, not knowing how Katy got home, and not knowing if Bill and Laura are in bed yet. My mind is reeling.

Back at the hospital the 8:00 pm shift-change tests show Heidi has an elevated blood pressure at 160/100 and a temperature of 36.7 degrees. At this time her lungs are suctioned for a small amount of yellow secretions. Her mouth and nose are still oozing bloody secretions. At 10:15 pm, someone from PORT calls to get additional information in preparation for tomorrow's organ harvest. At 11:00 pm, Dr. W, the orthopaedic resident, comes in to see Heidi one last time. He never gets to meet the fully conscious Heidi.

3.46 Scents of my Children

The scents of our babies are smells we mothers never forget. Each child has his or her own unique, identifying scent. I can still smell Heidi today, both as a teenager and as a baby. She smelled as sweet and silky as her soft skin always felt. Those who have touched her face know what I mean. My three children have always been my favourite perfumes: their essence coming through their skin to communicate with this mother's heart through her nostrils. I miss those sweet baby smells. Once in a while I catch a whiff of Heidi's scent in the air, as if she is close by, her warm skin suffusing the air with her perfumed soul. I can taste her scent even now.

She is with me.

3.47 Thursday, October 9

Our telephone rings at 6:00 am this morning, October 9th, and it is the hospital calling. Heidi has been taken to the Operating Room. The call is to tell us she is in surgery, and we realize that she is truly gone now. Heidi's heart is being lifted out of her chest this morning, for transplantation into another person's body. Her liver, kidneys, corneas, as well as some tracks of skin, are also being harvested to save or enhance the lives of others. The organ harvesting begins at 6:10 am. The heart is flown to Ontario where it will be transplanted into the chest of an eighteen-year-old Indo-Canadian boy from Etobicoke; but of course I don't find this out for another year and a half. Her liver also goes to Ontario, but I never learn to whom it is given. Two individuals in British Columbia receive a kidney each, and I hope that they are two of the many people I passed waiting for kidney dialysis on my way to and from the ICU over the past 3 ½ weeks. The recipients of her corneas are getting their sight back and Heidi would be so proud to know she was able to do this for them. There is so much beauty to be seen in this world and I am happy that two people will be able to appreciate the splendour of vision once again. I do not know who received the skin but I might assume a burn victim may have needed skin-grafts. Heidi's body is spread out across the country. She is everywhere now, keeping strangers alive. I hope the recipients remain alive and well today. I would love to hear from them sometime, just to know Heidi is still helping others and that parts of her body, her DNA, are still alive. It comforts me to know this.

The harvest is over at 10:57 am. Heidi's body arrives at the morgue at 11:00 am.

Angel

The angel of hope has broken a wing
and flies in circles above my head

The angel of song has lost her voice
and sits beside me crying

The angel of love has shed her golden skin
and slithers at my feet

The angel of joy is bleeding to death
and nobody hears her screams

The angel of strength has none left in her
and died in my arms last night

The angel of light has been blown out
and darkness has fallen over me

November, 1997
Anonymous by request

PART FOUR:

The Aftermath

4.1   The Funeral

Heidi's funeral takes place a week later, on October 15th, at Christian Life Assembly on 56th Avenue, adjacent to LSS, the children's high school. This is the largest church in Langley and it's chosen because we anticipate several hundred people will attend. It turns out that over one thousand people come to Heidi's funeral. Three churches are involved in her service. The women's' groups from Sharon United and Langley United pool their resources to provide a huge selection of food that more than feeds the attendees after the service. These fabulous women make and serve coffee and tea and soft drinks to the thirsty crowds. They serve and they clean up afterwards. I don't remember asking, but they showed up and gave of themselves throughout this most difficult day. They are angels and I thank them now.

The week before the funeral I spend almost every day going back and forth between Christian Life Assembly and home, arranging the service, putting together a program for Heidi's service that will be handed out to everyone who attends, arranging the music and the performers. Horst Jassman, a friend who is an events planner, helps out by finding professional entertainers for the service. Thank you, Horst. It is quite a task, arranging a large funeral service, and I have to say the good people at Christian Life Assembly were especially kind and patient with me. We made several last minute changes and they never complained. We also put together a little altar of Heidi's special items to be displayed in front of the stage: her baseball mitt and softball, two little baby outfits, photos of Heidi at various stages of her life, photos of her with her friends, and her family, one of her baby shoes, and of course, lots of yellow roses. It was a nice tribute to Heidi.

My father doesn't want a big service and he asks me if we can have two services: one public, then a private service for the family. He is nervous about being in such an emotional atmosphere in front of the whole town. I tell him Heidi would have wanted everyone there, with lots of music, and that's what she'll get. He relents and finally agrees to come. This is a very hard process for my parents to go through, as they haven't attended many funerals in their lives, let alone a funeral for a beloved granddaughter. They are struggling to stay strong for my benefit. This death later takes its toll on both Heidi's grandmothers' hearts.

The audience fills with people who segregate themselves into comfort groups. I look up and see groups of parents from Bill's old Boy Scouts troop. Next to them are the Girl Guides with their mothers and the leaders I once served with. I see groups of girls from the softball teams that Heidi once played on. Air Canada employees seat themselves together. Many in Langley's ECE community (Early Childhood Education) are here to support my mother and my sister Dawn. Bill and Laura's friends are here to support them, in full force. The schools are well represented. Every Langley Central Fundamental elementary school teacher Heidi had is present, as well as the principal and his wife. Most of her high school teachers are here, as are hundreds of the students. The staff, Administrators and the Trustees from the Langley School Board are all here. The mayor and councillors are also here, as are Rich Coleman and his wife Michelle.

Our family members gather in the back room while we wait for the service to start. When we file out to take our place in the front row, I see that the seats are filled to capacity with people standing at the back and in some of the aisles. I look up in amazement at the many groups I recognize through the past community involvements of my children. In the front, before the table holding Heidi's keepsakes and photos, sit Courtney and Vanessa in their wheelchairs, surrounded by all of Heidi's closest friends. A few others from the accident are there in leg casts. Love begins to fill the room and eventually take us past the pain.

Two Reverends conduct the service. Christian Life Assembly's Reverend Brent Cantelon welcomes everyone to Heidi's celebration of life. Scriptures are read, and then Reverend Douglas Alexander of Langley United Church, my mother-in-law's church, leads prayers. A large photo of Heidi is projected on an overhead screen above the sanctuary. My sister, Heidi's Aunty Margie, stands before this assembly and reads the eulogy she has written on behalf of our family. Our sister Sandy (Hubble) joins Margie on stage for support. Margie is shaking in front of this big crowd but nevertheless does an excellent job. A group of Heidi's girlfriends go up on the stage and one of them steps forward to read a tribute to Heidi on behalf of the others. The Langley Fine Arts School Chamber Choir sings two numbers: "Close Now Thine Eyes," and "Adoramus Te." They sing like angels. Heidi's teacher and mentor, Lynn Tansey, gives a stirring tribute to one of her favourite math students. She and Heidi were close and because of her Heidi ended up tutoring math when she was in grade eleven. Heidi's childhood friend, Marin Reith, sings a solo on stage: "That's What Friends Are For." Her voice quivers a little at first, but then she grabs hold of the song and finishes with strength. She is very brave, and I am so grateful to her for her generosity and courage in doing this for Heidi. Heidi's cousin Danielle, my sister Dawn's eldest daughter, gets up to make her tribute to Heidi on behalf of her ten cousins. Reverend Alexander has to step in and read her words for her as she suddenly cannot find her voice. She shares some of her sweetest memories of Heidi and tells us how important Heidi was to our extended family. Two Vancouver performers, Kenny Wayne and Sibel Thrasher, perform Nat King Cole's "Unforgettable" and incorporate Heidi's name into the lyrics. Kenny Wayne plays the piano while Sibel Thrasher sings a duet with him. It is an incredible, prickles-on-your-skin performance that takes our breaths away. Nat King Cole himself would have been proud of this rendition of his famous song. Reverend Alexander reads some thoughts that Heidi's father, then myself, have written down. We speak through these letters because we are incapable of speaking publicly at this time. Afterwards we all sing "Amazing Grace." Reverend Cantelon gives the closing remarks and invites the crowd into the large reception room at the back of the building for refreshments and the opportunity to speak with Heidi's family. We file out to the joyful, recorded voice of Louis Armstrong singing "What a Wonderful Life."

The reception, for me, is an endless round of hugs from friends and family. I stand in the middle of the room receiving one body after another, pressing into mine, holding me and giving me a moment of genuine love. I appreciate the gestures. A few people ask me why there was no urn or coffin at the service and I find it difficult to explain that Heidi is still being autopsied. Her body won't be released for cremation for another few days. A few hours later, I realize I have been standing the entire time and I need to sit down and drink something cold. I am thoroughly exhausted by the end of it, but grateful to all the people who took the time to say goodbye to Heidi.

After the service and reception a few of our friends join us at our home. John and Kathy Elden, Jean and Stu Livingstone, and Art and Susan Shortreid keep us company until finally we are all too exhausted to say anything more. We prepare to go to bed and I find this is the loneliest night of my life. My two children are here, my husband is here, yet I feel all alone in this strange universe I don't recognize anymore.

4.2   Memorials at Stokes Pit

When they hear the news, a few boys at Heidi's high school gather in Mr. Andrews' woodworking classroom and ask him to help them build a sturdy wooden cross for Heidi. Adam Reynolds, Blake Scott, Tim Farris, Mr. Reynolds and Mr. Emery all work together to fit two 4x4 Douglas Fir timbers together; they carve out her name and dates with a router. The boys finish the cross by using wood-burning tools to darken the routed letters and numbers: "HEIDI—May 5/80—Oct 8/97." Heidi's cross, built by the boys who loved her, becomes a significant and important, even healing, landmark in the coming days, months and years. I hereby wish to sincerely thank Adam, his friends Blake and Tim, and the two instructors, Mr. Paul Andrews and Mr. Emery for graciously providing this important memorial at such a critical time. Your kindness warms my heart. Thank you, thank you.

The boys take the finished cross to Stokes Pit and plant it firmly upright in the ground on the roadside. Ashley Reber's cross has been well attended by her friends and family for the last month, and now it is joined by Heidi's cross. New groups of the bereaved gather around it later that day. Large crowds gather at this site after the funeral service; Heidi's friends are joined by various members of Heidi's family and they all cry together. Candles are set alight on all available surfaces on the cross and into the earth at its base. Trinkets are placed on this cross, and over the months Laura and I add an angel sitting atop the main beam. I tack a laminated photograph of Heidi on the cross, and her friends add beaded necklaces, a rosary, flowers, and little ceramic figurines. Lots and lots of melted wax drips from the many candles. The cross catches on fire twice from the melted wax, but is extinguished by passers-by. One school friend, a boy, moves a picnic table over from the park and places it in front of Heidi's cross. He sleeps under this table for over a week; he spends his days and nights crying and tending to her cross until his parents finally intervene and take him home. Dozens of students miss weeks of school. Many of them struggle to complete their grade twelve, and some have to take extra semesters the next fall. The site of the accident becomes a meeting place for Heidi and Ashley's friends for the rest of the 1997-1998 school year.

I visit the site almost every day until we find a final resting place for Heidi's ashes. When the rains come in November, I erect a little water-proof shelter for the candles so that they can continue to burn throughout the night. I am there every day to see that my baby isn't alone, and to ensure there is always a light for her in the dark. Heidi didn't like sleeping in the dark; she always left her bedroom door ajar to allow the hall light to enter her room and keep her company. I worry about this a lot. I worry that my baby is all alone in the dark, frightened; and there is no way for me to reach her, to comfort her and to hold her. The lighted candles make me feel I'm reaching her somehow.

The roadside memorial at Stokes Pit becomes my grieving centre for the first year. When I realize there are large numbers of other people visiting this site each day, I place a journal at the cross for all of us to use, to write down our thoughts. I place the journal inside a Tupperware container, along with a pen, and this seems adequate for keeping the rain out. The journal soon fills up with poetry, thoughts, and anguished grieving written by a vast variety of people. Not only do friends and family write in it but also strangers and passers-by who pull their cars over to see the memorials. Heidi's friends attach large signs, messages and poems to the chain-link fence behind the cross, and for awhile this becomes something akin to a tourist attraction.

Ashley and Heidi's roadside memorials are well-tended and both girls have active journals. I take Heidi's first full journal home and replace it with a new one in late August of 1998. A few weeks later, in September 1998—close to the one-year anniversary of the accident—some vandals take all of Ashley's journals and Heidi's one new journal. They damage the crosses by tearing off the trinkets and smashing the candles. Someone (I still can't believe this!) pries off the seated angel from the top of Heidi's cross. Who would do such a thing? Nevertheless, the memorial site continues to receive visitors even to this day. I moved the journals to Heidi's burial site in November of 1998. I treasure these journals because they are filled with pages of authentic and pure longing and love for Heidi.

The cross is again vandalized in July of 2002, and this time it disappears altogether. I am puzzled as to why anyone would want to remove this active memorial (people are still dropping off fresh flowers for Heidi). I search the ditches and the area behind the fence to see if they tossed it aside, but I cannot find it. I conclude the vandals must have taken it with them. But for what purpose? I don't understand. Two weeks later Heidi's friend Chrissie Williamson builds, paints and erects a new cross on the same site. She has been disturbed, as have I, by the emptiness of Heidi's memorial site and she decides to do something about it. So, thank you Chrissie, for keeping the roadside memorial alive for Heidi. You are a true and dear friend. Heidi's cross that Chrissie built is still standing as I write this, in July of 2004.

4.3   LSS Graduation 1998

Looking back on the expensive graduation date Heidi attended in June, I am so thankful now that I allowed her to go. She grasped this opportunity to attend a graduation with all the bells and whistles, never thinking that she wouldn't live to see her own. In my capacity as a School Trustee, I attend what should have been Heidi's graduation ceremony at Langley Secondary School in June of 1998. It is a hard ceremony to sit through but I'm glad I am there. The valedictorian honours Heidi in her speech and it is a stirring tribute to my daughter. When the graduates are called up on the stage to receive their diplomas, I stand to hand each one a rose as I congratulate them. When the first of Heidi's friends comes up, she gives me a big hug. Then the next grad hugs me and then the next. By the end of the ceremony almost every one of the two hundred graduates, and most of whom I do not know, give me a warm hug. It was wonderful and I thank them now. It means a lot to me to see Heidi remembered so fondly and to have so many of you show me such affection. This truly was a special graduation at Langley High. We all felt Heidi's presence in the room.

4.4 The Burials

Heidi's ashes are placed inside the two blue urns that Dianne Wilson makes especially for us. Dianne is Courtney's mother and also a renowned potter involved in the Langley arts scene. She readily agrees when I ask her to make Heidi's urns. The urns come in two sizes: a small one to use at the tree planting service at Langley High, and a larger one to contain the bulk of her ashes that will be buried in a cemetery. Courtney chooses a beautiful blue glaze for the urns, remembering that Heidi had earlier admired this glaze on other pieces of Dianne's pottery. Thank you, Dianne, for making Heidi's beautiful urns. I'm sure her spirit takes comfort in knowing her ashes are kept safe in something you made with your hands. She loved your family almost like her own.

The students at Langley Secondary School want to plant a tree in Heidi's honour, and a lovely flowering Japanese plum tree is donated by LSS student Brad Hutchinson's father. A small ceremony is held in late October to plant the tree on the front lawn of the high school. I sprinkle Heidi's ashes from the small urn onto the roots before they are covered up with soil. Mr. Shipley, Vice-Principal of LSS, reads a passage from the Bible and prayers are said. We all cry. Most of Heidi's friends, siblings, and extended family members are there. Mayor John Scholtens, most of the Councillors, and the School Trustees are there to support me. When I release the ashes I am shocked at the tinkling noises they make, and I realize that little fragments of bone are making the unsettling sounds; my knees turn into rubber. After emptying the container I stumble towards John and collapse sobbing against his chest. My mother runs over to wrap me in her arms. It is a hard moment for everyone. A few people say some kind words about Heidi and we all agree she would have loved the flowering plum tree.

Heidi's friends, Tiffany Bernemann, Leigh McRae, Courtney Wilson and Jamie Hyde arrange for a bronze plaque to be imbedded in a beautiful piece of pink stone to commemorate the passing of their friend. The plaque reads: "In loving memory of Heidi Dawn Klompas/ An unforgettably vibrant L.S.S. student/ May 5, 1980–October 8, 1997/ Party of Five Forever." (The party of five refers to the above four girls plus Heidi and is a take-off on a television show about five friends). This stone is placed on the ground beside the plum tree the following spring. I'd like to thank the three companies that contributed to this effort: Hutchinson Nurseries, Ornamental Obco Bronze Ltd., and Seymour's Rock and Water Gardens. Your generosity is greatly appreciated. For the past six years I have been driving by the high school every March and April to enjoy the sight of this fully blossomed tree swaying in Heidi's glory, filling the air with her fragrance.

* * * * * * * * * * *

Six months after Heidi's death, I start researching burial sights for the large urn. The nearest cemetery is the municipal site on 208th Street at 44th Avenue, and I ask the person at Township Hall who oversees such things if we could put a large stone grave marker over her buried ashes. She says no. Apparently the Township has a policy that only flat ground-level grave markers are allowed in all its cemeteries. I am told that if they make an exception for our family, then people might make a fuss about favouritism, and they couldn't allow that to happen. Well, I wasn't going to settle for a standard flat marker just because the grounds-keepers find them convenient to run over with their lawn mowers. So I start searching outside of Langley. Most cemeteries refuse my idea of a large rock as a grave marker, citing that they're too much work for the grounds keepers, and also because they are often vandalized. Phooey!

Finally, in late September, I meet the cooperative staff at Victory Memorial Park cemetery on King George Highway in South Surrey. And they give me what I want. They tell me they have recently been considering allowing upright memorials and so they decide to let Heidi's rock be the inaugural upright in a new section of the cemetery. I choose a site that sees her nestled in between tall cedars and Douglas firs. Heidi liked playing amongst the mature trees in our front yard when she was little, so I feel this little paradise is the perfect spot for her. It is across from a pond, overlooks the grassy lawns, and the breeze keeps the canopy of trees in constant motion. This place is very calming and peaceful.

Next, I meet with my son Bill's friend, Carl Stevens, at his workplace at Langley Landscaping Depot on 56th Avenue. We spend some considerable time choosing just the right stone. We eventually select a large, round, speckled granite boulder. (Thank you, Carl, for helping me choose the perfect stone; I appreciated your patience with me as I selected, unselected, and reselected many boulders in your yard before I settled on the above stone). I make arrangements for J.B. Newall Memorials, a memorial stone-carving company in Vancouver, to pick it up for engraving. Next, Laura and I shop around for the perfect figurine to sit atop the stone; and we find it in a garden shop in Surrey. The little cherub with leafy wings is squatting down to touch a flower: perfect! Heidi never met a pretty flower she couldn't resist touching. Next, I bring a black and white photo of Heidi into Newell's so they can imbed it into the stone and cover it with a protective, clear sealant. They sandblast Heidi's name, birth and death dates into the stone. We ask her brother

Bill to come up with the right words to be included on the stone, and he quickly comes up the perfect reflection of how we are all feeling about Heidi: "Taken too soon, remembered eternally in our hearts." It's nice to have this input from Heidi's two siblings; I think she would have liked that. Originally, I had wanted Heidi to be buried on October 8th, the date of her death, but the arrangements take much longer than expected, so we set the date for November 10th, between my birthday and Remembrance Day.

Heidi's ashes are buried on November 10th, 1998, thirteen months after she dies. A week or two before this date I put out the word that anyone wanting to put something into the vault that holds the urn will be welcome to do so. I am thinking of letters and cards that can be buried with her that no one else will ever see. This proves to be a popular idea. A large crowd (100+) shows up for the burial, and hears a few words from a friend of Heidi's father, and then from myself. I finish saying what I need to then hand the urn to Bill. He kisses it before placing it inside the open vault that is buried two feet under the earth beneath the trees. I take out a small collection of photos and letters and tell the attendees they are from Heidi's dresser drawer, and assure them that I haven't read the personal letters from her friends. I place them one at a time into the vault, pausing to share a laugh or two with the crowd over some of the photographs. There is a photograph of Judd, and I comment that he looks about six years old in it. Judd shouts out, "I was in grade eight!" Everyone bursts out laughing and it feels so good. Then there is the photo I had snapped by leaning out of a window; it shows Heidi, Courtney and Melissa sneaking a cigarette on our front porch and they have shocked looks on their faces as they try to hide their cigarettes. We all laugh over that. Most are high school photos with messages written on the back and I wanted them to be with Heidi. I ask the crowd if anyone else wants to include something in Heidi's vault and, before my amazed eyes, they form a very long line-up that starts at the vault and circles around the crowd. All of Heidi's friends have letters to give her, some have lockets with pictures, and some have cards, candies or flowers. The vault, which has lots of room around the central urn, gets filled to capacity. These are such heartfelt gestures of love being given to Heidi that I am overwhelmed with joy for her. She was loved, she is loved, and remains loved by so many.

Now that Heidi is properly laid to rest, I feel better. Not having her buried was unsettling for me, and now it is done. I continue with the journals I started at the first memorial at Stokes Pit. The fourth, and current, journal still waits inside a plastic container at Heidi's gravesite, welcoming all who visit to write a few thoughts down.

4.5   Criminal Court

The first court date for "John" is held on November 26th, 1997, at the Provincial Courthouse in Surrey. This is a brief session in which the charges are read out and the accused makes his plea. He is charged with dangerous driving causing death, and dangerous driving causing bodily harm. He pleads guilty to all charges. Our family does not attend this hearing and to date, I have not spoken with anyone who did attend, except for the youth himself.

The second court date is for sentencing, and this is held on Friday, January 30th, 1998. The courtroom is scheduled from 9:30 in the morning to 4:30 in the afternoon. By 9:00 am, a large crowd is gathered outside the courtroom waiting for the doors to open. I see many of Heidi's friends and their parents in the crowds. John's father makes his way through the crowd to speak with us. His eyes are wet and he is looking down a lot as he tells Heidi's father and I how sorry he is for what his son has done. He tells us his son knew Heidi and never meant to hurt her or anyone else that night. He apologises again and shakes our hands. I thank him for his apology and ask how his family is coping with this tragedy. He says, "Not well." He moves away from us as others approach. He is clearly a devastated, broken man. Scanning the crowd, I see mixed emotions on the faces of the others: fear, anger, pain, and exhaustion. No one knows what to expect once we are inside. This is the first time inside a courthouse for most of us.

It is a long, emotionally exhausting day. There is a nervous energy inside the courtroom and I'm feeling queasy. Once proceedings begin, we sit back and absorb what is being said. First there are the numerous police reports that are read aloud. Then there is the long list of injuries and I am surprised by some of them because I haven't yet heard about all of the teens hurt that night. Judge Scarlett announces a lunch break and we all make our way outside. We don't know where to go for lunch, but no one in our family is really hungry. We grab something in a nearby cafe. I don't feel up to speaking with anyone this day and try to avoid the crowds going back in after the break. My heart feels so heavy, like it's filled with lead.

The last part of the day, and the hardest to bear, involves listening to the long list of Victim Impact Statements submitted by many of the injured. My son, Bill, writes the impact statement on behalf of our family. Our lawyer asked me to write this statement but I am unable to articulate any coherent words at this time. I am helpless to describe how Heidi's death has affected my life because my mind is still in a haze of shock. Bill's short statement is printed in the newspapers later in the week, and most people still remember this particular quote from it: "In a world full of coal you have managed to destroy one of the very few diamonds." How true.

The crown council makes sure to remind the judge that the driver's blood alcohol level was over twice the allowed limit on the early morning hours of September 13th, 1997. The judge announces he will present the sentence ruling on February 18th, 1998.

The Judge makes his ruling on Wednesday, February 18th, 1998. This boy is sentenced to three months in open custody to be served in a youth detention centre in Burnaby, two years probation, and a three-year driving ban. He must serve 175 hours of community service, and write letters of apology to each of the victims. He has already started his community service by giving one talk, so far, to a grade seven class attending the courthouse; he hopes to continue speaking to groups of youths about the devastation that can happen when people drink and drive.

While he is incarcerated for three months, John writes his letters of apology and turns them in to his youth worker for mailing. But she puts them in a pile on her desk and promptly forgets about them. Months later, many of the victims are disappointed they never received an apology and they assume he has ignored the judge's orders. After John is back home he hears complaints that his letters were never received, so he and his mother investigate the whereabouts of said letters. Months later they discover what has happened and it is only after they file a complaint that a different youth worker somehow finds the letters and pops them into the mail. People receive their letters almost a year after they are written and any sincerity these letters may have contained is now watered down by the extended time it takes to reach the addressees. This mistake by a crown's employee adds to the pain and hurt felt by the victims, and in my opinion, this employee should write her own letters of apology to each of the original letters' recipients. Instead, resentment is allowed to build towards this boy who made a terrible, life-altering mistake one night. This one employee missed an opportunity to help (even in a small way) a large group of physically and emotionally injured people to heal. Instead, she adds to their pain by fostering bitterness and resentment over a delay that John takes the blame for.

* * * * * * * * * * *

I feel the Young Offenders' Act does a great disservice to both the young offenders and to Canadian society in general. In our system the underage criminal usually receives a much lighter sentence than does an adult. Often the sentence is just some community work, apologies, and in the above case, very minimal time spent in a juvenile detention centre.

When a seventeen year old boy gets drunk, smokes a joint, then gets behind the wheel, he is making decisions that could affect the rest of his life and endanger the lives of others. Sixteen and seventeen year-olds know right from wrong and can expect to be punished for misdeeds *outside* our legal system. For example, when students are caught smoking marijuana on school grounds, in most Canadian school districts they are suspended for at least a month or expelled from the school altogether. When someone is caught shoplifting he or she is banned from that store and/or shopping mall for years. But when a youth injures fifteen people and is found responsible for the deaths of two more, he goes away for only three months to a youth detention facility and then is released back into society. What is wrong here? The Canadian justice system is an oxymoron. There is no real justice within our legal system.

As citizens, in our endeavours to be compassionate and forgiving, we commit a moral crime. We are letting down our young offenders by not allowing them to serve real time for the harm they cause others. Psychologically, our feelings of self worth are connected to our ability to overcome hardships; when we prevent people from working through these hardships—when we let them take the easy road—we rob them of the opportunity to grow and improve as a person. By giving light sentences for serious crimes in which others have died, our courts prevent these criminals from realizing any sense of self-worth. If this boy had served five or six years in jail—a time when he could really reflect on his decisions—and used this time to complete his high school education and learn a trade, or earn a college diploma, he would have come out of it knowing he had paid his dues to society. He would be smarter and better equipped to re-enter society after five or more years of education and training than if he was just tossed back into the mainstream after only three months. He would feel a sense of redemption. And most importantly, for society, an educated man is less likely to re-offend compared to an uneducated offender who gets a slap on the wrist for a serious crime. We need to think about this. Some people may disagree with me and say that criminals should not be provided with free post-secondary educations. But let's remember that this youth would still be incarcerated: no meeting friends at the 7-11, no weekend parties, no driving cars, and no girlfriends for five years. I have recently seen the effects of philosophy and psychology courses on the minds of young men and women at university, and it is a wonderful thing to behold. They rediscover thinking! They eagerly debate the many different philosophies and theories about the human condition, and with great enthusiasm. I believe everyone could benefit from these types of courses. I believe education is the key to releasing these young offenders from what is often a pre-ordained life of crime because education opens the mind to new ways of seeing the world.

Not only would the criminal feel better about himself after serving some serious time but also the victims and their families would sense justice had been served after seeing he had done his time. Both sides benefit in a situation like this. There is already a great deal of anger and frustration felt by Canadians regarding our legal system. We need to see tougher sentences handed out without early parole: for both young offenders and adults. It's a standing joke in Canada that you can murder someone, be sentenced to "life" in prison but be out in less than ten years for "good behaviour." We need to abandon our Young Offenders' Act and start sentencing all criminals alike, regardless of their age. (Having said this, I believe the younger prisoners should be segregated from older, hardened criminals). Any early releases should be connected to the completion of degrees, diploma programs, or trade certifications. They could use education to earn their way out of jail. I would love to see this idea tested over a ten year period, and in the follow-up see how differently the lives of the educated longer-term young offenders turn out compared to those who only get a few months. It would be interesting to also examine the psychological effects of short-term incarceration on the offenders as they re-enter a community that shuns them for getting off easy. What kind of damage is incurred when a young person feels his whole town hates him? What does this do to his feelings of self-worth, his self-esteem? Does low self-esteem lead to the abuse of drugs and alcohol? Depression and suicide? How do we expect a young person to grow into a mentally healthy adult under these conditions? I wonder about this a lot.

Teenagers act badly, in part, because they know they'll get away with it and they are confident their names will be kept out of the media. Why are we denying these underage criminals the opportunity to feel public shame? I say let their names be published and let them suffer the consequences. My daughter's name was not withheld from the press, nor were any of the other Stokes Pit victims' names withheld. I had to deal with reporters calling on the phone, television crews showing up at my door, and photographers taking pictures on some of the most difficult and painful days of my life. Why don't our young criminals get the same treatment? Everyone involved in a tragedy, and not just the victims, should receive equal amounts of news coverage. Let's see some fairness here. Dealing with public shame through exposure should be a part of every criminal case, and not just for adult offenders. If young people considering criminal acts knew that their names and faces would make headline news, plastered on the front pages of newspapers and featured on the six o'clock news, they might reconsider their plans to break the law. Public exposure is another opportunity our lawmakers are missing in their efforts to curb crimes committed by youths.

Our lawmakers clearly need to make changes to the youth justice system. We need a level playing field for our young offenders that should reflect the sentences given for serious crimes committed by adults. I say no more coddling of young offenders, because it robs them of the opportunity for redemption. Let them do their time. Give them the opportunity to show the people in their communities that they have earned the right to walk among them with their heads held high. Don't you think we owe it to them? And to us? And to their victims?

She Walks In Beauty

She walks in beauty, head held high
She walks with passion, in her blue eyes
She walks beyond clarity, letting you see
She walks on the faith from you & me

She walks in compassion, lending a hand
She walks with kindness, across our land
She walks beyond hope to help you live
She walks on in the memories we all have to give

She walks in peace through heaven above
She walks with joy, for having been loved
She walks beyond fear not batting an eye
She walks on in dreams her final good-bye

Christina Williamson
January 16, 2001

4.6   Coroner's Investigation

Medical Investigator for the Office of the Chief Coroner: Kathleen B. Stephany, RN, BScN. Report dated March 31, 1999.

Peace Arch District Hospital

In January of 1998, three months following Heidi's death, the Coroner's office assigns Kathleen Stephany to conduct an investigation. Ms. Stephany phones to arrange a meeting with me, and I invite my friend Kathy Elden to join us. Our first meeting is on January 6ᵗʰ, 1998, and we spend some considerable time going over the more troublesome concerns I have with Heidi's hospital care. Ms. Stephany is thorough with her questioning and we expand the scope of her investigation to include inquiries for the Langley RCMP, the doctors and nurses at Peace Arch District Hospital, and some doctors, nurses and technicians at Royal Columbian Hospital. By the time the meeting is over I've given her about six pages of questions I want answered, photocopies of the journal I kept in the hospital, and a photograph of Heidi: her tasks are set. She promises to keep in touch throughout her investigation, and I am pleased to report that she keeps her word.

Ms. Stephany phones me several times over the next year and a half. She meets with me off and on for the duration of the investigation and at one point she informs me she can no longer look at Heidi's photograph: it upsets her and she has to turn it over. She is increasingly shocked and appalled by what she is discovering, and becomes alarmed over the treatment Heidi received at Peace Arch Hospital. In particular, she is concerned about the excessive time it took for an orthopaedic surgeon to arrive. More than once she tells me her investigation has the express purpose of finding out the exact cause(s) of Heidi's death, and that the Coroner's Office is not allowed to assign blame to any doctors or nurses. She must be very careful in wording her final report and not point any fingers at individuals. Included in the report are her interviews with several doctors and nurses, and it is within these accounts of her interviews that some interesting and alarming inconsistencies are revealed.

Ms. Stephany interviews Dr. H as part of her investigation. The following is the interview as recorded in her final report:

> Dr. T[] H[] is an Orthopedic Surgeon. He believes that he was probably on Orthopedic call at Peace Arch Hospital on September 13, 1997. Dr. H[] thinks that Dr. L[] either telephoned or paged him during the early morning hours on September 13th. He thinks that he was notified by her sometime around 4am. Dr. H[] recalls that during telephone contact with Dr. L[] that she informed him that there were several accident victims from a gravel pit incident in the ER and that there were two patients with fractures for him to see. One patient had a closed fractured tibia and another had two closed fractured tibias. Dr. H[] is almost 99% certain that Dr. L[] did not notify him about Ms. Klompas more than one time. He recalls that he arrived to the ER slightly before 9am. He recalls that when he examined Ms. Klompas she was somewhat sedated and "groggy" but that she could respond. Both of her lower legs were swollen and splinted. Circulation was good, but because Ms. Klompas was somewhat sedated sensation was not evaluated. Although Dr. H[] noticed that both of Ms. Klompas' lower legs were swollen, one leg was worse than the other although

he could not remember which leg. Because of the leg swelling Dr. H[] decided to make Ms. Klompas a surgical priority as soon as it was reasonably possible. Ms. Klompas had early signs of compartment syndrome and therefore he thought she might be the surgical priority of the day, although he thought there was no real urgency. Dr. H[] explained that he saw the other boy with a fractured leg before he saw Ms. Klompas, however once he examined Ms. Klompas he decided she should have surgery first. Dr. H[] pointed out some of the classic symptoms of compartment syndrome: significant amount of pain, pain beyond the type of injury experienced and lastly, neurovascular compromise. If neurovascular compromise occurs the patient needs to have surgery as soon as possible (Stephany, 19-20).

The Coroner's Report reveals a different perspective on the events in Peace Arch Hospital that morning, based on the following interview with Dr. L:

Dr. [] L[] is an Emergency Room physician. She was the attending physician at Peace Arch Hospital ER during the early morning hours on September 13, 199[7]. Heidi Klompas was one of Dr. L[]'s patients. Dr. L[] explained that she remembers calling the Orthopedic surgeon on the telephone a total of four times that night, respectfully at approximately 0230, 0445, 0500 and again at 0700, just before she went off duty. Dr. L[] recalls expressing extreme concern to the Orthopedic Surgeon, Dr. H[] about the extensiveness of Ms. Klompas' bilateral lower leg fractures. According to Dr. L[], each time she telephoned Dr. H[] he apparently told her he would be coming in soon

yet he never came into the ER while Dr. L[] was still
on duty. At one point in time Dr. H[] requested that
she order lateral xray views of Ms. Klompas' legs prior
to his arrival. Dr. L[] explained to him that the bones
were shattered and that lateral views would likely not
make a difference to diagnosis (Stephany, 18-19).

Dr. L was very concerned about the fact that the Orthopaedic
surgeon on call would not come into hospital when requested.
She notified Dr. Y, the Department Head of ER, in writing
expressing her concerns. Dr. L explained why she did not transfer
Ms. Klompas to another hospital facility. After examining Ms.
Klompas Dr. L did not note any neurological deficit or other
injury that would require a specialty not available at Peace
Arch Hospital. She pointed out that each time she telephoned
the Orthopaedic surgeon, Dr. H, he kept telling her that he
would be coming into hospital soon (Stephany, 18-19).

The Coroner's investigator's interview with Dr. L confirms
my experience in the Peace Arch Hospital ER regarding the
telephone calls to Dr. H. I was becoming increasingly agitated
because he failed to show up each time he said he was coming
in. I remember shouting at Dr. L to call him again and again.
In speaking with JR's father years later, he reminded me that he
too had kept pressing Dr. L to bring in an orthopaedic surgeon
for his injured son. I distinctly remember Dr. L being very
upset with Dr. H.

Another testimony to the repeated phone calls to Dr. H comes
from the interview with one of the nurses working at Peace
Arch Hospital that night:

Ms. P[], RN was on duty at Peace Arch Hospital
ER during the early morning hours on September
13, 1997. Ms. P[] went off duty at 0700 hours that

morning.... . Ms. P[] pointed out that Dr. [] L[]
was very concerned about Ms. Klompas' fractures.
According to Ms. P[], Dr. L[] telephoned the
Orthopedic Surgeon, Dr. T. H[] more than once. She
apparently called him when Ms. Klompas arrived
to the ER as well as immediately following the xrays
being completed (Stephany, 18).

Furthermore, from her interview with Dr. Y, Ms. Stephany
reports that "Dr. Y[] discussed this particular case with
one of the other Orthopedic surgeons on staff at Peace Arch
Hospital. The Orthopedic surgeon he spoke to felt that given
the extensiveness of Ms. Klompas' bone injuries, there might
have been some expectation that the Orthopedic surgeon see
the patient when called" (Stephany, 21).

In the Conclusion to her Coroner's Investigation Report, Ms.
Stephany writes:

Bell et al. point out that the best treatment for fat
embolism syndrome is prevention which consists of
early fixation of long bone fractures. ten Duis (1997)
states that although the physiological pathway of the
fat emboli syndrome is obscure, full attention should
be paid to preventive measures which include the
following: "in the pre-hospital phase and Emergency
Room long bone fractures should be handled with
great care, with the minimum of movement and
splinting at the earliest possible opportunity, because
early immobilization is known to have a positive
influence on reducing the incidence of the syndrome"
(p.81)
(Stephany, 27).

So, here's how I see this problem. Clearly, the information on fat embolism syndrome tells us that early fixation of long bone fractures can prevent this syndrome that causes brain damage and death. The emergency crew at Peace Arch Hospital, including Dr. L, should have been aware of the dangers of this syndrome that is directly connected to long bone fractures; and they should have known that the probability of acquiring this syndrome increases dramatically—by 30%—if there are multiple long bone fractures, such as in Heidi's case. When Dr. H failed to show after the second time he promised he'd be right in, I feel the staff should have transferred both Heidi and JR to another hospital such as Royal Columbian, Vancouver General, or Children's for immediate orthopaedic care. Once Dr. H demonstrated that he couldn't be relied upon, the ER staff should have taken action regardless of any further promises from Dr. H. I had asked to have Heidi transferred and they refused me based on Dr. H's promises. They should have known better. They should have taken that opportunity to remove two patients from Dr. H's care and provide them with a chance at better treatment. This was a big opportunity missed by Dr. L and her staff. She should have had the courage to stand up to Dr. H and transfer these patients to another hospital.

Having said this, I feel that I am the person most responsible for missing this opportunity to remove Heidi from Peace Arch Hospital. I should have screamed, ranted, raved, and threatened them until they moved her to another hospital. I should never have trusted each successive promise by a man, whom I discovered much later, has one of the worst reputations in B.C. medicine (Ouston, Vancouver Sun, Nov.11/2000). My gut, or my intuition if you will, was telling me that Heidi should have been moved elsewhere. But I allowed myself to be talked into letting her stay at Peace Arch Hospital throughout the early morning hours against my better judgement. And Heidi died, in part, as a result of this decision to keep her in White Rock. This haunts me even now.

The Coroner's investigation reveals even more about the questionable treatment Heidi received at Peace Arch Hospital. Heidi's legs were grotesquely swollen and misshapen, and the longer they were left without help, the worse the compartment syndrome became. Also, the information on fat embolism syndrome indicates that the fractured limbs should be immobilized to prevent any movement; they should be held firmly in place with the appropriate splints. Dr. L didn't want to move Heidi's legs any more than necessary; therefore she did not send Heidi for the additional lateral x-rays that Dr. H had requested during one of their early morning telephone conversations. The x-ray technician, Ms. T, also refused to do the lateral x-rays on Heidi, but for different reasons. The following is an excerpt from her interview with the Coroner's investigator:

> Ms. T[] is a Radiology Technician at Peace Arch Hospital. She performed the first set of xrays on Ms. Klompas during the early morning hours on September 13, 1997. Ms. T[] did not understand why Ms. Klompas' legs were not splinted separate from her body. In Ms. T[]'s opinion Ms. Klompas' legs were not properly supported. Because Ms. T[] feared that the bones might protrude through the skin due to lack of proper support, she elected not to attempt to perform lateral xray views of Ms. Klompas' legs (Stephany, 20).

> Furthermore, Nurse P tells the Coroner's investigator that she "could not recall exactly what type of leg splints were used to immobilize Ms. Klompas' legs.

However, Ms. P pointed out that the only type of leg splints used in the Peace Arch Hospital ER are "back slabs" made of casting material.... She could not recall if ice packs were applied" (Stephany, 19).

In addition, another nurse was interviewed and she shared her concerns with the investigator:

Ms. K[] RN came on duty at the Peace Arch Hospital ER at 0700 hours on September 13, 1997. Ms K[] was assigned to care for Ms. Klompas. Ms. K[] recalls that Ms. Klompas' legs were very swollen but her pedal pulses were good. Ms. K[] was worried about the neurovascular status of Ms. Klompas' legs and the danger of compartment syndrome developing. Ms. K[] thinks that initially ice packs were applied to Ms. Klompas' legs to decrease swelling, but she could not recall for sure if the ice packs were maintained (Stephany, 19).

And last but not least are the comments from the interview with Dr. Y, the Chief of Emergency Medicine at Peace Arch Hospital:

Dr. Y[] explained that Peace Arch Hospital ER has fiberglass for use in molding nicely fitted limb splints for fractures but that they were not used in this case. Dr. Y[] feels that it is primarily a physician['s] responsibility to ensure that a patient's fractured limb(s) are splinted properly. In Dr. Y[]'s opinion ice treatment was not that important in Ms. Klompas' case and that ice packs are really only useful for sprains. According to Dr. Y[] the treatment modality of choice for fractured lower limbs is: elevation of the affected limbs [not done], reducing the fractures [not done], and splinting them [not done]. He pointed out that in this case elevating the legs was not possible because the fractures were so unstable (Stephany, 21).

The above Chief of Emergency Medicine at Peace Arch Hospital names three treatments most commonly used for fractured limbs, and Heidi receives none of them. How could this be? Not only does she have to wait nine hours to be seen by an orthopaedic surgeon, but she doesn't even receive the most basic and obvious care for her broken limbs. What galls me even further is the knowledge that anyone can go on the internet and find information on fat embolism syndrome and compartment syndrome and learn how to prevent and/or treat them within minutes. How is it possible that these medical "Professionals" don't seem to know that multiple long bone fractures can lead to dangerous and deadly complications? How could they be so complacent? Or was it simply ignorance?

Throughout her investigation for the Coroner's office, Ms. Stephany keeps me informed of her progress and her discoveries. She is brutally honest with me and I appreciate her frankness when discussing some of the events that happened to Heidi. I have always had a driving need to know all the details of Heidi's care while in these two hospitals, and Ms. Stephany holds nothing back as she responds to my relentless questioning. Again, I appreciate the openness and honesty in her delivery of information.

One of the complications of Heidi's care at Peace Arch Hospital was the mismanagement of her lungs. Firstly, only one nurse, late in the day, drew attention to the fluid overload problem. This was Nurse K, and she emphasized the discrepancy in fluid levels by underlining them in her notes around the time she rode in the ambulance with Heidi enroute to Royal Columbian. Ms.

K came on duty at 7:00 a.m., so most of the damage was done by the time she was assigned to Heidi. What bothers me about this fluid overload is that not one of the doctors at Peace Arch Hospital noticed it while Heidi's legs were swelling up, while Heidi's oxygen levels were dropping, and while Heidi's brain was seizing in reaction to the fat embolism, which, according to the literature I found, is extrapolated by excessive fluids in the system.

Secondly, the aspiration of vomit seems to have been a confusing issue within this hospital. In her interviews, Ms. Stephany obtains two different accountings of whether or not Heidi aspirated. Two more accounts are found within the hospital's records, yet no one notified the doctors at Royal Columbian. However, the doctors at Royal Columbian quickly confirmed she had earlier aspirated, and they subsequently battled the aspiration pneumonia in Heidi's lungs for the remainder of her stay in hospital—or more accurately—for the rest of her life. The staff at Peace Arch Hospital had some curious things to say about Heidi vomiting:

From the Coroner's Report:

> Ms. [] S[] LPN... [was given] the "okay" to transport Ms. Klompas by stretcher to Radiology. On the way over to xray Ms. Klompas was talking to Ms. S[]. However upon arrival to the Radiology Department Ms. S[] noticed that Ms. Klompas' eyes were rolled back. Ms. S[] knew that something [was] terribly wrong. She left Ms. Klompas unattended for only a few moments while she ran through an Xray door to call for help. A technician said she would call ER "stat." Ms. S[] then returned back at Ms. Klompas' side. Ms. K attended a short while later and together

they turned Ms. Klompas's top half of her body to
one side. According to Ms. S[], Ms. Klompas did not
vomit while she was in the Radiology Department.
She could not recall seeing any evidence of vomit. She
suspects that Ms. Klompas may have vomited when she
returned back to the ER (Stephany, 20).

From the Coroner's Report:

> Ms. []T[] is a Radiology Technician at Peace Arch
> Hospital.... Ms.T[] was in the xray room when Ms.
> Klompas seizured later that same morning. She recalls
> that Ms. Klompas was lying in the Hallway outside
> of the Radiology Room on a stretcher when Ms. S[]
> called Ms. T[] for help. Ms. T[] could not recall what
> position Ms. Klompas was lying in but she remembers
> seeing Ms. S[] hovering over Ms. Klompas' upper body.
> Ms. T[] did not recall whether Ms. Klompas vomited
> or not. She also did not directly witness any seizure
> activity. She did remember that she phoned the ER and
> that ER staff met her and Ms. S[] half way when they
> were transferring Ms. Klompas back to the ER from
> Radiology (Stephany, 20).

From Peace Arch District Hospital Records:

> While in the x-ray department she suffered a grand
> mal seizure and vomited and may have vomited [sic].
> History from her mother indicated there was no prior
> history of epilepsy and she is generally healthy. She was
> brought back to the resuscitation room and rolled into
> the left lateral position. There was no further vomiting.
> She continued to seize... ([] P[], MD, September 13,
> 1997).

From Peace Arch District Hospital Records:

> 9:40—To x-ray. Apparently starting to have seizure,
> vomited large amt. brown fluid as stated by technician.
> Positioned on Rt. side. Returned to ER limbs rigid and
> jaw clamped down. Seen by Dr. P[]. (Ms. [] K[], RN,
> September 13, 1997).

The two people who were asked the question by the Coroner's investigator could not "recall" any vomiting from their patient. But in the hospital records, a doctor reports that Heidi vomited prior to coming into the resuscitation room of the ER. Furthermore, a nurse reports in her notes that Heidi "apparently" vomited while seizing, based on what a technician told her. But which technician? The notes do not indicate the person she was referring to, so I don't suppose we'll ever know. Nevertheless, these four conflicting tales of vomiting raise serious questions about the communication between staff members at Peace Arch Hospital's ER. Aspiration, or the inhalation of highly acidic vomit, causes serious damage to the lungs. This is important information that should have been relayed to the doctors attending Heidi at Royal Columbian, as indicated in the notes made by one of the first of her consulting physicians at RCH:

> Opinion: This lady obviously needs surgery as
> proposed. I don't clearly see why she is having a
> problem with her oxygenation. I consider... [that]
> possibly she had an aspiration at some time, maybe
> during her convulsion or around the time of
> intubation.... She will be ventilated postoperatively
> and her respiratory progress assessed from there on. I
> suspect she will need ventilating for some little while...
> ([] Q[], M.D., RCH 29, 30).

I find it inexcusable that the above doctor had to guess what was wrong with Heidi's lungs as she lay in a coma with broken, swollen legs. This information should have been included with the paperwork that accompanied Heidi to Royal Columbian Hospital so that they could immediately treat the damage already started by the acid. Why was this information withheld? I can only shake my head in amazement at this omission.

Royal Columbian Hospital

Ms. Stephany's report contains a Conclusion that I would like to share with you verbatim:

Conclusion

Approximately 13 hours after arrival to hospital Ms. Klompas experienced a grand mal seizure with loss of consciousness. The initial CT scan of the head did not reveal any evidence of abnormality. The diagnosis that was made was that of fat emboli syndrome related to multiple long bone fractures. This diagnosis was supported by the initial clinical findings of loss of consciousness, fever and chest petechiae and the later findings of compromised lung function, increased intracranial pressure, reduced hemoglobin and reduced platelet count. Fat emboli syndrome is a potentially fatal condition. The distinction must first of all be made between fat emboli, which are present in every trauma patient, and "fat emboli syndrome" which is a deteriorating clinical course that necessitates aggressive therapeutic intervention. The incidence of fat emboli syndrome ranges from 1–17% of patients and classically occurs in patients with long-bone fractures but also occurs in patients suffering from various other illnesses (Bell, Enderson & Frame, 1994

& ten Duis, 1997). Fat emboli syndrome usually manifests itself within 12 to 72 hours after admission. Eighty-five percent of the patients who develop this disorder will recover in less than three days and only 10 % of the patients will require ventilatory support (Bell, Enderson & Frame, 1994). Mortality has been reported at ranging from 0 -35% (Ganong, 1993).

In the case of Ms. Klompas the onset of symptoms of fat emboli syndrome occurred quite rapidly, only approximately nine hours after initial injury. The physicians caring for Ms. Klompas thought that the rapid onset of fat emboli syndrome was due to a heart defect in the form of either a patent foramen ovale or atrialseptal defect. However neither of these heart conditions were confirmed by diagnostic tests. ten Duis (1997) points out that rapid onset of the symptoms associated with fat emboli syndrome are not exclusive to these two heart problems but has been known to occur in patients with multiple long bone fractures.

Bell et al point out that the best treatment for fat embolism syndrome is prevention which consists of early fixation of long bone fractures. Ten Duis (1997) states that although the physiological pathway of the fat emboli syndrome is obscure, full attention should be paid to preventive measures which include the following: "in the pre-hospital phase and Emergency Room long bone fractures should be handled with great care, with the minimum of movement and splinting at the earliest possible opportunity, because early immobilization is known to have a positive influence on reducing the incidence of the syndrome" (p.81).

Although Ms. Klompas suffered from significant morbidity due to fat embolism syndrome she was on route to recovery in that her pneumonia was resolving and her neurological functioning was improving. Her death was caused by anoxic brain injury sustained from a cardiac arrest due to rupture of the innominate artery from a fistula. The tracheo-innominate fistula had not been diagnosed until the cardiac arrest occurred. In retrospect the purulent discharge that was noted to be coming from the tracheostomy tube site may have been a possible indication that a fistula had formed. Paparell, Shumrick, Gluckman & Meyerhoff (1990) point out that the pathogenesis of fistulas involving the tracheostomy tube are felt to be due to the tracheostomy tube cuff or from the tip of a malpositioned tracheostomy tube. An additional factor may be the presence of an indwelling nasogastric tube or presence of an infection. They state that the following steps should be taken to prevent erosion of the innominate artery:

1) an adequate skin incision to allow visualization or palpation of normally situated vessels.

2) avoidance of a low tracheostomy by prevention of hyperextension of the neck, prevention of excessive upward traction of the trachea using the tracheal hook at the time of stabilization of the trachea, and accurate placement of the tracheal incision no lower than the second and third tracheal rings.

3) the use of nonirritating synthetic tubes without pressure cuff, if possible; and

4) constant humidification and sterile technique in

the care of the tracheostomy to prevent local infections with the attendant increased risks of mucosal ulceration. (Stephany, 27-28)

Ms. Stephany discusses the problems related to tracheostomy tubes and the development of fistulas by quoting from well-respected medical journals and texts. She points out that the persistent purulent discharge oozing from Heidi's tracheostomy site was a "possible indication that a fistula had formed" (Stephany, 27). The hospital records show that this infectious discharge was present immediately following the tracheostomy operation. It continued to ooze without stop from the time of the initial trachea incision on September 27th to the time of the bleed on October 4th: about seven full days. The nurses' notes indicate that they smelled the foul odour from her tracheostomy site when changing her dressings and cleaning the tubes. Upon reading the hospital records, it is clear to me that this virulent infection was present at the time of the tracheostomy operation, and I question how it is possible that no one thought to physically look inside her tracheal wall while they had the chance, especially after fourteen days of having endotracheal tubes irritating the lining of her trachea. Was the operation done in such a hurry that this oversight occurred? Dr. M, the neurosurgeon, and his team missed this opportunity to check the tissues inside her trachea for infection, irritation and erosion; and this omission was the beginning of the end for Heidi.

I never noticed the smell before October 3rd because whenever I visited Heidi the nurses had the t-piece connected to the ventilator. She was disconnected from the ventilator on October 3rd because she was starting to breathe on her own, and that's when I first smelled the foul odour. Had I detected the odour days earlier I may have had the chance to discuss it with one of her doctors. But this didn't happen. I question why the nurses didn't bring it to the attention of the doctors and why it was allowed to persist for such a long time (one week). I did, however, question the nurses about the large amount of discharge coming out of the site, but each time they just said "It's normal, don't worry about it." I trusted they knew what they were doing, and by trusting I failed Heidi. At the point on October 3rd when the two nurses were preparing Heidi for the transfer to the Maxi ward and they laughed out loud at my questions, I should have called for a doctor and brought to his attention my concerns about the bad smell and the persistent discharge. Perhaps then something might have directed them to the presence of the fistula. Perhaps a senior physician with more experience would have recognized the signs showing evidence of a fistula. Perhaps, perhaps, perhaps. I feel I missed this opportunity to do something. In retrospect, I should have made a fuss. It bothered me that the *reason* she was being removed from the ICU was because a heart patient needed her bed. It bothered me to see four empty beds in an Intensive Care quad unit as Heidi was slowly wheeled out. It bothered me that she was taken out of the Intensive Care Unit the same day her brain shunt was removed. And it REALLY, REALLY bothered me that those two nurses had the gall to laugh at me. Especially after what happened the next day. What a horrific way to be proven right.

In her interviews with the staff at Royal Columbian Hospital, Ms. Stephany reports the following:

> Ms. [] S[] RN works at RCH. She was the nurse
> who transferred Ms. Klompas to the Maxi ward on
> October 3, 1997. Ms. S[] cannot recall any details of a
> conversation that may have occurred between herself
> and Ms. Klompas' mom during the transfer. The only

thing that stands out clear in her memory is that she remembers Ms. Klompas coughing up green sputum (Stephany, 22).

Furthermore:

> Ms. L[] S[] RN works at RCH. She was the nurse who admitted Ms. Klompas to the Maxi ward on October 3, 1997. She recalls that she was concerned about the patient's heart rate being elevated at 120–130/minute. Because Ms. S[] was concerned she called Dr. B[] and informed her of the elevated heart rate. Ms. S[] recalls that Ms. Klompas' mom accompanied her during the transfer from the ICU and that she was a bit anxious about the transfer. Ms. S[] cannot recall if Ms. Adamson mentioned anything to her about the odour coming from Ms. Klompas' tracheostomy site (Stephany, 22).

It would seem that working in a hospital causes selective memory loss for some doctors and nurses. Another nurse in the Maxi ward was interviewed and she reports this:

> Ms. [] W[] RN works at RCH. She was Ms. Klompas' primary nurse on the night shift (1900–0700) beginning on October 3rd, Ms. Klompas' first evening on the Maxi ward. Ms. W[] remembers that Ms. Klompas' condition was fairly stable although her heart rate was elevated and she had a fever. Dr. B[] came in to see Ms. Klompas that evening and said she was okay. As night shift wore on Ms. W[] observed that Ms. Klompas was getting lighter neurologically. Ms. W[] performed tracheostomy care and a dressing

change. She didn't notice anything unusual about the tracheostomy site although she was concerned about the central IV line [in her neck] being red and inflamed looking (Stephany, 23).

So, Heidi's neck was inflamed, she had a high temperature, her tracheostomy site was oozing pus, and her heart was beating faster than normal. But I had been told not to worry because this was "normal." It appears that there was no investigation into the cause of the high temperature or the odorous discharge oozing from the tracheostomy site. Is it really possible that no one thought to look inside her trachea for the cause or the source of the infection? To this day I don't understand how these symptoms could escape the notice of so many doctors assigned to Heidi's care. Surely someone should have considered the possibility of a fistula.

The location of the tracheostomy incision was an important factor as well. With good intentions for a teenaged girl who would be self-conscious of visible scars, Dr. M placed the incision lower than what is recommended. This proved to have deadly consequences because the infection that ate through her trachea came through at the point the innominate artery passes in front of the trachea. Subsequently, the fistula continued to consume the tissues in its path and ate through the lining of the innominate artery. Hence the bleed.

The type of trachea cuff is also discussed above. In her interview with the neurosurgeon, Ms. Stephany reports:

> Dr. [] M[] is the Neurosurgeon who was caring for Ms. Klompas while she was at RCH. Dr. M[] was asked to comment on Ms. Klompas' potential for neurological recovery had she not sustained the anoxic brain insult due to the arrest. Dr. M[] explained that

two consequences usually occur due to fat embolism syndrome, the patient becomes confused and recovers or they die from complications of the syndrome. Ms. Klompas almost died from direct complications of the syndrome. Her condition was very guarded for quite some time in that she experienced increased ICP [intracranial pressure] levels and lung compromise from the syndrome. However, Dr. M[] pointed out that a young person like her would not likely have any evidence of primary brain injury once all of the symptoms of the fat emboli syndrome subsided.

Dr. M[] explained why the tracheostomy tube was inserted. After a patient has had an ET tube in place for longer than 10 days there is a real concern about damage occurring to the vocal cords as well as a tracheostomy tube is more appropriate than an ET tube, in that it facilitates better removal of lung secretions. Dr. M[] chose a cuffed tracheostomy tube as opposed to a non cuffed one because a cuffed tube would not be easily dislodged during coughing. Dr. M[] pointed out that the tracheostomy fistula had not been diagnosed until the time of the cardiac arrest (Stephany, 23).

According to Ms. Stephany's research, a tracheal hook is used with an unpressurized tracheal tube to keep the tube firmly in place. A non-cuffed tracheal tube causes less irritation inside the trachea, thereby reducing the incidence of erosion and infection. Again, as stated in Ms. Stephany's report, " the pathogenesis of fistulas involving the tracheostomy tube are felt to be due to the tracheostomy tube cuff or from the tip of a malpositioned tracheostomy tube" (Stephany, 27).

Is it possible the trachea was mismanaged from the beginning? I wonder if the infections, and perhaps the erosion of her trachea, were present before the tracheostomy was performed. Remember the nurses having trouble inserting the endo-tracheal tubes? Perhaps this tracheostomy tube was not positioned correctly simply because the wall of her trachea was badly infected and eroded. Certainly, on the day of the bleed, Heidi's father brought this to the attention of the attending nurse by pointing out the malpositioned T-piece, and he was shocked at how roughly she jerked it back into an upright position. The whole purpose of a pressurized cuff is to prevent dislodgement, so the fact that this cuffed tube was askew should have raised alarm bells with the nurses and doctors that something was terribly wrong with Heidi's trachea. But it didn't until it was too late.

The purpose of the investigation ordered by the office of the Chief Coroner is to find, conclusively, what caused the untimely death of an otherwise healthy seventeen year-old girl. In her report, Ms. Stephany states the following:

> An autopsy was performed on October 15, 1997 [date
> of Heidi's funeral] at Royal Columbian Hospital.
> Immediate cause of death was found to be due to
> anoxic brain injury as a result of massive blood loss
> from erosion of the innominate artery due to a
> tracheostomy tube. Proximal cause of death was due to
> complications of treatments as a result of being struck
> by a motor vehicle while a pedestrian and included:
> multiple blunt force injuries and long bone fractures
> resulting in fat emboli syndrome (Stephany, 26).

Heidi did not die because her legs were broken. She died because her trachea was allowed to erode and rot away. She died because the people caring for her "just didn't think to look" (quote from a nurse two weeks after Heidi's death) for a fistula. I believe her death was preventable. Her death resulted from a series of missed opportunities by medical personnel to intervene and to save her life.

I thank Ms. Kathleen Stephany for her investigation into Heidi's death. She accurately identified the problems in Heidi's medical care that needed addressing and she made appropriate recommendations for educational rounds for each of the two hospitals.

Thank you, Ms. Stephany.

Till Death Did Us Part

Do you know how I feel, when I feel this way
The hurt, the sorrow, and the pain I live through each day.
For even if I try my hardest,
I shall not regain.

People say they know how it feels
But I'm sorry I can't believe
Because I've never hurt so much
When somebody leaves.

It's been said that a heart heals itself in time
But forgetting you right now is the last thing on my mind
I will always remember your face, your laugh, your cry,
And I'll learn to live without you as the time goes by.

That's not to say it'll be easy
I'll shed a million tears
But your memories will keep me busy
And quiet all my fears.

I'm sorry that I didn't have the chance to say good-bye
Or that I'll love you and I'll miss you every second that goes by.
So please remember always, that this is how I feel,
And when I want to talk to you, beside my bed I'll kneel.

Christina Williamson
1998

4.7 RCMP

The Coroner's investigator asks me if there are any specifics I want addressed within the scope of her investigation; I give her several pages of questions. Some of these questions involve the actions of the Langley RCMP on the evening of Friday, September 12th, 1997. She promises to investigate whether or not the police officers who broke up the house party on 208th Street checked any of the drivers for alcohol consumption before sending them off in their cars. I ask her to find their reasoning behind not ensuring the drivers left the property sober. I need to know these answers.

Almost a year after she starts her investigation for the Chief Coroner's Office, Ms. Stephany meets me for an update on her progress. Although she does not include the verbal comments in her final report, she does tell me of her conversations with some members of the Langley RCMP who were on duty the night of September 12th, 1997. According to her accounts of their conversations, the officers tell her that they didn't check the drivers for alcohol because there were no indications that alcohol was being consumed that night. They say there was no evidence of drinking. This is their response to the questions I asked Ms. Stephany to pose. No evidence of drinking they say.

When Ms. Stephany repeats the above response from the RCMP I know that something isn't right. A few months later, after really thinking about it, I know I need more conclusive evidence about the way the police broke up that first important party. On June 25, 1999, I filed a freedom of information request with the RCMP in Ottawa. Specifically, I asked for information on three incidents, and here's what I wrote:

1) Langley RCMP—Sept. 12, 1997—Request time of call reporting loud party at a home on 208 street near

28ᵗʰ avenue. Request time of police arriving at party, how many officers and cars responded and details of how they broke up party and dispersed the people, including if any breathalyzers for alcohol were taken.

2) Langley RCMP—Sept. 12, 1997—Second call to break up large group of teens at 208 St., and 36 Ave. gravel pit. Request time of call, response time, number of police cars and officers who attended plus how they dispersed the crowd. Were any breathalyzers taken?

3) Surrey and Langley RCMP—Sept. 13, 1997— around
12:30am—Request times and number of 911 calls to accident on
28 Ave.—Stokes Pit.

It takes almost six months for the RCMP in Ottawa to respond, but respond they do. Here is their letter in full:

Aug. 4, 1999

Dear Ms. Adamson:

This is in response to your request for information under the Access to Information Act which was received on July 12, 1999.

I first wish to point out that the specific information you have requested is not recorded in such a way as to be retrieved. I should also point out that the Act does not require us to "create" records/information for the purpose of responding to a request. However, I will try and address your requests and I hope the following may be of some use to you.

With respect to two incidents occurring in the Langley Detachment area of 208 St. and 28ᵗʰ then 36 Ave. we have been unable to locate any one specific incident report pertaining to these locations. A search of several "crime types" for the date of 97-09-12 has surfaced only three incidents which are recorded on the Police Information Retrieval System (PIRS) which may or may not match the incidents you are inquiring about.

Attached are copies of all the accessible records from these incident reports. Please note that a portion of the records have been severed, pursuant to subsection 25 of the Act. The portions severed have been exempted under subparagraph 16(1)(a)(i) of the Act. I have enclosed a copy for your easy reference. Again these were the only recorded incidents which may or may not be the incidents you have identified.

With respect to the time and number of 911 calls received by the Langley and Surrey Detachments, Langley Detachment advises that from their records they can only state that between 0001 and 100 hour on 97-09-13 they received seventeen (17) 911 calls via the "Greater Vancouver Regional District (GVRD)" response centre. Langley cannot determine how many, if any, were in response to the Stokes Pit incident. They have further advised that they received eight (8) telephone calls directly to the Detachment during the same time period but again it is not known if any relate to the Stokes Pit incident. Lastly, Langley advises that audio tapes, which record police radio communications are only retained for four (4) months and then erased.

Our Surrey Detachment advises that they only retain a printed copy of the 911 calls received from the GVRD for a period of 30 days at which time they are destroyed. Further, that their audio tapes which record police radio communications are only retained for four (4) months and then erased.

I am advised that the GVRD response centre is a provincially funded unit which receives all 911 calls for the greater Vancouver district and then reroutes the call to the fire, ambulance or police agency responsible for the area in which the incident has occurred. You may wish to contact or access their records in the event they have the information you are seeking.

I have enclosed a copy of the PIRS printout as well as a copy of a briefing note prepared on the Stokes Pit incident. Please note that portions of the records have been severed, pursuant to subsection 25 of the Act. The portions severed have been exempted under subparagraph 16(1)(a)(i) of the Act.

Should you wish clarification on any matter concerning your request, Cpl. J.J. C[] may be reached at (613) 993-8758. Please ensure you provide the file number which appears on this letter.

You have a right to bring a complaint before the Information Commissioner concerning any aspect of your request. Notice of complaint should be addressed to:

> The Information Commissioner of Canada
> 112 Kent Street, 3rd Floor
> Ottawa, Ontario
> K1A 1H3

Your application fee receipt in the amount of
$5.00 is attached.

Yours truly,
G.W. C[], Sgt.
A/Departmental Privacy and
Access to Information Coordinator
1200 Vanier Parkway, Ottawa, Ontario K1A
0R2

Attached to the above introduction was the following
"Briefing Note" with file number 97-87455. I have
indicated the above-mentioned "severed" text with
asterisks (*******).

To: Commissioner, Ottawa
        C.O. "E" Division

Surrey Detachment responded to a report of a motor
vehicle/pedestrian accident with multiple victims at
00:25hrs., Saturday, April [should read September!]
13, 1997. The accident occurred near the intersection
of 192 St. and 28 Ave. Surrey, B.C., which is located
in a largely rural area of Surrey, very close to the
Surrey/Langley city limits. Upon arrival members
found numerous victims at the scene suffering from a
variety of injuries which ranged from very serious to
minor cuts, bruises, and abrasions. One seventeen year
old ******* determined to be dead at the scene while
fifteen other young people were transported to various
hospitals throughout the Lower Mainland. Some were
treated and released, others were held overnight and

then released and six remain in hospital. One seventeen year old ****** suffered serious neck and spinal injuries ******************. Another seventeen year old ****** suffered two broken legs and is experiencing some serious medical difficulties of an, as yet, undetermined cause. At this time it is not believed that any are suffering from any life-threatening complications.

It would appear that these youths were some of the same people who had previously been ejected from a very large house party by members of Langley Detachment and subsequently moved on again from yet another site within Langley Detachment area. Ultimately, most of them found their way to the location where the accident occurred in Surrey Detachment area. In all likelihood these youth, who were estimated to number one hundred and fifty (150) to two hundred (200) had just arrived at the location in order to continue their party. Many were on various parts of the roadway and some were in possession of alcohol. The house party attended by Langley members earlier in the evening required approximately twenty-five personnel in order to disperse the crowd and our members were reportedly pelted with beer bottles and other debris during that incident.

A ********* male has been arrested and charged with the following charges under the Criminal Code:

1. Criminal Negligence Causing Death

2. Dangerous Operation of a Motor Vehicle

3. Impaired Driving

4. Fail to Remain at the Scene of an Accident

Further charges are likely once our investigation is complete.

*******************. Our investigation is continuing however, it would appear that we have substantial evidence to support the charges which have been layed to this point.

At 13:00 [on Sunday, September 14th, at H.D. Stafford School] C/Supt T.P. SMITH, O.I.C. Surrey Detachment along with members of Surrey and Langley Detachments and representatives of the Langley School District held a public meeting to which all concerned youth and parents were invited, as were the media. The purpose of the meeting was to:

1. Provide factual information regarding the extent and nature of injuries as we know them.

2. Dispel rumours that were circulating.

3. Provide an opportunity and encourage members of the general public to come forward with any additional information that might be helpful.

It had been determined that there were a number of completely erroneous reports circulating that in fact three youths were dead, not just one, and others such as at least one person had suffered an amputation of a limb. These rumours were leading to a growing sense of anger among the young people and some threats of retaliation and violence. Victim Services personnel were on hand from both Langley and Surrey Detachments and members of Surrey Traffic Unit attended ready to accept additional information from the public. The meeting met with resounding endorsement from the school district and the parents and approximately 10 young people have come forward to offer more information as a result of the meeting. Members and Victim Services personnel from both detachments will continue to work with school district staff and counsellors to assist in whatever capacity is required.

It is anticipated that this incident will receive both local and national media coverage.

(T.P. S[]) C/Supt.
O.I.C. Surrey Detachment

I find it interesting to read in the above report that RCMP "members were reportedly pelted with beer bottles," especially after one or more RCMP officers told the Coroner's investigator that there was no evidence of alcohol consumption at the party on 208 Street. This bothers me, but then again, there is nothing I can do about it. Or is there? Nothing from the Coroner's investigator's conversation with Langley RCMP is in writing, so there is no proof of that conversation except her word. However, I can try to make the Langley Detachment aware of their culpability for this tragedy. And so I do.

On July 13, 2000, I meet with Langley RCMP Inspector C.W. B, Sergeant J. McN, and Corporal M. S, at the Langley Detachment in Murrayville. In this meeting I detail the events of September 12th and 13th, 1997, and explain how the actions of our police officers in Langley contributed to the carnage at Stokes Pit. I suggest that their fellow officers—twenty-five in total—might be, in part, responsible for my daughter's death.

I relay how these young people were standing on land and drinking, confident they would be staying there for awhile. Most of these drinkers had no intention of driving at that specific hour, but were put on the road by the police much sooner than they had anticipated. When one of the officers suggests that the drivers had to be held accountable for their own decisions, I countered with: "What seventeen year-old boy, who is drinking illegally, is going to confront a burly police officer and refuse to leave a party when ordered to do so?" Really, what teenager is going to get in the face of, and argue with, a police officer, especially when they've been drinking? I'll bet very few. I suspect most teens would slip away and remove themselves from the presence of the police as quickly as possible. And that's exactly what happened. I ask these three officers what we are going to do about this apparent practice of putting drunks on Langley's roads late at night?

The officers are very polite and seem interested in doing something about this problem. Inspector B promises to work on a new policy for the Langley RCMP that will address this issue and hopefully end this dangerous practice. He says I will be hearing back from him soon. And I do:

July 21, 2000

Dear Ms. Adamson,

This letter is further to your meeting on July 13, 2000 with Sergeant J. McN[], Corporal M. S and me. First, I would like to thank you for taking the time to attend the office and speak with us and make your concerns known. As a result of our meeting I have distributed a memo to our officers reminding them of the need to be ever vigilant when dealing with persons, particularly youth, if our officer's intention is to have the persons they are dealing with drive a vehicle. As discussed at our meeting, there are a number of factors that must be taken into consideration when trying to disperse a large group of people and sometimes the most expedient method is not always the safest.

Should you have further concerns or would like to discuss this or any other issues further please feel free to contact me at 532-3293.

Yours truly,

C.W. B[], Inspector
Operations Officer

I am pleased to receive this letter from Inspector B, but disappointed over his use of the word "memo" instead of a written policy that would directly identify the procedures to be used in breaking up a large party of teens. I am being asked to take this police officer at his word and I wonder if he is just paying me lip service to keep me quiet; but then, thankfully, I am proven wrong.

A couple of weeks into August, 2000, and a few weeks after I receive the above letter, my daughter Laura is at a house party with her friend Nicole. According to the two girls, aged eighteen and nineteen at the time, several police cars pull up and the officers start to break up the party. The party-goers are ordered to leave the property because the neighbours are complaining about the noise. As people start up their cars in preparation to leave, Laura and Nicole approach a female Langley RCMP officer and ask her if she's going to check the drivers' sobriety before sending them on the road. This officer's response is to wave her hand in the air and state, "That's their problem!" Laura and Nicole are shocked and disappointed at this attitude from someone who is paid to "Serve and Protect." Her callousness merits mention in this book. Laura drives Nicole and herself home safely that night (she has not been drinking), but she worries all the way home about the sudden surge of drunk drivers on the road from this one party.

The next day when Laura tells me what happened, I am outraged. I feel that the officers I met with were just placating me, just nodding their heads and smiling while pretending to care. I need to think first on what I am going to do about this, and I decide to sit on it for a few weeks before storming into the Langley Detachment to complain. Good thing I waited.

In early September, four or five weeks after Laura's party-raid, my nephew Steven has a completely different experience with the Langley RCMP during a house party. He tells me how impressed he is when the RCMP check each and every driver for alcohol consumption before letting them leave the property. He says the police actually stop some people from leaving until they can get a sober driver for their cars. I am thrilled to hear this. A year later he is at another house party in Langley that is interrupted by the arrival of our local police, and once again they check all the drivers for impairment before sending them on the road. I am proud to report that this nephew of mine, now a young adult, is currently applying to become an RCMP officer.

I am so relieved with this turnaround. I guess this "policy" took some time to take hold, but it now seems that it is common practice with Langley RCMP to stop any vehicle from leaving a house party until the driver is cleared for intoxication. Thank God. Maybe I did make a difference. I hereby extend my apologies for initially distrusting our local RCMP. I most sincerely thank the above three RCMP officers for taking my concerns seriously and, consequently, helping to make Langley a safer place in which to drive at night.

4.8   Children's Commission Fatality Review Report

Two investigations were conducted simultaneously into Heidi's untimely death. The Coroner's Office spent a year and a half investigating the circumstances surrounding Heidi's death, and then the Victoria-based Children's Commission spent over two years putting together their report on an even broader range of circumstances surrounding Heidi's tragedy. The Children's Commission Fatality Review Report, finished and released in January of 2000, examines not only the hospital treatment she received, but the events of the evening of the accident, as well as drunk driving issues and the boy's sentencing. The original report is twenty pages long and I'm providing it here in full, with one exception. I removed the extensive hospital portion because, in most parts, I find it replicates the Coroner's Report

Children's Commission Fatality Review Report

Year of Death: 1997

Sex: Female

Age at Death: 17 years

Legal Status of Child: Living with at least 1 biological/adoptive parent

Child in Care: No

MCF [Ministry of Children and Families] Services: No (within last 12 months)

Aboriginal: No

Police Investigation: Yes

Manner of Death: MVA Traffic Accident; Pedestrian; Vehicle driver

Alcohol: involved

Cause of Death: Crushing injuries; multiple

Premise of Death: Institutions; Hospital; Acute Care

Classification of Death: Accident

What the Children's Commission Learned from this Review

- Ongoing educational efforts emphasizing the dangers of combining alcohol and driving are necessary.

- This review identifies issues related to medical care which require further review.

1. IMMEDIATE CIRCUMSTANCES OF DEATH

In late evening, a group of 100-200 young persons was gathered at a site adjacent to an east-west rural roadway. This is a remote, wooded location with no residences in the vicinity and no artificial lighting. The site was popular for weekend and evening parties. Land to the south of the road is municipally owned and is designated parkland [Stokes Pit]. The property to the north of the road is privately owned. The roadway is a municipal thoroughfare. The posted speed limit at the site is 50 kph.

Shortly after midnight a crowd of youth was dispersed along both sides of the roadway. A vehicle travelling westward along the roadway suddenly swerved into the assembled crowd, striking numerous bystanders. The vehicle stopped momentarily, reversed and then continued westward, colliding with another vehicle before leaving the scene of the accident.

The following is an eyewitness account of the actual occurrence, as recorded by police:

"About 15-20 minutes after arriving at [the scene], [the witness] observed [the suspect vehicle] parked on the south side of the road. [the witness] observed a guy get into the [vehicle] by himself... the guy was joking with his friends then got into the vehicle. Next thing the guy pulled out almost onto the roadway facing eastbound.

[The witness] saw an unknown male person sitting on top of the vehicle's trunk and stating words to the effect 'I'm not getting off, I'm not letting you drive.' The vehicle left with one occupant eastbound and drove off quickly. [The witness] continued talking with his friends for approximately 10 minutes and recalls walking westbound towards a crowd of people. [The witness] saw headlights coming from behind him and turned around. He grabbed a friend and said, 'let's get off the road.'

The two kept walking and when they were about 20 feet from the crowd heard people screaming and saying 'Oh my God.' [The witness] observed the vehicle hitting a whole bunch of people and persons were flying into the ditches. The vehicle came to a stop, braking, then reversed backwards one or two feet. The scene was chaos—lots of screaming, people yelling call 911. The vehicle took off again forwards, squealing its tires westbound. The vehicle swerved and hit a parked vehicle on the left side of the roadway. The vehicle sideswiped the [parked vehicle] with its front left fender and took off westbound and... turned right on [street].

[The witness] met up with a friend and both looked for another friend. They saw people lying on the shoulder of the roadway. [The witness] observed [the deceased youth] lying face up, with her head towards the north on the shoulder of the roadway. [The witness] approached the deceased girl because he is first-aid trained. He observed blood coming out of her nose and the sides of her mouth. Someone grabbed [the witness] and said she was dead. Other injured persons were noticed in the ditch and on the shoulder of the road. Everyone was helping everyone."

From a statement made by another witness, police ascertained that the (minor) driver of the vehicle had spent most of the day preceding the incident with a friend. They had driven to school in the morning, spent time together after school and met again in early evening. The driver and his friend were able to acquire alcohol from a local establishment, and went to a park to consume it.

They next drove to a nearby school, and from there to a house party where more alcohol was apparently consumed. Approximately two hours before the incident, the driver and his friend left the house party, following arrival of the police, and drove to a larger party at an isolated site. They left this party shortly afterwards and arrived at the incident site approximately 60-90 minutes before it occurred.

At this location the driver was seen to get out of his

vehicle and speak to several persons. About 20 minutes prior to the incident, the driver had a disagreement with a friend over his state of intoxication and his ability to drive safely. The friend insisted that he give over his car keys but the driver maintained that he was not intoxicated. He retained his keys and drove away from the scene alone.

The driver returned to the gathering shortly afterwards, travelling westbound along the roadway. He then swerved without warning into the crowd of persons standing along the roadway, killing one youth immediately and injuring 15 others. Numerous witnesses gave varying estimates of the vehicle's rate of speed. Several asserted that it appeared to be exceeding the speed limit of 50 km/h at the time the bystanders were struck.

The youth who is the subject of this review [Heidi Klompas] was found at the scene with severe leg injuries and was taken to hospital. Another youth [Ashley Reber] died immediately at the scene and her death is the subject of a previous Children's Commission review (File No. 97-01473). One victim [Vanessa Glasser] suffered a serious spinal injury, while eight others were treated at hospital for cuts, abrasions and other injuries. Other victims were treated for less serious injuries at the scene by an EHS triage unit, and did not require transport to hospital.

The youth who is the subject of this review was transferred to a tertiary care hospital shortly after admission to the first hospital. While at the first hospital, she experienced a grand mal seizure. At the second hospital, the youth underwent orthopedic surgery on her legs and later developed complications for which she was treated. Three weeks following admission the youth suffered a massive hemorrhage, from which she did not recover. Brain death was confirmed four days later.

2. BACKGROUND INFORMATION

Victim:

The youth was a grade 12 student who lived with her parents and siblings. She was an active and well-liked student. She had no identified problems and had no involvement with the Ministry for Children and Families.

Hospital: [this portion has been removed]

Driver:

According to police, the 17-year-old driver of the vehicle did not have a criminal record and had no record of driving infractions. He recently purchased his vehicle using funds that he had earned and saved. The driver had been previously detained for being a minor in possession of liquor. These incidents did not result in a charge and were not motor-vehicle related.

The driver was an average student who did not have a troubled school record. Following the incident, he did not return to school. Instead, the school district provided him with an alternative educational program for the balance of the school year. He has received counselling to assist him in coping with the impact of the event. The driver was not known to the Ministry of Children and Families.

As a result of the incident, the driver was subsequently charged with dangerous driving causing bodily harm and dangerous driving causing death.

The driver later pled guilty to these charges, and was sentenced as a young offender to three months open custody, a three-year driving prohibition and two years probation. He was also ordered to perform community work service hours comprised of presentations to other youth on aspects of driver safety. In addition, this individual was ordered by the court to formally apologize to the injured victims of the incident and to their families.

The driver of the vehicle and the youth who is the subject of this review attended the same school. According to the principal, this had a divisive effect upon the student body, particularly following the death of the youth and during the ensuing criminal proceedings.

Grief Response:

This incident had a significant impact upon students, their families and the community in general, as most of the victims attended schools within the same school district. In response, the district deployed its Trauma Response Team, assisted by counselling staff from a community agency and the local mental health centre. These supports remained in place during the week following the incident, and were reinstituted when it was learned that the youth who is the subject of this review had died in hospital. Several of the district schools held memorial services.

3. OTHER REVIEWS/INVESTIGATIONS

Police:

Police were called to the scene approximately 20 minutes after the incident had occurred. One officer recorded his impression of the confusion he found upon arrival:

> "Attended at scene of fatal MVA at [location]. Upon attendance, I viewed a scene of total chaos. There were a number of ambulances, fire-trucks and other police personnel from both [community] detachments. There were hundreds of teenagers on the roadway interspersed with the emergency personnel. Efforts were immediately made to clear out the teens from the injured so as to move the ambulances out of the area.
>
> Once the scene was under control, observations were made of the area. The roadway was dry, the air was cool and damp but a clear night. On the roadway, there were distinct acceleration marks along with a swerve indication. A body covered with a yellow blanket was on the north side of the road and several persons with various injuries were scattered throughout the ditch."

A police traffic analyst attended the scene and concluded there was little available evidence to assist in his investigation:

> "The scene had been so contaminated by the number of people that were at the scene at the time of the incident that they may have walked many times over some of the evidence effectively obliterating it. Add to this that several people, civilians and police picked up several pieces of the suspect car from where they found them on the road, as well as the fact that the second car

involved [make] was moved away from the scene to the side of the road prior to police arrival."

Police interviewed scores of witnesses in connection with this incident, most of whom were in agreement concerning the sequence of events immediately prior to, during and after the collision.

At the scene, police were able to locate several persons who identified the owner of the vehicle. Other witnesses stated that the owner was driving the vehicle at the time of the incident, and also identified this person to police.

Approximately one hour after the incident occurred, police received a telephone report that a vehicle corresponding to the one involved in the incident had been stolen and damaged earlier in the evening. This report was made by the owner of the vehicle. When police arrived at the owner's residence the vehicle was parked outside. The owner stated that he had found the vehicle and driven it home. Police arrested this individual and charged him with offences related to the incident. This person was later confirmed to be the driver of the vehicle at the scene of the incident.

A breathalyzer test administered to the driver three hours after the incident yielded a blood alcohol level of 0.16 per cent, and the same reading twenty minutes later. The vehicle was seized and transported for inspection.

Two days after the event occurred, police held a public meeting at a local school, as the incident had had a significant impact on members of the community. Approximately 40 people attended. The purpose of this meeting was to inform the public of the status of the investigation and to encourage witnesses to come forward. The tone of the meeting was subdued but positive in terms of the public's willingness to assist.

Police also held a later meeting with the victims and their families. At this meeting, information was provided concerning the progress of the investigation and likely charges. Representatives of ICBC attended and spoke to questions of insurance liability. A lawyer engaged by one of the families addressed the civil litigation process. Victim Services personnel attended this meeting and were also at the previous public meeting. This service had been actively involved with the victims from the outset of the incident.

A senior police office interviewed in connection with the review has commented that there is an active party scene in the community and that youths regularly gather at one or more of several known sites, some of which are at or near a municipal park. These sites are routinely patrolled, particularly if a gathering is underway or known in advance. Patrols are also increased in the summer months and at school graduation time. Police patrolling is intended to be preventive in nature and is not limited to response to specific complaints. The frequency of such patrols depends upon the frequency of other calls for service occurring at the time. These are calls from the public for immediate police assistance which take precedent over routine patrol duties. The frequency with which youth gatherings are patrolled is also a function of available police resources, which were in short supply in this community at the time the incident occurred. A police helicopter is used occasionally to identify and patrol large gatherings.

The site where the incident occurred is chosen by youth for its relative remoteness, which lessens the chance that a member of the public will make a complaint. The great majority of the youth present at the site that evening were from an adjoining community, and the gathering at the site was unknown to local police until the incident was reported. Many of the youth present had been dispersed by police from an earlier gathering in the adjoining community, and had subsequently reassembled at the incident site in late evening.

Although alcohol was present, witness to the event reported that the gathering was orderly, with arrival of the speeding vehicle constituting the only incident of the evening.

Twenty-two months following the motor vehicle incident, police report that the youth gatherings remain an ongoing problem in the community. Police units dedicated to patrolling known sites are in use, and these have resulted in increased penalties for driving and liquor infractions. The site where the youth who is the subject of this review was injured is apparently less of a problem now than other gathering sites known to police.

Vehicle Mechanical Inspection:

The vehicle involved in the incident was inspected for any mechanical defects or malfunctions in the steering and braking systems that have caused the driver to lose control. None were found.

Coroner:

The Coroner attended the site of the incident and described the aftermath as "one of the worst scenes of carnage" she has seen. Debris was everywhere and the many injured bystanders were being treated by EHS staff and carried to waiting ambulances. Three hours after the event, the Coroner described the scene as still resembling a "war-zone."

An autopsy yielded the following principal findings:

1. Bilateral tibiofibular fractures with open reduction and internal fixation

2. Clinical fat embolism syndrome with adult respiratory distress syndrome, prolonged cerebral edema and multifocal vascular injury

3. Tracheostomy with erosion of anterolateral tracheal wall, right side and tracheo-innominate artery fistula

The Coroner's Judgement of Inquiry gives a brief account of the incident, followed by a summary of the results of an extensive medical investigation completed by the Coroners Service. This summary discusses the treatment that the youth received for her injuries at two hospitals and corresponds to the account given in Section 2 of this report. The Judgement of Inquiry includes the following conclusion and recommendations:

"The circumstances surrounding this fatality were investigated extensively by [the police]. Additionally, the medical management has been carefully reviewed in detail. I find therefore the [named deceased] came to her death on [date] from unnatural causes; to wit, "anoxic brain injury due to massive blood loss due to complications of treatment for multiple blunt force injuries and long bone fractures by means of impact with motor vehicle." I find the death of [named deceased] is unnatural and accidental. I make the following recommendations:

1. To the Medical Director of [the first hospital]: That Educational Rounds be conducted in the Emergency Department concerning the assessment, treatment and risks associated with patients who present to the Emergency Room with multiple, comminuted long bone fractures.

2. To the Medical Director of [the tertiary care hospital]: That Educational Rounds be conducted in the Intensive Care Unit and the Department of Respirology to review the measures that can be taken to prevent erosion and rupture of the innominate artery that may result from placement of a tracheostomy tube."

4. ANALYSIS

This youth died in hospital as a result of complications arising from the treatment of injuries sustained as a pedestrian in a motor vehicle incident. She was among a group of young persons standing at the side of a road when the driver of a vehicle swerved into the crowd, seriously injuring numerous pedestrians and immediately killing one other youth.

Medical Care

Finding: Issues relating to medical care have been identified.

The youth arrived at hospital with severe fractures to both her legs.

The investigation of the medical management in this case conducted by the B.C. Coroners Service found that an orthopedic surgeon was notified of the youth's injuries approximately 35 minutes after she arrived at hospital but did not attend until seven hours later. This finding is confirmed by a notation on the youth's chart indicating the time that this physician was called. X-rays of the youth's injuries had been taken 15 minutes earlier and were available for interpretation.

The orthopedic surgeon's examination of the youth on the following morning indicated the need for an immediate operation. However, a series of seizures occurred while the youth was being prepared for the procedure and surgery did not commence for another seven hours, after transfer to a tertiary care hospital.

Following surgery, the youth was diagnosed with fat emboli syndrome. This condition results when globules of fat obstruct blood vessels, and frequently occurs after fracture of long bones. The condition can cause disseminated intravascular coagulation and convulsions, especially during the first 12 to 24 hours following injury, when fat emboli are most likely to occur. It is not known if a more timely surgical response could have prevented the development of fat emboli syndrome, however the delay between the time an orthopedic specialist was notified of the youth's injuries and her examination approximately seven hours later, seems to have been excessive.

A review of literature related to orthopedic surgery by a pediatric consultant to the Children's Commission found no standard for commencing repair of long bone fractures, only that fixing of the fractures should occur "as soon as possible within 24 hours to prevent the development of fat emboli syndrome."

The medical director for the hospital reported to the Children's Commission that they are in the process of completing an internal review of this case and that it will be presented at educational rounds to the hospital, including the orthopedic surgery division, in the fall of this year.

Recommendation # 1

That the College of Physicians and Surgeons of B.C. review the medical care provided to this youth with reference to the delay in examination by an orthopedic surgeon.

Finding: The development of a tracheo-innominate fistula with rupture to an innominate artery leading to the trachea was unusual and unforeseen. The cause of erosion at the site is not known.

Two weeks following the motor vehicle incident the youth underwent surgery for placement of a tracheostomy tube, intended to prevent complications associated with extended ventilation. One week later, she suddenly began to bleed effusively through the tracheostomy dressing site.

Her airway and lungs filled with blood and she arrested, requiring prolonged resuscitation to restore a pulse. As a consequence of this event the youth suffered extensive brain damage and was removed from life supports four days later.

Recommendation #2

That the College of Physicians and Surgeons of B.C. review the procedure followed during surgery for placement of a tracheostomy tube.

Road and Weather Conditions

Finding: Road and weather conditions were not factors in this incident.

It was dark at the time of the incident, with no artificial lighting in the vicinity. The sky was clear, and pavement was dry.

Mechanical Condition of the Vehicle

Finding: This was not a factor in this incident.

The vehicle was mechanically inspected and found not to have defective or malfunctioning steering or braking systems.

Speed

Finding: This was reportedly a factor in this incident.

Due to severe contamination of the incident scene by the estimated 100-200 people present, a collision analysis could not be carried out by police. The speed of the vehicle at the time of impact could not therefore be accurately determined. Several bystanders who witnessed the incident reported that the vehicle appeared to be travelling in excess of the posted speed limit of 50 km/h when it struck the pedestrians.

ICBC considers young motorists to be an important target group for its safe-driving education strategies and programs. Drivers in British Columbia who are between the ages of 16 and 20 years comprise only 6% of all licensed drivers, but this group accounted for over 15% of all police-attended collisions in 1997 (latest year for which data is available).

By comparison, drivers in the 21-50 age group comprise 64% of all licensed drivers and accounted for 64% of collisions, while those drivers over the age of 50 comprise 30% of all drivers, but accounted for only 17% of all police-attended collisions in 1997. More males were involved in collisions than females in all age categories.

Moreover, the percentage of drivers who became involved in a personal injury or fatal collision in 1997 is inversely proportional to age throughout the entire range, with the highest rate at 2.5% for 16-18 year old drivers, decreasing to a rate of 1.64% for 21-25 year olds, compared with a collision rate of 0.85% for drivers in the 36-40 range.

Youth are at even greater risk when only motor vehicle fatalities are considered. The 16-20 age group accounted for 13% of all driver fatalities in 1997, and 29% of all vehicle passenger fatalities.

Concerning the category of fatal collisions where unsafe speed was a contributing factor; in 1997, 21% of all drivers and 51% of all passengers killed while in a vehicle travelling at unsafe speed were in the 16-20 age group. Unsafe speed was the single most frequently contributing factor, occurring in 36% of all 1997 fatal collisions.

When alcohol-related collisions are examined, the fatality rates for youth are similarly over-represented to a significant degree. The 16-20 age group accounted for 16% of all driver fatalities and 39% of all passenger fatalities in alcohol-related collisions in 1997.

In another recent fatality report (File # 97-01350), the Children's Commission made the following recommendation:

> "That ICBC incorporate a zero tolerance policy to any traffic violations involving excessive speed, as well as other dangerous driving offences, during both the six month learner period and the 18 month intermediate period of the new Graduated Licensing Program."

In May, 1998, ICBC provided the following response:

> "Any driving prohibitions or withdrawal of driving privileges is within the jurisdiction of the Office of the Superintendent of Motor Vehicles (OSMV).

> In the development of the Graduated Licensing Program [GLP], ICBC consulted with the OSMV to consider changing the threshold at which a driver within the GLP will be prohibited from driving. For example, currently a driver must accumulate seven to ten driver penalty points in a single year before they are prohibited from driving. ICBC has suggested a

revision to this policy so that drivers within the GLP would in fact be prohibited from driving at four to six penalty points.

Further, the OSMV is conducting a full review of the driver penalty point structure to determine whether the penalty points assigned to various offences are appropriate. For example, offences such as excessive speeding and failure to stop for police result in three penalty points. After the review of the driver penalty point structure, these and other offences may result in more penalty points thereby resulting in a driver prohibition for a single offence of the nature."

In October, 1998, ICBC provided the following follow-up response:

"Any driving prohibitions or withdrawal of driving privileges is within the jurisdiction of the Office of the Superintendent of Motor Vehicles (OSMV).

To date, the OSMV is still conducting its review of the driver penalty point system. Considerable research has been conducted, and a number of high-level recommendations are currently being considered. These recommendations require a significant amount of policy analysis before they can be finalized and submitted to government for decision."

Driver Impairment

Finding: This was a factor in this incident.

A sample taken from the driver three hours following the incident showed a blood alcohol level of 0.16 per cent.

Driving Record/Driver Experience

Finding: This was not cited by police as a factor in this fatality, however the driver was relatively inexperienced.

He was 15 months past his sixteenth birthday at the time of the incident and therefore could not have had more than this amount of legal driving experience in British Columbia, in addition to time spent driving under a learner's permit. The vehicle involved in the incident belonged to the driver, and had been recently purchased by him.

Had this individual applied for his driver's license after August 1, 1998, he would have entered the Learner stage of the Graduated Licensing program and been subject to the following driving restrictions for a minimum of six months (three months if an ICBC-approved driver education course is completed):

– Must be accompanied in the vehicle by a fully-licensed, adult supervisor.

– Must maintain zero blood alcohol content at all times when driving.

– Must display a "new driver" sign in the vehicle.

– Is permitted to carry only two passengers at any time, one of whom must be the adult supervisor.

– Is permitted to drive only between five o'clock in the morning and midnight.

Other Human Factors

Finding: Human error was a factor in this fatality.

The driver of the vehicle pleaded guilty to dangerous driving offences in connection with this incident, indicating that he did not exercise due caution when attempting to pass through the large number of bystanders assembled along both sides of the road at the site. Numerous witnesses stated that the driver actually swerved into the crowd, for unknown reasons.

Access to Trauma Services

Finding: Emergency response to notification of this incident was prompt and adequate.

The 911 call was received approximately 20-30 minutes after the incident is believed to have occurred. This gap in time remains unexplained. However, confusion at the scene, coupled with the immediate needs of so many injured persons, may have accounted for the delay. There are no residences or telephone booths in the immediate vicinity, and the source of the 911 call is not known.

Nine ambulances responded to this emergency, and transported ten patients to four hospitals. One youth was found dead at the scene, and was not transported to hospital.

The first ambulance arrived at the scene five minutes after being dispatched. The next arrived nine minutes later. Six additional ambulances arrived within the following 13 minutes. The last ambulance arrived half an hour later.

Thirty-six minutes after the arrival of the first ambulance, seven ambulances had departed the scene for different hospitals, carrying a total of ten injured victims, while two ambulances remained at the scene to act as triage units. Transport time from the site to hospital took between 10 and 40 minutes, depending upon the destination.

The youth who is the subject of this review was transported to the hospital nearest the site. She was then transferred by ambulance between hospitals several hours after the incident occurred, in order to receive more specialized medical services.

5. SUMMARY OF CHILDREN'S COMMISSION RECOMMENDATIONS

Recommendation # 1

That the College of Physicians and Surgeons of B.C. review the medical care provided to this youth with reference to the delay in examination by an orthopedic surgeon.

Recommendation # 2

That the College of Physicians and Surgeons of B.C. review the procedure followed during surgery for placement of a tracheostomy tube.

6. SUMMARY OF RESPONSE TO RECOMMENDATIONS

Re: Recommendation # 1

College of Physicians and Surgeons of B.C.—November 1999

"The College will obtain information from the hospital and from Dr. [name] allowing for review of this matter."

Re: Recommendation # 2

College of Physicians and Surgeons of B.C.—November 1999

"The College will contact the Medical Director of the hospital to determine who the physicians were who were involved in the care of the patient and to seek responses from the hospital and those physicians with regard to the above matter.

When the information has been received and analyzed, the College will provide you with a detailed response."

NEXT STEPS

The Children's Commission will request additional infor-mation about the status of implementation of the recommendations at regular intervals, for up to a year. as required.

END OF DOCUMENT: Children's Commission Fatality Review Report dated January 26, 2000, pages 1 through 20.

This is another good example of a comprehensive investigation into Heidi's death by a government agency. I am satisfied the investigator did a thorough job in identifying the areas needing improvement and, therefore, I do not feel the need to comment on this report. I thank the Commissioner for taking the time, almost two years, to conduct his investigation and complete this report.

Untitled

I was wondering how you're doing,
And if it's really nice up there?
I've really, really missed you,
I feel a chill in the air.

I'm wondering if you're happy,
And we're all hoping that you are.
Is it really true that now,
You're up amongst the stars.

Ya, I'm still pretty bitter,
That he cut your life so short.
I'm feeling pretty guilty though,
But those feelings I can't yet sort.

There's a lot of unanswered questions,
And so much left unexplained.
So pardon us if we still cry,
Sometimes we just cannot refrain.

Christina Williamson
1998

4.9   College of Physicians and Surgeons of B.C.

The College of Physicians and Surgeons of B.C. is an organization comprised of licensed doctors; it has the mandate to oversee the licensing of doctors and surgeons in the province of British Columbia. One of the purposes of this organization is to protect the public from incompetent and dangerous doctors by removing licences to practice medicine in this province. The elected members of each year's board examine the complaints made by the public and respond to these complaints in the form of a written review. The College also responds to inquiries made by other institutions, such as the Children's Commission and the Coroner's Office.

The Judgement of Inquiry is a five page document that summarizes the full Coroner's Report and gives recommendations to both hospitals. It is completed May 13th, 1999, but is not released to the media until July 9th, 1999. It causes a virtual news frenzy. I receive my copy of this report just days before it is made public, and only after hounding the Coroner's office for this document for months. I understood that it would be completed by the end of March, so since then I have been phoning the Coroner's office for a copy. The official, and final, copy is dated May 13th, 1999, so I don't know why it takes so long to be made public. The day it is released to the public I am out doing errands and come home to find two television news vans parked on my front lawn awaiting my return. The crews from BCTV and CBC news set up on my front and backyards, respectively. This takes me by surprise and I am quite unprepared to appear on the six o'clock news this evening. But there I am, telling the world how I feel about this Coroner's report that details how my daughter died needlessly after being taken to a couple of lower mainland hospitals with only two broken legs. How does one prepare for this?

Once the shock of the released report hits the television news, the newspapers follow up with stories on Heidi and the mismanagement of her injuries. My telephone answering machine is filled with calls from sympathetic members of the public who want me to know I am not alone and that many of them have also suffered at the hands of incompetent doctors. I am overwhelmed with calls and can't return many of them because there are just too many. The public is concerned. So am I but I feel I need to review the final investigation before deciding what I am going to do about it.

I know that people in Victoria are still working on the Children's Commission's investigation, so I patiently wait another six to seven months for the release of this Report. The Children's Commission Report is dated January 26, 2000, and is released in February 2000. When I have a chance to really absorb the thirty-page full Coroner's Report, the five-page Judgement of Inquiry, and the twenty-page Children's Commission Report, I write to the College of Physicians and Surgeons of B.C. I ask them several questions about Heidi's care based on what I've read in these Reports:

RE: Peace Arch District Hospital:

1. I ask the College to investigate why the only orthopaedic surgeon "On Call" on September 13th, 1997, did not come in when repeatedly called to do so.

2. I ask the College to explain why the attending physician did not transfer Heidi to another hospital.

3. I ask the College to investigate the allegations that a certain surgeon planned an "immediate" operation for Heidi when he had told me he was going first to another hospital. (I specifically ask the College to "obtain the surgery and operating room

records for that morning from both Peace Arch and Langley hospitals." I ask them not to rely on hearsay).

4. I ask the College to investigate the mismanagement of Heidi's lung function and fluid levels by medical personnel.

Re: Royal Columbian Hospital:

5. I ask the College which doctor was specifically in charge of Heidi's tracheostomy site, and why the infection was so badly mishandled; for example, how could a 3cm hole in her trachea go undetected? I ask what measures are now in place to prevent this from happening to other patients.

In my letter, I include my concerns about the RCH doctor who told me they don't "keep vegetables alive in their hospital." I ask the College to think about how his words affected this mother who, just the day before, had seen her daughter safely transferred out of the ICU. My letter is dated March 21, 2000.

The College of Physicians and Surgeons spend nine months putting together their response to my inquiries. I finally receive a ten-page letter from the College, dated December 15, 2000. It has now been three years and two months since Heidi died and the doctors are finally having their say. Their comments are interesting, especially those comments that contradict the findings of the two investigators.

I am printing the complete letter from the College here for your perusal. I have included my rebuttals and comments in square brackets amidst their paragraphs. Fasten your seatbelts.

COLLEGE OF PHYSICIANS & SURGEONS OF
BRITISH COLUMBIA

December 15, 2000

CPSID: CQ 2000-0241

PERSONAL & CONFIDENTIAL

Ms. Catherine S. Adamson

.... Langley, B.C....

Dear Ms. Adamson:

RE: Drs. S.P.B[], J.G. H[], T.E. H[], C.J.N. L[], J.W.
P[], & K.A. Z[]

Further to your letter of concern with regard to
the emergency orthopaedic care provided to your
late daughter, Ms. Heidi Dawn Klompas, and the
subsequent ventilatory care through a tracheostomy
that she received, the College has reviewed this matter
in two ways.

In the first instance the College reviewed your
daughter's care at the request of the Children's
Commission and I believe that a copy of the report
of the Children's Commissioner was sent to you,
although it is not clear whether or not you received a
copy of the College report to the Commissioner. For

your information I enclose a copy of that report with the permission of the Children's Commission.

In addition the College received your own letter of concern and therefore conducted a further review, utilizing the procedures of the complaints process and the expertise of the Quality of Medical Performance Committee of the College. The committee consists of a number of physicians of various disciplines, including orthopaedic surgery and anaesthesia, and two members of the general public appointed by the Minister of Health. In reaching a conclusion, the committee reviewed your letter of concern, the responses of Dr. S.P. B[], J.G. H[], T.E. H[], C.J.N. L[], J.W. P[] and K.A. Z[], and also the relevant portions of the clinical record together with the Coroner's Judgement of Inquiry and the report of the Coroner's investigator.

At the onset the committee members would like to express to you their sympathy for the terrible loss that you have suffered. To lose a child at any time of their life is a tragedy, but Heidi was clearly on the threshold of a successful young life and her death, and the manner of it, was clearly a terrible experience for you and your family.

The committee did identify the main questions within your letter and would like to consider the two critical areas of Heidi's care, the immediate care in the Peace Arch Hospital, and the subsequent management of her tracheostomy and her subsequent death due to a complication of the tracheostomy.

The College understands that Heidi was admitted to Peace Arch Hospital shortly before 0200 hours on the

13th of September, 1997. She had been involved in a motor vehicle accident and had sustained fractures of both bones of both lower legs. These fractures are known as comminuted fractures, that is they were fractures where the bone had been rendered into more than two fragments, but the overlying skin was intact, that is they were not compound fractures.

The orthopaedic surgeon on call, Dr. [] H[], was contacted shortly before 0230 hours and was advised of the clinical situation. He was advised that Heidi's condition was stable, that her fractures were splinted, that the circulation and sensation to her feet was intact, that is there had been no damage to the arteries supplying the lower leg, nor to the nerves involving the lower leg. Heidi was fully alert and orientated and although she had a small swelling over the left forehead and a laceration on the right temple, together with an abrasion of the right cheek bone, there was no evidence that she had a closed head injury. Her oxygen saturations at the time of admission were 97% on room air, that is, she had no respiratory difficulties at that time.

Appropriately Heidi was given morphine intravenously for the pain in her legs prior to the x-rays being performed.

I note from the clinical record and the Coroner's report that you were present in the emergency room at 0215 hours.

As I have indicated, Dr. H[] was contacted at 0230 hours by Dr. [] L[], the emergency room physician at the Peace Arch Hospital and was appraised of Heidi's

clinical condition and the results of the x-rays. Dr. H[]
made no further recommendations for Heidi's care at
that time, as her clinical assessments were reassuring
and the care that she had received up to that time was
completely appropriate.

It is understood from Dr. L[] that she placed a further
call to Dr. H[] sometime over the next four hours
and that it was her understanding that he would be
in shortly to see Heidi. The College has reviewed
the emergency record on this point and would note
that Dr. L[] had excellent clinical records that would
demonstrate a full and appropriate assessment and
appropriate treatment for bilateral comminuted
fractures of the tibia and fibula. In addition, in Dr.
L[]'s handwriting, it states: "Dr. H[] aware 0230—
states will see in am."

In his letter to the College Dr. H[] states:

> "... I have a recollection of receiving only one
> telephone call advising me of the referral. Being
> almost three years ago, it is possible I received
> another telephone call and do not remember it
> today. If I had been under the impression there
> was any urgency to Ms. Klompas' orthopaedic
> management, I would have attended the hospital
> earlier."

Certainly the clinical record would indicate that Dr.
H[] was contacted at 0230 hours, and that he had
stated that he would see Heidi in the morning. There is
no subsequent entry in the clinical record, either in the
nursing notes or in Dr. L[]'s notes that would indicate
that there was any further contact with Dr. H[], nor

that here was any urgent need for him to attend sooner than planned.

Whilst there may have been a subsequent conversation between Dr. L[] and Dr. H[], it is not recorded or commented upon in the material that was reviewed by the College, but Dr. L[] has clear recall of more than one telephone conversation with Dr. H[] and the committee does accept that more than one telephone call was made.

The committee members do recognize that this is an issue of concern for you. The clinical record was carefully reviewed, with particular attention paid to the nursing record. There is no question that initially Heidi was in a great deal of pain. Appropriately, as she was a motor vehicle accident victim, she received morphia in small increments until adequate analgesia was obtained. She was given intravenous antibiotics, as was appropriate. Her oxygen tension was monitored and importantly this remained completely satisfactory right up until the time that she was transferred to the x-ray department for follow up x-rays at the request of Dr. H[].

There is no evidence of any vascular damage or neurological damage, or any other orthopaedic reason for her to be subjected to emergency surgery on an immediate basis. The College is advised [by whom?] that in any hospital in British Columbia, including a tertiary facility, Heidi's injuries would have dictated that she should receive timely surgery as a 12 to 24 hour priority case. It would not have been possible for Dr. H[] to summon the operating room staff in order to operate immediately in the middle of the night, as there was no indication for such an immediate intervention.

Similarly the College is advised that it would have been inappropriate to transfer a patient with uncomplicated bilateral fractures of the tibia and fibula to another centre for immediate surgery. Such a transfer would not have resulted in the surgery being performed sooner elsewhere.

[Courtney Wilson's fractured tibia and fibula (one leg only) from the same accident were surgically corrected by an orthopaedic surgeon at Royal Columbian Hospital at 0500 hours that same morning: four and a half hours after the accident.]

Similarly, given that Heidi's condition was stable and given that the emergency physician had no concern about the status of her fractures, there was no requirement for Dr. H[] to have attended the hospital immediately. Had he done so, then no doubt that would have been comforting to the family, and to Heidi herself, but it would not have resulted in the surgery being performed any earlier, and would not have had any effect upon the subsequent clinical events.

The College is advised that in a similar clinical situation, it would be unusual for an orthopaedic surgeon to attend on an immediate basis anywhere in British Columbia, unless specifically requested to do so. There is no evidence within the clinical record that such a specific request was made of Dr. H[], nor was there any evidence in the clinical record of a clinical need for his immediate attendance.

[I witnessed Dr. L going back to the phone to call in Dr. H several times throughout the early morning, as did JR's father. The parents' agitation over his repeated promises to come in and then not showing up was exacerbated by the distress exhibited by Dr. L and the nurses over his assurances that he'd be right in. This resulted in everyone waiting anxiously for his imminent arrival. The repeated phone calls to Dr. H were, in my opinion, urgent and clear indications by emergency room staff that an orthopaedic surgeon should attend immediately.]

> Heidi's condition was monitored throughout the night and I note that at 0440 hours she was sleeping, but awoke at 0540 hours complaining of leg pain and received a further small dose of morphine intravenously at 0610 hours.

> By 0620 hours she was sleeping again and her oxygen saturation remained satisfactory at 97%.

> Again at 0635 hours she was continuing to sleep, had a normal respiratory rate and a satisfactory oxygen saturation at 96%.

> Heidi was awake at 0730 hours and stated that she felt better and that the pain in her legs was less. The circulation and sensation to both feet were noted to be satisfactory, although it is recorded that the right foot pulses were difficult to palpate.

[The College contradicts itself here: first they state her feet were "satisfactory," then, her "foot pulses were difficult to palpate."]

> At that time her chest was clear to examination and her oxygen saturation was again at approximately 97%. She continued to be drowsy, but remained in satisfactory condition, although at 0800 hours her

temperature was 38.5 C. She was receiving intravenous antibiotics and a fever such as this is sometimes seen in multiple trauma victims, although it does also occur with fat embolism.

Essentially, Heidi presented with the clinical picture of a fit young person who had suffered fractures of the legs and who was appropriately managed through the small hours until she was assessed by the consultant orthopaedic surgeon as was planned.

In his consultation Dr. H[] expressed concern with regard to the possibility of a development of a condition known as a "compartment syndrome." He describes the left lower extremity to have significant swelling with relatively tense skin and it was his impression that the pulses in the feet were somewhat diminished. The examination of her right leg was somewhat similar, but of less concern.

[This is the opposite of what is found later at Royal Columbian: her right leg needed the immediate fasciotomy, and the left leg was done later]

Dr. H[] identified that Heidi needed to be taken to the operating room as soon as that could be arranged, with a view to performing a procedure known as a "fasciotomy" on both sides and a fixation of the fractures using plates.

[In his statement to the College, Dr. H claims she needed surgery "as soon as that could be arranged." Aside from telling us he was going to Langley Hospital to perform a lengthy hip operation and that he'd fix Heidi in the afternoon, he actually goes upstairs at Peace Arch and performs the hip operation there. He left Heidi so he could perform an operation on someone else in the same hospital where a full operating team was assembled and ready to go, yet he tells the College Heidi was his priority.]

> The consultation states that he discussed the complications and consequences of compartment syndrome with you prior to arranging for Heidi to be taken to the operating room. In addition Dr. H[] ordered some further x-rays and Heidi was taken to the x-ray department between 0915 and 0940 hours. At 0940 hours she suddenly had a seizure, vomited a large amount of brown fluid and was returned immediately to the emergency room where emergency care was provided by Dr. P[].
>
> As I have detailed above, this seizure and altered level of consciousness was a sudden event that was not anticipated by the medical or nursing staff.

[Heidi was in extreme pain; her legs were not properly splinted and they kept jostling them when moving her, causing her more pain. It is not uncommon for people to vomit and/or pass out from extreme pain: two events that emergency staff should have been prepared for.]

> Given the circumstances of her injury, a motor vehicle accident in which several pedestrians were run down, there was concern that Heidi's seizure activity could be secondary to an undiagnosed head injury. Her oxygen saturations remained satisfactory prior to and following this seizure.

[According to hospital records, Heidi's oxygen saturation levels dropped after the seizure as follows: at 10:10am to 97%;

at 10:20am to 93%; and at 10:30am to 92%. She required
ventilation to maintain adequate oxygen levels from the time
of her seizure to almost three weeks later. When taken off the
ventilator a few hours later, her oxygen levels dropped as low as
86% (RCH 386).]

Appropriately, portable x-rays were taken of the
cervical spine and the chest and the chest x-ray report
is of particular note. The radiologist noted the lung
fields to be clear. This is a particularly important
finding that I will refer to again later, but essentially
fat embolism usually first affects the lungs and presents
a very typical pattern on chest x-ray. There was no
such change in Heidi's x-ray, although it must be said
that a portable chest x-ray, whilst appropriate in this
emergency setting, is not a very good medium for
anything but emergency diagnosis.

With a working diagnosis that now included a head
injury, Dr. P[] made an immediate telephone call to
Dr. M. M[], the neurosurgeon on call at the Royal
Columbian Hospital, and arrangements were made for
Heidi to be transferred there. Dr. P[] also discussed
the situation with the receiving emergency room
physician at the Royal Columbian Hospital. Heidi was
monitored carefully for any change in her neurological
condition, and by 1110 hours her neurological status
had lightened to the point where she opened her
eyes in response to her name being called. Dr. P[]
very appropriately arranged for a good airway to be
maintained for the process of transfer and Heidi was
transferred at 1130 hours to the Royal Columbian
Hospital. Dr. [] C[] accompanied Heidi in the
ambulance for the purpose of the transfer.

If I may return to the question of when Dr. H[] was going to operate on Heidi, it is clear that he was planning to operate on her at the earliest opportunity. I would like to quote Dr. H[] on this issue:

> "Ms. Adamson has raised concerns about my involvement in other surgeries on September 13, 1997. Although I do not have a recollection of my precise schedule for that day, I have reviewed the records from both the Peace Arch Hospital and Langley Memorial Hospital. These indicate that I was preparing for hip surgery at the Peace Arch Hospital at about the time Ms. Klompas had the seizure. The hip surgery began at 10:15, and I have a recollection of being advised of Ms. Klompas' seizure as I was scrubbing. The records from Langley Memorial Hospital indicate that I performed another hip surgery at that facility beginning at approximately 15:35 on September 13, 1997. I do not know what I said to Ms. Adamson which might have given her the impression that I planned to leave for Langley Memorial Hospital before completing Ms. Klompas' surgery, but it was always my intention to proceed with Ms. Klompas' surgery and with that of the other patient involved in the incident, before travelling to Langley Memorial Hospital to perform the afternoon hip procedure."

[The above is the College's response to my direct request for hospital records that would confirm Dr. H's whereabouts. I specifically asked for something other than hearsay, but they gave me hearsay. It would take me another three years before I obtained the proof of his whereabouts from the Medical

Directors of both hospitals. He was indeed upstairs at Peace Arch performing a hip operation when Heidi was awaiting her surgery. When he told my family members and myself that he was going first to Langley Memorial Hospital before operating on Heidi, he must have been confused about his scheduling for that day. I feel my confusion over his whereabouts is justifiable.]

> The committee would like to make some general comments about fat embolism. It is not a condition that is completely understood, and there remains a debate about a number of features involved in the diagnosis and treatment of fat embolism. In more recent years, the prevention of the fat embolism syndrome by early fracture fixation and patient mobilization has become the focus of a wave of clinical investigation. The clinical signs and symptoms associated with the fat embolism are evident in 0.5% to 2% of patients with long bone fractures.

[The College neglects to cite which medical study these numbers come from, which is interesting simply because they are about 30% lower than the numbers from my sources, with regards to **multiple** fractures. For example, H.J. ten Duis states in his 1997 article, "The fat embolism syndrome," that FES presents itself in "0.5% to 3% of patients who sustained a single long-bone fracture. In multiply injured patients, percentages of up to 30% have been reported. The incidence increases with the number of fractures." Heidi's legs had a total of six separate fractures, according to the radiologist's report. (See the photographs of her x-rays). In addition, Dr. R.B. Ganong, in his 1993 paper, "Fat Emboli Syndrome in Isolated Fractures of the Tibia and Femur," states that in an eleven-year study of otherwise healthy skiers, "thirty-three percent of displaced transverse tibial fractures developed FES." Furthermore, Dr. K. Odegard, in her article, "Fat Embolism: Diagnosis and Treatment," (circa 1993) explains that "Multiple fractures release a greater amount of fat into the marrow vessels than do single fractures, increasing the likelihood of FES."]

However, systemic embolization of marrow fat as a subclinical event occurs with nearly all fractures of long bones, and its direct clinical effect is measured most readily by monitoring the arterial blood gas level. That is, the clinically apparent fat embolism syndrome is rare, but the subclinical embolization of fat into the bloodstream is seen after nearly all lower extremity fractures. The signs and symptoms of fat embolism syndrome are predominately those of adult respiratory stress syndrome. That is the patients develop marked respiratory difficulties, poor oxygen perfusion and have characteristic changes on the chest x-ray. As you will recall, the measurement of Heidi's oxygen saturation throughout the night was entirely satisfactory, and her chest x-ray in the morning, shortly before the seizure, was reported as normal. Certainly there were not the classical changes of fat embolism on the chest x-ray.

Heidi's sudden seizure was the first sign that she had a problem that could be attributed to fat embolism syndrome, and given the nature of her accident, it was not the first diagnosis that was entertained. The College would have no criticism of the emergency staff for their supposition that this was an unrecognized head injury. The recognition of fat embolism syndrome remains a diagnosis of exclusion dependent on a high index of suspicion. The commonest way that the syndrome presents is with evidence of poor oxygen perfusion, respiratory difficulties and poor oxygen saturation. These Heidi did not have.

[Heidi did indeed have poor oxygen saturation. In addition, she also presented with other signs of fat embolism syndrome: rapid heart rate (tachycardia), high temperature, abnormal T-waves, restlessness, drowsiness and confusion (present prior to the seizure, although at the time I thought it was the morphine).]

She did have a raised temperature, noted for the first time at 0800 hours and such a finding is sometimes found in fractures without fat embolism, but in her case it was probably the first subtle sign that the syndrome was developing.

[I agree. "The onset of FES is sudden, with Restlessness [Heidi was squirming] and vague pain in the chest [she complained of upper back pain]. Fever occurs, often in excess of 38.3 C (101 F), with a disproportionately [high] pulse rate. Drowsiness with oliguria [a condition characterized by the excretion of an abnormally small amount of urine (Webster's)] is almost pathognomonic [typical of a disease (Webster's)]" (Prazeres 1). Heidi experienced all of the above. In addition to Prazeres' definition, H.J. ten Duis explains:

"Although it has been mentioned by almost every author, very little attention has been paid to the meaning of fever as an early symptom in fat embolism patients. In injured and burn patients, fever is strongly correlated with plasma interleukin-6 (IL-6) values. IL-6 is a hormone-like protein that plays a key role in the induction of the acute phase response (113, 114). The acute phase response is considered to be a physiological reaction to injury. The severity of the response is directly related to the extent of the injuries

(115). Is there a pathophysiological relation with the
fat embolism syndrome? Besides the induction of fever,
IL-6 stimulates the production of acute phase proteins,
such as C-reactive protein (CRP) and fibrinogen. (As
mentioned above, elevated CRP levels are related to the
formation of fat globules from chylomicrons.) High
IL-6 plasma values are found in injured patients within
1 h[our] after the accident (116, 117). Macrophages,
endothelial cells and fibroblasts are potent IL-6
producers. Nevertheless, the origin of increased IL-
6 synthesis remains unclear. Its production has been
ascribed to TNF-x and IL-1B stimulation. This implies
that in the first few minutes after the injury, sufficient
quantities of TNF-x and IL-1B have to be produced
to induce the increase in IL-6 production. However,
until now no detectable amounts of these cytokines
have been found in injured patients soon after the
accident. Deitch (118) emphasized the importance of
local cytokine production within various tissues as a
possible source of TNF-x. So if we consider that the
high incidence of fever in patients who develop the fat
embolism syndrome is related to increased levels of IL-
6, then the tissues that can produce TNF-x and IL-1B
(skin, subcutaneous tissue) must play a decisive role
in the induction of the fat embolism syndrome. This
means that future attempts to unravel this syndrome
should not focus on the further analysis of breakdown
pathways of triglycerides or differences in their origin,
but instead should pay full attention to differences in
the extent of accompanying soft-tissue injuries that
surround a long-bone fracture" (ten Duis 82,83).]

[The above is the concluding paragraph in ten Duis' extensive paper on Fat Embolism Syndrome. I find it interesting that he directs our attention to the damage done to the surrounding soft tissues when long bones are fractured. Heidi's legs had six severe fractures that were displaced and, therefore, I assume they were poking into the tissues. The ragged, sharp edges of bone must have been slicing into flesh; and the longer she waited, and the more she was moved around (remember her legs were improperly splinted and unstable), the more internal damage was done. Her legs were grossly swollen—think of a fully extended blowfish—and they were a vivid purple in colour, so it seems apparent that her legs were bleeding under the skin and filling with fluids. She had massive soft-tissue damage, which soon manifested into compartment syndrome. Immediate fixation of her displaced broken bones would have reduced, if not prevented, the compartment syndrome, and according to ten Duis, prevented or reduced the fat embolism syndrome. Based on the above article, I agree with the College that her high temperature was definitely an early indication that she was in trouble; however, it is unclear, by their letter, whether or not *they* fully understand why.]

> For a fat embolism syndrome to present with sudden seizures and no other warnings is very uncommon, and certainly in Heidi's case the onset was really quite soon after the accident, occurring at 0940 hours. More commonly the effects of fat embolism syndrome upon the central nervous system follow on from the symptoms of adult respiratory distress syndrome.
>
> The initial treatment of fat embolism is directed at decreasing the hypoxemia that occurs as a result of the respiratory distress, and in Heidi's case she was given oxygen from the moment that she arrived in hospital and her oxygen tensions were satisfactory throughout.

[I do not remember seeing an oxygen mask on Heidi; she was freely speaking with us throughout most of the night and early morning.]

> The debate of the management and prevention of the fat embolism syndrome surrounds the issues of specific drug therapy and the role and timing of definitive fracture fixation. The incomplete understanding of the pathology of the process and the difficulty in making an early clinical diagnosis have not assisted in reaching definitive conclusions in this matter. Over the past decade a body of evidence has accumulated which is in support of early fracture fixation within 24 hours after injury, based on a demonstrated decrease in the incidence of fat embolism syndrome and an improvement in pulmonary function, if such an early intervention is made. It is important to note that this is what would have occurred in Heidi's case, as it was fully anticipated that her fractures would be surgically treated within the 24-hour period. Thus in summary, while it is true that an early orthopaedic intervention in the care of multiply injured patients does appear to reduce the incidence of fat embolism syndrome, early intervention is quite different from immediate intervention. In fact, immediate surgery is stated to be associated with a higher infection rate, and thus is not without its own considerable problems.

[Again, the College neglects to cite which studies their information comes from. My research reveals differing opinions on the timeliness of fixation of fractures. For example: "The most effective prophylactic measure is to reduce long bone fractures as soon as possible after the injury" (Odegard 3); "Prompt surgical stabilization of long bone fractures and correcting or preventing decreased systemic perfusion, reduce the risk of the syndrome" (Prazeres 2); "In trauma patients FES complications can be minimized by rapid splinting and immobilization of the injured limbs. Another factor... is the time of operative fixation of the fracture. Several studies have observed a decrease incidence of FES in fracture patients treated with early internal fixation" (Anon 6); "In the prehospital phase and in the emergency room, long-bone fractures should be handled with great care, with minimum of movement and splinting at the earliest possible opportunity, because early immobilization is known to have a positive influence on reducing the incidence of the syndrome" (ten Duis 81); and last but not least: "fat embolism associated with the release of intramedullary [bone marrow] fat into the venous circulation... can occur at any time following fracture, but is more common if surgical fixation is delayed for longer than 8 hours" (WFSA 9).

With regards to the College's last line in their above paragraph that suggests a higher infection rate with immediate surgery, my sources again contradict their sources. For example, "Early open reduction... [is] believed to reduce the risk of developing major pathophysiological disturbances, such as the fat embolism syndrome, ARDS, MOF and sepsis" (ten Duis 78); and, "Early fracture management also was associated with reduction of systemic infection and mortality" (L.B.Bone et al/Johnson et al, 57).]

> In your letter you expressed concern with regard to the management of Heidi's lung function and fluid balance within the Peace Arch Hospital. The committee members noted that Heidi received approximately 4 1/2 litres of fluids intravenously during her stay there, with a 500 cc's urinary output. The committee would state that this is in fact not an excessive load in a young

woman with normal renal function, and the urinary output might even suggest that Heidi required more fluid.

[I am shocked at the College's misunderstanding of Fat Embolism Syndrome and its relationship with fluids because as reported above, low urinary output (oliguria) is one of the symptoms of fat embolism syndrome. Moreover, one of the papers on FES states that "Restriction of fluid intake and the use of diuretics can be done (if systemic perfusion can be maintained), to minimize fluid accumulation" (Prazeres 2).]

> The committee stated that this fluid load would not be enough to induce pulmonary edema in a young woman with normal lung function [FES takes the 'normal' out of lung function] and would add also that with the injuries that Heidi suffered, she could have easily lost a litre or more fluid into the tissues of the legs. That she did have a loss of tissue fluid into the legs is certainly evidenced by the bilateral compartment syndrome that she subsequently developed.

> As was stated above, the committee members were of the opinion that Heidi's airway control was appropriate and was well maintained through to the time of her transfer to the Royal Columbian Hospital.

> Once Heidi arrived at the Royal Columbian Hospital, although the diagnosis of fat embolism was made, it was not immediately evident, either at the time of Heidi's collapse or at the time of her transfer. Heidi arrived at the Royal Columbian Hospital emergency department at 1152 hours on the 13th of September, 1997 and was seen immediately by Dr. B.J. M[] in the emergency department. Whilst her vital signs

were stable, she was unresponsive and in coma and was attached to a ventilator. Her right lower leg demonstrated signs of a compartment syndrome and a portable chest x-ray was repeated again and was reported to show some mild perihilar congestion.

As I have already indicated to you, a portable chest x-ray is not a good diagnostic medium from which to reach a firm conclusion with regard to fluid overload, aspiration pneumonitis or fat embolism.

In the emergency room Heidi was assessed by Dr. M[], a neurosurgeon, who ordered a CT scan of her head which did not show any abnormality.

Heidi was taken to the operating room for treatment of her right compartment syndrome and Dr. O[], the orthopaedic surgeon, performed the appropriate surgery to both fracture sites, together with a right sided fasciotomy to treat the compartment syndrome. During the surgery Heidi received four units of blood and remained stable throughout.

Heidi was transferred to the recovery area at 2330 hours and continued to be ventilated on a respirator. Her vital signs remained stable and her urinary output was good.

Unfortunately Heidi developed signs of a full blown compartment syndrome in the left leg and was therefore taken back to the operating room at 0005 hours on the 14th of September, 1997 for a fasciotomy to relieve the pressure in that limb.

She was transferred back to the recovery area at 0100 hours and portable chest x-rays at that time were interpreted as normal.

At 0730 hours that morning Heidi was transferred to the intensive care unit.

Unfortunately Heidi's neurological status did not improve and at 0905 hours a repeat CT scan of her head showed signs of swelling of the brain, or cerebral edema. These appearances were in keeping with a diagnosis of fat embolism, which was now recognized to be the cause of her acute seizure and comatose state.

At 2300 hours that day Heidi was returned to the operating room and had a ventricular drain and intracranial pressure monitor inserted by Dr. M[] in order to closely observe her intracranial pressure.

A repeat chest x-ray on the 15th of September, 1997 showed some consolidation in the left lung, and although it was thought that these findings might be due to aspiration during the vomiting episode, the differential diagnosis would also include a resolving fat embolism to the lung.

As you have stated, Heidi's care continued on at the Royal Columbian Hospital in a satisfactory manner, although her condition remained grave and her neurological status was unchanged. By the 17th of September, any signs of fat embolism to the lungs had resolved. Unfortunately, the changes to the brain continued on.

The intracranial pressure was monitored and in the early hours of the 18th of September, 1997 there was concern as the pressure had risen significantly. The repeat CT scan performed at 0700 hours that morning showed an increase in the abnormal changes induced by the fat embolism.

During this time Heidi remained deeply comatose and the changes on CT scan of the brain were persistent. She ran a fever intermittently and was appropriately treated with intravenous antibiotics. On the 27th of September, 1997 she was taken back to the operating room and the fasciotomy wounds were surgically closed by Dr. B[]. During this surgical time Dr. M[] performed a tracheostomy in order that her airway might be better managed and in order that her ventilation might be more efficient.

Following the insertion of the tracheostomy Heidi's neurological status remained unchanged and her tracheostomy care was routine and appropriate. Importantly, the tracheostomy cuff pressures were recorded and the measurements were constantly within the normal range.

The physician with the prime responsibility for the management of Heidi's airway was Dr.[]B[], a consultant in respiratory and critical care medicine. Dr. B[] cared for Heidi from the 29th of September through to the 10th of October, 1997 and made daily rounds on all patients in the ICU, including Heidi.

It is important to understand that all patients with a tracheostomy have problems with infection around the tracheostomy wound, which is usually limited to the skin, together with swelling of the region and bleeding from the wound edges. This is usually most evident in the first three weeks following the tracheostomy.

Heidi had appropriate cultures taken from her
tracheostomy site and also from the secretions
aspirated from the tracheostomy itself.

[But no cultures were ever taken from the area between the
cuff and the inside of the trachea wall].

These cultures were positive and Heidi was receiving
the appropriate broad spectrum anitbiotics to deal
with these infections. Indeed her temperature subsided
over the ensuing days[,]

[Heidi was diaphoretic (sweaty), her face remained flushed,
her white blood cell count was high, and her heart-rate was
elevated.]

and she was weaned off the ventilator and it was finally
possible to transfer her to the 3N Maxicare unit on the
3rd of October, 1997.

[This is the tape from Heidi's heart monitor on the morning of
October 3rd, 1997:]

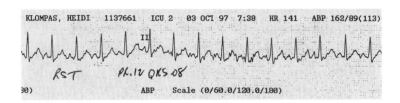

It was the committee's opinion that Dr. B[] provided
appropriate care to Heidi's tracheostomy, and that
the tracheostomy cuff pressures were appropriately
monitored and the infection [but not the fistula]
appropriately treated. The committee noted that the
Autopsy Report would indicate that there was no

evidence of infection of the tracheostomy regions, either to culture or microscopy, at the time of death.

[Wait a minute! The time of Heidi's death was almost five days after the rupture of the innominate artery and the subsequent sterilization and surgical repair of the 3cm hole in the trachea that the infection had eaten through. The autopsy was performed on Oct. 15ᵗʰ, a full week after her death and eleven days after the fistula was cleaned and the area sterilized.]

> Dr. B[] visited Heidi in the ward on the morning of the 4ᵗʰ of October and at that time she appeared to be quite stable. There was no indication of any problem with the tracheostomy tube, and particularly there was no evidence of any bleeding recorded that would have given the physician any warning of the catastrophic events that were to occur that day.

[Records show that the central IV line in her neck had "purulent drainage -area quite reddened—pt (patient) has pustule [raised] rash to face & chest" (RCH 620). This was written in the nurse's notes at 8:00 am, a full three hours before Dr. B, the Respirologist, visited Heidi at 11:00 am.]

> As I am sure you are aware, the whole purpose of monitoring the tracheostomy cuff pressure was to prevent the complication known as "pressure necrosis" where the tracheostomy cuff erodes through the trachea and other adjacent structures. Even with the best monitored tracheostomy tube, pressure necrosis does occur and results in incidental hemorrhage in about 4% of cases. Erosion into the innominate artery, the College is informed [by whom?], occurs in less than 1% of those cases that bleed, and in such a situation the survival rate is less than 20%. Coughing

often precipitates the bleeding and it occurs without warning, and when it occurs it is a clinical problem that is extremely difficult to manage.

[My research turned up the following on pressure necrosis: (italic type is mine)

"Tracheal injury is mostly associated with high-pressure tracheal cuffs... Tracheal capillary pressure ranges between 20 and 30 mm Hg. In humans, tracheal blood flow is impaired at 22 mm Hg and is totally obstructed at 37 mm Hg (13). Therefore, to avoid mucosal pressure necrosis, the use of low-pressure *tracheal cuffs inflated to < [less than] 20 mm Hg is recommended.* In addition, intermittent deflation of the cuff during long-term ventilation may reduce the risk of mucosal ischemia (4)... Approximately 50% of patients with TIF [tracheo-innominate fistula] have relatively minor bleeding that stops spontaneously before the diagnosis... The key to preventing TIF formation is careful management of tracheotomized patients, prompt treatment of tracheostomy site infection, prevention of tracheal injury by avoiding prolonged cuff overinflation, and prevention of excessive head movement" (Kapural, et al, 778-9).]

[According to hospital records, Heidi's trachea cuff pressures were: 24 mm Hg on Sept. 27th, just after the tracheostomy surgery, and later that day, 22 mm Hg at 8:10 pm; 24 mm Hg on Sept. 28th; 24 mm Hg on Oct.2nd; 22 mm Hg on Oct. 3rd; and 22 mm Hg on Oct. 4th (prior to the bleed) (RCH, 335, 561,599, 359). It would appear Heidi's trachea cuff was consistently kept at higher than the above recommended pressure of less than 20 mm Hg.

Furthermore:

> "The incidence of tracheoinnominate artery fistula
> has been reported to be 0.4 to 4.5%. Innominate
> artery rupture has been associated with tracheal
> necrosis secondary to infection and from erosion
> from the tracheostomy tube. While the most
> frequent site of fistula formation is at the distal end
> of the tube, low placement of the tracheotomy as
> well as a high innominate artery is also associated
> with tracheoinnominate artery fistula. In a series
> of ten and a review of the literature containing 127
> documented cased, Jones noted that 50% of the
> cases had sentinel bleeds and that one-half of those
> which had tracheotomy bleeding of the greater than
> 10 ml at 48 hours or later after surgery would have
> a tracheoinnominate artery fistula.... Suspicion of a
> tracheoinnominate artery fistula mandates removal
> of the tracheostomy tube and bronchoscopy" [visual
> examination of trachea's interior using a bronchoscope:
> small tubular instrument with electric light
> (Webster's)] (Sicard, 4).

In addition:

> "Evacuation of pooled secretions from the subglottic
> space [near vocal chords] above the endotracheal tube
> (ETT) cuff is a strategy to help prevent ventilator-
> associated pneumonia. Removing oropharyngeal
> secretions from the subglottic area is thought to
> reduce occult aspiration of secretions containing
> high bacterial loads... Tracheal-innominate artery
> erosion is rare... and is almost exclusively associated
> with tracheostomy. With tracheostomy tubes, lesion

sites have been associated with both the cuff and the tube tip. Tracheo-innominate artery fistula requires emergency surgical intervention, and the mortality rate from the condition is high. To our knowledge, we are reporting the second case of a fatal tracheal-arterial erosion caused by an ETT and the first report of this complication at the site of the ETT tip" (Siobal et al, 1012-1018).

It is my belief that Heidi's trachea was eroding prior to her tracheostomy (caused by the endo-tracheal tube), and that when the pressurized tracheostomy cuff covered over the erosion, it dramatically worsened her condition. Supporting this theory is the following:

"The fundamental problem that is common to all endotracheal tubes is that they must have some rigidity in order to be effective conduits that do not kink or collapse. Given this rigidity, there will be some force applied to the mucosa of the mouth, pharynx, larynx, and trachea. The smaller the area of contact, the higher the pressure, since pressure is directly proportional to the area over which that force is applied. In studies of the pressures exerted by endotracheal tubes in the larynx, Weymuller et al found that at the points of contact with the mucosa overlying the cricoid and arytenoid cartilages, endotracheal tubes routinely exert pressures far in excess of the mucosal perfusion pressure of approximately 30 mm Hg (4). Endotracheal tubes routinely result in ischemic [damage from lack of blood supply] areas of the laryngeal mucosa and this ischemia routinely results in ulceration within days (5)" (Bishop, 1).

On September 26th, 1997, the day before Heidi's tracheostomy, the following was included in the nurses' notes: "1520—(o) RN trying to sxn [suction] pt. but catheter not advancing far enough. Tried deflating and reinflating cuff in case of herniated cuff—seemed to work." And: "1631—(o) RN again having difficulty [with] sxn catheter—tried scn [suctioning] [with] smaller catheter" (RCH 538). Clearly something was wrong with Heidi's trachea but no one thought to look inside it.

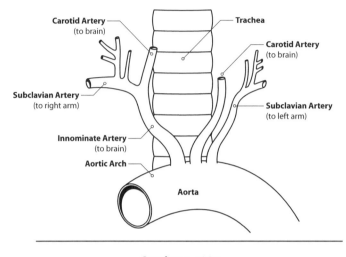

September 13, 1997

October 4, 1997

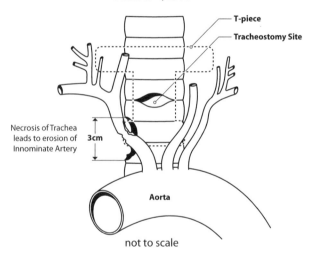

not to scale

The above is my rendition of the before and after state of Heidi's trachea and innominate artery. The anatomy may not be exactly correct, but it is close enough to give you a visualization of what occurred.

[Heidi's temperature remained consistently high on the days before and directly after the tracheostomy. Also, her face remained flushed, her skin diaphoretic (sweaty), and her heart rate rapid. All these 'signs' correlate with what the nurses later recorded on her trachea care:

September 27th, just back from the OR at 11:24: "Sxn for whitish yellow creamy secretions" (RCH 335).

14:30: "Small amt sang oozing noted from trach site" (RCH 553).

20:30: "Suctioned for thin, ...secretions" (RCH 558).

September 28th, at 06:00: "Large amount of purulent, foul-smelling drainage from trach site" (RCH 559).

10:45: "Dk. sang ooze noticed on trach drsg [dressing]"(RCH 562).

12:00 [noon]: "Lg. amt. very, very foul smelling drainage, greyish brown in colour" (RCH 563).

15:00: "Fever persists ...trach site continues to ooze foul smelling greyish brown drainage" (RCH 563).

18:00: "Creamy coloured drainage noted coming out of R. nare [right nostril]" (RCH 563).

19:00: "Creamy foul drainage suctioned from back of mouth" (RCH 563).

20:00: "Trach drsg [with] some yellowish drainage" (RCH 556).

23:00: "Trach care on L/A [large amount] foul smelling yellow drainage" (RCH 557).

23:20: "Suctioned for fair amt. thick purulent looking yellow secretions" (RCH 557).

September 29th, at 03:30: "Suctioned for large amts.

purulent looking yellow secretions" (RCH 557).

06:45: "Trach care copious foul smelling purulent looking drainage from trach stoma [opening]" (RCH 557).

12:40: "Trach site oozing purulent drainage" (RCH 572).

16:00: "Trach site continues to drain Lge. amount purulent secretions" (RCH 573).

19:45: "Purulent looking drainage at IV site [in neck] ...suctioned for thick yellow secretions" (RCH 573).

22:15: "Trach drsg chgd for mod. thick purulent yellow drainage" (RCH 576).

24:00: "Suctioning thick yellow" (RCH 576).

September 30th, at 01:15: "Suctioned for thick yellow" (RCH 576).

04:00: "Suctioning yellow" (RCH 576).

05:00: "Trach drsg chgd for mod thick yellow drainage" (RCH 576).

05:45: "Suctioned for thick yellow secretions" (RCH 576).

08:30: "Mod amount yellow secretions obtained" (RCH 582).

16:15: "Suctioned for mod, sticky yellow secretions" (RCH 583).

19:05: "Trach site changed for + + purulent drainage" (RCH 583).

23:00: "Trach care done for mod thick yellow secretion—site red" (RCH 586).

October 1st, 00:30: "Suctioning lg. thick creamy & yellow pus" (RCH 587).

05:25: "Trach drsg changed as above" (RCH 587).

07:55: "Suctioned ...for moderate mucoid purulent secretions" (RCH 343).

08:00: "Trach site oozing yellow secretions" (RCH 593).

16:00: "[Less] secretions to suctioning" (RCH 593).

20:45: "Suctioned by RT [Resident] for mod thick creamy yellow secretions" (RCH 594).

24:00: "Continue to suction thick yellow secretions per trach" (RCH 597).

October 2nd, 06:35: "Trach care done for lg yellow secretions—site red" (RCH 597).

07:35: "Suctioned for scant amounts of clear secretions" (RCH 345).

08:50: "Nurse suctioned and instilled and got copious amounts of yellow secretions" (RCH 345).

12:00: "Mod. Amts. Yellow secretions when coughing" (RCH 603).

20:00: "Suctioned for sm amts yellow secretions" (RCH 604).

24:00: "Sm amts yellow secretions (RCH 604).

October 3rd, 04:00: "Mod amts thick yellow "plugs,"
..."Trach care done—prod amt thick creamy beige
drainage @ site" (RCH 607).

08:00: "Coughing up mod amts thick green sputum.
Instilled & suctioned for small amt loose white
sputum" (RCH 612).

08:45: "Suctioned for scant amounts but pt
spontaneously coughs up small–mod amounts of
greenish secretions" (RCH 347).

20:50: "Sxn'd for mod amt yellow tinged secretions"
(RCH 359).

23:30: "Suctioned" (RCH 618).

October 4th, 02:00: "Suctioned for same" (RCH 618).

03:50: "Suctioned for same secretions" (RCH 618).

11:00: "Dr. B in to see pt" (RCH 620).

12:00: "Dr. C in to see pt" (RCH 620).

13:45: "pt coughed and started to bleed profusely ..."
(RCH 620).]

[As demonstrated above, this "purulent" drainage from
Heidi's tracheostomy site was evident from the time of her
tracheostomy surgery on September 27th to the time of the big
bleed on October 4th. There are no records of anyone EVER
looking inside her trachea with a bronchoscope prior to the
bleed. The College of Physicians and Surgeons offers no viable
explanations for this oversight.

The Lab results for the day following the tracheostomy, September 28th, 1997:]

- Right nares: no growth: Group A Streptococcus or Staphylococcus aureus.

- Stool: no Clostridium Difficile toxin detected.

- Trachiostomy: from Stoma [opening]

- Gram Stain: +3 Gram pos cocci; +4 Gram neg bacilli; +2 Pus cells

- Wound Culture: +2 Mixed Enteric organisms; +3 Haemophilus influenzae; few colonies only Staphylococcus aureus; +2 Normal respiratory flora (RCH 279).]

[Because these lab samples were taken the day after her tracheostomy surgery, they indicate to me that the infections must have been present before the tracheostomy was performed.]

On the afternoon of the 4th of October, 1997, Heidi suffered a catastrophic bleed from the tracheostomy site and Dr. B[] arrived on the ward after she had been resuscitated. Dr. B[] had advised the College that he spoke with members of family prior to Heidi being taken to emergency surgery and indicated at that time that she had had a prolonged period of cardiac arrest and that there was a likelihood of additional brain damage as a result. Dr. B[] continued to look after Heidi in the ICU following her surgery and did so up until the time of her death on the 8th of October, 1997. Following that emergency surgery Heidi's neurological condition deteriorated further despite aggressive support, and it was evident by the 8th of October that she had suffered irreversible brain damage to the point of brain death. Appropriately, the family was involved in the decision to discontinue life support [I was neither involved nor aware of this decision], and the committee members were most concerned in reading your letter that the attending physician in the Maxi ward at the time of the bleed advised you that Heidi would be brain dead, and you report that this person used the word "vegetable" in that discussion.

Dr. B[] had advised the College that he did not use that expression in his discussions with you. He states:

"I can unequivocally state that I have never used the term "vegetable" in conversation with families or other medical personnel. I have looked after many patients with severe neurological injuries and have never considered them "vegetables." The term is abhorrent to me and I am completely certain that I would not have used it."

The committee members accept that Dr. B[] did not use this offensive term to you and are unsure who actually did. If this term was used it is completely inappropriate, and the committee could well understand your distress and anger.

[To date I do not know which doctor uttered those words; but "vegetable" was certainly used by a doctor and heard by Heidi's father, brother, sister, and myself. More on this later.]

Finally, the committee would emphasize that this sudden bleed from the tracheostomy site occurred completely without warning, and that the major cause

of this sudden bleed was pressure necrosis, which I
have explained above, and not infection. The erosion of
the tracheostomy tube into the innominate artery was
impossible to observe and was completely unpredicted.

[I was told by the surgeon who repaired Heidi's trachea that
an infection had eaten a large hole through her trachea and
had continued to work its way through the lining of the
innominate artery. Also, as to this last statement that "erosion
of the tracheostomy tube... was impossible to observe," I'd like
to state again that had someone removed the tracheostomy
tube and actually looked inside the trachea, then the erosion
and the fistula, or at least the source of the infection, would
have been detected prior to disaster.]

In summary, it was the committee's opinion that
Heidi suffered a tragic accident on the highway,
and received appropriate emergency care. She then
had the misfortune to suffer a significant and severe
fat embolism to the brain, which led to significant
brain damage. Subsequently she had the further
misfortune to suffer an uncommon complication of
her tracheostomy which led to a massive bleed from
the innominate artery in the neck, which was followed
by a prolonged period of cardiac arrest, resulting in
further brain damage from which it was impossible to
recover.

[The brain damage from the fat embolism was resolving itself
and Dr. M was optimistic for a full neurological recovery. If
the bleed hadn't occurred, she would have had minimal to no
brain damage at all. It was the bleed that ultimately killed her:
not the fat embolism, not the persistent pneumonia, and not
the leg fractures].

The committee would like to thank you for the

patience that you have shown during this lengthy and complicated review, and to offer you every sympathy in your loss.

Given that this has been a lengthy and complex letter, I would be happy to meet with you to discuss its content if you have any further questions. Please contact my secretary, Ms. [], at [] to arrange a mutually convenient time if you would like this meeting to occur.

Yours sincerely,

B.T.B. T[], M.B., B.S.
Deputy Registrar

cc: Dr. S.P. B[]   Dr. C.J.N. L[]
    Dr. J.G. H[]   Dr. J.W. P[]
    Dr. T.E. H[]   Dr. K.A. Z[]

I find it curious that Dr. M., Heidi's neurosurgeon, Dr. McC., Head physician of Royal Columbian's ICU, and Dr. O., Heidi's orthopaedic surgeon, are not on this list of recipients for the above letter from the College.

During my ongoing quest for information regarding hospital practices, I sent letters to six area hospitals requesting information on policies they might have regarding the timeline between declaring a patient brain-dead and organ retrieval for transplantation. As it turns out, Vancouver General, Surrey Memorial, St. Paul's, UBC, Lions Gate, and Royal Columbian hospitals all concur that there is no set policy that exists outside of the guidelines of the Transplant Society. They all agreed that most organs are retrieved for transplantation as soon as possible after brain-death is declared.

I include the email letter I received from Royal Columbian Hospital for your enlightenment:

Sent: Tuesday, November 04, 2003 1:02PM

> Dear Ms. Adamson,
>
> There has never been to my knowledge an arbitrary period of time before organ retrieval. In those cases that are in a vegetative state, it is standard to get two EEG's 24 hours apart, to confirm that there is no improvement, but that would only be done where the clinical course is not obvious.
>
> None of these are 'policies' in the strict sense, so they do not go to the Board. They are medical practice patterns that change from time to time, and are dictated by what is in the literature, and what is common practice within the community.
>
> Hope that is helpful. Sorry, no smoking gun.
>
> > [] V[] MD, MHSc, FRCPC
> > Medical Director
> >
> > Royal Columbian Hospital

Hmmm... did he say "vegetative state"? This is from the hospital that considers *vegetable* an "offensive term." And what is implied by "Sorry, no smoking gun"? Thank you Royal Columbian Hospital for your illumination. This letter says it all.

Response to the Children's Commission:

The College of Physicians and Surgeons of B.C. were kind enough to provide me with three additional letters. The first is their letter to Mr. John Greschner, Deputy Commissioner and Chief Investigator for the Children's Commission of B.C., in which they outline the positions of their doctors and hospitals. Namely, they defend themselves in their response to the Commission's recommendations about the delay in time for fixation of her leg fractures, and the treatment surrounding Heidi's trachea. The second is a letter from Dr. N, then Medical Director of Royal Columbian Hospital, to the College, and he details the review of the tracheostomy disaster that his hospital conducted. The third letter is a copy of Dr. N's letter to the Chief Coroner of B.C., Mr. L.W. Campbell (currently known as Larry Campbell, Mayor, City of Vancouver), which contains similar explanations for Heidi's care at Royal Columbian.

In their letter to the Commission, the College includes a written statement from Dr. H, and he states in part: "Had I been under the impression that there was any urgency to her orthopaedic management, I would have attended the hospital earlier. If so, if anything, earlier surgery would have likely accelerated the release of the fat emboli." The College concludes its section on the care at Peace Arch District Hospital by stating: "In summary, therefore, at the time that Dr. H[] saw the patient at 9:00 am there was no indication for emergency treatment, but as stated in the consultation and in the notes, definitive treatment should be initiated as soon as possible."

All the documentation I reviewed on fat embolism syndrome indicates, absolutely, that early and open fixation of multiple long bone fractures reduces, and *does not* "accelerate," the incidence of fat embolism syndrome.

The other recommendation from the Commission is for Royal Columbian Hospital regarding the tracheostomy and the eventual tracheo-innominate fistula. The College maintains that "the complication which led to the patient's death occurred sometime after the tracheostomy was placed, and in the interval there had been no problems with the tracheostomy tube." They add, "There was no suggestion at any time that there was a problem with the tracheostomy cuff or that there was necrosis of surrounding tissue, or any similar signs." [Were not the foul odour, the constant ooze coming from the tracheostomy opening, the high temperatures, the sweating, and the t-piece sitting askew just minutes before the bleed surely *signs*?] The College concludes its letter to the Commission with the following:

> "As is evident from the enclosed material, the review at Royal Columbian Hospital, both internal and as requested by the Coroner, was very comprehensive and involved a number of medical disciplines. Its intent was to determine whether there was anything to be learned from this disastrous complication, so that its occurrence could be further minimized in the future. Unfortunately, this remains an unexplained phenomenon and it is rare and could not have been anticipated.
>
> I hope the College has satisfied the Commissioner's recommendations. Our conclusions are that the complications suffered by the patient were inherent in the nature of the injury and the subsequent complications and disease process. The College is unable to conclude that the medical care, or the alleged lack of or delay in definitive care, contributed to the patient's death."
>
> (M. V[], M.D., Deputy Registrar for the College of Physicians and Surgeons of B.C.).

Wow. Sometimes I just have to tell myself to keep breathing. Inhale, exhale. I'll get through this. In complete denial of both the Coroner's and Children's Commissioner's findings, the "College is unable to conclude that the medical care ... contributed to the patient's death." Again I say, Wow. God help us all.

The second letter is from Dr. N, Medical Director for Royal Columbian Hospital, addressed to the above Dr. V, Deputy Registrar for the College of Physicians and Surgeons of B.C., and is dated December 7, 1999. In his letter, Dr. N states in part:

> "There was a fairly complete review of this case for educational purposes on October 19th [1999] but I am also aware that the case was reviewed at Respiratory Rounds shortly after the patient's expiry. In addition, Dr. M[] informs me that this case was discussed at Neurosurgery rounds or/and at meetings of the Department of Neurosciences. However, this was not reported to the Quality Committee as part of the mandatory Morbidity/Mortality Rounds of the Department of Neurosurgery. Unfortunately I do not have reports from those rounds, and those present cannot remember the dates. I would note that it is not at all unusual, following such a clinical misadventure, that there be repeated discussions among medical and nursing staff along the lines of "could we have done anything different"? I, myself, on August 11th, 1999, requested the pathologist who did the autopsy to review the slides of the innominate artery involved, to see if there might be any anatomic irregularity predisposing to such an erosion and rupture. The pathologist could find no evidence of any significant

predisposing factor… A chart review shows no evidence
of any problems associated with the surgical procedure
of tracheostomy or placement of the tube. Moreover,
cuff pressures were reviewed on an ongoing basis and
were always within the acceptable range."

The third letter is also from the above Dr. N and is addressed to
Mr. L.W. Campbell, Chief Coroner for the Province of British
Columbia, and it is dated October 19, 1999. He states in part:

"At the direction of Coroner Stewart Respiratory
Rounds were conducted on October 19th, at 4:00pm,
in Conference Room T047, of the Columbia Tower
of Royal Columbian Hospital by the Division of
Respiratory & Critical Care Medicine. Rounds
were chaired by the Chief of the Division, Dr. S.
B[] [Heidi's primary tracheostomy/respiratory care
physician], and case presentation was by the Medical
Director of the Intensive Care Unit. In attendance
were other respiratory medicine specialists,… members
of house staff, the nursing staff and registered
respiratory therapists who attended Ms. Klompas
during her stay in the Intensive Care Unit."

The letter goes on to discuss the care given Heidi's tracheostomy
that is similar to the previous two letters. Dr. N adds:

"As Medical Director, I asked all assembled at the end
of the presentation, whether they could identify any of
the outlined precautions which they felt had not been
adhered to, and no member of the medical/surgical,
nursing or other staff could identify such a lapse in
monitoring or in continuing care."

In other words, no one spoke up.

Several weeks after Heidi's funeral, I visited the Intensive Care Unit at Royal Columbian with the purpose of thanking the nurses for the care they gave Heidi during her time there. My "Yellow Roses" stitchery was framed a few days earlier, and I presented this to the Head Nurse of the ICU (I don't know her name). This tall, serene woman was kind enough to speak with me outside the ICU doors, and we discussed Heidi's care and her subsequent death. When I mentioned the fistula and the big bleed, she said to me, "I am so sorry. We knew about those but we just didn't think to look." That is quite an admission, especially after reading the above words from Dr. N who insists that no member of his staff spoke up during this very important meeting. I do not know whether this particular head nurse was present at his meeting but I hope she would have said something had she been there. Nevertheless, I appreciate her honesty with me.

Dr. N concludes his letter to the Chief Coroner with:

"In summary, therefore, careful review of this unfortunate lady's care at Royal Columbian Hospital does not identify any measures or any modification of medical management which could be reasonably assumed to have changed her clinical course."

This scares me. The hospital staff had several opportunities in their "Rounds" to discuss improvements for treatments, yet they appear to dismiss the concerns of both the Coroner's investigator and the Children's Commissioner. And by their acceptance, does the College of Physicians and Surgeons endorse this blatant disregard for honest analysis? And what about the Chief Coroner and the Children's Commissioner; is there no follow-up? Do they not care that their investigative reports have been so handily dismissed? How can doctors improve their medical skills when they persist in denying any culpability in this unusual death of an otherwise healthy seventeen-year-old girl? Aren't we supposed to learn by our mistakes? Who benefits by burying them in the sand? I don't know the answers to these questions, but I put them out there for you, dear reader, to ponder.

I am sadly disappointed in our medical community. The only act of courage I've witnessed so far has been by the head nurse who apologized for her part in the staff's omission; she accepted that more should have, and could have, been done to save Heidi's life. Why do the rest of them appear to be running for cover? Smoking guns indeed.

Still

Crowded into small dark places
Lies the hurt I force deeper inside
I can't sleep, haunted by the memories
That I can't seem to push aside

I watched pain and hurt shift to helpless and hollow
Over and over on your mother's face
I've seen all the anger and dreams
Disappear without a trace

Searching and yearning to hear your voice
Hoping and praying you'd come around
There is a silence I constantly hear
And I tell you it's a god awful sound

Questions repeated over and over
Still I do what I have to do
Trying to find some peace and comfort
In a world that robbed us of you

Christina Williamson
January 16, 2001

4.10 The Lawsuit

The Coroner and Children's Commission reports offered up new evidence of medical malpractice that I'd never imagined before. While awaiting these reports, our lawyer, G. Garry MacDonald, keeps up communications with ICBC (Insurance Corporation of British Columbia) and our "claim." When I receive the above two reports I start asking questions regarding the addition of a malpractice lawsuit. Garry looks into it for me and then advises against it for many reasons, not least of which are our existing laws pertaining to the death of a child. Because Heidi's injuries began with a car crash, ICBC has to be the initial focus of a claim for loss. If we want to sue for malpractice then we will have to include everyone all at once because our laws do not permit anyone to sue more than once for the same death. Therefore, we would have to sue both hospitals, all the doctors and nurses involved, and ICBC together in one lawsuit. This would be a huge undertaking and the legal fees could cost at least $200,000. The expected compensation is less than $50,000, which will mean we might stand to lose a minimum of $150,000. We are not a wealthy family and cannot afford such a staggering financial loss. Nevertheless, I pressure Garry to go forward, mostly because I want the public to know what really happened to Heidi in the hospitals. He directs me to a large firm in Vancouver that deals with malpractice suits; after discussing Heidi's case with me their lawyer confirms what Garry has said: a malpractice suit is not feasible unless I am wealthy and able to spend hundreds of thousands of dollars and five to ten years of my life, just to make a point. Defeated, I agree to go ahead with just the single lawsuit against ICBC. This is not a pleasant experience.

In monetary values, a child's life is virtually worthless in Canada. Our legal guidelines for the death of a child come from the *Family Compensation Act;* and the amounts recoverable are usually for medical costs, funeral costs and the loss of income we would have expected from our daughter had she gone on to earn a living for the rest of her life while supporting us. Obviously, this is negligible as we have never expected our children to support us financially once they start working. There is no compensation allowable for the pain and suffering of parents when they lose a child. There is no compensation for the marriages that fall apart after the death of a child. I read once that the divorce rate is as high as 75% for couples who have lost a child. Our marriage succumbed and joined this sad majority within a year. The loss of half my husband's income (airline pilot) is not a consideration for compensation by ICBC's lawyer.

Two days before Christmas in 1999, Garry MacDonald's law office fax machine spits out an offer for settlement from ICBC's lawyer in the amount of $5000 (five thousand dollars).

They explain:

> "It is clear from the evidence of the mother and father that there was no quantifiable dependency of them upon their deceased daughter at the time of her death. It is also clear from their evidence that they never anticipated having any dependency upon her in the future. Although we all may be somewhat critical of the Family Compensation Act, the statute seems to remain and the claim of the surviving mother and father is limited to the pecuniary losses which they have sustained. As best as we can determine those pecuniary losses are minimal."

During the next year and a half several offers and counter offers go back and forth between my lawyer and ICBC's lawyer.

Finally, and against my wishes, we agree to mediation. I will not see my day in court where I had hoped to tell the world (through the media) all that Heidi endured as the doctors slowly dragged her towards her death. In August of 2001, nearly four years after Heidi's death, we settle the claim in mediation. We sign a non-disclosure agreement with ICBC; and therefore, I am not permitted to disclose the amount we received. Just let me say that the amount I personally received was far less than $100,000. At this point I am a single mom going to university; the money allows me to repay my parents for the down payment on my little house, pay off my car loan, and almost pay off the credit card debt. Four years after Heidi's death I am still penniless but oh, so relieved that the two years of bickering with ICBC are over.

Our courts, our lawmakers, need to take a broader look at the actual damages a family suffers after the death of a child. In Heidi's case, the two government investigations clearly point to medical errors and omissions as the cause of her death. Where is the apology? The emotional toll on us has been huge. Bill and Laura each lost three years of schooling. I lost my marriage, my security, my spark. I am forever a changed woman. Some viable financial security at this time in my life would have been most welcome.

I feel there should be two ways of calculating compensation to victims. Certainly people should be reimbursed for costs incurred, but I feel there should also be larger awards given to act as *deterrents* for those that harm. The courts should charge the doctors and hospitals amounts that exceed their comfort zones. By this I mean that if the doctors, hospitals and the College of Physicians and Surgeons knew they could be successfully sued for millions, do you think they'd take more care in dealing with their patients' health? Malpractice insurance providers might then start refusing to insure doctors with repeated losses in court; and then these doctors wouldn't be able to practice in B.C., at least not without their malpractice insurance. How else to cull the bad doctors from the good? The College doesn't seem to be in any hurry to do the right thing. Currently, doctors in B.C. are virtually untouchable. Our legal system is set up to allow them to harm—even kill—with impunity. This is wrong and this system must be changed to better protect patients and their families. Dr. H from Langley and Peace Arch Hospitals is B.C.'s perfect case in point. Change the law to allow patients to sue for millions and we would finally be rid of these menaces to medicine.

In the meantime, all I can do is write this book and reveal the details of Heidi's slow death. Maybe then enough people will pressure the government to make some real changes in the medical community by restructuring licensing and taking it out of the protectionist hands of the Old Boys Club known as the College of Physicians and Surgeons. It's also time to open them up to devastating, albeit deserving, losses through malpractice suits. Some changes cannot occur without great pain. I say it is time.

4.11   Drunk Driving: MADD, Laws and Reform

In the weeks following Heidi's death we receive many phone calls from a member of Victims' Services, and this kind stranger on the phone wants to know how I am "feeling." Unfortunately, I am in no condition to speak with a complete stranger about how I feel and whether or not I am depressed and need help. The first year is like a vacuum to me and I simply need time to adjust to this new life without Heidi. About six months into my grieving I receive an invitation to attend a MADD meeting. Mothers Against Drunk Driving is an organization that was initially formed by a few mothers in the United States, with a mandate to provide comfort and advice to families of victims of drunk drivers. They help traumatized people find the organizations and services they need to see them through the court cases, insurance negotiations, and psychological stress involved in dealing with tragedy. The MADD group is a non-profit society that has grown tremendously in both the U.S.A. and Canada, with memberships in the tens of thousands.

When I sign up as a member of MADD, I think to myself, "This particular club has the highest membership fees in the world: the death of a loved one." I attend several meetings, but with no regularity over the next few years. I enjoy getting to know some of the members, but the meetings are, to me, a trip back down Grieving Lane and I cannot handle too many in a year.

In the spring of 2002 I am invited to attend the North American MADD conference in Toronto; the conference is held at the Constellation Hotel near the Toronto airport. As I enter this hotel I feel an enormous rush of deja vu. My head is reeling as I walk through the lobby and I can't figure out what is wrong with me. I feel like I am going to faint! I go up to my room and it seems the same as any other hotel room. I have my MADD package with instructions for where to go for breakfast the next morning, along with the conference rooms for the series of seminars I have signed up for; and the next morning I walk past an area overlooking the hotel's pool on my way to the main convention room. That's when it hits me! Oh my gosh, this is the same hotel we stayed in when we took the children to Walt Disney World in Florida in 1989. Our flight from Vancouver had a stopover in Toronto before connecting with a Tampa Bay flight the next morning, and this is where we spent our lay-over. The pool! It was winter (February) when our family was last here and I remember how the children and I were so thrilled to discover that the indoor pool had a portal to the outdoor pool; we could swim from the warm inside area and under an archway to the outside where snow blanketed the pool deck and landscaping. The children were so excited to be able to swim first inside and then outside in the snow. Heidi, Billy and Laura spent what seemed like hours in that pool before I dragged them off to bed late at night. Heidi was not quite nine years old; Billy was ten and Laura was seven and a half. My children were so happy here in that moment, and it all comes rushing back to me, almost knocks me off of my feet! It is weird enough to be back in Mississauga, where Heidi and Laura were born, but to be staying back in the only hotel I ever stayed at in Toronto was mind-blowing. Nevertheless, I eventually make my way to breakfast and the conference that first morning.

As I walk through the huge double doors I am taken aback at the sight of hundreds of people milling around the room. We fill our plates at the buffet tables then find a place at a table with strangers. Over the three days of this conference I meet many new people, all of whom have lost a loved one (or several family members) to a drunk driver. When the master of ceremonies speaks, all is quiet and I scan the room, recognizing the grief they wear on their faces as my own. This assembly is unique. Everyone in this room has been traumatized by personal tragedy and I see it on their faces, in the slump of their shoulders, in the shuffle of their feet, and in the total lack of laughter normally present when people converse over a meal. It is almost eerie. I think there may be over six hundred people here, but it might be more. The Americans are here in full force and have lots to say on the subject of drunk driving. The seminars and workshops are pleasant, helpful, and informative, and I am grateful to the Vancouver chapter of MADD for sending me here. I thank you again.

My most memorable discussion happens in one of the seminar rooms when an American woman says something that really shocks me. This conference takes place about eight months after the September 11th, 2001, terrorist attacks on the United States that destroys the twin towers of the World Trade Center and part of the Pentagon building. About 3000 people die as a result of those attacks and the world still mourns for America. This woman tells us that she was pregnant with her fourth child (and first daughter), and was driving her car with her three small boys in the back strapped into car seats and with her mother in the front passenger seat when she was struck by a drunk driver who ran a red light as she was entering an intersection. Her mother died, her sons were injured, but survived, and her seven-month foetus was ripped from her belly, almost costing her life. She not only lost her mother and her baby daughter, but also her uterus. She almost died several times over the next few weeks and did not return home from the hospital for six months. The drunk driver died at the scene. Although she is glad the drunk driver died at the scene, this young mother is still angry over his long history of repeated offences for driving under the influence (DUI). He was let out of jail the day before he struck her. She tells us she is angry, in part, because of what is being given to the families of the victims of September 11th. Each 9/11 family was to receive about a million dollars from the federal government. She feels abandoned by her government in her time of grief, as she watches the news about the squabbling over the one million dollar compensation packages that many September 11th families are saying is insufficient. Her family received a new car and financially crippling medical bills. This is just one of many horrific stories I listened to at this conference.

Hundreds of families attend these conferences every year and the numbers keep growing. The candlelight vigil held at a community church Saturday night stirred up lots of emotions and many tears were shed. An artist worked on a memorial mural during the conference and many attendees contributed to it, including myself. Our fallen children, parents, and grandparents' photographs lined both sides of the display boards that ran the length of the massive corridor outside the conference room. Heidi has now joined an extraordinarily large group of people whose lives were cut short by a drunk driver.

In 2001 in the United States, about 3000 people died from the September terrorist attacks. In the same year 17,400 people died from contact with drunk drivers. The question is, WHO ARE THE REAL TERRORISTS?

In Canada, 3,021 people died in driving accidents in 2001, and it is conservatively estimated (by MADD Canada) that 1,213 of these deaths resulted from drunk driving. This means an average of 3.32 Canadians die each day because someone chooses to drink and drive. Our numbers are obviously a great deal smaller than the U.S.A.'s, but so is our population: 31.6 million versus 292 million (Population Reference Bureau). British Columbian statistics on drunk driving are discussed earlier in the Children's Commission's Report, so I will not repeat them here. Let's now look at what's happening in the United States.

The U.S. website for MADD (www.madd.org) contains some interesting statistics related to alcohol:

–   In 2002, an estimated 17, 419 people died in alcohol-related traffic crashes—an average of one every 30 minutes. These deaths constitute 41% of the 42, 815 total traffic fatalities. (NHTSA, 2003)

–   In 2001, more than half a million people were injured in crashes where police reported that alcohol was present—an average of one person injured approximately every 2 minutes. (Blincoe, Seay et al., 2002)

–   Alcohol is closely linked with violence. About 40% of all crimes (violent and non-violent) are committed under the influence of alcohol. (Bureau of Justice Statistics, 1998)

–   Alcohol is society's legal, oldest and most popular drug. (Narcotic Educational Foundation of America, 2002)

–   Beer is the drink most commonly consumed by people stopped for alcohol-impaired driving or involved in alcohol-related crashes. (IHS, 2003)

–   Those drivers 21 to 24 years old were most likely to be intoxicated (BAC of 0.08 g/dl or greater) in fatal crashes in 2002. Thirty-three percent of drivers 21 to 24 years old involved in fatal crashes were intoxicated, followed by ages 25 to 34 (28%) and 35 to 44 (26%). (NHTSA, 2003)

– The impact of alcohol involvement increases with injury severity. Alcohol-involved crashes accounted for 10% of property damage only crash costs. 21% of nonfatal injury crashes; and 46% of fatal injury crash costs. (NHTSA, 2002)

– The intoxication rate (those over 0.08 BAC) for male drivers involved in fatal crashes was 25%, compared with 12% for female drivers. (NHTSA, 2003)

– The average person metabolizes alcohol at the rate of about one drink per hour. Only time will sober a person up. Drinking strong coffee, exercising or taking a cold shower will not help. (Michigan State University, 2002)

– For fatal crashes occurring from midnight to 3:00a. m., 79% involved alcohol (NHTSA, 2001)

– Drunk driving is the nation's most frequently committed violent crime, killing someone every 30 minutes. (NHTSA, 2003)

– In 2002, motor vehicle crashes were the leading cause of death for people from 2 to 33 years old. (NHTSA, 2003)

– In 2002, 31% of all fatal crashes during the week were alcohol-related, compared to 54% on weekends. For all crashes, the alcohol involvement rate was 4% during the week and 11% during the weekend. (NHTSA, 2003)

– All states and the District of Columbia now have 21-year-old minimum drinking age laws. It is estimated that these laws have reduced traffic fatalities involving drivers 18 to 20 years old by 13% and have saved an estimated 21,887 lives since 1975. In 2002, an estimated 917 lives were saved by minimum drinking age laws. (NHTSA, 2003)

Read again the first statistic: a drunk driver kills a person in the U.S.A. every 30 minutes. Two per hour. Forty-eight per day. If the United States government had evidence that foreign terrorists were systematically killing two Americans per hour, 24 hours a day, seven days a week, don't you think they'd do something about it? And, if a foreign terrorist was caught in the act of killing an American, do you think he'd only get two years in jail? A killer is a killer, no matter his or her country of origin and no matter his or her choice of weapon. Premeditated murder starts when the bullets are put in the chambers of the gun the murderer knows he's going to be shooting into a crowd, and just as the drinker swallows that first of many mouthfuls of alcohol knowing she is soon going to be driving her car into traffic. Both are premeditated crimes that are potentially fatal for anyone getting in the way of the bullet or the car, and both criminals should be treated as potential murderers. That's my opinion.

So, how are we doing in Canada? The drunk driver who was responsible for the deaths of two girls and the severe injuries of fifteen others at Stokes Pit got three months in youth detention. Kind of takes your breath away, doesn't it? We need to rethink our relationship with this drug, alcohol, and re-examine how our laws protect our citizens, through both preventative measures and punishment-as-deterrent measures. We have a long way to go. In Canada, raising the legal drinking age to 21 would be a good start. Acknowledging the three to four people killed each day by drunks might make us rethink our casual relationship with alcohol. Would we Canadians be so complacent if we were made aware of terrorists who were killing three to four Canadians each day? I would hope not. But it seems we are when it comes to alcohol.

The government of British Columbia drafted new legislation in November, 2004, that will tighten up our drunk driving laws. The discussion paper is available on the internet at: www.pssg. gov.bc.ca/legislation/drinking-driving/strategies.htm. In brief, the province is looking at the following strategies: Education and awareness; Influencing the decision to drive; Enforcement; Sanctions; and Rehabilitation. They plan to increase education in secondary schools, enhance the "Serving it Right" provincial server intervention program; enhance enforcement by providing more officers and giving them more training in recognizing impairment and more flexibility in enforcement. For example: "Use existing roadside blood alcohol screening devices to collect evidence in support of an ADP rather than have to take the driver to a police station for a breathalyzer." Under Sanctions, they propose lowering the criminal blood alcohol count (BAC) to 0.05 instead of the current 0.08 BAC to impose 90-day driving suspensions.

In addition, in 2002, "25% of all the [criminal] trials scheduled in Provincial Court were for impaired driving"(4), therefore in order to reduce the motivation to contest charges, the government is proposing allowing convicted drunk drivers a provisional driver's license for work purposes only, and to install ignition interlock devices in their cars for the duration of the suspension. This Strategy reads: "Establish provincial offences under the Motor Vehicle Act for impaired driving and refusing a Breathalyzer that would entail a short (90 day) driving prohibition, provisional licensing during the prohibition period for work purposes, a fine and ignition interlock [car won't start unless alcohol-free air is blown into device]." They explain, "The new offence would give police a new alcohol-related tool that could be used. The new offence would also be available to Crown Counsel when an accused is prepared to plead guilty rather than go to trial on a criminal offence."

British Columbia was the only province without a mandatory rehabilitation program for drunk drivers. Our government hopes to rectify that by implementing a user-pay rehabilitation program for B.C. drivers who have:

"– Any Criminal Code drinking and driving conviction.

– Any 24-hour driving prohibition or 90-day ADP within two years after a Criminal Code drinking and driving conviction.

– Any combination of three 90-day ADPs and 24-hour driving prohibitions within two years.

A program of this scope would apply to approximately 14,000 suspended or prohibited drivers annually. To re-obtain their license, they would have to complete education or treatment and pass an addiction assessment."

From my point of view, this is all good news for British Columbians. This government is moving in the right direction, even if it sometimes appears to be in baby-steps. From the State of New Mexico in the U.S.A., Governor Bill Richardson's office sent me their *Ignition Interlock Task Force Final Report*. This report supports legislation that requires mandatory Interlocks for convicted drunk drivers for years at a time. For example, on the first conviction the driver must use the Interlock for one year; for the second conviction the driver must use the Interlock for two years; for the third conviction the driver must use the Interlock for three years; for four or more convictions the driver must use the Interlock for life. The Task Force also calls for the development of "tax and insurance incentives for voluntary use of ignition interlocks." They also are calling on their government to amend the law to "develop penalties for tampering with an Interlock device," and to increase "90-day driver's license revocation to one year for first time offenders... 2 years for second; 3 years for 3rd; and lifetime with a 5-year review for 4th arrest." We, here in British Columbia, still have a long way to go.

Remember driving forty, thirty, twenty and ten years ago? No seatbelts, no anti-lock brakes, no safety glass, no headrests and no air-bags. All these safety features evolved over time due to our increased awareness of easily preventable injuries. That's how I feel about ignition Interlock systems. In July of 2003, I began communicating with Ian Marples, President of *Guardian Interlock Systems* (now *Alcohol Countermeasure Systems, Director of research and development*) of Toronto, and he now seems confident that we may soon be able to purchase a smaller, more efficient model of the ignition Interlock for voluntary use. The current model that Alcohol Countermeasure Systems is working on is called the *WR3*. Mr. Marples anticipates that the prototype of the WR3 will be ready by June or July of 2005 and available for public use by late 2005. This is exciting news. Can you imagine how many parents would install these in their teenagers' first cars? I expect most would. But I have an even bigger dream: I envision a future where ignition Interlocks are standard equipment in *all* motor vehicles. Imagine the drop in deaths from drunk driving, let alone the savings to automobile insurance companies. Mr. Marples thinks these devices might sell for around $500, which some people will think is high;

but what if insurance companies reduced the car insurance fees by the same amount? Insurance companies would more than make up for the costs in reduced claims; and these devices can be checked every year or two when car-owners take their cars through our already mandatory AirCare (air-pollution checks on exhaust emissions). Forty years ago the only people using seatbelts were racing car drivers and stuntmen. Now they are mandatory equipment. In the United States a person is killed by a drunk driver every 30 minutes. In Canada a person is killed every 7 ½ hours. How long will it take before ignition Interlocks are mandatory? If we can put a dune-buggy on Mars surely we can fine-tune the technology needed for this very important device that could put an end to this relentless vehicular terrorism committed by drunks.

Ian Marples recently sent me an article from Autoweb.com.au . It is a press release from the Saab car company in Sweden and I would like to share it with you:

Saab Develops "Alcokey" Breathalyser, 15 June, 2004

SAAB IS DEVELOPING an innovative car key that doubles up as a miniature breathalyser to prevent potential drunk drivers from starting their cars.

What makes the Saab 'Alcokey' unique is its size and that it will be integrated into the car key—unlike more costly and complicated alcohol detecting devices fitted to a car's dashboard or door locks.

Saab Alcokey is being trialed in Sweden with the support of the influential Swedish National Road Administration.

Alcokey's ease of use and relative affordability—around $400—means it could be offered as an accessory through Saab dealers if the trials prove successful.

The Saab Alcokey concept features a small mouthpiece in the car's key fob. When the driver presses the 'doors open' button on the car key fob, the alcohol sensor is also switched on.

The driver then blows into a small mouthpiece at the end of the fob to provide a breath sample which passes down a small internal tube containing a semi-conductor.

The sample is then analysed, and a small green or red light on the fob is illuminated. If the green light is shown, the key will transmit an 'all clear' signal to the car's electronic control unit to allow the engine to be started.

However, if a red light is shown, the 'all clear' signal will not be sent and the engine will, therefore, remain immobilised.

The software instructing the engine immobiliser can be adjusted according to statutory alcohol limits.

The current prototype Alcokey is a separate unit, about 10cm long and 4cm wide [4 x 1 ½ inches], additional to a conventional Saab key. It is envisaged that the final production version of the Alcokey will see both the key and alcohol detector contained in a single, pocket-sized unit.

Mounting concern about drink [sic] driving in Sweden as well as other countries has prompted Saab to develop the Alcokey concept.

Companies operating large car fleets could be anxious to demonstrate their social responsibility by having an alcohol-detecting device such as Alcokey fitted as standard. Insurance companies may also provide incentives for drivers of cars fitted with Alcokey.

"Saab is an innovative brand and in that tradition the Alcokey concept is a very practical and efficient solution," says Saab's global President and CEO, Mr. Peter Augustsson. "Saab Alcokey will help those who want to be sure they should only get behind the wheel when they are fit to drive."

Last year alcohol was a factor in 29 per cent of driver deaths on Swedish roads.

* * * * * * * * * * *

Imagine a world that has no need for organizations like MADD. Imagine the police not having to spend their valuable time conducting road-blocks for drunk drivers. Imagine a 25% reduction in criminal court cases in the province of British Columbia alone. Imagine how this device would lighten the loads on our over-stressed hospitals, our paramedics, our doctors and nurses, and on our waiting lists for surgeries. Imagine the reductions in car insurance due to the reduced claims. Imagine not worrying about driving after midnight. Imagine attending fewer funerals for teenagers. Imagine our world just one device, one law away.

4.12 The Other Victims from Stokes Pit:

In my quest for the truth about the events of September 13th, 1997, I made several attempts to find the fifteen surviving victims from Stokes Pit. I was able to find almost half of them, but I soon realized that most of these young people did not want to talk about what was the single most traumatic event of their lives. I spoke with many of their parents, and even they were very emotional when speaking with me. I realized that in contacting them I inadvertently stirred up all those old buried emotions; and most of them could not handle speaking directly with me. I sincerely apologize to those I upset. I did not anticipate the strong emotional reactions from some of the parents and their children and I truly apologize for this.

I did manage to speak with a few of the victims and witnesses from Stokes, and from our conversations I was better able to piece together the events of the night at Stokes Pit and weed out the rumours to get a clearer picture. I thank these young people now and acknowledge the courage it took to speak with me and to dredge up all those old horrors. I appreciate your candour and your courage and wish you well. Heidi knew most of you, and loved some of you, and she'd be thanking you now if she could. I thank you again.

Courtney Wilson, 2004

I was seventeen years old and a student at Langley Secondary School at the time of the accident. I think the last person I was talking to was Jason, about what we were going to be doing when we graduated. I don't remember much of that night and sometimes I think my memory is mostly from what other people have told me. I received a compound fracture of my tibia and fibula on my right leg. I fractured my pelvis in front and back. I fractured my left shoulder, and broke several ribs on both sides. I suffered soft tissue damage, whiplash, and psychological trauma. I have suffered from P.T.S.D. (Post Traumatic Stress Disorder), clinical depression, headaches, sleep disturbances and anxiety.

I was taken directly to Royal Columbian Hospital in New Westminster. My leg was operated on at about 5:00 a.m., by Dr. O, the same orthopaedic surgeon who later fixed Heidi's legs. I stayed in hospital for two weeks and returned home on September 26th. I have never fully recovered from these injuries. I do not have full range in my left shoulder and still suffer from this ongoing pain. I cannot do high impact sports with my leg, so there will be no jumping or fast running for the rest of my life. If I do, then I deal with the pain. The missing bone tissue in my tibia did not initially knit together when the titanium rod was inside, so I had to have some bone taken from my hip and transplanted to my tibia after the rod was removed. These operations have been very painful and upsetting, and the long recovery times have been very frustrating for me.

I was never able to attend high school full time after the accident. I went part-time, then supplemented with distance education and L.E.C. (Langley Education Centre). I finished my grade twelve diploma half a year later than expected. I still have recurring nightmares, many different ones that won't go away.

On the subject of the drunk driver who caused my injuries and my best friend's death, I would have liked him to talk to high schools and speak about the incident (like I do), but I can understand how hard it would be for him.

Not one part of my life is the same now. This car crash affected every part of my life. I don't talk to anyone who was at the accident any more. I attended Heidi's funeral in a wheelchair, and a year later I was at her burial. I have an Associate of Arts Degree in Psychology, and I'm still going on with my university studies while I work at a private elementary school, teaching autistic children. I volunteer at high schools with my presentation on drinking and driving, and this I do about once a month. If the accident had never happened, I would be a different person and a lot further in my schooling.

One of the things I remember from the hospital is that Heidi's Mom came to see me all the time and brought me fresh juice. I felt so bad when I left the hospital that day and left Heidi there. I remember when I was crying and she was comforting me I thought it should be the opposite.

I have had five operations since the car crash. I had to have a blood transfusion; my bones went right through and out of my leg, both the tibia and fibula. I don't remember that night and what I do I don't know if I remember it myself, or from stories. I have had water therapy, physiotherapy, chiropractic manipulation, massage and horse therapy. I am still in pain.

Heidi and I were very close and her death has had a profound affect on me. She was like a sister to me and I loved her very much. I will always love Heidi.

Jamie Hyde, 2004

I was at Stokes Pit when the accident happened, and the events of that night changed my life forever. I was sixteen years old and just starting grade eleven that fall. I was talking with Heidi and Courtney just before they were struck by the car and if not for a few seconds, I could have been one of the injured or dead. I remember seeing lots of sparks as the Eldorado sideswiped the Honda, and people were yelling and screaming and throwing things at the car as it sped away. It was very dark and therefore hard to find my friends. Bodies were lying all over the road and everyone was trying to find their friends during the frenzied first few minutes. I ran over to Heidi and she said her legs hurt. I remember looking at the odd way Heidi's feet were positioned: her knees were facing upwards as she lay flat on her back, but her feet were splayed open and lying on the road on their sides – an impossible position. It took me a few seconds to realize why her feet were flopped over on their sides. This image still haunts me.

I saw Courtney crumpled at Heidi's feet and watched as she used her one good arm to drag herself along the length of Heidi's body. Courtney kept passing out, but each time she woke up she dragged herself closer to Heidi's head. Finally, she stopped moving after she curled herself around Heidi's head. I couldn't stop her. Vanessa was a few feet away and when I found her she said she couldn't feel anything in her hands or feet. She asked me to lift up her arm and drop it. I did this for her without thinking of her injuries. She cried out that she couldn't feel anything in her arms or legs; she was very scared. I saw some people doing CPR on Ashley. People were calling 911 on their cell phones, and then the police cars, fire trucks and ambulances started to arrive.

When I finally got home that night I went to bed without washing up. The next morning I woke up to discover my arms were covered in blood. It was Heidi's blood from her head when I was cradling it in my lap, and now it was dried and caked all over my arms and hands. I washed the blood off. I have had many nightmares in which I am trying to wash the blood off my arms, but it won't come off. Heidi's blood stays with me. I had horrible nightmares for many years after Heidi died, but they are better now.

Heidi was one of my best friends and I felt like she was a part of my family. Everything was different from then on. School was a struggle to complete. Our group of friends split apart and now we hardly ever get together. No one wants these terrible memories to come back and each time we see each other, Stokes Pit comes flooding back. But I have many happy memories of Heidi that make me smile, and these are what I like to remember most.

I was angry at "John" for the longest time and I have had a hard time forgiving him. I don't think he should ever be allowed to have his driver's license back. He should not drive again. I think his sentencing was too light; three months is nothing.

I have moved on with my life. I graduated from Langley Secondary School in 1999 and went on to Cosmetology School where I earned my diploma as a Hair Stylist. I worked in Calgary, Alberta, for a while, but have recently come back to Langley, and my family. I am living on my own now and working as a full-time stylist. I am trying to put some order into my life. I am happy and my life seems to be moving forward again. I will never forget Heidi and the good times we shared. I love you Heidi.

Victor Martin, 2004

I was an eighteen year old student at D.W. Poppy High at the time of the accident. I was at Stokes Pit with a group of my friends that night and I had my back turned towards the car and didn't even see it coming. I flew into the bushes beyond the ditch and I lay there for what seemed an eternity until my friends found me. I suffered soft tissue damage in both knees, and one fractured knee cap. My right leg suffered a fractured fibula. I was taken to Langley Memorial Hospital, but I don't remember what time I got there or at what time I received my surgery. I only stayed in the hospital for two nights. I came home on September 15th. I couldn't return to school until the end of September, and then I had a lot of catching up to do before I graduated. I didn't play in any sports during my grade twelve year. Six years later, my injuries are all healed and my leg is close to being back to normal.

I have had some really detailed nightmares since the accident. I dream of my family members getting hit by a car, or some of my closest friends. Things are really rough, with a friend (Heidi) passing away, and all the inquiries about the accident, but you have to move on. September 13th, 1997, that day has been stamped into my head and will never be forgotten. I met Heidi through Jamie Hyde a few years before the accident. She was a very beautiful, loving, warm spirit that was always happy to see you. Smile worth a million bucks. I attended the funeral service and it was very emotional. I said my goodbyes to Heidi there, so I didn't attend the burial a year later.

On the subject of "John," I feel the punishment was quite light, but if you're under nineteen you can do pretty much anything these days.

I have just moved back from the Kootneys and I'm getting involved with the City Fire Department. I graduated from College a couple of years ago and I'm doing okay now. I live with a roommate and we're getting by as well as can be expected. I have lost touch with a lot of the people that were involved in Stokes Pit, injured or not. I just want to thank them for giving me the strength and support I needed to overcome this tragedy. A day that will never be forgotten.

Ryan Kilby, 2004

I was seventeen at the time of the accident, and a student at D. W. Poppy High School. I was with Jamie the night of September 12th and 13th. We were talking with Courtney, Heidi, Vanessa and Jason. I walked across the road and called for Jamie to join me. Then the car came ripping behind us and all I heard was people screaming. It was very dark out and I had trouble finding our friends. People were running everywhere in a panic and crowding around the injured. Bodies were lying on the road, in the ditches and in the bushes. It was crazy. Jamie and I stayed with Heidi, Courtney and Vanessa until the ambulances took them away. We wanted to go with our friends to the hospitals, but the paramedics wouldn't let us ride in the ambulances. Jamie and I got a ride to my home and then we went to Jamie's. It was a long, horrible night.

I have had nightmares about this night, where I was always seeing the incident reoccur, but it was a little different each time. I can't really explain these dreams. This tragedy will never be forgotten; I will think of it forever. People that are important to you might be gone tomorrow, but better judgement and decision-making can prevent such innocent deaths and save lives.

The drunk driver is a friend of mine and I know him as a

good, honest person. I know he would have accepted any punishment.

I was at Heidi's funeral and at her burial a year later. I put a photograph of myself and Jamie and our closest friends into the vault with her urn.

I finished my grade twelve and am enrolled at BCIT (British Columbia Institute of Technology) to become an electrician. I am a Langley City Firefighter and I'm enjoying this work.

Heidi was a good friend and before the accident those three girls (Heidi, Jamie and Courtney) were inseparable and the funnest people to hang out with. But unfortunately, Heidi's death broke everyone apart; I guess it was too much. But for the better part of four years, Jamie and I stayed together: a relationship that Heidi started. So many things have changed since the accident but I'll never forget Heidi's loving personality. I still have the '97 Grad picture of Heidi, Courtney and Jamie on my mantle to remember those times.

And last but not least, here is a statement of apology we received from "John," the drunk driver responsible for the tragedy at Stokes Pit:

Dear Klompas Family,

I never pictured myself having to ever do something like this; it's as hard for me to write this as it is for you to read it. This whole tragic incident has totally changed my life. It has probably changed yours too and I'm sorry it has. I never meant to do what I did, but because of my impairment it happened and I can't even remember any of it. Even though I was impaired while the accident happened it doesn't mean that it's okay because I wasn't myself. I believe I am fully responsible for my actions even though I wish it would have never happened. I have caused much grief, pain and sorrow and when I think about it it's hard to believe that it was me who caused it all. I think about what happened every day and can't believe what a fool I was. I have to deal with this the rest of my life knowing what I've done. I can't say how sorry I am for causing the passing of Heidi as well as the pain you must feel from losing someone you love so much. I never meant for any of this to happen. I'm not the type of person who would ever think of doing this on purpose. I know I have committed a crime as well as betrayed my friends and community. But I have to be ready to handle whatever I have to. In this letter I'm not asking for your forgiveness. I just want to let you know how sorry I am as well as how I'm feeling about what I did to your family. I apologise sincerely.

Yours Truly,

[... .] ["John"]

4.13 Saying Goodbye

Five and a half years after Heidi's death I finally find the courage to read the autopsy report. Imagine my surprise when I discover that not only are her corneas, kidneys, liver and heart donated, but also large tracts of skin from her thighs. No one had mentioned this to me before and I have to wonder why? After reading the autopsy report I now understand why they wouldn't let me view Heidi's body before she was cremated. Her eyes are gone, her heart, liver and kidneys are gone, her skin has been stripped off, and again to my surprise, her brain and spinal cord have been removed and taken to another facility for examination. She is but a shell of a human being at the time of her cremation.

As hard as it might be to see her in this state, I feel viewing her body would allow me some closure and give me the absolute confirmation I need that she is truly dead. It will dispel these thoughts of denial I have that she is not really gone. The last time I see Heidi is on the morning of October 8th. She is breathing through a respirator; she is warm and pink and appears sound asleep. How do I reconcile her death if I never see her body when it's not breathing? I am haunted by this image of my daughter sleeping in a hospital bed, very much alive.

I have recurring nightmares about this. Shall I tell you?

> I am sitting in a chair beside Heidi's hospital bed watching her sleep. Medical personnel (three or four of them), come into the room, flank her bed and start wheeling her towards the Operating Room doors. It is time to remove her beating heart. Heidi turns to me, extends her arm out towards me and pleads, "Mom, don't let them take my heart! Please Mom, I'm awake now, see? See me, Mom, I'm awake now!" She screams,

"Don't let them take my heart, don't let them kill me!" as they wheel her out the doors and away from me. I am frozen in my chair and cannot move. I try to scream but my voice is gone and I keep straining to use it. I am screaming but no sounds are coming out. I am paralysed and unable to stop them from killing my daughter. I struggle and struggle but I cannot move, cannot lift myself up out of the chair to save her. I can't save her.

I usually wake up screaming and moaning and soaking in sweat. My heart is pounding and I am crying in huge, gulping sobs. This nightmare always rattles me for days afterwards. I have had this dream many times and it is persistently the same: it never varies and it is always deeply disturbing. I have spoken with Courtney about this dream and she reports she has had the very same dream herself. This is what we have to live with now.

Why do these dramatic dreams plague me? Is it because of the trauma I experienced? Or are the dreams from some place else? Perhaps an intuition, if you will, that all was not right; that maybe something unusual has occurred regarding my daughter's death. Where is this ominous feeling coming from? I doubt that I will ever really know the answer to this. It is year six as I write this, and thankfully, the nightmares are becoming less frequent and less upsetting.

Date of Death

Two doctors separately tested Heidi for brain death. They each followed a fifteen minute procedure that tests deep pain response and other brain functions at the deep coma level.

They turn off the respirator and wait a few minutes to see if she spontaneously makes an effort to breathe on her own. On the morning of October 8th, after Heidi's family took their turns saying goodbye, the doctors began their tests. She was officially declared brain dead at 11:20 am, October 8th, 1997.

The next morning at 6:00 am, the heart team from Ontario began their work and Heidi's heart was lifted out of her body and flown to Toronto's Sick Kid's Hospital. I imagine her true time of death should have been when her heart was disconnected and lifted out of her chest: somewhere between 6:00 and 7:00 am. The rest of the organ harvesting was finished by 10:30 am.

Later that day a hospital employee phoned me to ask which date I wanted recorded as her official date of death for her death certificate: October 8th or 9th? As Heidi's sister Laura and I have birthdays on the ninth of September and November, respectively, I opted for the October 8th date. This date is now on Heidi's death certificate and is carved into her grave stone. But after some reflection I realised that it really wasn't the truth. Heidi 'actually' died, or her body ceased to live, or her heart stopped beating, on October 9th and not the 8th. I regret my decision at the time because it was not the absolute truth. Brain death is not body death. Her blood was still flowing, her heart was still beating, and her lungs were still breathing air well past midnight on October 8th. There is nothing I can do about this except to declare the mistake publicly, here and now in this book. Heidi actually died on October 9th, 1997.

How many devastated parents are asked to make such a choice as this? Forgive me, Heidi.

I Remember

I remember memories,
The ones that do not fade.
I remember Heidi,
And the memories that we made.

I remember crying,
Until the bitter end.
I remember screaming,
At the loss of my friend.

I remember dreaming,
That it was all a big mistake.
I remember feeling,
The intensity of the heartache.

I remember hoping,
That I'd see her face today.
I remember bitterly,
That October day.

I remember painfully,
The look on her mother's face.
I remember carefully,
The girl we can't replace.

Christina Williamson
1997

4.14   Kidney Dialysis Patients

At Royal Columbian Hospital, the private family rooms start on a corner, a junction if you will, that serves as a main intersection. One hall leads to the maternity ward and delivery rooms. One hall leads to the operating theatres. Another leads to the Kidney Dialysis centre. The other hallway leads to the other wings of the hospital and the other towers. The hall I walk every day from the family room to the ICU ward takes me past the Kidney Dialysis ward and then left towards the Cardiac Unit. The ICU doors are halfway down the hall between the Cardiac and Kidney Dialysis wards. At first I don't notice the people waiting outside the Kidney Dialysis centre but after a few days I start to notice patterns. The same people are back every two or three days and they are noticeable by their yellowish skin and their lethargy. They come in all sizes, races and ages, and they sit slumped in their chairs while waiting for their turn on the dialysis machines. When I start to recognize certain faces, I finally look up at the sign above the doorway and realize what they are there for. As a lot, they look so sickly, so disheartened and so very tired.

I'd never before given much thought about the world of daily or weekly kidney dialysis, but seeing these poor souls waiting their turns gives me pause to consider what their lives must be like: to schedule their work, schooling and home life around these gruelling dialysis appointments. Most of them are waiting for kidney transplants, and most of them know they will eventually die if they don't receive a new kidney. This makes me think about organ donation and how important it is to sign the papers authorizing donation. Everyone in my family has done so, especially after what happened to Heidi and her organs.

Dear readers, it takes just a moment to register as an organ donor with the B.C. Transplant Society. Their toll-free number for registration is: **1-800-663-6189**. Also, you can register online at: **www.transplant.bc.ca**

Each province in Canada has a transplant organization, or

society, and I am sure they are listed in your local telephone books. Most countries in the world also have transplant societies, as well as blood donor clinics, and I urge you to participate in both of these. Heidi needed a lot of blood and blood products during her three and a half weeks in hospital, and in the end she gave others her organs. Blood donors kept her alive, and her organs are now keeping a few other people alive, or at least are enhancing their lives.

Please give blood, and please, please, register for organ donation at your Provincial, or State, transplant society. You may never know the lives you save, but know that you *will* save lives. Thank you.

4.15   A Boy Named Vicram

On October 1st, 1979, a baby boy is born to Mrs. Ralh and her husband, Dr. Surender Kumar Ralh, in Vancouver, British Columbia. They name him Vicram. The young Dr. Ralh has recently immigrated to Canada from India and is settling in with his young bride: starting up a family practice and a new family all at the same time. When baby Vicram is six months old his mother suddenly develops a heart condition known as Postpartum Cardiomyopathy; and it subsequently robs her of her young life on March 18th, 1980. Dr. Ralh is devastated, and knowing how difficult it will be to raise a baby while working the full-time, chaotic hours of a new doctor, he and his family decide to send the infant to India to be raised by his paternal grandparents until Dr. Ralh can provide a traditional home for him in Canada.

Vicram Ralh grows up in the capital city of India, New Delhi; and for the next fifteen years he is lovingly cared for by his doting grandparents. He proves to be a good student at a private English school where he perfects his second language in preparation for coming to Canada some day. Vicram's father visits his son in India several times over the next fifteen years, and the two become very close. His father visits him once when he is still a toddler. A few years later Surender's family arranges a new bride for him, and he sends her to Delhi to meet his son prior to their wedding. The young woman and the little boy instantly bond; she is his new mother. A year later Mrs. Rajinder Kaur Ralh produces a son, Manish Kumar, and then a few years later a daughter, Neeharika Raakhi, is born. The expanding family visits Vicram in India three or four times before he finally joins them in Canada. In India, Vicram's beloved grandfather passes away when he is fifteen years old and it is decided he will now rejoin his father in Canada. Vicram is thrilled to be living with his father, his new mother, his younger brother and his adorable little sister, whom he affectionately nicknames "Motti" (chubby). Vicram quickly adapts to life in Canada. After a stint in Newfoundland, the doctor finally settles his growing family in Etobicoke, Ontario, and this busy suburb of Toronto soon proves to be a good location for Dr. Ralh's family practice; they buy a nice home in a good neighbourhood. The parents enrol their children in a large private school, and the children all excel in their education while actively participating in a variety of sports. Vicram enjoys softball (wins MVP in 1996), basketball, volleyball, badminton and tennis.

In June of 1997, Vicram is playing in a tennis tournament when he first notices something is wrong with his heart. He makes it to the finals, but two days after the tournament he starts to feel a shortness of breath. Vicram has just started work at a door factory and there is a lot of sawdust in the air. His father feels Vicram's wheezing is a direct result of inhaling the fine sawdust. He asks his son not to go back to work, but just like a typical teenager, Vicram defies his father and returns to work in the dusty factory. His wheezing and shortness of breath become acute by the end of the next day. He uses an inhaler for asthma, but this does little good. Vicram cannot sleep and is very restless. His father decides to take him to the hospital at 4:00 in the morning, and there they sit and wait for over two hours. Finally, Dr. Ralh cannot wait any longer and at 7:00 am he decides to take Vicram to his own clinic for chest x-rays. They go home afterwards and Vicram catches up on his sleep. The next day the x-ray report is completed and Dr. Ralh is horrified to read that his son has an enlarged heart. He tells Vicram he is not going back to work, but instead is going to the hospital. When Dr. Ralh reads the x-ray report it reminds him of what he experienced with Vicram's birth mother. He tells Vicram what happened to his first wife.

At the hospital, the ECG shows some changes in Vicram's heart. He is showing PVC's, or Premature Ventricular Contractions and he is in congestive heart failure. They try to get in to see a Cardiologist right away but are told he'll have to wait at least a week before seeing one. Vicram's father calls a Paediatric Cardiologist who works out of Toronto's Hospital for Sick Children and convinces him to see Vicram the next day. That night Vicram wants to go home so that he can attend a party with his friends. They argue about it until his father agrees to drive him to the party on the condition he can wait in his car out front. And so they do.

The next day Vicram and his father see the Cardiologist and an Echocardiogram is done on his heart. It shows a heart in very poor condition and Vicram is told to get to Sick Kid's Hospital as soon as possible. The Cardiologist makes immediate arrangements to have Vicram admitted the same day. Dr. Ralh knows how bad this is going to be from his experience as a doctor and as the husband of a woman who succumbed to heart disease. He keeps the information mostly to himself as he doesn't want to upset his wife and two younger children. He knows what the prognosis is going to be for his son. Vicram's disease is known as Cardiomyopathy: enlargement of the heart. There is no known cure. He is slowly going into heart failure and is hospitalized. After some weeks, the doctors at Sick Kid's give Vicram some experimental medicine for his heart and send him home, telling his dad, "Don't worry, he'll be okay." But he is not okay.

Vicram is having difficulty breathing when climbing the stairs, so his parents have the basement quickly outfitted with a small kitchen, bedroom and bathroom so that he doesn't have to worry about exerting himself. The family takes their meals downstairs with Vicram over the next few days. His physical activities are restricted and he can no longer run, walk fast, climb stairs or go downstairs; he must also restrict his water and salt intake. As his condition deteriorates, Vicram is registered for a heart transplant at Toronto General Hospital. If he stays at home then his position is lower on the transplant list; but if he is in the hospital he has a better chance at receiving a new heart. If he's in the ICU, then he is close to the top of the transplant recipient list. He gets sicker and sicker by the week and quickly makes his way to the top of this terrifying list.

Vicram goes home only a couple of times during the summer, but each time, within two or three days, his condition worsens and he has to return to the hospital. He stays in a regular ward room at first but he soon needs the services of the ICU (Intensive Care Unit). Vicram tries to count the lines, but he has so many IVs connected to his limbs he loses count. His mother, Rajinder, stays with him 24 hours a day, every day. She reads him passages from religious books that give him courage and strength, teach him spirituality and acceptance of his condition, and prepare him for what is to come, be it life with a new heart, or death. On October 1st his eighteenth birthday is celebrated in the ICU. Vicram is so weak he cannot drink even the tiniest bit of water. When he tries to swallow a mere 5ml with his pills, he quickly throws it back up. This is typical of people with congestive heart failure, this inability to tolerate fluids and the increased vomiting. He is put on IV fluids to keep him hydrated, although he complains that he is thirsty and wants a sip of water. His doctors forbid him to drink, but he sometimes sneaks in a sip when he asks for water to rinse out his mouth. And again he throws it up. By October of 1997, his condition deteriorates to the point he can no longer sit up or breathe on his own, and he is put on a Bi-Pap machine to breathe for him. His blood pressure is dropping and he needs additional IV medication to keep his blood pressure up at a safe level. His health steadily deteriorates during his ten days in the ICU.

By October 7th, Dr. Ralh is told his son is not going to survive for much longer without a new heart. In the Intensive Care Unit, another boy Vicram's age awaits a new heart as well, and soon the two boys are deathly sick with just days to live. The other boy is scheduled to receive his new heart ahead of Vicram, if and when one becomes available. Vicram struggles to breathe with the respirator and can no longer speak easily. Surender's heart is completely broken at the thought of losing his son, and this grieving brings back memories of losing his first wife to heart disease (a slightly different condition than Vicram's). The family is distraught, not knowing what will happen next.

In the early morning hours of October 9th, the miracle call comes in from Vancouver: a seventeen year old girl has just been declared brain-dead and her heart will soon be made available. At 9:00 am the doctor calls Vicram's father into the hospital because there is the possibility of a heart for his son. The doctor can't promise suitability or guarantee anything but wants both parents there just in case. Rajinder wants to place a photograph of their guru, Baba Gi, under Vicram's pillow, but Vicram says, "No, Mom, I have him here in my heart. I will be fine." The two transplant teams scramble to assemble. Dr. Ralh joins his wife within the hour and together they wait the long agonizing hours until they get word. When the heart arrives it is Vicram's team that is fully prepared to operate immediately. This heart has travelled a great distance, from Vancouver to Toronto, and it is kept "on ice" for longer than the optimum time length for transplantation; but the situation is desperate and the boys need this heart now. Vicram is taken to the Operating Room at noon. His team is ready and so he is chosen to receive this very special heart.

The doctors ask the Ralhs to council the parents of the other boy who was also waiting for a new heart. This boy was driven for four or five hours to Toronto's Sick Kid's Hospital even though he was never on the list to receive a transplant. Whatever his problem was it must have come on much faster than Vicram's condition. He has the same blood group as Vicram and is a match for this heart. And this poor sick boy won't survive long without a new heart. His parents are suffering just as the Ralhs are suffering.

The heart is brought into the OR at noon. It must be tested first outside the body to see if it still works, then when it's deemed acceptable, they'll remove Vicram's defective heart and replace it with this new one. Hours later the surgeons insert a plate behind Vicram's sternum and close up the long incision with a thick row of staples. The operation takes nearly seven hours. After what seems like an eternity of anguish, Vicram's father is told the good news: the new heart is functioning well and his son is starting to wake up. Vicram is taken to the PACU, Post Anaesthesia Care Unit, until he is fully awake and aware. It takes him some time to come out of the anaesthesia as there is often a great deal of discomfort and nausea associated with "waking up." He is well aware the same evening, although he is drowsy from all the painkillers and sedation medications. He hallucinates for awhile. The next day he is fully conscious and knows what has happened to him. It really is a miracle: it looks like Vicram will survive after all. The Ralh family rejoices and from that day onward, they celebrate Vicram's birthday on two dates: October 1st for when he is born, and October 9th for when he is given the gift of life with his new heart. Sadly, the other boy waiting for a new heart dies the next day.

Within two days they let him try to stand up. Over the next few months Vicram works hard at learning how to walk again as he has some trouble balancing. The months of inactivity in hospital have atrophied his muscles and it takes some time for him to regain control of his limbs. He goes back to school to finish his grade thirteen, and in June of 1998, he wins the Governor-General's award for excellence in academic achievement in his graduating class, along with several other awards and scholarships. He is accepted into both the University of Toronto and London's Computer Engineering programs. Because Toronto General is the only hospital for transplant patients, Vicram decides to attend the U of T (University of Toronto) because it is close to the hospital. He takes up residency at his university, close to his classrooms, and is provided with reasonably priced food. This is deemed best for his heart. He excels at university and the next summer he works for a computer engineering company where he designs and constructs computers.

During the next few years Vicram is actively involved with NIMDAC: Northern India Medical and Dental Association of Canada. NIMDAC holds annual three-day events in which the doctors attend continuing education seminars and their families enjoy a variety of activities and entertainment. They go on cruises, play golf, hold tennis tournaments, and go bowling. Vicram often DJs for the parties on the cruise ship and helps organize many events, especially for the children. He designs the web page for NIMDAC and assists in any way he can. These are fun events for the Ralh family and they look forward to them every year. First there were just a handful of doctors participating, but over the years close to forty doctors have joined the association and the three-day event now accommodates over 250 family members. NIMDAC is based in Toronto, Ontario.

In February of 1998, four months after Heidi dies, I receive a letter from Vicram. The B.C. Transplant Society edits out his name and his hometown in compliance with privacy regulations, so I have no idea at this time who he is. I contact a woman at the Transplant Society and ask to be put in touch with this person who has written me such a wonderful letter. She refuses, stating they have rules against relaying personal information between donor families and organ recipients. Problems can arise, which I'll get into later. 1998 is an especially hard year for me and it isn't until after my separation from my husband in October that I decide to try writing back to this young person. The letter has to go through the B.C. Transplant Society, so I request they leave my letter intact and instead allow the Ontario Transplant Society to decide whether or not the heart recipient should receive my name and address. I send my letter on January 21ˢᵗ, 1999. (By this time my marriage has ended, I have moved to a new address and I have reclaimed my maiden name, Adamson). Determined to find this person with Heidi's heart, I write a letter to the editor of the Toronto Star newspaper two months later, asking for this recipient to contact me. It doesn't work. Meanwhile, some angel at the Ontario Transplant Society works her magic.

Late one night, in June of 1999, I receive a telephone call that rocks my world. The voice on the phone asks if I am Catherine Adamson; he introduces himself as Vicram Ralh, heart recipient. I can't believe it. Five months after I sent the letter, here he is! We talk for more than two hours on the phone (his bill must have been huge!). He calls again a few weeks later and over the course of our conversations we discover both he and Heidi loved softball and mangoes; they both were taking courses in photography and liked to draw. Vicram and I discuss our newfound spirituality and our appreciation of the sublime in everyday things. We talk like we've always known each other.

This boy is walking and breathing with my daughter's heart inside his chest; it is too wonderful for words, this discovery of Vicram. Later on, I speak with his mother and father and they thank me profusely for their son's extended life. We speak of organ donation and I learn that Vicram has been very active with the Ontario Transplant Society, often giving speeches to roomfuls of doctors and students. We discuss visiting and it's decided their family of five will travel to B.C. this summer of 1999. Arrangements are made and I am jumpy with pins and needles awaiting their arrival.

The father decides that our first meeting should be in a public restaurant and accompanied by his long-time friend from their Newfoundland days, a well-known Vancouver forensic psychiatrist who teaches at UBC (University of British Columbia). Laura and I meet with Dr. and Mrs. Ralh and their friend at a restaurant on South Granville Street in Vancouver in July of 1999. We don't know what to expect but are pleased to discover that the Ralh family is sweet and loving and wonderfully emotional. Unfortunately, the week before they were due to leave for Vancouver Vicram came down with an infection that required hospitalization; therefore, he had to postpone his visit out west. The parents had already purchased non-refundable airline tickets so they decide to make the trip anyways, to still enjoy visits with their relatives and friends on the west coast. Vicram is left in the capable hands of his doctors and relatives in Toronto while his family is gone. Vicram's parents want to meet with me beforehand so that they can assess whether I am mentally and emotionally stable enough to meet with their son. They are being very cautious, and rightly so. I have read or heard of a case pending in the Ontario courts in which a donor's mother wanted partial custody of the nine-year-old recipient of her daughter's heart. I guess this is one of the reasons the transplant societies keep identities secret: some grief-stricken parents behave irrationally and cause problems unforeseen by doctors and the recipient families. I think our first meeting reassures all parties that we are dealing with intelligent, rational and kind-hearted people here. It's all good.

We spend a couple of hours chatting in the restaurant and then make plans for a daytrip out to Langley to visit my home with their two younger children. Rajinder says the children want to go horseback riding and asks if Langley has any riding stables they can avail themselves of. I laugh because my hometown of Langley claims to be the "Horse Capital of British Columbia." Our community has many riding stables, and there are several to choose from in the Campbell Valley Park area of South Langley, which is close to my home. So, a few days later, that's what we do. I am introduced to Manish, age thirteen, and Neeharika, age nine; and I escort them to the stables. The two children and their mother each ride a horse and are taken on a guided tour of the trails in and around Campbell Valley Park. They are gone for about an hour and Dr. Ralh and I spend this time talking about his family and Vicram. The near-loss of his eldest son was quite a traumatic event for him and he is so grateful for our decision to donate Heidi's organs. I know Heidi would be pleased to know she has saved this boy's life. This is a nice family.

The next summer, in August of 2000, I decide to drive my car across Canada to meet Vicram in Toronto. My sister, Heidi's Auntie Dawn, agrees to accompany me on the provision that we go all the way to Nova Scotia, "while we're in the neighbourhood." Laughing, I readily agree. So off we go on our transcontinental trek. We do not stop and sightsee like most tourists; instead we drive straight through stopping only for fuel, food, coffee, and sleep. We arrive in Toronto on the fourth day of our trip, and on the way to Etobicoke we pass through the towns of Milton and Mississauga so I can revisit the two homes my little family lived in during the first few years of our marriage. It feels bittersweet to see those homes with the mature trees now shading the properties. My babies' first years were spent in the province of Ontario, with both girls being born in Mississauga.

We arrive at the Ralh residence around noon, and the family pours out onto the front porch to receive us. (We are a little dusty by this time!). I see Vicram and my heart leaps in my chest. I know him! We smile and hug and it is as if we've always known each other. We are very calm in each other's presence. There isn't much we need to say to each other; just being in the same room seems enough. Vicram asks if I'd like a tour of their home and we soon part with the others and make our way upstairs. Vicram shows me his room, the main living area and the kitchen. We gaze out over the backyard and he tells me of the games he plays with his younger brother and sister. He loves his family deeply. He adores his mother and truly respects, and loves, his father. He is vividly aware of the trauma his illness has caused his family and he is especially conscious of the attention he is getting (from both myself and his extended family members) that is over and above the attention given to Manish and Neeharika, and he feels bad about it. He feels they deserve just as much attention as he does and is embarrassed that everyone is fussing over him so much.

Vicram has such a generous spirit, a life filled with love for others. I like to think his new heart has something to do with it, but Vicram is Vicram, no matter who his second heart came from. When we return to the ground floor we walk in on a peculiar scene. My sister, along with Rajinder, her friends and relatives, are all crying. Vicram and I just laugh. Even his father is teary-eyed. The emotions become too much for them and they all enjoy a good cry together. Somehow, Vicram and I are beyond the crying. We know this is as it should be: he and I standing in the same room together, knowing each other.

Rajinder, and her friend from Newfoundland who was visiting them at the time, make a beautiful meal for us that consists of a vast variety of Indian foods. It is absolutely delicious, and I appreciate the tremendous effort she must have put forth to prepare such an array of scrumptious food. I wish I could tell you the names of the dishes, but I cannot recall, or even pronounce, the names. What kind and generous people they all are. Dawn and I politely decline the Ralh's generous invitation to stay overnight, optioning instead to keep rolling towards the Atlantic. I feel the three hours we spend with their family is about all everyone needs for this visit. Perhaps the next time we meet we'll be able to withstand a longer visit, but for now I find the emotions we are experiencing to be exhausting. The Ralh's are a wonderful, wonderful family that I am so glad to know.

Dawn and I eventually make our way to Halifax and back to Langley, all within fourteen days. That's right; in two weeks we drive from the Pacific Ocean to the Atlantic and back again. We come back through the United States and visit Bangor, Maine (I'm a big Stephen King fan), and Fargo, North Dakota (remember the movie?). There is a Joni Mitchell painting exhibition in Saskatoon, so we stay overnight there on our way home. We visit a friend of mine in Calgary, a sister of our sister-in-law's (Karen, wife of our brother Darren) in Halifax, a friend of Dawn's in Prince George, and our brother Bill in Quesnel. No flat tires, no accidents, and no overheated radiators: it is an excellent road-trip.

Two years later, in July of 2002, the entire Ralh family comes to B.C. This time I arrange for a big family gathering in which my parents, brothers and sisters, nieces and nephews, Heidi's brother and sister, and some of Heidi's friends can all meet together over dinner at my place. Due to a previous commitment, Courtney Wilson cannot attend the dinner-party, therefore, two days before the party I take her into South Vancouver to meet Vicram at the home where he and his family are staying: the psychiatrist's home. We visit with the family for a few minutes then leave, as previously arranged, with Vicram to drive into Vancouver to find someplace private to talk. We settle on Kits Beach (in Kitsilano), and talk the afternoon and evening away while watching the sun slowly set over the water. It is a beautiful Vancouver evening and Courtney and Vicram have the chance to get to know each other. They talk about their post-secondary schooling, cars, music, and other such stuff that is important to twenty-somethings. When we arrive back at Vicram's hosts' home, his mother has prepared a large batch of authentic Chai Tea for us. My favourite! Courtney and I stay awhile longer, enjoying the delicious tea and, of course, their good company. On the way home, Courtney expresses her feelings about meeting Vicram, and how awkward she felt in his presence. She kept thinking, "This is Heidi's heart, this is Heidi's heart." She is pleased to have finally met the keeper of her best friend's heart, but is saddened over the circumstances. In retrospect, I am happy I brought Courtney to meet Vicram, regardless of the emotional toll.

Two days later, it is hot outside so I set up a buffet table in the kitchen and arrange for our families to sit around the patio in the backyard. My parents are thrilled to meet this boy with Heidi's heart, and to also meet his parents and siblings. The Ralh's and the Adamson's get along so well we feel like one great big multi-cultural family. By this time Manish has grown into a tall and muscular sixteen-year-old, and Neeharika is now twelve and about a foot taller. They all dress in nice clothing and Vicram looks as handsome as ever. The Ralhs stay for the afternoon and evening and we enjoy their visit immensely. Heidi's extended family has just grown by five more people and we are so happy for this new connection. Heidi's friends are nervous in Vicram's presence and don't know what to say to him. I think he feels bad as he realizes the effect he's having on them. They are awestruck watching this big tall handsome young man walking around with their friend's heart beating inside his chest. Some of Heidi's friends stay on after the others leave and we talk long into the night. Jamie Hyde, Tiffany Bernemann, and Leigh McRae were all so close to Heidi and they are having a hard time dealing with the reality of Vicram. Chrissie Williamson arrives late because she has been erecting a new cross at Stokes Pit to replace the original cross that vandals recently removed. She couldn't bear to see Heidi's memorial gone, and as a consequence she almost misses meeting Vicram. The evening ends late and in due course everyone returns to their respective homes happy and content with the day's events.

Later that summer, just before school is about to start, Vicram is playing baseball when he sprains his ankle. It is a bad sprain and he is put in a walking cast for six weeks. He had been living at home since he gave up his residency at U of T last spring (preferences for residencies are given to first and second year students). Now he is travelling to university via subway train, but this soon becomes too hard on him. He needs physiotherapy on his ankle two or three times a week at Toronto General and all this travel exhausts him. His parents find him an apartment just a five minutes' walk from his classes at U of T: a nursing residency close to both the hospital and university. This works well for Vicram, allowing him to ease up on the ankle's stress load; he travels home on the weekends.

In December of 2002, Vicram starts to feel some discomfort in his chest. He is taken to Toronto General Hospital and it is found that he has had a heart attack. They do an angiogram and it shows some blockage of the coronary arteries; three coronary arteries need an angioplasty to open them up. He feels better after this is done. His cholesterol is high due to the medicine he takes to suppress his immune system. This is common for most transplant patients because these drugs increase blood cholesterol levels; hence, he is put on cholesterol-lowering medication. Vicram is also put on Prednisone, a synthetic hormone that reduces inflammation and suppresses the immune response to foreign matter. One of the side effects of Prednisone is increased blood sugar levels. Vicram develops diabetes, then high blood pressure (hypertension) and high cholesterol, all of which are symptomatic of people with heart problems. Post transplant heart patients are at increased risk for high blood pressure, but he is still able to do most things. He is put on a restricted diet, but he finds this is hard to stick to. He likes to go out with his friends and party like most people in their early twenties. He mostly sticks to his new diet regimen but not always. Since his hospitalization leading up to the transplant, Vicram has been a strict vegetarian and non-drinker, in keeping with his faith. But he still likes the occasional junk food.

The Ralh family goes on vacation to Nova Scotia in 2003, and it is here that Vicram finds trouble in climbing steep stairways. The family is at a park and Vicram hesitates to go down the steps to the park because he is worried he won't be able to climb back up. His father offers to go down and videotape the scenery for him, but this bothers him and later depresses him because he wants to be able to do all the things that other young men his age are doing. These limitations bother him. He tries to take good care of his heart, but still, his prognosis is guarded. He is told to not overexert himself but to continue doing what he wants to do without pushing himself too hard. He is put on the list for another transplant. This is very hard on him, but he tries to focus on the positive things in life and he manages to keep upbeat about his life. He avoids talking about his heart because it depresses him to speak about it too much. His family respects his wishes and try not to bring it up too often.

A few months later, on August 14th, 2003, there occurs a massive power outage that stretches from the eastern United States towards the north and into central Canada. The lights go out at 4 pm at Dr. Ralh's clinic in Etobicoke but he assumes this outage is just temporary because they have had blackouts here before. Vicram calls his father at 4:15 pm to tell him that all of Toronto is in the dark. Manish is volunteering at a tennis tournament and no one can reach him. Cell phones are not working. They find a radio with batteries and listen to the news: the power outage is absolutely massive. All of New York City is out, as are all of Toronto and many places in between the two largest cities in the United States and Canada. All the traffic signals are out, as are most of the telephones. The city is at a standstill. Vicram reaches his mom at home at 6:30 pm and tells her he is okay and is coming home by bus. She offers to pay for a taxi but he refuses, saying he's enjoying this day because the weather reminds him of India. He wants to take his time. His father calls him a little later to tell him a friend will pick him up, but he's too late; Vicram has already left his apartment.

On this day, a Thursday, Vicram is experiencing some discomfort in his chest but he doesn't tell his parents this. He makes his way through the chaotic Toronto city traffic and into the Emergency Room of Toronto General Hospital. But he finds the ER extremely busy and filled with many injured people; Vicram decides to leave and perhaps come back tomorrow. His parents have no idea his heart is bothering him today.

It takes his mom a long time to drive to the tennis tournament to pick up Manish. Traffic is a nightmare; it is getting dark and the power is not back on. Traffic signals are still out at 9 pm when Rajinder finally arrives home with Manish. Vicram calls just after 9 pm from the subway station and tells his parents he is coming home and they are not to worry about him. The parents wait anxiously for him. It is 10:30, now 11:00 pm and there is nothing they can do. They have no way of contacting him and they are getting very worried. Vicram eventually shows up just after 11:00 pm. He had tried calling home but the phone is no longer working: it needs to be charged. He tells his mother he feels so depressed. He tells her this night reminds him of his home in India, the nice weather, the full moon. It's a beautiful night, so dark and quiet. The stars are out in their full glory due to the blackout. They take themselves outside and talk for hours. Vicram's friend comes over and they sit outside chatting until nearly 2:00 am. They are talking and laughing well into the night, enjoying this uniquely tranquil night in the city. His father has to work the next morning so he tells Vicram and his friend to go to bed sometime after 2:00 am. His family has no inclination of the events about to occur the next day. They are at peace this long dark night.

The next morning Dr. Ralh is working in his garden when a neighbour tells him the power is now back on. He decides to go into the clinic. Rajinder is invited to spend the day at a relative's air conditioned home which hasn't been affected by the power outage. It is another hot day and they aren't supposed to use their cooling systems yet because the power is not yet fully restored, so she readily agrees to visit her family in the cooler house. Vicram wants to stay home and rest.

Vicram is coughing and feels discomfort in his chest throughout the morning so he calls his father at noon and asks him to take him to the hospital. His father gets angry and asks him why he didn't go to the hospital yesterday when he was so close to it. Vicram tells him he did but it was too crowded so he left. His father is irritated; he has no gas in his car and must fill it up before returning home to fetch Vicram. The gas stations have huge line-ups of people needing gas who couldn't get any yesterday when the pumps stopped working. He needs time to see the patients in his clinic. He suggests Vicram go to another, closer hospital to get chest x-rays; but Vicram doesn't want to go to a hospital that doesn't specialize in transplant patients. His dad agrees to drive him into Toronto General but warns him it will take some time to first fill up the car. Dr. Ralh finishes up at work and heads out to find some gas before going home. He keeps checking his cell phone every half hour or so, just in case it starts working again. Vicram cannot reach him once he leaves his office. It takes Dr. Ralh 45 to 50 minutes to reach home even though he didn't get a full tank: there were thirty to forty cars ahead of him at the gas station. But Vicram is not at home when he gets there. The house is empty and he tries to reach his wife but there is no answer at the relative's home either. He tries but fails to contact Vicram via cell phone. He assumes Vicram has had a friend drive him into the city. Rajinder arrives home a little later and asks, "Where's Vicram?" She calls the hospital and is told Vicram is not there yet. She calls again and this time locates Vicram. The nurse tells them not to come into the hospital just yet because they are very busy right now, and they will get Vicram to call home when he can.

They say they are taking good care of him and not to worry. Being a doctor, the father feels they should not go there and get in the way. He doesn't feel it's going to be so too bad because Vicram has been coughing for several days now.

Vicram calls from the hospital at 5:30pm and tells them everything is fine. Blood tests have been taken and he is being seen by a Cardiologist. Dr. Ralh is mad at him and tells his son that's not the way to treat his life: delaying important medical care when he's feeling ill. Vicram argues with his father and tells him he doesn't know how he feels. But his father insists that when you are feeling ill you should go see your doctor in a timely fashion. Vicram apologises to his dad and then reveals what the test results show. His Troponin is high: this is a protein present in the blood after a heart attack; he must have been in pain for at least 24 hours. Dr. Ralh asks his son if he is having chest pains and Vicram confesses that yes, he's not been feeling well for several days now. His dad asks him why he didn't go into the hospital earlier. Vicram doesn't answer him. His father is not surprised; young people his age are still immature and this is typical to deny he is in trouble. He tells him he needs to take better care of himself. He should have come earlier and Dr. Ralh wonders if perhaps heart transplant patients don't feel the pain as others would because the nerves are severed during the transfer of organs. He tries to be understanding of his son's delay in seeking treatment. People tend to seek treatment faster when they are having most of the other symptoms of a heart attack such as coughing, shortness of breath, and severe pain. Vicram tells his dad he is being admitted and they'll do an ECG and an Echocardiogram. He tells his dad they can come in to see him once he's admitted upstairs. Dr. Ralh asks if he can come now, but Vicram says, "No Dad, don't come, it's busy. Whenever they're done I'll give you a call."

This day, Friday, the Ralh's were planning to travel to an uncle's place for birthday celebrations, but they don't want to go without Vicram. Vicram insists his parents not miss this much-anticipated party just because he isn't feeling well. He implores them to attend the party and they reluctantly agree. They leave for the party with Vicram agreeing to call them there. Rajinder doesn't want to go to the party but her husband insists because that's what Vicram wants them to do. Vicram asks them not to tell the relatives he's in the hospital; he doesn't want to spoil the party. He phones his uncle's home and speaks to his relatives at the party. He wishes his uncle a Happy Birthday and apologises for not being there. He calls some of his friends to let them know where he is and how he's doing, insisting they not come to the hospital but wait and visit him tomorrow. When the Ralhs are half way to the party Vicram calls his mother and tells her, "I love you, Mom. I love you." This is around 9:00 pm. He tells his dad he feels like he is drunk, drunk from the medicine, and that he thinks he's going to throw up. Dr. Ralh says they can come right to the hospital, but Vicram insists he's only feeling a little sick to his stomach. His dad asks if he's been given Morphine, and if so he should also take some Gravol to combat the nausea. He tells Vicram to ask for some Gravol and to call him back after he's taken it. That is the last time they could call because after 9 pm they cannot call into the hospital from the outside: calls can only come from the inside. This is the last time they speak to their son. When they reach the house they hear how Vicram has called to wish his uncle a Happy Birthday and to wish the same on another girl who was also celebrating her birthday on this date. He speaks with many others at the party. He speaks with his brother, Manish, and this is the last his family hears from him. His last call is to a friend, and the time recorded on the cell-phone records show the call ended at 9:15 pm.

According to hospital records Vicram vomits just after 9pm and then he asks for Gravol. The nurse goes to get the Gravol and that's when his heart starts beating irregular and he goes into cardiac arrhythmia. The doctors and nurses try valiantly but unsuccessfully to save his life. They cannot revive him. His time of death is recorded as 10:01 pm, August 15th, 2003.

The Ralh family leaves the party around 10:30–11 pm. They decide to wait for Vicram in the basement where it is cooler. (Residents of the Greater Toronto area are asked not to use their air conditioners due to the power not being fully restored yet.) His dad is surprised he hasn't called yet and they sit and wait for over an hour. They think they'll just wait for him to call. They assume he's gone to sleep, especially knowing Vicram has been given Morphine. They assume all is well. They don't go upstairs when they first arrive home; that is where the answering machine is and there is a message waiting for them: his condition is not good. Just after midnight they receive a call from a nurse at the hospital asking to speak with his mother, Rajinder, listed as his next of kin. Dr. Ralh wants to speak but the nurse insists she speak with the mother. That's when he knows something is terribly wrong. The nurse speaks with Dr. Ralh only to say that the doctor wants to speak with him and that he'll call them back. The nurse calls back in a few minutes to say the doctor wants Vicram's father to come to the hospital to speak directly with him. They drop Neeharika off at her grandparents' and the husband spends the drive into Toronto General trying to prepare his wife for the worst. He knows Vicram has either taken a turn for the worse, or that he is already "no more."

Two nights later I receive a tearful telephone call from Vicram's parents. They each take turns speaking with me and they are clearly distraught and exhausted. I can hear many voices in the background and know that their home must be filled with dozens of relatives and friends. I know this too well. They explain that Vicram had a minor heart attack the previous December and that he was put on a strict diet and new medications to reduce his cholesterol levels. He hadn't been the same since, and was going in and out of depression with the added restrictions on his lifestyle. They never realized how serious his chest pains were as Vicram never let on. They are making funeral arrangements and invite me to attend: an invitation I politely refuse (I am having serious health problems of my own at this time but I don't tell them this). They thank me again for the almost six additional years they got to spend with their beloved Vicram.

Vicram's body is first embalmed and then taken to his family home. He spends time in his home, as per tradition, before going to the crematorium. After cremation, Vicram's ashes are taken to the Sikh Temple for his funeral, which takes place on August 20th, 2003. Over 500 people attend, including every member of NIMDAC. The family begins seven days of prayers for their beloved son. Rajinder calls me a few weeks after the funeral to explain that their family plans to take Vicram's ashes back to India for a full Hindu ceremonial funeral. His ashes will be set afloat on a Holy river as part of the funeral rites.

The members of NIMDAC decide to honour Vicram by naming a trophy after him, to be awarded to the winner of the children's talent games at their annual conference. (The first year winner of this trophy was a boy in grade eleven. His compassionate family insisted on having their photos taken with Vicram's family, to remember and honour the Ralh's and Vicram).

In October of 2003, Dr. and Mrs. Ralh travel to the north of India into the Punjab area and make their way to the Holy

City of Beas, situated on the Beas River. The Beas River flows from the Himalayas, across northern India and travels through Pakistan on its way to the Arabian Sea. During the arduous trip that takes eleven hours by airplane, they hold Vicram's ashes on their laps, filling his ashes, and his spirit, with their love. They speak to him and include him in everything they are doing: meals, prayers, resting, and travelling. They try to be strong for Vicram as he nears his final resting place. The city of Beas is considered a religious centre in India and it is a fitting place for Vicram's last rites. At certain times of the year the temple offers free accommodations for foreigners; the various religious ceremonies are often conducted in both Hindi and English because so many Caucasians attend. The Holy Men take the time to explain all the myths, the stories and the history behind each portion of the ceremonies. The Ralh family arranges for a traditional Hindu funeral ceremony in its full glory, and on October 23rd they come away satisfied that Vicram's soul has been duly honoured. Later outside, they watch as Vicram's ashes are sent floating down the beautiful flowing waters of the Beas River.

Heidi's heart, the ashes forever mingled with Vicram's, is now somewhere in India, blended into the sacred waters of the Beas River. Someday soon I hope to visit this site of her heart's send-off and offer up a bouquet of glorious yellow roses to float downstream to meet her. I promise my Heidi this.

Afterword

This book was written with a purpose in mind: to create dialogues about the issues raised within its pages. Changes can only be brought about after we first acknowledge there are problems; and when we expose these problems to public scrutiny, only then can we, collectively, set to work on viable solutions. Let's talk.

If you feel strongly about what you have read, please let your voice be heard. Write letters to the editors of your local, provincial and national newspapers and express your point of view on the issues. Suggest ideas for change. Our medical community needs to hear from the public, as do our police and our politicians. You may contact Catherine Adamson through the website listed below. This site contains a Reader's Forum to give you a voice. Please log on, read the comments from other readers, and by all means, add your thoughts.

Thank you for reading Heidi's story.

Catherine S. Adamson

Website: www.catadampublishing.com

References and Works Cited:

Anonymous, MD., Professor of Clinical Anesthesiology, Associate Professor of Clinical Medicine and Surgery University of Miami School of Medicine. "Fat Embolism—The Trauma Victim's Bad Break." This essay is a compilation of other doctors' medical research and the writer has requested his name not be used because his article was intended for a lecture series only and not for publication. He used the following sources in his paper:

1. Bone, R.C., "Pulmonary microvascular fat in lung injury: an epiphenomenon?" Critical Care Medicine, 1993. 21(5): p.644.

2. Byrick, R.J., J.C.Kay, and J.B. Mullen, "Capnography is not as sensitive as pulmonary artery pressure monitoring in detecting marrow microembolism. Studies in a canine model." Anesthesia & Analgesia, 1989. 68(2): p. 94-100.

3. Byrick, R.J., et al., "Prostanoid production and pulmonary hypertension after fat embolism are not modified by methylprednisolone." Canadian Journal of Anaesthesia Journal Canadien d Anesthesie, 1991. 38(5): p. 660-7.

4. Byrick, R.J., et al., "Ibuprofen pre-treatment does not prevent hemodynamic instability after cemented arthroplasty in dogs." Anesthesia & Analgesia, 1992. 75(4): p. 515-22.

5. Castella, X., et al., Fat embolism syndrome and pulmonary microvascular cytology. Chest, 1992. 101(6): p. 1710-1.

6. Chastre, J., et al., "Bronchoalveolar lavage for rapid diagnosis of the fat embolism syndrome in trauma patients." Annals of Internal Medicine, 1990. 113(8): p. 583-8.

7. Deppe, S.A., R.R. Barrette, and D.R. Thompson. "Other embolic syndromes, in Critical Care," J.M. Civetta, R.W. Taylor, and R.R. Kirby, Editor. 1992, Lippincott: Philadelphia. P. 1303-11.

8. Fabian, T.C., et al., Fat embolism syndrome: prospective evaluation in 92 fracture patients. Critical Care Medicine, 1990, 18(1): p. 42-6.

9. Fabian, T.C., "Unravelling the fat embolism syndrome." New England Journal of Medicine, 1993. 329(13): p. 961-3.

10. Ganong, R.B., "Fat emboli syndrome in isolated fractures of the tibia and femur." Clinical Orthopaedics & Related Research, 1993. 291: p. 208-14.

11. Gitin, T.A., et al., "Pulmonary microvascular fat: the significance?" Critical Care Medicine, 1993. 21(5): p. 673-7.

12. Gurd, A.R. and R.I. Wilson, "The fat embolism syndrome." Journal of Bone and Joint Surgery, 1974. 56B: p. 408.

13. Levy, D., "The fat embolism syndrome. A review." Clinical Orthopaedics & Related Research, 1990. 261: p. 281-6.

14. Lindeque, B.G.P., H.S. Schoeman, and G.F. Dommisse, "Fat embolism and the fat embolism syndrome." Journal of Bone and Joint Surgery, 1987. 69B: p. 128.

15. Moed, B.R., D.W. Boyd, and R.E. Andring, "Clinically inapparent hypoxemia after skeletal injury. The use of the pulse oximeter as a screening method." Clinical Orthopaedics & Related Research, 1993. 293: p. 269-73.

16. Murray, D.G. and G.B. Racz, "Fat-embolism syndrome (respiratory insufficiency syndrome)." Journal of Bone and Joint Surgery, 1974. 56A: p. 1338.

17. Pape, H., et al., "Influence of different methods of intramedullary femoral nailing on lung function in patients with multiple trauma." Journal of Trauma, 1993. 35(5): p. 709-16.

18. Patel, K.P. and L.M. Capan, "Musculoskeletal Injuries, in Trauma anesthesia and intensive care," L.M. Capan, S.M. Miller, and H. Turndorf, Editor. 1991, Lippincott: Philadelpia. P. 511-46.

19. Pell. A.C., et al., "Brief report: fulminating fat embolism syndrome caused by paradoxical embolism through a patent foramen ovale." New England Journal of Medicine, 1993. 329(13): p. 926-9.

20. Riska, E.B. and P. Myllyne, "Fat embolism in patients with multiple injuries." Journal of Trauma, 1982. 22(11): p. 891-4.

21. Schnaid, E., et al., "The early biochemical and hormonal profile of patients with long bone fractures at risk of fat embolism syndrome." Journal of Trauma, 1987. 27(3): p. 309-11.

22. Schonfeld, S.A., Y. Polysongsang, and R. Dilisio, "Fat embolism prophylaxis with corticosteroids: a prospective study in high-risk patients." Annals of Internal Medicine, 1983. 99: p. 438.

23. Stanley, J.D., et al., "Specificity of bronchoalveolar lavage for the diagnosis of fat embolism syndrome." American Surgeon, 1994. 60(7): p. 537-41.

24. Talucci, R.C., et al., "Early intramedullary nailing of femoral shaft fractures: a cause of fat embolism syndrome." American Journal of Surgery, 1983. 146: p. 107-11.

25. Vedrinne, J.M., et al., "Bronchoalveolar lavage in trauma patients for diagnosis of fat embolism syndrome." Chest, 1992. 102(5): p. 1323-7.

26. Wheelwright, E.F., et al., "Hypotension during cemented arthroplasty. Relationship to cardiac output and fat embolism." Journal of Bone & Joint Surgery—British, 1993. 75(5): p. 715-23.

27. Wilkins, K.E., "Fat embolism, in Anaesthesia for orthopaedic surgery," H.L. Zauder, Editor. 1980, F.A. Davis: Philadelphia. P. 147-79.

Author unknown. Autoweb.com.au "Saab Develops 'Alcokey' Breathalyser." (Press Release). Dated June 15, 2004

Bishop, Michael J, MD. Anesthesia Service, Division of Pulmonary and Critical Care Medicine, Veterans Affairs Puget Sound Health Care System, University of Washington, Seattle, Washington. "Unintended Consequences of Artificial Airways: Replacement Parts Are Never As Good as the Factory-Installed." *Respiratory Care Journal,* October 2001 issue. >www.rcjournal.com< With permission.

Ganong, Richard B., M.D., F.A.C.P. "Fat Emboli Syndrome in Isolated Fractures of the Tibia and Femur." *Clinical Orthopaedics and Related Research,* Number 291, June 1993, pp. 208 – 214. Copyright 1993. J.B. Lippincott Company. With permission.

Greschner, John, Deputy Commissioner and Chief Investigator, Children's Commission. *Children's Commission Fatality Review Report,* File no. 97-01547, January 26, 2000.

Helm, Ann, RN, JD. "Heidi Dawn Klompas: Summary of Approximately 710 pages of Medical Records." March, 2000. (Independent forensic report completed at the request of G. Garry MacDonald, lawyer). Referenced but not cited.

Homer. *The Odyssey.* Robert Fagles translation. Page 271. Penguin Putnam Inc., New York, New York. 1996.

Kapural, Leonardo, MD; Sprung, Juraj, MD, PhD; Gluncic, Ivo, MD; Kapural, Miranda, MD; Andelinovic, Simon, MD; Primorac, Dragan, MD; and Schoenwald, Peter K., MD. "Tracheo-Innominate Artery Fistula After Tracheostomy." Case Report. Anesth Analg 1999; 88: 777-80. Copyright 1999 by the International Anesthesia Research Society 0003-2999/99/. With permission.

Mader, Sylvia, S. *Human Biology,* Sixth Edition. McGraw-Hill Higher Education, New York, NY. 2000. Reprinted with permission from McGraw-Hill.

Mattice, Connie, RN, MS, ANP. "When Fat Coalesces in a Patient's Bloodstream." *RN,* Vol. 63, No. 5, May 2000. >www.rnweb.com< With permission.

MEDLINEplus Medical Encyclopedia: "Compartment Syndrome." Updated by: Andrew L. Chen, M.D., M.S., Department of Orthopaedic Surgery, Hospital for Joint Diseases, New York, NY. Review provided by VeriMed Healthcare Network. >http://www.nlm.nih.gov/medlineplus/ency/article/001224.htm<

Neufeldt, Victoria, Editor in Chief; Guralnik, David B., Editor in Chief Emeritus. *Webster's New World Dictionary, Third College Edition.* Simon & Shuster, New York, NY.1986.

Odegard, MD, Department of Anesthesiology, New York University Medical Center. "Fat Embolism: Diagnosis and Treatment." New York, NY. >http://gasnet.med.yale.edu/gta/fat_embolism.html<

Ousten, Rick. "What Happened To Heidi? The untold story of her tragic death." *Vancouver Sun Newspaper,* November 11, 2000, pages: front cover, A8, A9. Part Two: November 13, 2000, page A6. (Referenced only).

Peace Arch District Hospital Records. Compilation of nurses' notes, doctors' orders, lab reports and x-ray films. Twenty nine pages. September 13, 1997.

Prazeres, Gisele De Azevedo. "Fat Embolism Syndrome." *Internal Medicine*. (No date found). (References: *Cecil Textbook of Medicine*, 20th edition. W.B. Saunders Company, 1996) >http://www.medstudents.com.br/medint/medint2.htm<

Royal Columbian Hospital Records. Compilation of nurses' notes, doctor's notes/orders, lab results, consultants' reports, CT scans, x-rays and autopsy report. Approximately 700 pages. September 13, 1997–October 15, 1997.

Sicard, Michael W., M.D. "Complications of Tracheotomy." *The Bobby R. Alford Department of Otorhinolaryngology and Communicative Sciences; Grand Rounds Archives*. Baylor College of Medicine. December 1, 1994. >www.bcm.tmc.edu/oto/grand/12194. html< With permission.

Sinclair, Ray, MD; Wrathall, Gareth, MD. "The Management of Major Trauma." From "Update in Anaesthesia" in *Practical Procedures*, Issue 6 (1996), Article 2, page 9 of 9. Copyright World Federation of Societies of Anaesthesiologists. WWW implementation by the NDA Web Team, Oxford, England. With permission. >http://www.nda.ox.ac.uk/wfsa/html/u06/u06_011.htm<

Siobal, Mark, RRT; Kallet, Richard H, RRT; Kraemer, Roger, CRT; Jonson, Emmanuel, CRT; Lemons, Donald CET; Young, David, MD; Campbell, Andre R, MD; Schecter, William, MD; and Tang, Julin, MD.
"Tracheal-Innominate Artery Fistula Caused by the Endotracheal Tube Tip: Case Report and Investigation of a Fatal Complication of Prolonged Intubation." *Respiratory Care Journal*, October, 2001. With permission. >www.rcjournal.com/ contents/10.01/10.01.1012.asp<

Stephany, Kathleen. Medical Investigator, Office of the Chief Coroner. *B.C. Coroners Service Medical Investigative Report*, Case # 97-203-1466. Completed March 31, 1999.

Ten Duis, H.J., Department of Surgery, University Hospital Groningen, The Netherlands. "The Fat Embolism Syndrome." *Injury*, Vol. 28, No. 2, pp. 77–85, 1997. Copyright 1997, Elsevier Science Ltd. Reprinted with permission from Elsevier.

Williamson, Christina. *Poems for Heidi*. 1997-2004.